A TUTORIAL ON THE ADVENT OF DIVINE JUSTICE

SPIRITUAL VALUES FOR A NEW WORLD ORDER

Fazel Naghdy

Other books by Fazel Naghdy

A Tutorial on the Dispensation of Bahá'u'lláh: Exploring the Fundamental Verities of the Bahá'í Faith, 2012.

A Tutorial on the Kitáb-i-Íqán: A Journey Through the Book of Certitude, 2012.

Knowing My Inner Self: Applied Spirituality for Teenagers, 2014.

A TUTORIAL ON THE ADVENT OF DIVINE JUSTICE

SPIRITUAL VALUES FOR A NEW WORLD ORDER

Fazel Naghdy

This book was approved by the review committee of the
National Spiritual Assembly of the Baháʼís of Australia on 22 April 2019.
Cover design by Zohreh and Naysan Faizi, Designers Inc.
ISBN–13: 9781876322533

Dedication

To Golshah, my children and grandchildren

Contents

Acknowledgments

I would like to express my deep appreciation to Michael W. Thomas and Yvonne I. Woźniak who did the general editing of the book.

Preface

The beloved Guardian wrote *The Advent of Divine Justice* as a letter to the North American Bahá'ís in 1938, at a critical time in the history of the Faith and the affairs of the world. The North American Bahá'í community was chosen by 'Abdu'l-Bahá to initiate the plan set out in the Tablets of the Divine Plan, the charter revealed by 'Abdu'l-Bahá for the spiritual conquest of the planet. 'Abdu'l-Bahá and later Shoghi Effendi nurtured the development of the North American Bahá'ís, preparing them to embark on the mission conferred on them by 'Abdu'l-Bahá. A year before writing *The Advent of Divine Justice*, Shoghi Effendi provided the North American Bahá'í community with a Seven Year Plan as the first stage in bringing the Light of the Cause to the American continent.

The messages written by Shoghi Effendi during this period clearly indicate that he foreshadowed the breakout of another world war, signalling further the unfoldment of the convulsion prophesied by Bahá'u'lláh. In *The Advent of Divine Justice*, he identifies four signs of that convulsion as: the extinguishing of the lights of liberty, the increase of the clamour of discord, the growth of fanaticism and the continuing rise of irreligion.

Against the background described above, Shoghi Effendi pursued a number of objectives in *The Advent of Divine Justice*. He defined the moral standards that were essential for the success of the tasks 'Abdu'l-Bahá had set for the North American Bahá'ís in the Tablets of the Divine Plan. He provided them with some practical guidance on how to conduct the Plan, particularly in teaching the Cause and in pioneering. He warned the North American Bahá'ís against the corrosive materialism of their society, and counselled them not to be threatened or subdued by the extraordinary events that would occur during the course of the Plan. He identified rectitude of conduct, a chaste and holy life, and freedom from racial prejudice, as the three weapons that the American Bahá'í community must possess in their twofold crusade; first to regenerate the inner life of their own community and next to fight against the evils that have corrupted the life of American society.

Worldwide, the Bahá'í community, under the guidance of the Universal House of Justice, is currently engaged in a spiritual enterprise to propagate "the Faith in local communities and among multitudinous peoples of all continents"[1]. Thus, they are striving to transform individuals and their communities through the life-giving teachings of Bahá'u'lláh. The evils of moral laxity, excessive materialism, corruption and prejudice identified by Shoghi Effendi in 1936 as afflicting the North American society, are now prevalent features of many societies around the world to an appalling degree.

In a message dated January 18, 2019 to the Bahá'ís of the world, the Universal House of Justice signals that the forces of disintegration have regrouped and gained ground since the beginning of the 21st century and new challenges have begun to emerge. "Certain shared ethical principles, which seemed to be in the ascendant at the start of this century, are eroded, threatening the prevailing consensus about right and wrong that, in various arenas, had succeeded in holding humanity's basest tendencies in check. And the will to engage in international collective action, which twenty years ago represented a powerful strain of thinking among world leaders, has been cowed, assailed by resurgent forces of racism, nationalism, and factionalism."[2] The increasing problems of the world bring an urgency to the study of *The Advent of Divine Justice*. It is critical for all Bahá'ís at this time, to assimilate its contents into the patterns of their behaviour as individuals and as communities, no matter in what part of the globe they live.

This tutorial is designed to assist you to study *The Advent of Divine Justice* and absorb its contents. It is called a tutorial to emphasize the concept underlying its development. In a tutorial, a tutor facilitates learning for an individual or a small group by providing the scaffolding and the structure around the content. Accordingly, this tutorial is an attempt to simulate as much as possible, in distance learning mode, the tutor-tutored relationship in a self-paced personal study scheme.

The tutorial identifies the main themes covered in the Guardian's book, and maps the related paragraphs into chapters. Accordingly, the 124 paragraphs of *The Advent of Divine Justice* are apportioned for study across 24 chapters. The size and complexity of each chapter reflects the content and intricacy of the issues addressed in the paragraphs included therein. The title chosen for each chapter reflects the main theme covered in the paragraphs under study.

Each chapter starts with an introduction that highlights the key concepts addressed. Those paragraphs from *The Advent of Divine Justice* covered in the chapter are then listed. Quotes from Bahá'u'lláh and 'Abdu'l-Bahá within those paragraphs (if referred to later on) are sequentially annotated with letters within square brackets to save subsequent repetition. For example the tenth quote within paragraph 42 will be referred to as "quote 42:J".

---

[1]   The Universal House of Justice, Message to the followers of Bahá'u'lláh in Írán, 10 May 2013.

[2]   The Universal House of Justice, retrieved from https://www.bahai.org/library/authoritative-texts/the-universal-house-of-justice/messages/20190118_001/1#276724432.

The paragraphs from *The Advent of Divine Justice* are followed by a description of the background information on the terminologies, references and mystical concepts contained in those paragraphs. At the end of each chapter, there are a series of activities provided to consolidate your learning and to assist you to develop a deeper understanding of the content.

To derive the most benefit from your study, please follow the procedure explained below:

1. Read carefully the paragraphs covered in each chapter and reflect on them.
2. Identify the concepts and issues that you do not fully understand. Formulate them as a set of questions.
3. Read the content of the chapter and look for answers to your questions.
4. Reflect on the answers to obtain a deeper meaning.
5. Read the paragraphs of the book covered in the chapter again and ensure that you have a clear understanding of the issues raised.
6. Complete the activities given in the chapter.

Fazel Naghdy
May 2019

1.
Overview and significance

1.1 Introduction

Shoghi Effendi wrote *The Advent of Divine Justice* in 1938, as a letter to the North American Bahá'ís, the community chosen by 'Abdu'l-Bahá to undertake the tasks of the Tablets of the Divine Plan. Understanding the standards set in *The Advent of Divine Justice* is fundamental to building an inclusive community based on spiritual principles and a pattern of behaviour enunciated by Bahá'u'lláh in His writings. In this chapter, an overview of the book is provided, its significance and historical context are explained, and the concept of "divine justice" that is the underlying theme of the book is explored.

In this chapter, you should reflect on and understand the following key points:

a) Two major themes in the book relate to the life of the individual Bahá'í and the interaction between the American Bahá'í community and the wider society.
b) The book deals with the faults, habits, and tendencies that the American Bahá'í community must weed out.
c) The book also deals with the distinctive qualities and characteristics that the American Bahá'í community must cultivate and acquire.
d) Shoghi Effendi chose the American Bahá'í community as the chief instrument for building the Bahá'í Administrative Order and expanding the Faith based on the guidance of 'Abdu'l-Bahá in the Tablets of the Divine Plan.
e) Justice has a lofty rank in the Bahá'í teachings.
f) Bahá'u'lláh refers to His revelation as the advent of divine justice.
g) In *The Advent of Divine Justice*, Shoghi Effendi identifies some of the major ideals and standards in the revelation of Bahá'u'lláh that underline divine justice.

1.2 Historical context and significance

1.2.1 *Tablets of the Divine Plan*

'Abdu'l-Bahá revealed 14 Tablets during 1916–17 as a worldwide teaching plan for the Bahá'ís of the United States and Canada, known as the Tablets of the Divine Plan. The first eight of these Tablets were revealed between 26 March and 22 April 1916 during a violent period of the First World War in Europe. The final six Tablets were revealed between 2 February and 8 March 1917, a month before the entry of the United States into the war.

Four of these Tablets were directed to the Bahá'ís of the United States and Canada, and two were addressed to the Bahá'ís of Canada and Greenland. The remaining eight Tablets were addressed to the believers in the Southern States, the Central States, the Western States, and the North-eastern States of America. In the Tablets addressed to the North American Bahá'í community, 'Abdu'l-Bahá guided them to teach the Faith and gave them the mandate to take the Bahá'í Faith to every corner of the earth.

Five Tablets in the first group reached the United States and were published in the *Star of the West*.[1] The remaining Tablets could not be sent from Haifa as all communications with the Holy land were stopped due to the war. All the Tablets were kept in a vault under the Shrine of the Báb on Mt. Carmel for the duration of the war. The Tablets were sent to the United States after the war and were presented to the "Convention of the Covenant" held at Hotel McAlpin in New York City on 26–30 April 1919.

The believers were excited, uplifted and inspired by the Tablets and a few individuals such as John and Clara Dunn, and Martha Root immediately responded to the call of 'Abdu'l-Bahá and set off travel teaching or to pioneering posts. However, the systematic implementation of the Plans was not possible since the North American Bahá'í community was in its infancy and the mission described by 'Abdu'l-Bahá in these Tablets was well beyond their capacity. Although the Faith was introduced in the United States in 1894, the community still lacked the necessary instruments and institutions to systematically undertake and administer those lofty plans.

Following the passing of 'Abdu'l-Bahá on 28 November 1921, Shoghi Effendi took over the affairs of the Faith as the appointed Guardian. He identified *The Will and Testament of 'Abdu'l-Bahá* as one of the Charters[2] of the World Order of Bahá'u'lláh[3] and embarked on developing and establishing the embryonic institutions mentioned by 'Abdu'l-Bahá in that document. In His Will and Testament, 'Abdu'l-Bahá provided clear guidance on how the Local and the Secondary Houses of Justice,[4] and the Universal House of Justice must be elected.

---

[1] *Star of the West*, Vol. VII, no. 10, pp. 87–91.
[2] In *God Passes By*, p. 213, Shoghi Effendi also identified *The Kitáb-i-Aqdas* as another Charter of the World Order of Bahá'u'lláh.
[3] Shoghi Effendi, *God Passes By*, p. 213.
[4] The Local and the Secondary Houses of the Justice are currently known as the Local and National Spiritual Assemblies.

Shoghi Effendi also considered the Tablets of the Divine Plan as his mandate for propagating and expanding the Faith throughout the various territories and countries of the world. The first step was to empower the North American Bahá'ís as the recipients of these Tablets to build the capacities needed to discharge the tasks they were given by 'Abdu'l-Bahá. It was equally important to guide the Bahá'í community in North America to develop the institutions that were to implement the Plans.

The 14 Tablets of the Divine Plan are provided in the Appendix for you to study and develop an appreciation of the mission that 'Abdu'l-Bahá entrusted to the Bahá'ís of North America.

1.2.2   Guardian's messages to North American Bahá'ís

From the earliest years of his ministry as the divinely appointed Guardian of the Cause of God, Shoghi Effendi conferred upon the Bahá'ís of North America a very special bounty in communicating to them a series of inspiring and challenging messages, and carefully delineating the tasks they were called upon to discharge. He set specific goals for them, emphasizing that through the achievement of those goals they would fulfil their destiny as the chosen instruments for the execution of the Divine Plan of 'Abdu'l-Bahá.

Among these messages, *The Advent of Divine Justice* stands out because of its frank and direct analysis of the basic ills afflicting American society, which threatened the spiritual life of individual Bahá'ís and the well-being of the Bahá'í community. These maladies have not only intensified in their scope, implications and influence since the time of Shoghi Effendi, but they have been promoted and propagated by the powerful American entertainment industry and modern social media, and accepted globally by many societies as the norm for personal and social behaviour.

The above conditions are described in the later communications of the Guardian. In a message dated 28 July 1954, while referring to the maladies afflicting the American Society, Shoghi Effendi states:

> The steady and alarming deterioration in the standard of morality as exemplified by the appalling increase of crime, by political corruption in ever widening and ever higher circles, by the loosening of the sacred ties of marriage, by the inordinate craving for pleasure and diversion, and by the marked and progressive slackening of parental control, is no doubt the most arresting and distressing aspect of the decline that has set in, and can be clearly perceived, in the fortunes of the entire nation.[1]

It is reasonable to suggest that the guidance provided by Shoghi Effendi in *The Advent of Divine Justice* to the American Bahá'í community is equally valid and applicable to many Bahá'í communities around the world. At the same time the spiritual principles and counsels provided by Shoghi Effendi on how to purge such maladies from the behaviour of the individual and the habits embedded in the Bahá'í community are critical in building Bahá'í communities that truly reflect

---

[1]   Shoghi Effendi, *Citadel of Faith*, p. 124.

the spiritual qualities and characteristics prescribed in the revelation of Bahá'u'lláh, and are pre-requisites to serving the Bahá'í Cause.

Hence, studying *The Advent of Divine Justice* and assimilating its contents into the patterns of behaviour of the individual Bahá'í and into the general community is critically important for all Bahá'ís, no matter in what part of the world they live. In a letter written on behalf of Shoghi Effendi to an individual believer, dated 20 May 1939, it is stated:

> The principles and methods laid down by the Guardian in his 'Advent of Divine Justice' on this vital subject of Bahá'í ethics, should indeed prove of invaluable inspiration and guidance to all the students and friends attending the Summer School classes, and thus prepare them to better appreciate the privileges, and more adequately discharge the responsibilities, of their citizenship in the World Order of Bahá'u'lláh.[1]

1.3 Overview of *The Advent of Divine Justice*

Shoghi Effendi wrote *The Advent of Divine Justice* at the end of December 1938, while he was staying in Europe because of the threat of terrorist activities in Palestine. This was the time that Europe itself was in such strife and discord that it eventually led to the outbreak of the Second World War a year later. Some of his statements in *The Advent of Divine Justice* clearly indicate that Shoghi Effendi anticipated the war and accordingly he directly and indirectly referred to the impending convulsions in his book, warning the Bahá'í community of their devastating consequences and impact.

The book was addressed to the Bahá'ís of the United States and Canada, the community that is praised by Shoghi Effendi in the book as the "chief remaining citadel" of the Bahá'í Faith in the 1930's. However, the issues raised and the guidance provided are applicable to any Bahá'í community, particularly at this time when the pace of disintegration of the old order has significantly increased and its negative influence on the followers of Bahá'u'lláh has intensified. Understanding the standards set in *The Advent of Divine Justice* is fundamental to building a vibrant community based on the spiritual principles and pattern of behaviour revealed by Bahá'u'lláh in His Writings.

Three major themes stand out in the book: the qualities characterizing the life of individuals in the American Bahá'í community; the nature of the systematic plans and actions required for the expansion and consolidation of the Bahá'í Faith in that community towards its destiny as envisaged by 'Abdu'l-Bahá; and the interaction between the American Bahá'í Community and the wider society.

During the course of the book, Shoghi Effendi identifies the "faults, habits, and tendencies" that the North American Bahá'ís have "inherited from their own nation", while he highlights the necessity of weeding out such harmful vices. He also describes the "distinctive qualities and characteristics" that the North American Bahá'í community must "patiently and prayerfully" cultivate and acquire. Shoghi Effendi specifically pinpoints the most challenging issues prevailing in the wider American society as moral laxity, corruption and racial

---

[1]   Written on behalf of Shoghi Effendi, in *Lights of Guidance*, p. 562.

prejudice. He highlights the need for the American Bahá'ís to root out such evils from their community and strive to conduct a chaste and holy life that is adorned with rectitude of conduct and free from all types of prejudice.

Shoghi Effendi further describes the spiritual prerequisites for success in teaching and provides detailed guidance on how teaching campaigns to achieve the goals of the first Seven Year Plan should be conducted. He specifically addresses the role that the handmaidens of Bahá'u'lláh and the Bahá'í youth should assume. He also places all the activities of the American Bahá'ís in the context of the destiny of America.

Amatu'l-Bahá Rúḥíyyih Khánum provides the following overview of *The Advent of Divine Justice*:

> In it Shoghi Effendi set forth, as never before, the role this Community was destined to play in the unfolding destiny of man on this planet. It defined the objectives of the recently opened Seven Year Plan, the first step in implementing the provisions of 'Abdu'l-Bahá's Divine Plan, and pointed out that upon the success of this greatest joint enterprise ever undertaken by Bahá'u'lláh's followers must depend the fate of all future activities in the promulgation of His World Order throughout the other continents of the globe. With a kind but firm hand Shoghi Effendi held up before the face of the North American Community the mirror of the civilization by which they were surrounded and warned them, in terms that riveted the eye and chilled the heart, against its evils, pointing out to them a truth few of them had ever pondered, namely, that the very evils of that civilization were the mystic reason for their homeland having been chosen by God as the Cradle of His World Order in this day. As the warnings contained in *The Advent of Divine Justice* are an integral part of the vision and guidance Shoghi Effendi gave to the faithful throughout his ministry, they cannot be passed over in silence if we are to obtain any correct understanding of his own mission. In no uncertain terms he castigated the moral laxity, political corruption, racial prejudice and corrosive of their society, contrasting it with the exalted standards inculcated by Bahá'u'lláh in His Teachings, and enjoined by Him upon His followers. It warned them of the war so soon to come and admonished them to stand fast, in spite of every trial that might in future afflict them and their nations, and discharge their sacred trust by prosecuting to a triumphal outcome the Plan they had so recently inaugurated throughout the Western Hemisphere.[1]

Because of its emphasis on teaching and the practical guidance it provides, *The Advent of Divine Justice* was known as "the Bible of Bahá'í pioneers" among the early Bahá'ís in the West.[2]

In summary, the major themes covered in the book can be summarized as:

- The spiritual attributes that should adorn every individual Bahá'í to ensure the success and progress of the Bahá'í Faith.

---

[1] Amatu'l-Bahá Rúḥíyyih Khánum, *The Priceless Pearl*, p. 93.
[2] Marzieh Gale, *Arches of the Years*, p. 307.

- The importance of human and social relationships, referred to as the spiritual outer life, which should be reflected in the daily life of every Bahá'í, in addition to the spiritual inner life.
- The basic ills afflicting the American body politic.
- The new challenges and opportunities that are created for the American believers as a result of world events.
- The role of the American believers in the advancement of the Bahá'í Cause in the years to come.

1.4 Advent of divine justice

In a number of His Tablets, Bahá'u'lláh refers to His revelation as the advent of divine justice. He summons the people of the world: *"Bestir yourselves, O people, in anticipation of the days of Divine justice, for the promised hour is now come. Beware lest ye fail to apprehend its import and be accounted among the erring."*[1] In another Tablet, Bahá'u'lláh asserts: *"In this Day the Straight Path is made manifest, the Balance of divine justice is set and the light of the sun of His bounty is resplendent, yet the oppressive darkness of the people of tyranny hath, even as clouds, intervened and caused a grievous obstruction between the Daystar of heavenly grace and the people of the world."*[2]

The Báb also refers to the days of His revelation and the revelation of *"He Whom God shall make manifest"*, i.e., Bahá'u'lláh, as the days of the advent of divine justice: *"These are the appointed days which ye have been yearningly awaiting in the past—the days of the advent of divine justice. Render ye thanks unto God, O ye concourse of believers."*[3]

In describing the nature of the divine justice brought about through the revelation of Bahá'u'lláh, Shoghi Effendi illustrates its effects as a flame cleansing and uniting a stubbornly erring humanity:

> The flames which His Divine justice have kindled cleanse an unregenerate humanity, and fuse its discordant, its warring elements as no other agency can cleanse or fuse them. It is not only a retributory and destructive fire, but a disciplinary and creative process, whose aim is the salvation, through unification, of the entire planet. Mysteriously, slowly, and resistlessly God accomplishes His design, though the sight that meets our eyes in this day be the spectacle of a world hopelessly entangled in its own meshes, utterly careless of the Voice which, for a century, has been calling it to God, and miserably subservient to the siren voices which are attempting to lure it into the vast abyss.[4]

In *The Advent of Divine Justice*, Shoghi Effendi identifies some of the major ideals and standards in the revelation of Bahá'u'lláh that underline divine justice, which are severely compromised by American society. He specifically elaborates on racial prejudice and immoral conduct as the most pressing issues in a society

---

[1] Bahá'u'lláh, *Gleanings for the Writings of Bahá'u'lláh*, p. 17.

[2] Bahá'u'lláh, *Tablets of Bahá'u'lláh*, pp. 255–256.

[3] The Báb, *Selections from the Writings of the Báb*, p. 161.

[4] Shoghi Effendi, *The Promised Day is Come*, p. 116.

that is diametrically opposite to the standards of divine justice enshrined in the revelation of Bahá'u'lláh. Shoghi Effendi states that these issues must be addressed by every individual Bahá'í and by the Bahá'í community collectively.

Shoghi Effendi maintains that racial prejudice "has attacked the whole social structure of American society. It should be regarded as constituting the most vital and challenging issue confronting the Bahá'í community at the present stage of its evolution."[1] At the same time, the "rectitude of conduct, with its implications of justice, equity, truthfulness, honesty, fair-mindedness, reliability, and trustworthiness, must distinguish every phase of the life of the Bahá'í community."

Later chapters of this tutorial on *The Advent of Divine Justice* will cover these topics in more detail.

---

[1]   Shoghi Effendi, *The Advent of Divine Justice*, p. 33.

1.5 Activities

1.5.1 Short answer questions

1. What are the major themes in *The Advent of Divine Justice*?

_____

_____

_____

_____

2. What does the "spiritual inner life" represent?

_____

_____

_____

_____

3. What does the "spiritual outer life" represent?

_____

_____

_____

_____

4. What are the common features of the spiritual inner life and spiritual outer life?

_____

_____

_____

_____

5. What are the Tablets of the Divine Plan?

_____

_____

_____

6. What were the two major goals of Shoghi Effendi when he assumed the Guardianship?

_____

_____

_____

7.   Why did Shoghi Effendi choose the American Bahá'í community as the instrument to achieve these goals?

_____

_____

_____

_____

8.   What is your understanding of the term "divine justice"?

_____

_____

_____

_____

9.   Why did Shoghi Effendi use the title *The Advent of Divine Justice* for this book?

_____

_____

_____

_____

1.5.2   *Mini-project*

Study the Tablets of the Divine Plan provided in the Appendix. Develop a list of key points in each Tablet in bullet form. Analyse the differences and similarities between the key points you have identified for each Tablet. Organize your findings as a presentation and share it with your Bahá'í community.

2.
Feelings of irresistible joy

2.1 Introduction

This chapter covers paragraphs 1–3, in which the Guardian expresses his feelings of irrepressible joy about the progress made by the National Spiritual Assembly of the Bahá'ís of the United States and Canada in the first Seven Year Plan, and the generous support given by the Bahá'í community in supporting the National Assembly in its endeavours. A summary of the North American first Seven Year Plan and an outline of the victories achieved in this plan by 1938, the time that Shoghi Effendi wrote *The Advent of Divine Justice*, are provided.

In this chapter, you need to reflect on and understand the following key points:

a) Shoghi Effendi's first Seven Year Plan was his guidance for the North American believers to undertake a systematic response to the mandate they had received from 'Abdu'l-Bahá in the Tablets of the Divine Plan.

b) Shoghi Effendi channelled the efforts of the North American Bahá'ís in the 1920s and 1930s towards building the Bahá'í Administrative Order and completing the exterior of the Bahá'í House of Worship in Wilmette, Illinois.

c) The Seven Year Plan had three major goals.

d) Despite the challenges of the Second World War, the goals of the Plan were achieved by 1944.

e) The National Spiritual Assembly established an Inter-America Committee in 1936 to coordinate teaching activities in Mexico, Central America, South America and islands of the Caribbean Sea.

f) A schedule was developed to complete the external decoration of the Temple within the course of the Plan.

g) The apparent challenges faced by the Bahá'í community primarily demonstrate its unity and reinforce its inner strength.

h) The followers of Bahá'u'lláh must feel grateful for the interventions of a caring Providence, whether it appears as a blessing or an affliction.

i) The Bahá'í community should be alert and prepared to seize any opportunities that arise from crises or victories to advance the Bahá'í Faith.

2.2 Paragraphs under study

To the beloved of God and the handmaids of the Merciful throughout the United States and Canada.

Best-beloved brothers and sisters in the love of Bahá'u'lláh:

1   It would be difficult indeed to adequately express the feelings of irrepressible joy and exultation that flood my heart every time I pause to contemplate the ceaseless evidences of the dynamic energy which animates the stalwart pioneers of the World Order of Bahá'u'lláh in the execution of the Plan committed to their charge. The signature of the contract, by your elected national representatives, signalizing the opening of the final phase of the greatest enterprise ever launched by the followers of the Faith of Bahá'u'lláh in the West, no less than the extremely heartening progress recorded in the successive reports of their National Teaching Committee, attest, beyond the shadow of a doubt, the fidelity, the vigour, and the thoroughness with which you are conducting the manifold operations which the evolution of the Seven Year Plan must necessarily involve. In both of its aspects, and in all its details, it is being prosecuted with exemplary regularity and precision, with undiminished efficiency, and commendable dispatch.

2   The resourcefulness which the national representatives of the American believers have, in recent months, so strikingly demonstrated, as evidenced by the successive measures they have adopted, has been matched by the loyal, the unquestioning and generous support accorded them by all those whom they represent, at every critical stage, and with every fresh advance, in the discharge of their sacred duties. Such close interaction, such complete cohesion, such continual harmony and fellowship between the various agencies that contribute to the organic life, and constitute the basic framework, of every properly functioning Bahá'í community, is a phenomenon which offers a striking contrast to the disruptive tendencies which the discordant elements of present-day society so tragically manifest. Whereas every apparent trial with which the unfathomable wisdom of the Almighty deems it necessary to afflict His chosen community serves only to demonstrate afresh its essential solidarity and to consolidate its inward strength, each of the successive crises in the fortunes of a decadent age exposes more convincingly than the one preceding it the corrosive influences that are fast sapping the vitality and undermining the basis of its declining institutions.

3   For such demonstrations of the interpositions of an ever-watchful Providence they who stand identified with the Community of the Most Great Name must feel eternally grateful. From every fresh token of His unfailing blessing on the one hand, and of His visitation on the other, they cannot but derive immense hope and courage. Alert to seize every opportunity which the revolutions of the wheel of destiny within their Faith offers them, and undismayed by the prospect of spasmodic convulsions that must sooner or

later fatally affect those who have refused to embrace its light, they, and those who will labour after them, must press forward until the processes now set in motion will have each spent its force and contributed its share towards the birth of the Order now stirring in the womb of a travailing age.

2.3 America's first Seven Year Plan

In his first paragraph, Shoghi Effendi refers to the execution of the first Seven Year Plan undertaken by the National Spiritual Assembly of the Bahá'ís of the United States and Canada in 1937 under his care and guidance as "the greatest enterprise ever launched by the followers of the Faith of Bahá'u'lláh in the West ...." This endeavour represented the first systematic response by the North American believers to the mandate they received from 'Abdu'l-Bahá in the Tablets of the Divine Plan. As highlighted by Shoghi Effendi, it was also the first systematic teaching enterprise in the West launched to expand and consolidate the Bahá'í Faith.

It would require 16 years of nurturing by Shoghi Effendi before the spiritual seeds sowed by 'Abdu'l-Bahá during His journey to North America in 1912 developed into the capacities necessary for the American Bahá'í community to discharge the mission conferred on them in the Tablets of the Divine Plan. At the time of the launch of the Seven Year Plan, 51 of the 62 states, provinces and territories of the USA and Canada had resident Bahá'ís, most of whom were concentrated in or around big cities such as New York, Chicago and San Francisco. Of the 51 administrative regions inhabited by Bahá'ís, 34 had no Local Spiritual Assembly. Although, the response of the North American Bahá'ís to the Tablets of the Divine Plans was immediate, the initial progress was insignificant.

Shoghi Effendi channelled the efforts of the North American Bahá'ís in the 1920s and 1930s towards building the Bahá'í Administrative Order and completing the exterior of the Bahá'í House of Worship at Wilmette. The size and diversity of the community increased during this period. These developments prepared the community to take up the challenge of pursuing a systematic plan in 1937.[1]

The Seven Year Plan had three major goals:

a) The opening of every republic of Latin America to the Bahá'í Faith through the settlement of pioneers.
b) Completion of the exterior of the Bahá'í House of Worship in Wilmette, Illinois.
c) Establishment of at least one Local Spiritual Assembly in every state in the United States and in every province in Canada.

The community deployed three teaching methods to establish new homefront Local Spiritual Assemblies: firesides, teaching campaigns that were developed during 1930s, and homefront pioneering.

World War II had a significant impact on the progress of the Plan. Transportation was disrupted; it was difficult to acquire construction materials

---

[1] Roger M. Dahl, "Three Teaching Methods Used during North America's First Seven-Year Plan", *Journal of Bahá'í Studies*, Vol. 5, no. 3, 1993.

for the Temple; and Bahá'í pioneers had major problems to find housing in goal areas. Despite these challenges, the goals of the Plan were achieved by 1944. There was an increase in the number of North American Bahá'ís to around 4,800. Local Spiritual Assemblies were formed in every province of Canada, every state of the United States of America, and in 15 Latin American cities.[1] The exterior ornamentation of the House of Worship was completed.

2.4 Praise for the community

In the opening paragraphs of *The Advent of Divine Justice*, Shoghi Effendi praises the National Spiritual Assembly of the Bahá'ís of the United States and Canada and its National Teaching Committee for pursuing the Seven Year Plan "with exemplary regularity and precision, with undiminished efficiency, and commendable dispatch." He also admires the community for the generous support they provided for the National Assembly to discharge their duties. Such statements reflect the devoted response that the North American Bahá'í community and institutions gave to the appeals and guidance of Shoghi Effendi. Indeed, the response of the North American Bahá'í community to the earnest request of Shoghi Effendi to pursue the goals defined by 'Abdu'l-Bahá in the Tablets of Divine Plan was swift and overwhelming.

The United States National Convention in 1936 received the following cablegram from Shoghi Effendi:

> APPEAL ASSEMBLED DELEGATES POWER HISTORIC APPEAL VOICED BY 'ABDU'L-BAHÁ TABLETS DIVINE PLAN. URGE EARNEST DELIBERATION WITH INCOMING NATIONAL ASSEMBLY ENSURE ITS COMPLETE FULFILLMENT. FIRST CENTURY BAHÁ'Í ERA DRAWING TO A CLOSE. HUMANITY ENTERING OUTER FRINGES MOST PERILOUS STAGE ITS EXISTENCE. OPPORTUNITIES PRESENT HOUR UNIMAGINABLY PRECIOUS. WOULD TO GOD EVERY STATE WITHIN AMERICAN REPUBLIC AND EVERY REPUBLIC IN AMERICAN CONTINENT MIGHT ERE TERMINATION THIS GLORIOUS CENTURY EMBRACE LIGHT FAITH BAHÁ'U'LLÁH AND ESTABLISH STRUCTURAL BASIS OF HIS WORLD ORDER.[2]

This is how Horace Holley, describes the upliftment of the North American Bahá'í community upon the receipt of this message: American believers

> ... have made supreme and collective efforts to rise to that world of action and complete consecration revealed in 'Abdu'l-Bahá's words. Their realm of responsibility has widened to include Mexico, Central America, the islands of the Caribbean Sea and South America. A sense of intimate personal conviction has grown rapidly in the hearts. The feeling of crisis and challenge has galvanized the community. It has become realized that true faith means capacity for growth, that a passive and static acceptance of the Bahá'í teaching is sterile and unacceptable.[3]

---

[1] Robert Stockman, *United States of America: History of the Bahá'í Community*, 1995, cited at https://bahai-library.com/stockman_encyclopedia_usa.

[2] *This Decisive Hour: Messages from Shoghi Effendi to the American Bahá'ís 1932–1946*, p. 11.

[3] Horace Holley, "Survey of current Bahá'í Activities in the East and the West", *Bahá'í World*, 1936–1938, p. 17.

In response to the appeal of Shoghi Effendi, the National Spiritual Assembly established an Inter-America Committee in 1936 to co-ordinate teaching activities in Mexico, Central America, South America and the islands of the Caribbean Sea. Various Regional Teaching Committees were appointed in different parts of the United States and Canada to intensify teaching activities, particularly in goal areas. A schedule was also developed to complete the external decoration of the Bahá'í House of Worship at Wilmette during the course of the Plan.

During 1936–1937, Bahá'í pioneers settled in five of the 12 virgin states/provinces of Nebraska, Wyoming, Oklahoma, North Dakota and North Carolina. The Faith was also introduced into 42 new cities, and travel teachers visited a total of 38 cities. There were also eight new Local Spiritual Assemblies formed on 21 April 1938, increasing the number of assemblies in the United States and Canada to 78. In addition, 82 new cities opened to Bahá'í teaching activities in the period 1936–1937.

The significance of this period as well as the victories of the first Seven Year Plan become more pronounced when they are considered within the context of the development and evolution of the North American Bahá'í community, as illustrated in the American Bahá'í chronology note provided in section 2.8.

2.5 Bahá'í community vs. wider society

In the second paragraph, the Guardian refers to the complete cohesion, unity and harmony among various agencies of the American Bahá'í community as the basic framework of every properly functioning Bahá'í community. This was a remarkable contrast to the disruptive tendencies manifested in wider society. Shoghi Effendi then continues by making another comparison between the American Bahá'í community and the wider society around it. The challenges faced by the Bahá'í community primarily demonstrate its unity and reinforces its inner strength. On the other hand, each successive crisis afflicting society, illustrates more clearly than the one before, the destructive elements that are eroding its vitality and "undermining the basis of its declining institutions."

In paragraph two, Shoghi Effendi refers to the American society in the 1930's when it was moving from one crisis to the next. The stock market crashed on 29 October 1929. At the beginning of the 1930's, more than 15 million workers were unemployed. Since people were not earning, they stopped spending and the consumer society came to a halt. The ordinary recession suddenly became the Great Depression. In 1932, Franklin Delano Roosevelt was elected as the new president of the United States after he promised to change the life of all Americans. However, the Great Depression continued for another nine years and the crises worsened. In 1933, more than 9,000 banks were closed and more than $2.5 billion in deposits were lost in the US. As a result, workers grew more militant and, by 1937, 8 million workers joined unions and violently demanded their rights.

The US entered World War II in December 1941 after the Japanese air force bombed Pearl Harbour. American industry was stimulated by the war effort and this resulted in the ending of the Great Depression.

2.6 Seizing any opportunity

In the third paragraph, Shoghi Effendi affirms that the followers of Bahá'u'lláh must be grateful for the interventions of a caring Providence, whether perceived as a blessing or an affliction, finding in either case a source of great hope and courage.

The crises resulting from these processes will sooner or later fatally affect those who refuse to accept the Revelation of Bahá'u'lláh. At the same time, such crises would create fresh opportunities for the expansion of the Faith. Bahá'ís should be ready to seize these opportunities and to press forward.

The Revelation of Bahá'u'lláh has set in motion a series of processes with destructive and constructive effects on the world. Bahá'ís should persevere in their activities until each of these processes has exhausted its energy and contributed towards the birth of the Order which is now growing in the womb of this age.

2.7 Activities

2.7.1 *Short answer questions*

1. What were the foci of the efforts of the North American Bahá'ís in the 1920s and 1930s?

2. What were the major goals of the first Seven Year Plan of the North American Bahá'í community?

3. What were the three teaching methods deployed in achieving the goals?

4. What were the outcomes of the Seven Year Plan?

5. Why did Shoghi Effendi praise the National Spiritual Assembly of the Bahá'ís of the United States and Canada in the first paragraph of the book?

6. What was the Inter-America Committee?

_____

_____

_____

7. Briefly describe the numerical goals achieved in the first two years of the Plan?

_____

_____

_____

8. What are the two features identified by Shoghi Effendi that distinguish the Bahá'í community from the wider society?

_____

_____

_____

9. What were the major challenges faced by the American society in the 1930's?

_____

_____

_____

10. What were the "disruptive tendencies" in the wider society during the 1930's?

_____

_____

_____

11. In your opinion, what are the symptoms of a Bahá'í community that is not fully functioning?

_____

_____

_____

12. How does the statement made by the Guardian on a properly functioning community in paragraph 2 apply to your local community?

_____

_____

_____

_____

13. What is your understanding of the first two sentences in paragraph 3?

_____

_____

_____

_____

2.7.2 Mini-project

Study the American Bahá'í chronology note provided in section 2.8. Develop a 300 words commentary on it, addressing the following questions:

a) How did 'Abdu'l-Bahá nurture the growth and development of the American Bahá'í Community?
b) What was the community development focus during the 1910's?
c) What was the community development focus during the 1920's?
d) What was the community development focus during the 1930's?
e) What were the major milestones in the conception and construction of the Bahá'í House of Worship at Wilmette?

2.8 American Bahá'í chronology note[1]

1883 10 December—A letter titled, "The Bábís and Their Prophet" published in the *New York Sun*.

1893 23 September—Reference to Bahá'u'lláh in address by Dr Jessup in the Parliament of Religions, Columbian Exposition, Chicago.

1894 Formation of the first Bahá'í group in America, Chicago.

1894 Green Acre founded by Sarah J. Farmer, Eliot, Maine, as a universal platform for discussion of religions.

1898 Mrs Phoebe Hearst's party of pilgrims visited 'Abdu'l-Bahá in 'Akká.

1903 A petition was addressed to 'Abdu'l-Bahá signed by all American Bahá'ís requesting authority to construct a House of Worship.

1903 7 June—'Abdu'l-Bahá's Tablet was revealed to the American Bahá'ís through the Chicago Assembly, stating that the time had come to construct a Bahá'í Temple in America.

1904 A compilation of Bahá'í Writings in English was prepared and published by the Board of Counsel of New York

1907 26 November—The first Bahá'í convention convened in Chicago.

1908 9 April—Chicago Assembly purchased the first lots of the plot of land chosen for the House of Worship at Wilmette, Illinois.

1989–1909—The Bahá'í Publishing Society was founded in Chicago.

1909 Bahá'í Temple Unity, corporate body representing the American Bahá'ís in the construction of the Temple, was incorporated in Illinois.

1910 21 March—The first number of *Bahá'í News* was published in Chicago. This bulletin later became the *Star of the West*, then *The Bahá'í Magazine*, and is now *World Order* (in 1946).

1912 11 April—'Abdu'l-Bahá arrived at New York.

1912 1 May—'Abdu'l-Bahá dedicated the Temple grounds.

1912 5 December—'Abdu'l-Bahá departed from America.

1921 19–21 May—Race Amity Conferences were inaugurated by Mrs Agnes Parsons in Washington, DC, under the direction of 'Abdu'l-Bahá.

1921 28 November—Ascension of 'Abdu'l-Bahá.

1924 December—The first number of *Bahá'í News Letter*, later *Bahá'í News*, the organ of the National Spiritual Assembly, was published in New York.

1925 1 October—A National Bahá'í Office was established by the National Spiritual Assembly at Green Acre, Eliot, Maine.

1926 *The Bahá'í Year Book*, Volume One was published. Later volumes were entitled *The Bahá'í World*.

1927 4 April—The National Spiritual Assembly adopted its Declaration of Trust.

1927 The first session of a Bahá'í School was conducted on the Bosch property, Geyserville, California.

1928 13 November—The Indenture of Trust executed by the Bahá'í Temple Unity transferring the Temple Property to trustees for the benefit of the National Spiritual Assembly was recorded in Cook County, Illinois.

1930 1 January—The Indenture of Trust executed by Green Acre Fellowship transferring the Green Acre property to trustees for the benefits of the National Spiritual Assembly was recorded in York County, Maine.

1930 9 May—The National Spiritual Assembly of the Bahá'ís of the United States and Canada: Palestine Branch, was established as a religious society in Palestine.

---

[1] *The Bahá'í World*, 1944–1946, Vol. X, pp. 179–181.

1931 1 May—The superstructure of the Bahá'í House of Worship was completed.

1931 The first session of a Bahá'í School was conducted on the Eggleston property, Davison, Michigan.

1935 9 March—An Indenture of Trust was executed by Roy C. Wilhelm transferring property in West Englewood, New Jersey, to trustees for the benefit of the National Spiritual Assembly for the construction of a Memorial commemorating the American visit of 'Abdu'l-Bahá.

1935 27 September—The Indenture of Trust executed by Shoghi Effendi transferring the house Malden, Massachusetts, bequeathed to him by Maria P. Wilson, to trustees for the benefit of the National Spiritual Assembly, was recorded in Middlesex Country, Massachusetts.

1935 25 November—The Indenture of Trust Executed by John and Louise Bosch transferring the property used by the Geyserville Bahá'í School to trustees for the benefit of the National Spiritual Assembly was recorded in Sonoma County, California.

1936 1 July—Appointment of the first Inter-America Committee by the National Spiritual Assembly and the beginning of the organized and coordinated effort to establish the Faith in the Republics of Central and South America.

1939 1 October—National Bahá'í Offices established at 536 Sheridan Road, Wilmette, Illinois.

1939 10 October—The Indenture of Trust executed by Mrs Loulie A. Mathews transferring the property used by the International Bahá'í School at Pine Valley near Colorado Springs, was recorded in El Paso County, Colorado.

1943 8 January—Completion of the exterior ornamentation and circular steps of the House of Worship.

1944 28 March—Completion of Teaching plan to establish an Assembly in every State and Province of North America.

3.
Impact of upheavals on the community

3.1 Introduction

This chapter covers paragraphs 4–9. In this section, the Guardian describes how the violent forces released through the world upheaval throw every aspect of ordinary human life into chaos and confusion, and exert their influence, though temporary, on the Bahá'í community. He specifically mentions the restrictions imposed on the Faith in Germany; harassment of the Bahá'ís in 'Ishqábád; persecution of the Bahá'ís in Persia; and the limitations experienced by the small Bahá'í community in the Bahá'í World Centre as the result of religious and racial animosity, and hatred.

In this chapter, you need to reflect on and understand the following key points:

a)   The crises that were afflicting a large proportion of humanity with tremendous force in the 1930's signalled the beginning of a world upheaval.
b)   'Abdu'l-Bahá has attributed great importance to Germany.
c)   The rise of the Nazis and the world war that followed significantly impeded the advancement of European Bahá'í communities.
d)   The development of the German Bahá'í community resumed after World War II with the assistance of the North American Bahá'ís.
e)   The first Bahá'í House of Worship was built in 'Ishqábád, Turkmenistan, during 1902–1908 under the instruction of 'Abdu'l-Bahá.
f)   Within a short period, 'Ishqábád became a flourishing Bahá'í community.
g)   A new phase of persecutions in Turkmenistan during the 1920's and 30's followed the formation of the Soviet Union in 1917. The central government used its new constitution, and legal arguments and instruments, to systematically deny the Bahá'í community its basic rights.
h)   In 1934, many restrictions were imposed on the Persian Bahá'í community of Turkmenistan, such as shutting down of the Bahá'í schools, expulsion of Bahá'ís from government jobs, banning the printing or importing books, and prohibiting the Bahá'í marriage ceremony.

i) In 1928, the Soviet Union authorities expropriated the Bahá'í House of Worship in 'Ishqábád and leased it back to the Bahá'ís until 1938.

j) "The Great Revolt", that occurred in 1936–1939 in Palestine, was a nationalist uprising by Palestinian Arabs against the British Mandate authorities, demanding immediate self-determination and an end to the open-ended Jewish immigration policy.

3.2 Paragraphs under study

4   These recurrent crises which, with ominous frequency and resistless force, are afflicting an ever-increasing portion of the human race must of necessity continue, however impermanently, to exercise, in a certain measure, their baleful influence upon a world community which has spread its ramifications to the uttermost ends of the earth. How can the beginnings of a world upheaval, unleashing forces that are so gravely deranging the social, the religious, the political, and the economic equilibrium of organised society, throwing into chaos and confusion political systems, racial doctrines, social conceptions, cultural standards, religious associations, and trade relationships—how can such agitations, on a scale so vast, so unprecedented, fail to produce any repercussions on the institutions of a Faith of such tender age whose teachings have a direct and vital bearing on each of these spheres of human life and conduct?

5   Little wonder, therefore, if they who are holding aloft the banner of so pervasive a Faith, so challenging a Cause, find themselves affected by the impact of these world-shaking forces. Little wonder if they find that in the midst of this whirlpool of contending passions their freedom has been curtailed, their tenets contemned, their institutions assaulted, their motives maligned, their authority jeopardised, their claim rejected.

6   In the heart of the European continent a community which, as predicted by 'Abdu'l-Bahá, is destined, by virtue of its spiritual potentialities and geographical situation, to radiate the splendour of the light of the Faith on the countries that surround it, has been momentarily eclipsed through the restrictions which a regime that has sorely misapprehended its purpose and function has chosen to impose upon it. Its voice, alas, is now silenced, its institutions dissolved, its literature banned, its archives confiscated, and its meetings suspended.

7   In central Asia, in the city enjoying the unique distinction of having been chosen by 'Abdu'l-Bahá as the home of the first Mashriqu'l-Adhkár of the Bahá'í world, as well as in the towns and villages of the province to which it belongs, the sore-pressed Faith of Bahá'u'lláh, as a result of the extraordinary and unique vitality which, in the course of several decades, it has consistently manifested, finds itself at the mercy of forces which, alarmed at its rising power, are now bent on reducing it to utter impotence. Its Temple, though still used for purposes of Bahá'í worship, has been expropriated, its Assemblies and committees disbanded, its teaching activities crippled, its chief promoters deported, and not a few of its most enthusiastic supporters, both men and women, imprisoned.

8   In the land of its birth, wherein reside the immense majority of its followers—a country whose capital has been hailed by Bahá'u'lláh as the *"mother of the world"* and the *"dayspring of the joy of mankind"*—a civil authority, as yet undivorced officially from the paralysing influences of an antiquated, a fanatical, and outrageously corrupt clergy, pursues relentlessly its campaign of repression against the adherents of a Faith which it has for well-nigh a century striven unsuccessfully to suppress. Indifferent to the truth that the members of this innocent and proscribed community can justly claim to rank as among the most disinterested, the most competent, and the most ardent lovers of their native land, contemptuous of their high sense of world citizenship which the advocates of an excessive and narrow nationalism can never hope to appreciate, such an authority refuses to grant to a Faith which extends its spiritual jurisdiction over well-nigh six hundred local communities, and which numerically outnumbers the adherents of either the Christian, the Jewish, or the Zoroastrian Faiths in that land, the necessary legal right to enforce its laws, to administer its affairs, to conduct its schools, to celebrate its festivals, to circulate its literature, to solemnise its rites, to erect its edifices, and to safeguard its endowments.

9   And now recently in the Holy Land itself, the heart and nerve-Centre of a world-embracing Faith, the fires of racial animosity, of fratricidal strife, of unabashed terrorism, have lit a conflagration that gravely interferes, on the one hand, with that flow of pilgrims that constitutes the lifeblood of that Centre, and suspends, on the other, the various projects that had been initiated in connection with the preservation and extension of the areas surrounding the sacred Spots it enshrines. The safety of the small community of resident believers, faced by the rising tide of lawlessness, has been imperilled, its status as a neutral and distinct community indirectly challenged, and its freedom to carry out certain of its observances curtailed. A series of murderous assaults, alternating with outbursts of bitter fanaticism, both racial and religious, involving the leaders as well as the followers of the three leading Faiths in that distracted country, have, at times, threatened to sever all normal communications both within its confines as well as with the outside world. Perilous though the situation has been, the Bahá'í Holy Places, the object of the adoration of a world-encircling Faith, have, notwithstanding their number and exposed position, and though to outward seeming deprived of any means of protection, been vouchsafed a preservation little short of miraculous.

3.3 Beginning of the world upheaval

War, conflict and crises have always been a major characteristic of human history. However, the dynamics of the world upheaval that started in the early 19th century was fundamentally different. The forces released through those agitations, as mentioned by the Guardian in paragraph 4, have been gravely deranging "the social, the religious, the political, and the economic equilibrium of organised society", and throwing "into chaos and confusion political systems, racial doctrines, social conceptions, cultural standards, religious associations, and trade relationships ... on a scale so vast, so unprecedented".

Bahá'u'lláh, had discerned the signs of the convulsions and had warned humanity:

> The winds of despair are, alas, blowing from every direction, and the strife that divideth and afflicteth the human race is daily increasing. The signs of impending convulsions and chaos can now be discerned, inasmuch as the prevailing order appeareth to be lamentably defective. I beseech God, exalted be His glory, that He may graciously awaken the peoples of the earth, may grant that the end of their conduct may be profitable unto them, and aid them to accomplish that which beseemeth their station.[1]

However, humanity had ignored the Revelation of Bahá'u'lláh and His warnings. At the time *The Advent of Divine Justice* was written, the massive bloodshed of World War I (1914–1918) had ended but the nations of the world were relentlessly preparing for World War II (1939–1945).

In paragraph 4, Shoghi Effendi refers to those crises that were afflicting a large proportion of humanity with tremendous force as the beginning of the world upheaval. Undoubtedly, the Bahá'í world community and the young institutions of the Faith were bound to be affected by the adverse effects of such an upheaval.

In paragraph 5, Shoghi Effendi expounds on the impact of those "world-shaking forces" on those who follow the Bahá'í Cause.

> They find themselves affected by the impact of these world-shaking forces. Little wonder if they find that in the midst of this whirlpool of contending passions their freedom has been curtailed, their tenets contemned, their institutions assaulted, their motives maligned, their authority jeopardised, their claim rejected.

In other paragraphs covered in this chapter, the Guardian illustrates the impact of those crises by describing how they were afflicting the Bahá'í community at the time.

3.4 Restrictions on Bahá'ís in Germany

In paragraph 6, Shoghi Effendi refers to the spiritual significance of Germany and mentions restrictions that the Nazi regime had imposed on the Bahá'í community of Germany, primarily out of misunderstandings about the purpose and function of the Bahá'í Faith.

The development of the Bahá'í Faith in Europe began within a few years of the establishment of the Faith in North America. London and Paris were the first centres where the Bahá'í groups were formed. However, with the journeys of 'Abdu'l-Bahá to Europe in 1911 and 1912, the Faith was introduced to other parts of Europe. Over time, Germany became the centre of the Bahá'í activities, which continued after the interruption caused by World War I.

'Abdu'l-Bahá has attributed great importance to Germany. In a compilation of quotes regarding Germany, France, Italy and Switzerland there are a number of statements by 'Abdu'l-Bahá on the significance of Germany, some of which are

---

[1]   Bahá'u'lláh, *Gleanings from the Writing of Bahá'u'lláh*, pp. 216–217.

quoted in this section.[1] In a Tablet to an individual believer, He expresses no doubt "*... that the Faith of God will progress from day to day in that land* [Germany], *for it will be aided by the strengthening power of the Holy Spirit and the confirmation of the Word of God.*" In another Tablet, He promises that "*Germany will shine resplendent, inasmuch as its citizens are religiously minded. They are not subservient to the world of nature, for souls who are immersed in the material world are like mouldering corpses and remain unaffected by the quickening breath of the Spirit.*"

Furthermore, 'Abdu'l-Bahá affirms that "*There is much spiritual receptivity in Germany. Many souls evince a special disposition to receive the outpourings of heavenly grace. They have the capacity to become the recipients of divine teachings. Hence some individuals are attracted to the principle of the oneness of mankind and treat all the peoples and kindreds of the earth in a spirit of concord and fellowship.*" He foresees that "*[t]he Cause of God will make great progress in Germany. It will surpass all other regions.*" Finally, 'Abdu'l-Bahá cherishes "*... the greatest affection for the loved ones of God in Germany and fervently*" beseeches "*for them divine confirmation and blessing.*" He promises that "*[t]he Call of the Kingdom proclaimed in that country will surely produce tremendous results in the future.*"

In His journey to Europe in 1913, 'Abdu'l-Bahá spent eight days visiting Esslingen, Stuttgart and Bad Mergentheim in Germany, giving public talks and meeting the Bahá'ís. In 1916, the German Bahá'ís erected a public memorial in Bad Mergentheim in memory of 'Abdu'l-Baha's visit. Despite the effects of World War I, the German Bahá'í community grew to the stage that in 1923 it was able to form one of the world's first Bahá'í National Spiritual Assemblies.

The rise of the Nazis, and the world war that followed, significantly impeded the advancement of the European Bahá'í communities. In Germany, Heinrich Himmler accused the Bahá'ís of having "international and pacifist tendencies" and banned the Bahá'í Faith in 1937. Afterwards, the Nazi regime engaged in systematic persecution of the Bahá'ís. The public memorial to 'Abdu'l-Bahá in Bad Mergentheim was destroyed by the Nazis. In 1939, the former members of the National Spiritual Assembly of the Bahá'ís of Germany and many other members of the community were arrested and jailed without any charges. There were more mass arrests in 1942 and many prisoners were sent to Nazi concentration camps.[2]

However, these restrictions proved to be temporary as highlighted by Shoghi Effendi. The development of the German Bahá'í community resumed after World War II. The Bahá'ís of North America played a major role in this process as part of their second Seven Year Plan.

In a message that Shoghi Effendi wrote after World War II to the National Spiritual Assembly of the Bahá'ís of Germany and Austria he states:

---

[1]   Research Department of the Universal House of Justice, *Germany, France, Italy and Switzerland* in *Baha'i Studies Review* 4:1, 1994. http://bahai-library.com/pdf/compilations/germany_france_italy_switzerland.pdf.

[2]   Peter Smith, *A Concise Encyclopaedia of the Bahá'í Faith*, Oneworld Publications, December 1999.

It is such a joy, mingled with feelings of deep thankfulness to Bahá'u'lláh, to be able to resume direct correspondence with the elected national representatives of a community that has achieved so much in the past for our Faith, that has been so dearly loved by 'Abdu'l-Bahá, and is destined to spread, as He foretold, the light of God's sacred Revelation not only in the heart of Europe but throughout that dark, war-devastated spiritually famished continent. Now that the shackles imposed upon that community have been removed, and its chief and central administrative institution is again vigorously functioning, a concerted, sustained and systematic effort must be made, not only by its members, but by the rank and file of its supporters throughout that land, to expand, multiply and consolidate the community's nascent institutions, widen, considerably und rapidly, the range of its literature, establish, firmly and definitely, in however rudimentary a form its national headquarters in Frankfurt situated in the heart of that country, reinforce and develop the work assigned to its national committees, revitalize its summer-schools and other subsidiary institutions, maintain and develop its contact, through correspondence, with national and local administrative bodies throughout the Bahá'í world, devise effective measures for the proclamation, boldly and determinedly, of the message to the masses, fortify and enrich its corporate life and lay and unassailable foundation for its future development.[1]

3.5 Persecution of Bahá'ís in 'Ishqábád

Shoghi Effendi mentions the persecution of the Bahá'í community of 'Ishqábád in paragraph 7. 'Ishqábád was a new city established by the Russians in 1881 as the capital of the province of Trancaspia, the area captured from Turkmen tribes after a long war.

Bahá'ís were associated with 'Ishqábád after one of the relatives of the Báb visited the city in 1881 on his way to 'Akká. He saw the potential of the city and eventually purchased a piece of land.[2] Gradually, further professional Persian Bahá'ís, who had experienced severe persecutions in various villages and cities in Írán, moved to 'Ishqábád and established their businesses and trades. By 1902, there were about 1,000 Bahá'ís, including children, living in 'Ishqábád.[3]

The community began to build various facilities on a piece of land acquired in the centre of the town. These included public baths, a meeting house, a travellers' hospice, a dispensary and a hospital. The building of a boys school was completed in 1897. The Bahá'ís planned to build a House of Worship at the centre of the property. In mid-September 1902, 'Abdu'l-Bahá instructed Ḥájí Muḥammad Taqí Afnán to proceed from Yazd to 'Ishqábád to supervise the construction of the

---

[1] Shoghi Effendi, *The Light of Divine Guidance*, pp. 113–114.
[2] The source of materials in this Section are mainly from: M. Momen, "The Bahá'í Community of 'Ishqábád; Its social basis and importance in Bahá'í history", *Cultural Change and Continuity in Central Asia*, ed. Shirin Akiner, Kegan Paul International, London, 1991, pp. 278–305.
[3] Fáḍil-i-Mázindaráni, *Táríkh-i-Ẓuhúr al-Ḥaqq*, Vol. 8, pt 2, Ṭihrán, 132 Badí'/1975, pp. 981-1049.

House of Worship. Construction started on 31 October 1902 and it was basically completed in 1908.

The Russian revolution of 1917 proved to be a blessing for the Bahá'í community in its first decade as the restrictions imposed by the previous authorities were lifted and the community broke out of its social isolation. They started to hold public meetings and taught the Faith extensively. By 1928, there were 4,000 Bahá'ís living in 'Ishqábád.

During this period, the anti-religious propaganda of the government was spreading fast and the followers of all religions in the Soviet Union were under threat of persecution. The Bahá'í community started to experience these persecutions from 1928.

In 1928, the secret police started to raid Bahá'í meetings and arrest Bahá'ís as part of its anti-religious campaign initiated under Stalin. The Bahá'í printing press was confiscated, Bahá'í administration was suppressed, and the House of Worship was expropriated as all the religious buildings were declared to be government property. Bahá'ís had to rent the House of Worship from the government under a five-year lease. In 1929, the Bahá'í schools, which by then had around 1,000 students, were closed.

A large number of Bahá'ís were arrested in 1929: some were imprisoned, some sent to Siberia, and others deported to Írán. The persecution extended to taking over Bahá'í businesses and expelling Bahá'í students from universities. These severe restrictions continued until 1938. The lease of the House of Worship was renewed in 1933. Under new regulations, the Bahá'í community received full ownership of the House of Worship in 1935 and restrictions on the community eased.

However, in February 1938 the authorities suddenly arrested all the male members of the community as well as some women. Around five hundred men were imprisoned and six hundred women and children were deported to Írán. The House of Worship was expropriated again and was converted to an art gallery.

The House of Worship was badly damaged in an earthquake that occurred in Ishqábád in 1948. Its structure was further weakened by heavy rain in the following year. As a result, it was demolished and the area was converted to a public park.

3.6 Persecution of Bahá'ís in Írán

In paragraph 8, Shoghi Effendi highlights the ongoing repression of the Bahá'í Faith in Írán, "the land of its birth". Although it is the largest religious minority in the country, it has been deprived of the basic legal rights enjoyed by other religious groups such as the Zoroastrians, Jews and Christians. The civil authority has not only disregarded the fact that Persian Bahá'ís have proved themselves to be "among the most disinterested, the most competent, and the most ardent lovers of their native land", but also vilifies them for their elevated consciousness of world citizenship—a concept that is at odds with the regime's fanatically nationalistic paradigm.

The persecution of the Bahá'ís in Írán entered a new stage when a new constitution was approved in 1906, and later with the establishment of the Pahlavi dynasty in 1925. The new constitution did not recognize the Bahá'í Faith as a minority religion in Írán, in contrast to the recognition given to Zoroastrianism, Judaism and Christianity. In the past, mobs and local clergies were primarily the instigators of persecutions. In the new phase, the central government became the primary initiator and executor of oppressions using the new constitution, legal arguments and instruments to systematically deny the Bahá'í community its basic rights. In the face of persecution, the Bahá'í community became more mature and openly pursued its communal and infrastructural developments.

The permanent closure of Bahá'í schools in 1934 by the Pahlavi regime was a good example of this new wave of persecutions. A pronouncement issued on 8 December 1934 by the Prime Minister of Írán ordered the closure of two Tarbíyat schools and a number of other Bahá'í schools. The order argued that those schools disobeyed the Ministry of Education regulations governing the operation of schools by closing on 6 December 1934, which was not a national holiday. The Bahá'í community were commemorating the Declaration of the Báb on the 6th of December, as one of nine Holy Days strictly observed by the Bahá'í community all over the world. Accordingly, the Ministry of Education nullified the concession of the schools and ordered their permanent shutdown. Similar pronouncements were sent to other localities ordering the closure of around 60 Bahá'í schools.

Other legal constraints were forced on the Bahá'ís. The Bahá'í community was banned from printing books, importing books and registering their marriages. Many Bahá'ís were expelled from their government and military positions. In 1938, it became a criminal offence to marry under a religious ceremony not offered by one of the religions recognized in the constitution. This was a measure deployed primarily to suppress the Persian Bahá'í community.

3.7 Conflict and crisis in Holy Land

In paragraph 9, Shoghi Effendi describes the disturbances occurring in the Holy Land, preventing the flow of the pilgrims, suspending various projects underway at the Bahá'í World Centre, endangering the safety of the local Bahá'í community, challenging the neutrality of the Faith, and threatening to cut off all forms of communication. Despite their number, exposed positions and apparent lack of protection, the Bahá'í Holy places were miraculously protected and preserved.

The incident mentioned by Shoghi Effendi in this paragraph is a reference to the revolt, known as "The Great Revolt" that took place during 1936–1939 in Palestine. This was a nationalist uprising by the Palestinian Arabs against the British Mandate authorities, demanding immediate self-determination for the Palestine Arabs and an end to an open-ended Jewish immigration policy. At that time, Great Britain was entrusted with the Mandate for Palestine that was to facilitate the establishment of a Jewish National Home. The Mandate system had been established in the early 20th Century by the League of Nations for administration of non-self-governing territories as a temporary trust. Great Britain was entrusted with the Mandate in July 1922, after the dissolution of the Ottoman Empire in 1922.

In April 1936, the Mufti of Jerusalem called the Arabs in Palestine to observe an unlimited strike against British rule that finally ended in October 1936. The strike was supported by other forms of political protest led by an urban and elitist group called the Higher Arab Committee (HAB). This was later considered as the first phase of the revolt. The second phase of the revolt, led by peasants, was violent and lasted from September 1937 to August 1939.[1]

There are different estimates of the number of casualties in the revolt. According to British figures, more than 2,000 Arabs were killed in combat, 108 were hanged and 961 died as the result of terrorist activities. The Arab sources give an estimate of 19,792 causalities for the Arabs, of which 14,760 were wounded.[2]

---

[1] Jacob Norris, "Repression and Rebellion: Britain's Response to the Arab Revolt in Palestine of 1936–39", *The Journal of Imperial and Commonwealth History* 36(1), 2008, pp. 25–45.

[2] M. Hughes, "The Banality of Brutality: British Armed Forces and the Repression of the Arab Revolt in Palestine, 1936–39", *English Historical Review*, Vol. CXXIV, No. 507, 2009, pp. 314–354.

3.8 Activities

3.8.1 Short answer questions

1. What is your understanding of paragraph 5?

_____

_____

_____

_____

2. What factors distinguish World War I and World War II from other wars in human history?

_____

_____

_____

_____

3. Do you see any relationship between the convulsions experienced by humanity in the period of 1910–1945 and the following quote from Bahá'u'lláh? Comment?

   "The winds of despair are, alas, blowing from every direction, and the strife that divideth and afflicteth the human race is daily increasing. The signs of impending convulsions and chaos can now be discerned, inasmuch as the prevailing order appeareth to be lamentably defective."[1]

_____

_____

_____

_____

4. Why did 'Abdu'l-Bahá predict a significant (noteworthy) future for the Bahá'í community of Germany?

_____

_____

_____

_____

5. What are the distinguishing characteristics of the German Bahá'í community according to 'Abdu'l-Bahá and Shoghi Effendi?

_____

---

[1] Bahá'u'lláh, *Gleanings from the Writing of Bahá'u'lláh*, pp. 216–217.

_____

_____

_____

6. What did the Nazi regime fail to understand about the purpose and function of the Bahá'í Faith?

_____

_____

_____

_____

7. Why did so many Persian Bahá'ís move to 'I<u>sh</u>qábád?

_____

_____

_____

_____

8. Why was the Bahá'í community of 'I<u>sh</u>qábád persecuted?

_____

_____

_____

_____

9. What is the context of sentence two in paragraph 8 and what is your understanding of it?

_____

_____

_____

_____

10. How was the persecution of the Bahá'ís in Írán in the 1930's different from earlier persecutions?

_____

_____

_____

_____

11. Why were all the Bahá'í schools in Írán shut down in 1934?

_____

_____

_____

_____

12. What is Shoghi Effendi referring to by the statement "the fires of racial animosity, of fratricidal strife, of unabashed terrorism" in paragraph 9?

_____

_____

_____

_____

13. What were the specific impacts of the revolt in Palestine during the period of 1936–1939 on the Bahá'í World Centre and its functions?

_____

_____

_____

_____

3.8.2   Mini-project

Choose one of the four cases of persecution of the Bahá'ís described in this chapter and conduct further research on it. Develop a PowerPoint presentation on your research and share it with your community.

4.
Greatness of the Cause

4.1 Introduction

This chapter covers paragraphs 10–11, in which Shoghi Effendi further articulates the nature of the encounter between the infant Faith of Bahá'u'lláh and a world that is disintegrating from within. He identifies four signs of the convulsion afflicting humanity as the quenching of the lights of liberty, the increasing clamour of discord, growing fanaticism and a relentless rise of irreligion. The Guardian indicates that the crises faced by the Bahá'í community at that juncture of history was foreseen by 'Abdu'l-Bahá. He asserts that the reason for the assault of the religious leaders as well as material, cultural, or political forces on the Bahá'í community was the greatness of the Cause, which is clear and manifest.

In this chapter, you need to reflect on and understand the following key points:

a)   In paragraph 10, Shoghi Effendi further expands on the nature of the encounter between the infant Faith of Bahá'u'lláh and a world that is disintegrating from within.

b)   The decade of the 1930's was marked by an economic collapse known as the Great Depression.

c)   During the 1920's and the 1930's, humanity experienced unprecedented oppression and tyranny in different parts of the world.

d)   The political systems that were designed to be democratic in this period led to fascism, Nazism, royal dictatorships and other forms of authoritarian dictatorship.

e)   A review of the world history during the 1930's reveals many revolts, uprisings and wars in different parts of the world—including South America, Europe, Middle East, South East Asia and the Far East, leading eventually to the World War II.

f)   The early 20th century proved a period of continuous rise of irreligion, driven by the atheist theories of Darwin and various ideologies and political movements inspired and driven by communism and Marxism.

g)   In paragraph 11, the Guardian states that the crises faced by the Bahá'í community at that juncture of history were foreseen by 'Abdu'l-Bahá.

h)   'Abdu'l-Bahá asserts that the evident greatness of the Bahá'í Cause has provoked the attacks on the Bahá'í community not only by religious leaders but also by the proponents of current material, cultural, or political views.

4.2 Paragraphs under study

10   A world, torn with conflicting passions, and perilously disintegrating from within, finds itself confronted, at so crucial an epoch in its history, by the rising fortunes of an infant Faith, a Faith that, at times, seems to be drawn into its controversies, entangled by its conflicts, eclipsed by its gathering shadows, and overpowered by the mounting tide of its passions. In its very heart, within its cradle, at the seat of its first and venerable Temple, in one of its hitherto flourishing and potentially powerful centres, the as-yet unemancipated Faith of Bahá'u'lláh seems indeed to have retreated before the onrushing forces of violence and disorder to which humanity is steadily falling a victim. The strongholds of such a Faith, one by one and day after day, are to outward seeming being successively isolated, assaulted and captured. As the lights of liberty flicker and go out, as the din of discord grows louder and louder every day, as the fires of fanaticism flame with increasing fierceness in the breasts of men, as the chill of irreligion creeps relentlessly over the soul of mankind, the limbs and organs that constitute the body of the Faith of Bahá'u'lláh appear, in varying measure, to have become afflicted with the crippling influences that now hold in their grip the whole of the civilized world.

11   How clearly and strikingly the following words of 'Abdu'l-Bahá are being demonstrated at this hour: *"The darkness of error that has enveloped the East and the West is, in this most great cycle, battling with the light of Divine Guidance. Its swords and its spears are very sharp and pointed; its army keenly bloodthirsty."*[A] *"This day,"* He, in another passage has written, *"the powers of all the leaders of religion are directed towards the dispersion of the congregation of the All-Merciful, and the shattering of the Divine Edifice. The hosts of the world, whether material, cultural or political are from every side launching their assault, for the Cause is great, very great. Its greatness is, in this day, clear and manifest to men's eyes."*[B]

4.3 Signs of convulsion

In paragraph 10, Shoghi Effendi further expands on the nature of the encounter between the emerging and resilient Faith of Bahá'u'lláh and a world whose societal structures are crumbling. The Guardian also describes the difficulty the Bahá'í community has in resisting the negative forces generated by the failure of the old world order.

Shoghi Effendi refers to the crippling effect on the Bahá'í Cause of the world's degeneration—an effect that becomes more and more evident as "the lights of liberty flicker and go out, as the din of discord grows louder and louder every day, as the fires of fanaticism flame with increasing fierceness in the breasts of men, as the chill of irreligion creeps relentlessly over the soul of mankind". The Bahá'í community has been:

- Drawn into the controversies of the old world order.
- Entrapped in its conflicts.
- Overshadowed by the darkness surrounding it.
- Overcome by its increasing passion.

The catastrophic phenomena Shoghi Effendi is describing in this paragraph were driven by a succession of events and processes that started, strengthened or culminated after World War I—during the 1920's and the 1930s. In particular, the decade of the 1930's was marked by an economic collapse known as the Great Depression that followed the Wall Street Crash of late October 1929. The crash led to widespread unemployment and worldwide poverty. There were also major political aftermaths such as the emergence of authoritarian regimes in a number of countries in Europe and South America, the invasion of weak countries such as Ethiopia, China and Poland by imperialist world powers, and the break out of World War II just before the end of the decade.

In fact, the four signs of convulsion referred to by Shoghi Effendi were directly or indirectly driven by these processes. Hence, in order to acquire a better insight into the processes that were unfolding, a brief review of the major historical events and processes during that period is provided in the following sections.

4.4 Dousing of the lights of liberty

During the 1920's and the 1930's, humanity experienced unprecedented oppression and tyranny in different parts of the world. People lost their freedom and liberty[1] as the result of authoritarian regimes that emerged in many countries simultaneously.

This is how Shoghi Effendi describes the affairs of the world in a letter he wrote in 1924:

> We have but to turn our eyes to the world without to realize the fierceness and the magnitude of the forces of darkness that are struggling with the dawning light of the Abhá Revelation. Nations, though exhausted and disillusioned, have seemingly begun to cherish anew the spirit of revenge, of domination and strife. Peoples, convulsed by economic upheavals, are slowly drifting into two great opposing camps with all their menace of social chaos, class hatreds, and worldwide ruin. Races, alienated more than ever before, are filled with mistrust, humiliation and fear, and seem to prepare themselves for a fresh and fateful encounter. Creeds and religions, caught in this whirlpool of conflict and passion, appear to gaze with impotence and despair at this spectacle of unceasing turmoil.[2]

---

[1] "Speaking generally, Freedom usually means to be free *from* something, whereas Liberty usually means to be free *to do* something, although both refer to the quality or state of being free." See http://eyler.freeservers.com/JeffPers/jefpc026.htm

[2] Shoghi Effendi, *Bahá'í Administration*, pp. 67–68.

It was generally believed that after the bloody events of World War I, humanity was determined to build a peaceful world and the formation of the League of Nations was a strong indication of such a hope. Such expectations started to develop even during World War I. Woodrow Wilson, the 19th President of the United States, asked the congress to enter World War I by stating: "The world must be made safe for democracy." World War I was also seen as a war to end all wars.[1] History has shown that those assumptions were false and the political systems that were designed to be democratic in the 1920's and the 1930's led to fascism, Nazism, royal dictatorships and other forms of autocracy.

World War I was formally ended when the peace treaty known as Treaty of Versailles was signed by the Allies on 28 June 1919 without the participation of Germany. The Allies included Britain, France, Russia, Italy and the United States who fought against the Central Powers that consisted of Germany, Austria-Hungry, the Ottoman Empire and Bulgaria. There were many provisions in the Treaty, but the most important and controversial of them deemed Germany as the aggressor in the war and required Germany to accept the responsibility of having caused all the losses and damages incurred during the war. The Treaty compelled Germany to disarm, to make extensive territorial concessions, and to pay reparations. This treaty was put together by the Allies to prevent another war. However, its controversial articles and treatment of Germany fuelled the emergence of another world war.[2]

In the same year, the German Workers' Party was founded with the agenda to abandon the Treaty of Versailles and promote German nationalism. Later, the party changed its name to the Nationalist Socialist German Workers' (Nazi) party. Adolf Hitler, an army veteran, was unhappy with the defeat of Germany in World War I, so he joined the party in 1921. Through his charismatic speeches, Hitler soon became a prominent figure in the movement. He blamed Jews and Marxists for Germany's problems, and promoted the idea that Germans were pure descendants of the ancient Aryan race, which they considered to be a "superior" or "master race". Hitler's views attracted much attention and he became the leader of the party in July 1921.

Germany entered an economic depression in 1929. The Nazis exploited the situation and criticized the government in power. Eventually, in January 1933, Hitler became the German Chancellor. Through his strict dictatorship, all other political parties in the country were banned and Nazis took the control of every aspect of life in Germany. This gave Hitler and his party the opportunity to systematically pursue their ideologies of persecution and eradication from German society of Jews and other minorities, as well as expanding Germany's territory and halting the spread of communism. This agenda was a significant contribution to the start of World War II on 1 September 1939.[3]

---

[1] James M. Lutz, "The spread of authoritarian regimes in interwar Europe", *Politics, Religion and Ideology*, 18:3, 2017, pp. 243–263.

[2] *Encyclopaedia Britannica*, cited at https://www.britannica.com/event/Treaty-of-Versailles-1919.

[3] *History*, cited at https://www.history.com/topics/world-war-ii/nazi-party.

In Italy, another War World I veteran, Benito Mussolini, after being discharged from the army in 1917, established the National Fascist Party, in collaboration with Italian socialists and nationalists. In October 1922, Mussolini and his Fascist party marched on Rome. King Victor Emmanuel III asked him to form a new government and appointed him as the prime minister. Initially he collaborated with the parliament, but eventually he effectively became a dictator. In January 1925, Italy was declared a Fascist state with Mussolini as the leader. In 1935, Mussolini's army invaded and annexed Ethiopia.[1]

On 17 July 1936, Mussolini joined Adolf Hitler in support of Francisco Franco's Nationalist force in the Spanish Civil War against a left-wing republican faction backed by the Soviet Union and international communist parties. Franco's national forces defeated the republican forces in April 1939. Consequently, Franco became the head of state of Spain, forming an authoritarian dictatorship.[2]

In the Soviet Union, Joseph Stalin came to power after the death of Lenin[3] in the mid-1920s. He was committed to Marxist-Leninism and established a totalitarian regime based on this ideology. In 1934, he started purging the leaders inside and outside the communist party whose loyalty he doubted. This period is known as the Great Purge in the Soviet Union as many people were arbitrarily arrested, sent to labour camps or executed.[4]

Another dictatorship was established in Brazil by Getulio Dornelles Vargas in 1937. Vargas served as the president of Brazil for two terms from 1930 to 1937. According to the constitution, he had to step down as a president after two terms. Using fears of a communist revolution as an excuse, he announced on the radio on 10 November 1937 that he was seizing emergency powers. He dissolved the Congress and cancelled the election planned for 1938. He also changed the constitution to secure absolute power in the authoritarian "New State" corporist regime. He stayed in power until 1945.[5]

4.5 Growing discord, fanaticism and irreligion

A review of world history during the 1930's reveals many revolts, uprisings and wars in different parts of the globe—including South America, Europe, the Middle East, Southeast Asia and the Far East—leading eventually to World War II. The League of Nations was formed after World War I to prevent another war, but lost its credibility after some countries such as Germany, the Kingdom of Italy and the Empire of Japan pulled out of it.

---

[1] *Encyclopaedia Britannica*, cited at https://www.britannica.com/biography/Benito-Mussolini.

[2] *Encyclopaedia Britannica*, cited at https://www.britannica.com/biography/Francisco-Franco.

[3] Vladimir Ilyich Ulyanov, better known by the alias Lenin.

[4] *Encyclopaedia Britannica*, cited at https://www.britannica.com/biography/Vladimir-Lenin.

[5] *Encyclopaedia Britannica*, cited at https://www.britannica.com/biography/Getulio-Vargas.

In China, civil war for the control of the nation broke out in 1927 between the ruling Kuomintang and the rebel Communist Party of China. In the early 1930's, the communists announced a Chinese Soviet Republic. However, the Republic did not last long and collapsed following Kuomintang attacks, resulting in a mass retreat by the communists led by Mao Zedong, known as the Long March. In 1931, the Empire of Japan invaded and captured Manchuria. It established the puppet state of Manchukuo to control that region, managed by a puppet government headed by Puyi, the last Qing dynasty Emperor of China.[1]

The 1930's also witnessed the growth of fanaticism and fundamentalism manifesting as extreme political, racial, religious, and nationalistic biases and prejudices. The long period of economic hardship and anxiety known as the Great Depression led to fanaticism and the emergence of radical regimes.

The Great Depression in the United States affected every group of the society, but the African Americans suffered the most. By 1932, nearly half of the African Americans had lost their jobs and in some places the whites called for the sacking of blacks and giving their jobs to whites. Racial violence also became more widespread, particularly in the southern states.[2]

In Germany, as described earlier, antisemitism became a major policy for the Nazis after 1933 and resulted in the extermination of millions of Jews in Europe.

The early 20th century proved to be a period of continuing rise of irreligion, driven by the atheist theories of Darwinism and various ideologies and political movements inspired and driven by communism and Marxism.

With the Russian Revolution of 1917, the Bolshevik Party came to power and fully embraced Marxist ideologies. This resulted in the spread of communism in Europe during the 20th century and the establishment of communist governments in Eastern and Central Europe after World War II. The spread of communism was so extensive that by 1985, one third of the world lived under a communist system of governance.[3] This significantly contributed to the spread of materialist theories and undermined religious beliefs.

In some communist countries, there were systematic and aggressive campaigns against religion. For example, in the Soviet Union, a new phase of anti-religious persecution started in 1928 after legislation was introduced to severely restrict religious activities in order to promote atheism. The main target, with the largest number of followers, was the Russian Orthodox Church, though other religious groups, including the Bahá'í community in 'Ishqábád, were affected. This campaign continued until 1941.

An anti-Christian campaign started in China in 1922. This was driven by other factors such a strong nationalist movement as a reaction to the invasion and humiliation of China by many foreign forces.

[1] *Encyclopaedia Britannica*, cited at https://www.britannica.com/event/Chinese-Civil-War.

[2] *Encyclopaedia Britannica,* cited at https://www.britannica.com/topic/African-American/African-American-life-during-the-Great-Depression-and-the-New-Deal.

[3] Thomas Lansford, *Communism*, New York: Cavendish Square Publishing, 2007.

4.6 The Cause is great

In paragraph 11, the Guardian indicates that the crises faced by the Bahá'í community in the late 1930s were foreseen by 'Abdu'l-Bahá, as illustrated by the two statements he quotes from Him. In the first statement (quote 11:A), 'Abdu'l-Bahá refers to *"darkness of error"* that is battling with *"the light of divine guidance"*. In the second statement (quote 11:B), 'Abdu'l-Bahá asserts that the evident greatness of the Bahá'í Cause has provoked the attacks on the Bahá'í community not only by religious leaders but also by the proponents of current material, cultural, or political views.

The greatness of the Cause can be perceived in a number of contexts. The forces released through the Revelation of Bahá'u'lláh were already in operation to prepare the world for the establishment of His World Order. In one of His Tablets, 'Abdu'l-Bahá states:

> O my friend, verily the Cause is great and great, and the penetration of the Word of God in the temple of all the regions is similar to the pervasion of the soul in a sound body.

> By the life of Bahá, verily, the power of the Kingdom of God hath taken hold of the pillars of the world, and hath possessed all the nations. Thou wilt surely find the standards of the Testament waving in all regions, the chanting of the verses of unity raised in exalted assemblies, and the lights of the Sun of Truth and its heat dispersing the thick clouds massed on the horizon.[1]

The teachings of the Bahá'í Faith also represent lofty standards set for human thoughts, attitudes and deeds, which are an extreme contrast to the vices and iniquities that underlined the on-going oppression experienced by people during the 1930's. In one of His Tablets, 'Abdu'l-Bahá illustrates such contrasts when He urges us to endeavour with heart and soul

> ... until the world of war become the world of peace; the world of darkness the world of light; satanic conduct be turned into heavenly behaviour; the ruined places become built up; the sword be turned into the olive branch; the flash of hatred become the flame of the love of God and the noise of the gun the voice of the Kingdom; the soldiers of death the soldiers of life; all the nations of the world one nation; all races as one race; and all national anthems harmonized into one melody.[2]

---

[1] 'Abdu'l-Bahá in *Bahá'í World Faith*, pp. 393–394.

[2] 'Abdu'l-Baha, *Tablets of Abdul-Baha Abbas*, Vol. 1, pp. 39–40.

4.7 Activities

4.7.1 *Short answer questions*

1. What is your understanding of the first sentence in paragraph 10?

_____

_____

_____

_____

2. Consider the following statement from paragraph 10:

   "The strongholds of such a Faith, one by one and day after day, are to outward seeming being successively isolated, assaulted and captured."

   a) What does Shoghi Effendi mean by "outward seeming"?

   _____

   _____

   _____

   _____

   b) What is your understanding of this sentence?

   _____

   _____

   _____

   _____

3. Consider the following statement from paragraph 10:

   "... the body of the Faith of Bahá'u'lláh appear, in varying measure, to have become afflicted with the crippling influences that now hold in their grip the whole of the civilized world."

   a) What does Shoghi Effendi mean by "crippling influences"?

   _____

   _____

   _____

   b) What is your understanding of this statement?

   _____

   _____

   _____

4. Give three historical examples demonstrating how the lights of liberty were dimming in the 1930's.

    _____

    _____

    _____

    _____

5. What were the evidences of growing discord in the 1930's?

    _____

    _____

    _____

    _____

6. What were the evidences of rising fanaticism in the 1930's?

    _____

    _____

    _____

    _____

7. What were the evidences of rising irreligion in the 1930's?

    _____

    _____

    _____

    _____

8. The following questions relate to quote 11:B from 'Abdu'l-Bahá.

    a) What is your understanding of the term "darkness of error"?

    _____

    _____

    _____

    b) What is your understanding of the term "the light of Divine Guidance"?

    _____

    _____

    _____

    _____

9. How can the greatness of the Cause be a primary reason for outside forces to assault and attack the Faith?

_____

_____

_____

_____

4.7.2 *Mini-project*

Develop a timeline of the major events of the 1930s illustrating the growth of dictatorship, discord, fanaticism and irreligion. On the timeline, also show the impact of these convulsions on the Bahá'í community.

5.
Cradle of the New World Order

5.1 Introduction

This chapter covers paragraphs 12–15. In this section Shoghi Effendi identifies the North American Bahá'í community as the remaining fortress upholding the standards of the Cause of Bahá'u'lláh in the chaos surrounding the world at that time. He also calls that community the cradle and stronghold of the New World Order that is "the promise and the glory of the Dispensation" of Bahá'u'lláh (para. 12) and cites a statement from 'Abdu'l-Bahá to justify this assertion (quote 13:A).

In this chapter, you need to reflect on and understand the following key points:

a) In the Persian Bayán (Bayán-i-Fársí), the Báb announces the Order that is associated with the Revelation of Bahá'u'lláh.

b) In *The Kitáb-i-Aqdas*, Bahá'u'lláh makes reference to this Order as the New World Order.

c) The Guardian considers attainment to the New World Order as the only saviour for humanity in its dire condition.

d) Shoghi Effendi identifies the evolving Bahá'í Administrative Order as the nucleus and pattern of the New World Order.

e) The North American Bahá'í community will play a major role in the unfoldment of the New World Order towards its full glory.

f) There are two simultaneous but independent and closely linked processes occurring in America towards the realization of the New World Order.

   • The first process is associated with the mission of North American Bahá'í community as revealed by 'Abdu'l-Bahá in the Tablets of the Divine Plan.

   • The second process is associated with the role that the American nation—unaware of the Revelation of Bahá'u'lláh–plays in the establishment of the New World Oder.

g) The Golden Age is the stage of perfection and the realization of the goals of the Dispensation of Bahá'u'lláh.

5.2 Paragraphs under study

12 The one chief remaining citadel, the mighty arm, which still raises aloft the standard of an unconquerable Faith, is none other than the blessed community of the followers of the Most Great Name in the North American continent. By its works, and through the unfailing protection vouchsafed to it by an almighty Providence, this distinguished member of the body of the constantly interacting Bahá'í communities of East and West, bids fair to be universally regarded as the cradle, as well as the stronghold, of that future New World Order, which is at once the promise and the glory of the Dispensation associated with the name of Bahá'u'lláh.

13 Let anyone inclined to either belittle the unique station conferred upon this community, or to question the role it will be called upon to play in the days to come, ponder the implication of these pregnant and highly illuminating words uttered by 'Abdu'l-Bahá, and addressed to it at a time when the fortunes of a world groaning beneath the burden of a devastating war had reached their lowest ebb. *"The continent of America,"* He so significantly wrote, *"is, in the eyes of the one true God, the land wherein the splendours of His light shall be revealed, where the mysteries of His Faith shall be unveiled, where the righteous will abide, and the free assemble."*[A]

14 Already, the community of the believers of the North American continent—at once the prime mover and pattern of the future communities which the Faith of Bahá'u'lláh is destined to raise up throughout the length and breadth of the Western Hemisphere—has, despite the prevailing gloom, shown its capacity to be recognized as the torchbearer of that light, the repository of those mysteries, the exponent of that righteousness and the sanctuary of that freedom. To what other light can these above-quoted words possibly allude, if not to the light of the glory of the Golden Age of the Faith of Bahá'u'lláh? What mysteries could 'Abdu'l-Bahá have contemplated except the mysteries of that embryonic World Order now evolving within the matrix of His Administration? What righteousness if not the righteousness whose reign that Age and that Order can alone establish? What freedom but the freedom which the proclamation of His sovereignty in the fullness of time must bestow?

15 The community of the organized promoters of the Faith of Bahá'u'lláh in the American continent—the spiritual descendants of the dawn-breakers of an heroic Age, who by their death proclaimed the birth of that Faith—must, in turn, usher in, not by their death but through living sacrifice, that promised World Order, the shell ordained to enshrine that priceless jewel, the world civilization, of which the Faith itself is the sole begetter. While its sister communities are bending beneath the tempestuous winds that beat upon them from every side, this community, preserved by the immutable decrees of the omnipotent Ordainer and deriving continual sustenance from the mandate with which the Tablets of the Divine Plan have invested it, is now busily engaged in laying the foundations and in fostering the growth of those

institutions which are to herald the approach of the Age destined to witness the birth and rise of the World Order of Bahá'u'lláh.

5.3 Cradle and stronghold of the New World Order

In paragraph 12, Shoghi Effendi refers to the North American Bahá'í community as the remaining fortress upholding the standards of the Cause of Bahá'u'lláh in the chaos surrounding the world at that time. He suggests that it is fair, considering the works conducted by this community and the protection vouchsafed for it by Bahá'u'lláh, to suggest that the North American Bahá'í community can be considered as the cradle and stronghold of the New World Order that is "the promise and the glory of the Dispensation" of Bahá'u'lláh.

In the Persian Bayán, the Báb announces the Order that is associated with the Revelation of Bahá'u'lláh and exhorts *"... him who fixeth his gaze upon the Order of Bahá'u'lláh, and rendereth thanks unto his Lord. For He will assuredly be made manifest. God hath indeed irrevocably ordained it in the Bayán."*[1] In *The Kitáb-i-Aqdas*, Bahá'u'lláh makes reference to this Order as the new World Order and announces: *"The world's equilibrium hath been upset through the vibrating influence of this most great, this new World Order. Mankind's ordered life hath been revolutionized through the agency of this unique, this wondrous System—the like of which mortal eyes have never witnessed."*[2]

The Guardian considers the realization of the New World Order, "whose promise is enshrined in the Revelation of Bahá'u'lláh, whose fundamental principles have been enunciated in the writings of the Centre of His Covenant,"[3] as the only saviour for humanity in its dire condition. "It is towards this goal—the goal of a new World Order, Divine in origin, all-embracing in scope, equitable in principle, challenging in its features—that a harassed humanity must strive."[4]

Shoghi Effendi identifies the evolving Bahá'í Administrative Order as the nucleus and pattern of the New World Order. He affirms that with the expansion and consolidation of the Administrative Order, and "... as its component parts, its organic institutions, begin to function with efficiency and vigour, assert its claim and demonstrate its capacity to be regarded not only as the nucleus but the very pattern of the New World Order destined to embrace in the fullness of time the whole of mankind."[5] According to Shoghi Effendi, the structure of the New World Order "now stirring in the womb of the administrative institutions He [Bahá'u'lláh] Himself has created ... will serve both as a pattern and a nucleus of that world commonwealth which is the sure, the inevitable destiny of the peoples and nations of the earth."[6]

---

[1]   The Báb in *God Passes By*, p. 25; and *The Kitáb-i-Aqdas*, Note 189, p. 247.

[2]   Bahá'u'lláh, *The Kitáb-i-Aqdas*, p. 85.

[3]   Shoghi Effendi, *The World Order of Bahá'u'lláh*, p. 162.

[4]   Shoghi Effendi, *The World Order of Bahá'u'lláh*, p. 34.

[5]   Shoghi Effendi, *The World Order of Bahá'u'lláh*, p. 144.

[6]   Shoghi Effendi, *The Promised Day is Come*, p. 118.

Regarding the impact of the New World Order, Shoghi Effendi asserts that it will achieve "... no less than the complete unification of the entire human race. This unification should conform to such principles as would directly harmonize with the spirit that animates, and the laws that govern the operation of, the institutions that already constitute the structural basis of the Administrative Order of His Faith."[1]

The emergence of the New World Order and its "consummation will, by its very nature, be a gradual process, and must, as Bahá'u'lláh has Himself anticipated, lead at first to the establishment of that Lesser Peace which the nations of the earth, as yet unconscious of His Revelation and yet unwittingly enforcing the general principles which He has enunciated, will themselves establish. This momentous and historic step, involving the reconstruction of mankind, as the result of the universal recognition of its oneness and wholeness, will bring in its wake the spiritualization of the masses, consequent to the recognition of the character, and the acknowledgement of the claims, of the Faith of Bahá'u'lláh—the essential condition to that ultimate fusion of all races, creeds, classes, and nations which must signalize the emergence of His New World Order."[2]

In one of his messages, Shoghi Effendi briefly articulates the general character, the implications and features of the world commonwealth, representing the New World Order:

"The unity of the human race, as envisaged by Bahá'u'lláh, implies the establishment of a world commonwealth in which

- all nations, races, creeds and classes are closely and permanently united, and in which the autonomy of its state members and the personal freedom and initiative of the individuals that compose them are definitely and completely safeguarded.
- This commonwealth must, as far as we can visualize it, consist of a world legislature, whose members will, as the trustees of the whole of mankind, ultimately control the entire resources of all the component nations, and will enact such laws as shall be required to regulate the life, satisfy the needs and adjust the relationships of all races and peoples.
- A world executive, backed by an international Force, will carry out the decisions arrived at, and apply the laws enacted by, this world legislature, and will safeguard the organic unity of the whole commonwealth.
- A world tribunal will adjudicate and deliver its compulsory and final verdict in all and any disputes that may arise between the various elements constituting this universal system.
- A mechanism of world inter-communication will be devised, embracing the whole planet, freed from national hindrances and restrictions, and functioning with marvellous swiftness and perfect regularity.

---

[1]   Shoghi Effendi, *The World Order of Bahá'u'lláh*, p. 162.

[2]   Shoghi Effendi, *The Promised Day is Come*, p. 123.

- A world metropolis will act as the nerve centre of a world civilization, the focus towards which the unifying forces of life will converge and from which its energizing influences will radiate.
- A world language will either be invented or chosen from among the existing languages and will be taught in the schools of all the federated nations as an auxiliary to their mother tongue.
- A world script, a world literature, a uniform and universal system of currency, of weights and measures, will simplify and facilitate intercourse and understanding among the nations and races of mankind.
- In such a world society, science and religion, the two most potent forces in human life, will be reconciled, will cooperate, and will harmoniously develop.
- The press will, under such a system, while giving full scope to the expression of the diversified views and convictions of mankind, cease to be mischievously manipulated by vested interests, whether private or public, and will be liberated from the influence of contending governments and peoples.
- The economic resources of the world will be organized, its sources of raw materials will be tapped and fully utilized, its markets will be coordinated and developed, and the distribution of its products will be equitably regulated.
- National rivalries, hatreds, and intrigues will cease, and racial animosity and prejudice will be replaced by racial amity, understanding and cooperation.
- The causes of religious strife will be permanently removed, economic barriers and restrictions will be completely abolished, and the inordinate distinction between classes will be obliterated.
- Destitution on the one hand, and gross accumulation of ownership on the other, will disappear.
- The enormous energy dissipated and wasted on war, whether economic or political, will be consecrated to such ends as will extend the range of human inventions and technical development, to the increase of the productivity of mankind, to the extermination of disease, to the extension of scientific research, to the raising of the standard of physical health, to the sharpening and refinement of the human brain, to the exploitation of the unused and unsuspected resources of the planet, to the prolongation of human life, and to the furtherance of any other agency that can stimulate the intellectual, the moral, and spiritual life of the entire human race.
- A world federal system, ruling the whole earth and exercising unchallengeable authority over its unimaginably vast resources, blending and embodying the ideals of both the East and the West, liberated from the curse of war and its miseries, and bent on the exploitation of all the available sources of energy on the surface of the planet, a system in which Force is made the servant of Justice, whose life is sustained by its universal recognition of one God and by its allegiance to one common Revelation—

such is the goal towards which humanity, impelled by the unifying forces of life, is moving."[1]

5.4 North American Bahá'í community

Shoghi Effendi quotes from the Tablets of the Divine Plan (quote 13:A) in paragraph 13 to confirm the unique station of the North American Bahá'í community. In this assertion, 'Abdu'l-Bahá describes the continent of America as a land where

- the splendours of the light of God will be revealed,
- the mysteries of His Faith shall be known,
- upright people will abide in, and
- those who are free will gather together.

In paragraph 14, Shoghi Effendi explains the meaning and implications of this statement of 'Abdu'l-Bahá (quote 13:A) by pointing out that:

- The light is the glory of the Golden Age of the Faith of Bahá'u'lláh.
- The mysteries are the characteristics of the new World Order, evolving within the matrix of the Bahá'í Administration.
- The righteousness will be established by the New World Order.
- Freedom will be achieved in the fullness of time through the proclamation of the sovereignty of Bahá'u'lláh.

The statement of 'Abdu'l-Bahá in Shoghi Effendi's interpretation implies that America as a nation, and the North American Bahá'í community in particular, will play major roles in the unfoldment of the New World Order in its full glory.

Finally, in paragraph 15, Shoghi Effendi identifies the North American Bahá'í community as the spiritual descendants of the dawn breakers of the Cause in Persia who proclaimed the birth of the Revelations of the Báb and Bahá'u'lláh by their martyrdoms. Similarly, the North American believers must usher in the World Order of Bahá'u'lláh through their living sacrifice, not death, building the institutions that will herald the unfoldment of that order.

In *Citadel of Faith*, written in 1947, Shoghi Effendi sheds some light on the processes associated with America that would eventually lead to the realization of the New World Order. In this connection, he identifies two simultaneous but independent and closely linked processes.

The first process is associated with the mission of the North American Bahá'í community that started with the revelation of the Tablets of the Divine Plan, but was suspended for about 20 years while the North American Bahá'í community developed the necessary administrative structure to undertake its tasks. The administration evolved through two consecutive Seven Year Plans until 1953.[2] The development of the North American Bahá'í community continued during the Ten Year Crusade and will continue as a result of other systematic plans that will

---

[1] Shoghi Effendi, *The World Order of Bahá'u'lláh*, pp. 203–204. Bullets added for emphasis.

[2] Shoghi Effendi, *Citadel of Faith*, p. 32.

be devised and initiated by the Universal House of Justice. This evolution will be completed when the Bahá'í World Commonwealth emerges in the Golden Age of the Bahá'í Dispensation.

The second process is associated with the role that the American nation, though unaware of the Revelation of Bahá'u'lláh, plays in the establishment of the New World Oder. This process commenced when the American nation turned its attention to world affairs with the outbreak of World War I. This engagement grew stronger when the President Woodrow Wilson gave a speech to the United States Congress on 8 January 1918 outlining a statement of principle for peace, known as the Fourteen Points, to guide the peace negotiations at the end of World War I.

In order to prevent another world war, American and British statesmen established the League of Nations. However, Woodrow Wilson did not manage to convince Americans to join the League of Nations, although the United States continued to play an economically crucial role in advancing peace in Europe during the 1920's.

The United States became more deeply involved in the affairs of the world with the outbreak of World War II. On 14 August 1941, President Franklin Roosevelt and the British Prime Minister Winston Churchill issued a joint policy statement, known as the Atlantic Charter, for a post war world that was confirmed later by all the Allies involved in World War II. The Charter consisted of the following principles:[1]

1. No territorial gains were to be sought by the United States or the United Kingdom.
2. Territorial changes should not be made against the wishes of the people.
3. The right of people to choose their own form of government and the restoration of self-government for those who lost it during the war should be promoted.
4. Ensuring equal access to trade and raw materials by all nations to achieve economic prosperity.
5. Fostering international co-operation to improve labour standards, economic progress and social security.
6. Freedom for all nations to live safely within their boundaries without fear or need.
7. Participant nations would work towards the establishment of the freedom of the seas.
8. Abandonment of armed force and the disarming of aggressor states.

The Atlantic Charter was incorporated by reference into the Declaration of the United Nations on 1 January 1942 that was signed by 26 countries. This became the basis of the modern United Nations. The final Charter of the United Nations was discussed and accepted at the United Nations Conference on International Organization convened in San Francisco on 25 April 1945. The San Francisco conference was attended by 50 countries from all parts of the world. The United

---

[1] *Encyclopaedia Britannica*, cited at https://www.britannica.com/event/Atlantic-Charter.

Fazel Naghdy

Nations Charter was unanimously signed on 26 June and promulgated on 24 October 1945. The cornerstone for the permanent seat of the United Nations was laid in New York City in 1949.

During His journeys in the United States, 'Abdu'l-Bahá visited Sacramento, the capital of California about 120 km northeast of San Francisco. On 26 October 1912, He gave a talk on international peace at the Assembly Hall of Hotel Sacramento. In that talk He foretold the San Francisco conference by stating:

> *Inasmuch as the Californians seem peace loving and possessed of great worthiness and capacity, I hope that advocates of peace may daily increase among them until the whole population shall stand for that beneficent outcome. May the men of affairs in this democracy uphold the standard of international conciliation. Then may altruistic aims and thoughts radiate from this centre toward all other regions of the earth, and may the glory of this accomplishment forever halo the history of this country. May the first flag of international peace be upraised in this state. May the first illumination of reality shine gloriously upon this soil. May this centre and capital become distinguished in all degrees of accomplishment, for the virtues of humanity and the possibilities of human advancement are boundless.[1]*

'Abdu'l-Bahá also designated New York City as the "City of the Covenant".[2] In a talk 'Abdu'l-Bahá gave at a reception by the New York Peace Society on 13 May 1912, He stated:

> *The powers of earth cannot withstand the privileges and bestowals which God has ordained for this great and glorious century. It is a need and exigency of the time. Man can withstand anything except that which is divinely intended and indicated for the age and its requirements. Now—praise be to God!—in all countries of the world, lovers of peace are to be found, and these principles are being spread among mankind, especially in this country. Praise be to God! This thought is prevailing, and souls are continually arising as defenders of the oneness of humanity, endeavouring to assist and establish international peace. There is no doubt that this wonderful democracy will be able to realize it, and the banner of international agreement will be unfurled here to spread onward and outward among all the nations of the world.[3]*

Shoghi Effendi refers to other significant foreign policies of the United States and its engagement in world affairs, and then states that the journey of the American nation, however long and tortuous the way, must "... lead, through a series of victories and reverses, to the political unification of the Eastern and Western Hemispheres, to the emergence of a world government and the establishment of the Lesser Peace, as foretold by Bahá'u'lláh and foreshadowed by the Prophet Isaiah. It must, in the end, culminate in the unfurling of the banner of the Most Great Peace, in the Golden Age of the Dispensation of Bahá'u'lláh."[4]

---

[1]   'Abdu'l-Bahá, *The Promulgation of Universal Peace*, pp. 376–377.
[2]   Shoghi Effendi, *God Passes By*, p. 288.
[3]   'Abdu'l-Bahá, *The Promulgation of Universal Peace*, p. 125.
[4]   Shoghi Effendi, *Citadel of Faith*, p. 33.

Towards the end of the message, Shoghi Effendi further elaborates on the journey that the American nation will take towards its destiny:

> Many and divers are the setbacks and reverses which this nation, extolled so highly by 'Abdu'l-Bahá, and occupying at present so unique a position among its fellow nations, must, alas, suffer. The road leading to its destiny is long, thorny and tortuous. The impact of various forces upon the structure and polity of that nation will be tremendous. Tribulations, on a scale unprecedented in its history, and calculated to purge its institutions, to purify the hearts of its people, to fuse its constituent elements, and to weld it into one entity with its sister nations in both hemispheres, are inevitable.[1]

5.5 Glory of the Golden Age

The entire history of the Revelation of Bahá'u'lláh can be divided into three ages or stages known as the Heroic, Formative and Golden Ages. Each Age on its own consists of a number of epochs or periods.

5.5.1   *Heroic Age*

The first stage is the Heroic Age, otherwise referred to by Shoghi Effendi as the Primitive Age or the Apostolic Age. This stage began with the Declaration of the Báb on 23 May 1844 and ended with the passing of 'Abdu'l-Bahá on 28 November 1921, or "more particularly", as the Guardian states, with the passing of the Greatest Holy Leaf, the sister of 'Abdu'l-Bahá, in July 1932.

The Heroic Age of the Bahá'í Era is unique in its impact and spiritual power. The Guardian describes it thus:

> This Primitive Age of the Bahá'í Era, unapproached in spiritual fecundity by any period associated with the mission of the Founder of any previous Dispensation, was impregnated, from its inception to its termination, with the creative energies generated through the advent of two independent Manifestations and the establishment of a Covenant unique in the spiritual annals of mankind.[2]

The Guardian has identified "three distinct epochs, of nine, of thirty-nine and of twenty-nine years duration" in the Heroic Age which are "associated respectively with the Bábí Dispensation and the Ministries of Bahá'u'lláh and of 'Abdu'l-Bahá."[3]

5.5.2   *Formative Age*

The Transitional or Formative Age is the period of evolution of the Faith towards the unfoldment of its potentials and the emergence of the world order envisaged by Bahá'u'lláh. In the Bahá'í Writings there is no indication of the duration of the Formative Age. However, Shoghi Effendi indicates that the

---

[1]   Shoghi Effendi, *Citadel of Faith*, pp. 36–37.
[2]   Shoghi Effendi, in *Lights of Guidance*, p. 488.
[3]   Shoghi Effendi, in *Lights of Guidance*, p. 488.

Formative Age consists of a number of epochs[1] that will gradually emerge over time.

In one of his letters, Shoghi Effendi describes the major events to occur during the Formative Age. He foresees that during the succeeding epochs:[2]

a) The "last and crowning stage in the erection of the framework of the Administrative Order of the Faith of Bahá'u'lláh—the election of the Universal House of Justice—will have been completed,

b) *The Kitáb-i-Aqdas*, the Mother-Book of His Revelation, will have been codified and its laws promulgated,

c) the Lesser Peace will have been established,

d) the unity of mankind will have been achieved and its maturity attained,

e) the Plan conceived by 'Abdu'l-Bahá will have been executed,

f) the emancipation of the Faith from the fetters of religious orthodoxy will have been effected,

g) and its independent religious status will have been universally recognized."[3]

A number of these developments, including (a) and (b), have been fully accomplished and significant progress is made towards fulfilling (c) and (e).

Thus far the Bahá'í Faith has passed through the following epochs of the Formative Age:

a) The first epoch began with the ministry of Shoghi Effendi as the Guardian of the Bahá'í Faith in 1921 and ended in 1944–46, the closing of the first century after the Declaration of the Báb. This epoch witnessed "the birth and the primary stages in the erection of the framework of the Administrative Order of the Faith."[4]

b) The Second Epoch began in 1946 and ended in 1963 with the election of the first Universal House of Justice. "This epoch extended the developments of the first epoch by calling for the Consummation of a laboriously constructed Administrative Order, and was to witness the formulation of a succession of teaching plans designed to facilitate the development of the Faith beyond the confines of the Western Hemisphere and the continent of Europe .... The Second Epoch thus clearly demonstrated the further maturation of the institutions of the Administrative Order."[5]

c) The third epoch began in 1963 and ended in 1986. "The period of the third epoch encompassed three world plans, involving all the National Spiritual Assemblies, under the direction of the Universal House of Justice, namely, the Nine Year Plan (1964–1973), the Five Year Plan (1974–1979), and the Seven Year Plan (1979–1986). The third epoch witnessed the emergence of the

---

[1] Shoghi Effendi, in *Lights of Guidance*, p. 488.

[2] List form is added for emphasis and further reference.

[3] Shoghi Effendi, *Citadel of Faith*, p. 6.

[4] Shoghi Effendi, *Citadel of Faith*, p. 5.

[5] The Universal House of Justice, *Messages from the Universal House of Justice 1963–1986*, p. 713.

Faith from obscurity and the initiation of activities designed to foster the social and economic development of communities."[1]

d) The fourth epoch began in 1986. The Universal House of Justice announced the inception of this new epoch of the Formative Age in a letter dated 2 January 1986 to the Bahá'ís of the World.[2] The fourth epoch highlighted the significant developments that had occurred in the "organic growth of the Cause of God" during the third epoch. In the previous epochs, the national plans were largely derived from the Bahá'í World Centre. In the new epoch the specific goals for each national community were formulated within the framework of the overall objectives of the Plan through consultation between National Spiritual Assemblies and the Continental Board of Counsellors.

e) The fifth epoch started in 2001. The Universal House of Justice announced the inception of this epoch of the Formative Age in a letter dated 16 January 2001 to the Bahá'ís of the World: "... as the construction projects on Mount Carmel approached their completion, and as the internal processes of institutional consolidation and the external processes towards world unity became more fully synchronized. ... the extraordinary dynamics at work throughout the Conference [of the Continental Boards of Counsellors in January 2001] crystallized these indications into a recognizable reality."[3]

Additional epochs can be anticipated in the Formative Age, as the tasks to be completed in this Age are many and challenging. *The Will and Testament of 'Abdu'l-Bahá* provides the link between the Heroic Age and the Formative Age.

5.5.3   Golden Age

The Golden Age is the stage of perfection and the realization of the goals of the Dispensation of Bahá'u'lláh. The initial stages of the Golden Age will be synchronized with the "emergence of a world community", "the consciousness of world citizenship", and "the founding of a world civilization and culture."[4] Shoghi Effendi regards such developments as "the furthermost limits in the organization of human society" on this planet. Although "man, as an individual, will, nay must indeed as a result of such a consummation, continue indefinitely to progress and develop."[5]

In the course of the Golden Age, humanity will witness that "the banner of the Most Great Peace, promised by its Author, will have been unfurled, the World Bahá'í Commonwealth will have emerged in the plenitude of its power and splendour, and the birth and efflorescence of a world civilization, the child of that

---

[1] The Universal House of Justice, *Messages from the Universal House of Justice 1963–1986*, p. 715.

[2] The Universal House of Justice, *Messages from the Universal House of Justice 1963–1986*, pp. 715–716.

[3] The Universal House of Justice, *Messages from the Universal House of Justice 1986–2001*, p. 773.

[4] Shoghi Effendi, *The World Order of Bahá'u'lláh*, p. 163.

[5] Shoghi Effendi, *The World Order of Bahá'u'lláh*, p. 163.

Peace, will have conferred its inestimable blessings upon all mankind".[1] Such outcomes will be unfolded through "successive epochs" of the Golden Age.[2]

---

[1]   Shoghi Effendi, *Citadel of Faith*, p. 6.
[2]   The Universal House of Justice, *A Wider Horizon, Selected Letters from the Universal House of Justice 1983–1992*, p. 179.

5.6 Activities

5.6.1 Short answer questions

1. On what basis does Shoghi Effendi refer to the North American Bahá'í community as the cradle and the stronghold of the future New World Order?

    _____

    _____

    _____

    _____

2. What is the "living sacrifice" mentioned by Shoghi Effendi in paragraph 15?

    _____

    _____

    _____

    _____

3. What is your understanding of the following statement by Bahá'u'lláh?

    "The world's equilibrium hath been upset through the vibrating influence of this most great, this new World Order. Mankind's ordered life hath been revolutionized through the agency of this unique, this wondrous System—the like of which mortal eyes have never witnessed."[1]

    _____

    _____

    _____

    _____

4. Shoghi Effendi states that the Bahá'í Administrative Order will be "not only as the nucleus but the very pattern of the New World Order." What does he mean by "nucleus" and "pattern" of the New World Order?

    _____

    _____

    _____

    _____

5. What are the different stages of development that precede the emergence of the New world Order?

    _____

    _____

---

[1] Bahá'u'lláh, *The Kitáb-i-Aqdas*, p. 85.

6. The following questions relate to quote 13:A 'Abdu'l-Bahá:

   What does 'Abdu'l-Bahá mean by each of the following statements?

   a) *"the land wherein the splendours of His light shall be revealed"*

   _____

   _____

   _____

   _____

   b) *"where the mysteries of His Faith shall be unveiled"*

   _____

   _____

   _____

   _____

   c) *"where the righteous will abide"*

   _____

   _____

   _____

   _____

   d) *"and the free assemble"*

   _____

   _____

   _____

   _____

7. Briefly describe the role of the American Bahá'í community in bringing about the New World Order.

   _____

   _____

   _____

   _____

8. What are the features of the Bahá'í Golden Age?

   _____

   _____

5.6.2 *Mini-project*

Develop a mind map to illustrate the general character, the implications and features of the world commonwealth representing the New World Order as described by Shoghi Effendi in section 5.3.

6.
Marching forward despite obstacles

6.1 Introduction

This chapter covers paragraph 16 of *The Advent of Divine Justice*. In this paragraph the Guardian praises the achievements of the North American Bahá'í community despite the obstacles it has faced since its birth. In order to illustrate the magnitude of these hurdles, this chapter provides a brief background on some of them. Initially, the origin and the birth of the North American Bahá'í community are studied. Then "defection of prominent Bahá'ís" as one of the challenges of the community is explored. Finally, the rest of the chapter deals with the three forces of corruption, moral laxity and ingrained prejudice that the North American Bahá'í community has had to combat since its birth.

In this chapter, you need to reflect on and understand the following key points:

a) The Bahá'í Faith was introduced in the United States when two Bahá'ís from what is now Lebanon, Anton Haddad and Dr Ibráhím-i-Khayru'lláh, moved to New York in 1892 to find work.

b) The classes Dr Ibráhím-i-Khayru'lláh started in Chicago to teach the Faith in 1895 attracted a significant number of souls.

c) After visiting 'Abdu'l-Bahá in 1898, some of the American Bahá'ís realized that the curriculum taught by Dr Khayru'lláh was not a true representation of the Bahá'í scriptures.

d) In 1900, Dr Khayru'lláh decided to break away from 'Abdu'l-Bahá and to start his own sect in collaboration with Mírzá Muḥammad-'Alí.

e) Aḥmad Suhráb and Mrs Julia Lynch Chanler, who set up the New History Society in New York in 1929, confronted the American National Spiritual Assembly and as a result were expelled from the Bahá'í community.

f) Corruption is the use of power by people in authority for illegitimate personal gain, either for private enrichment or to stay in power.

g) Corruption in America is systemic and endemic. It influences the American system of government, the operation of corporations, and business and trade relationships.

h) The dramatic changes that occurred in the United States after World War I undermined the role of Christianity in society and its moral influence on people.

i) There is strong evidence indicating that racial prejudice is deeply entrenched in American society and in the minds of many of its citizens.

6.2 Paragraph under study

16 A community, relatively negligible in its numerical strength; separated by vast distances from both the focal-Centre of its Faith and the land wherein the preponderating mass of its fellow-believers reside; bereft in the main of material resources and lacking in experience and in prominence; ignorant of the beliefs, concepts and habits of those peoples and races from which its spiritual Founders have sprung; wholly unfamiliar with the languages in which its sacred Books were originally revealed; constrained to place its sole reliance upon an inadequate rendering of only a fragmentary portion of the literature embodying its laws, its tenets, and its history; subjected from its infancy to tests of extreme severity, involving, at times, the defection of some of its most prominent members; having to contend, ever since its inception, and in an ever-increasing measure, with the forces of corruption, of moral laxity, and ingrained prejudice—such a community, in less than half a century, and unaided by any of its sister communities, whether in the East or in the West, has, by virtue of the celestial potency with which an all-loving Master has abundantly endowed it, lent an impetus to the onward march of the Cause it has espoused which the combined achievements of its coreligionists in the West have failed to rival.

6.3 Obstacles

In paragraph 16, Shoghi Effendi highlights the significant advances made by the North American Bahá'í community over the previous 50 years in spite of the many obstacles and challenges that they have had to overcome. Their progress has exceeded the combined achievements of all the other Bahá'í communities in the West. He identifies the following obstacles faced by the community:

*   Insignificant number of believers.
*   Geographically remote from Persia, the birthplace of the Faith, and the Holy Land, its focal Centre.
*   A lack of material resources, experience and prominence.
*   Unfamiliar with Arabic and Farsi, the languages in which the sacred Books were originally revealed.
*   Unaware of the beliefs, concepts and habits of Persians among whom the Báb and Bahá'u'lláh emerged.
*   Relying on only a fragment of the literature providing the laws, tenets and history of the Faith.
*   Experiencing severe spiritual tests from the early days due to the defection of some of its most prominent members.

- Having to contend with the negative forces of corruption, moral laxity and prejudice dominating the wider community.

The introduction of the Bahá'í Faith in the United States had a very humble start. In 1892 two Bahá'ís of Christian background from a region that today is Lebanon, Anton Haddad and Dr Ibráhím-i-Khayru'lláh, travelled to New York to find work. Dr Khayru'lláh had become a Bahá'í in Cairo and had received a Tablet from Bahá'u'lláh. He had also been in communication with 'Abdu'l-Bahá.[1]

In 1984, Haddad went back to Europe to participate in the Antwerp International Art Fair and then he returned to Syria. Dr Ibráhím-i-Khayru'lláh decided to settle down in Chicago and earn a living as a spiritual healer. He also started some classes to teach the Bahá'í Faith to Americans. At that time the Bahá'í scriptures were not available in English. In addition, Dr Khayru'lláh was not fully aware of the Bahá'í social teachings and the fundamental verities of the Faith. Hence, he devised a curriculum based on his skill of spiritual healing, biblical prophecies referring to Bahá'u'lláh, and his impression of the teachings and fundamentals of the Faith. The classes proved quite popular and attracted many people. Within two years, Dr Khayru'lláh was informing 'Abdu'l-Bahá about his remarkable success.

In 1895, Khayru'lláh started weekly classes, teaching the Faith in Kenosha. By 1896, there were hundreds of believers in Chicago and Kenosha. In 1897, he visited Kansas City, New York City, Ithaca and Philadelphia attracting a significant number of souls. Shoghi Effendi names the most prominent among those who were converted to the Faith in that period as "... the stout-hearted Thornton Chase, surnamed Thabit (Steadfast) by 'Abdu'l-Bahá and designated by Him 'the first American believer,' who became a convert to the Faith in 1894, the immortal Louisa A. Moore, the mother teacher of the West, surnamed Liva (Banner) by 'Abdu'l-Bahá, Dr Edward Getsinger, to whom she was later married, Howard MacNutt, Arthur P. Dodge, Isabella D. Brittingham, Lillian F. Kappes, Paul K. Dealy, Chester I. Thacher and Helen S. Goodall."[2]

By 1899, the size of the American Bahá'í community had reached 1,500. Various Bahá'í communities emerged in Chicago, New York, Kenosha, Wisconsin, Cincinnati, Northern New Jersey, Philadelphia and Racine.[3]

In the remaining part of this chapter, some background is provided on the major points raised by Shoghi Effendi in this paragraph of *The Advent of Divine Justice*.

6.4 Defections of prominent Bahá'ís

In paragraph 16, Shoghi Effendi refers to "the defection of some of its most prominent members" as one of the challenges that the North American Bahá'í community had to deal with. These defections occurred during both the

---

[1] Shoghi Effendi, *God Passes By*, p. 256.
[2] Shoghi Effendi, *God Passes By*, p. 257.
[3] Robert Stockman, *United States of America: History of the Bahá'í Community*, 1995, cited at https://bahai-library.com/stockman_encyclopedia_usa.

ministries of 'Abdu'l-Bahá and Shoghi Effendi. In this section, some of these incidents up to 1938, the year *The Advent of Divine Justice* was written, are briefly explored.

6.4.1 During Ministry of 'Abdu'l-Bahá

One of the major incidents that resulted in the defection of some prominent Bahá'ís was the rebellion of Dr Khayru'lláh in the time of 'Abdu'l-Bahá. In 1898, Mrs Phoebe Hearst, who had been introduced to the Faith by Mrs Lua Getsinger, had plans to visit 'Abdu'l-Bahá in the Holy Land. She invited other believers to join her. The invitation attracted a number of people including Dr and Mrs Getsinger, Dr Khayru'lláh and his wife, May Ellis Bolles, Miss Pearson, Ann Apperson, Mrs Thornburgh and her daughter, and Dr Khayru'lláh's daughters and their grandmother.[1] This created an opportunity for the American believers to initiate direct contact and communication with 'Abdu'l-Bahá and to learn from Him about the verities of the Faith. They suddenly realized that the curriculum taught by Dr Khayru'lláh was not a true representation of the Bahá'í scriptures and many of his ideas contradicted the concepts enshrined in the Writings of Bahá'u'lláh.

This resulted in crisis and disunity as soon as the believers returned from the Holy Land in December 1899. Contrary to what the pilgrims had discovered, Dr Khayru'lláh insisted that his teachings represented orthodox Bahá'í belief and were correct. Others denied his claim and asserted that the friends should turn to 'Abdu'l-Bahá for guidance. After two years, in 1900, Dr Khayru'lláh decided to break away from 'Abdu'l-Bahá and to start his own sect. Only a small portion of the American Bahá'ís followed him. However, the disunity affected around half of the American believers who became alienated and left the Faith.[2]

Shoghi Effendi refers to this episode in the early years of the Ministry of 'Abdu'l-Bahá as "... the devastating crisis which the ambition of Dr Khayru'lláh had, upon his return from the Holy Land (December, 1899) precipitated; ... the agitation which he, working in collaboration with the arch-breaker of the Covenant and his messengers, had provoked; ... the attacks launched by him and his fellow-seceders, as well as by Christian ecclesiastics increasingly jealous of the rising power and extending influence of the Faith ...."[3] One of the messengers mentioned in Shoghi Effendi's statement was Shu'á'u'lláh, Mírzá Muḥammad-'Alí's son who travelled to the United States to specifically meet Dr Khayru'lláh.

Shoghi Effendi also denounces Khayru'lláh as "... the greedy and conceited Ibráhím-i-Khayru'lláh, who had chosen to uphold the banner of his rebellion in America for no less than twenty years, and who had the temerity to denounce, in writing, 'Abdu'l-Bahá, His 'false teachings, His misrepresentations of Bahaism, His

---

1   Shoghi Effendi, *God Passes By*, p. 257.

2   Robert Stockman, *United States of America: History of the Bahá'í Community*, 1995, cited at https://bahai-library.com/stockman_encyclopedia_usa.

3   Shoghi Effendi, *God Passes By*, p. 260.

dissimulation,' and to stigmatize His visit to America as 'a death-blow' to the 'Cause of God,' ...."[1]

6.4.2 During Ministry of Shoghi Effendi

One of the major goals of Shoghi Effendi from the beginning of his ministry was to develop the framework of the Bahá'í Administrative Order based on the guidance provided by Bahá'u'lláh and 'Abdu'l-Bahá. This was a major cultural change that some Bahá'ís in North America did not find easy to accept. Hence, some of the believers drifted away as reflected in the US Census that reports of the number of Bahá'ís in 1926 was 1,247 compared to 2,884 in 1916.[2]

There was also some open opposition to the initiatives of Shoghi Effendi. For example, Ruth White in 1926–1929 opposed the organizational changes pursued by Shoghi Effendi. She rejected the authority of Shoghi Effendi as the Guardian of the Faith appointed by 'Abdu'l-Bahá and claimed that *The Will and Testament of 'Abdu'l-Bahá* was a forgery.

Aḥmad Suhráb, 'Abdu'l-Bahá's secretary and interpreter, and Mrs Julia Chanler set up the New History Society in New York in 1929 to indirectly teach the Faith. They were told that they should operate within the Bahá'í institutions and the Local Spiritual Assembly of the Bahá'ís of New York was to have an input into how the New History Society promoted the Faith. Suhráb and Chanler declined to work with the New York Assembly. This resulted in a confrontation with the National Spiritual Assembly and their eventual expulsion from the Bahá'í community.

6.5 Corruption

Corruption is the use of power by people in authority for illegitimate personal gain, either for private enrichment, referred to as "extraction", or to stay in power, known as "power preservation". There are often connections between these two forms of corruption, particularly in major corruption scandals. Corruption can happen in many different contexts. Political corruption occurs at the highest levels of the political system. Administrative or bureaucratic corruption occurs at the legal implementation end of politics. Corruption can also be in the form of dishonesty in the conduct and business of an individual.

The ancient Greeks understood corruption as a problem of moral decay and deviation from a healthy system of government. In England during the 18th century, corruption was seen as the intrusion of the executive on the legislature by giving bribes or offering a favour. Corruption is often identified by one of the following behaviours:

- Bribery: The giving or offering of a bribe.
- Extortion: The practice of obtaining something, particularly money through force or the threat of force.

[1] Shoghi Effendi, *God Passes By*, p. 319.
[2] Mojan Momen, *A Change of Culture*, 2007, cited at https://bahai-library.com/momen_change_culture.

- Cronyism: The appointment of friends and associates to positions of authority, without proper regard to their qualifications.
- Nepotism: The practice of favouring relatives or friends, particularly by giving them jobs.
- Patronage politics: Distribution of favours or rewards such as public office, jobs, contracts, subsidies, prestige by a patron (who controls their dispensation) to a client.
- Influence peddling: The illegal practice of using one's influence in government or connections with people in authority to obtain favours or preferential treatment for another, usually in return for money.
- Graft: Dishonest use of political authority for personal gain.
- Embezzlement: Theft or misappropriation of funds placed in one's trust or belonging to one's employer.
- Gerrymandering: In the USA this is the practice, since the founding of the country, of allowing state politicians to set boundaries of electoral districts (not a possibility for Senate seats), often by an incumbent political party, to strengthen or weaken the power of a political party or a racial group (especially since the franchise to vote was extended to racial minorities). The courts have attempted with limited success to set legal and political standards to prevent the rigging of election boundaries.[1]

In the context of political corruption, accumulation and extraction include "bribes, commissions and fees taken from private sector businesses; undue extraction through taxation and customs; fraud and economic crime; politically created rent-seeking opportunities; politically created market favours benefiting businesses owned by political elites; off-budget transfers; manipulated processes of privatisation; and extorting party and campaign funding from the state, private sector and voters."[2]

On the other hand, corrupt means of power preservation consist of "buying political support and majorities from other parties and politicians; co-optation and maintenance of patron-client networks; buying decisions from parliament, judiciary, control and oversight bodies; favouritism and patronage in allocation of government resources; buying voters and votes; electoral fraud; use of public money for political campaigns; and buying off media and civil society."[3]

In general, corruption, and in particular political corruption, has been a dominant phenomenon in politics in nearly every country of the world throughout human history. Shoghi Effendi, however, highlights corruption in America because of its systemic and endemic nature, and its persistent influence on the American system of government, operation of corporations, and business and trade relationships.

---

[1] For more information on political corruption, see www.washingtonpost.com/news/global-opinions/wp/ 2016/11/25/the-american-political-system-is-broken/?noredirect=on

[2] Inge Amundsen, *Political Corruption*, Anti-Corruption Resource Centre, U4, Issue 6:2006, p. 9.

[3] Inge Amundsen, *Political Corruption*, Anti-Corruption Resource Centre, U4, Issue 6:2006, p. 9.

Political corruption in the US is as old as the nation. For example, in 1829 Samuel Swarwout, the Collector of Customs for the port of New York appointed by President Andrew Jackson, embezzled over $1 million in custom receipts and fled to Europe. Wherever corruption exists, there have been efforts to combat it through reforms. The most important events and transformation in American history, such as the American Revolution, the development of democracy, and the Civil War and period after that, i.e. reconstruction, have been fraught with corruption and reform.

Some aspects of political corruption as described above have remained unchanged in the United States throughout the centuries. Greed, secrecy and conspiracy are the dominant forces in politics. Public office is exploited for private interest. The law is searched for loopholes and political enemies are accused of corruption. On the other hand, some features of corruption have changed and practices that were acceptable in the past are now forbidden.

Political corruption is interwoven with American democracy to the extent that even some legal practices in US politics can be considered as corrupt. For example, Harvard law Professor Lawrence Lessig describes how special-interest money systemically corrupts American Politics.[1] The members of the United States Congress are heavily dependent on funding from large donors for their political survival. Lessig argues that such a practice, though legal, is a systemic problem and a form of corruption. The members of the Congress spend three of every five weekdays raising money for re-election. In this process, the members take up less-than-important issues in order to intimidate corporations and to force them to become campaign contributors. The complexity of the tax system and various special exceptions encourage this practice. Lessig writes:

> The clients of the lobbyists get a better chance at changing government policy. In a world of endless government spending and government regulation, that chance can be enormously lucrative. As researchers at the University of Kansas calculated, the return on lobbyists' investment to modify the American Jobs Creation Act of 2004 to create a tax benefit was 22,000 percent. A paper published in 2009 calculates that, on average, for every $1 that an average firm spends to lobby for targeted tax benefits, the return is between $6 and $20.[2]

The major scandals that have unfolded in the United States over the last few decades clearly highlight the depth and breadth of corruption in that country as was highlighted by Shoghi Effendi.

6.6 Moral laxity

Alexis de Tocqueville (1805–1859), French statesman, historian and social philosopher wrote: "In the United States the sovereign authority is religious ...; there is no country in the whole world in which the Christian religion retains a greater influence over the souls of men than in America; and there can be no

---

[1] Lawrence Lessig, *Republic, Lost: How Money Corrupts Congress—and a Plan to Stop it,* Twelve, Hatchette Book Group, NY. 2011.

[2] Lawrence Lessig, *Republic, Lost: How Money Corrupts Congress—and a Plan to Stop it,* Twelve, Hatchette Book Group, NY. 2011, p. 117.

greater proof of its utility, and of its conformity to human nature, than that its influence is powerfully felt over the most enlightened and free nation of the earth."[1]

Such an observation, however, lost its validity as the twentieth century unfolded. The dramatic changes that occurred in the United States after World War I undermined the role of Christianity in the society and its moral influence on people. Before the 1920's, values and morality were respected and everyone was expected to live by them. Women were trained to be sophisticated and reserved. There was no smoking or drinking permitted in public.

The family was the critical unit in early American society and comprised a husband, wife, biological children and extended family. Divorce was rare. It was generally illegal to live together or have children outside of marriage. In the early 19th century, the family gained more importance as a source of happiness but its nature started to change. Common-law marriage became an acceptable form of union. Companionate marriage, in which couples consented to have no children, and divorce by mutual consent with no financial or economic claim on each other, became widespread. This resulted in a rapid tripling of the divorce rate between 1860 and 1910.[2]

In the 1920's, Christian values and morality started to be replaced by a new morality under a social liberalism, emphasizing freedom and equality for everyone. These changes were particularly pronounced in the metropolitan areas of the Northern and Western US. Liberalism "is a political or social philosophy advocating the freedom of individual, parliamentary systems of government, nonviolent modification of political, social, or economic institutions to assure unrestricted development in all spheres of human endeavour, and government guarantees of individual rights and civil liberties."[3]

Concepts promoted by liberalism are generally positive and progressive, and can significantly advance a society. However, like any ideology when it is not pursued holistically, and in particular when some of its elements are taken to an extreme, it can become a source of harm. The liberalist movement in the United States in this period was also a reaction to the fundamentalism that started among conservative Presbyterian theologians at Princeton Theological Seminary in the late 19th century and spread to conservatives in Baptist and other denominations in 1920 to 1930.

Social liberalism gave rise to envy and greed amongst the lower classes of society. Hence, many Americans went into debt to buy consumer goods such as cars, radios and home appliances. Its impact on sexuality was quite observable. Prior to the 1920's, Protestant values of chastity and modesty dominated American culture. Sexual relationships outside traditional marriage were

---

[1] Alexis de Tocqueville, *Democracy in America*, 1841, Vol. 1, p. 332. Alexis de Torqueville. Democracy in America, Vol. I, tr. Henry Reeve. J. & H. G. Langley, New York. 1841.

[2] Tricia Hussung, *The Evolution of American Family Structure*, cited at https://online.csp.edu/blog/family-science/the-evolution-of-american-family-structure.

[3] Dictionary.com, cited at http://www.dictionary.com/browse/liberalism.

regarded as immoral and vile. However, in the 1920's, concepts about sexuality underwent a radical change. People became more receptive to explicit sexual behaviour outside of marriage as promoted by motion pictures, plays, songs, novels and advertising. A new generation of women in the 1920's, known as "Flappers", were stylish, and smoked and drank in public. They dressed "provocatively" and "revealingly" and sought independence and other social freedoms. These young women not only embraced their sexuality, but often publicly displayed it.[1]

Moral laxity has continued to affect more Americans in the decades that followed and intensified its negative impact on the fabric of the American society to the extent that Shoghi Effendi has considered it as one of the negative forces hampering the progress of the North American Bahá'í community.

6.7 Engrained prejudice

The American civil war of 1861–1865 was fought over two fundamental issues that had not been resolved during the American Revolution (1776–1783). The Northern victory in the war ensured the unity of the United States as one nation and legally ended the institution of slavery through the Thirteenth Amendment. In the South, African Americans found a new life after slavery, free from the brutality and indignities they experienced during slavery. However, prejudice and discrimination against African Americans persisted.

Southern state governments legislated Black Codes to give African Americans the rights to marry, own property and sue in court. However, coloured people could not serve on juries, testify against whites, or serve in state militias. Most southern African Americans lived in extreme poverty and were forced to rent land from the previous white slave owners and a portion of their crops were given to the landowner as rent.

During the Reconstruction era (1865 and 1877) Congress passed laws to promote civil and political rights of African Americans across the South. The opportunities provided were welcomed by African Americans. As a result, seven hundred African American men served in elected public office, two were elected as State Senators and 14 became members of the House of Representatives, and 1,300 African American men and women held government jobs.

A hate group against Reconstruction, called the Ku Klux Klan (KKK, the first movement), emerged in Pulaski, Tennessee in 1866. KKK members demanded the restoration of white supremacy through violence and intimidation against African Americans. White supremacy is a racist ideology that claims white people are the dominant race. Supremacy groups in the world vary according to whom they envisage to be white and which racial groups are considered as the primary enemy. Under pressure from the Federal government, the KKK started to disappear in 1871, particularly when their objectives were achieved in the 1870's.

From the late 1870s, Southern states passed laws to segregate whites from "persons of colour" in public transportation, schools, parks, cemeteries, theatres

---

[1] Shellie Clark, "The sexual revolution of the 'Roaring Twenties': Practice or perception?", *#History: A Journal of Student Research*, Vol. 1, Article 7, 2016.

and restaurants. The "persons of colour" referred to anyone with any degree of black ancestry. These laws were known as the Jim Crow laws and were enforced until 1954 when the Supreme Court declared them unconstitutional.

Racial prejudice and animosity towards those who were not considered as "real" Americans continued into the 20th century. The majority of African Americans did not benefit from the economic prosperity of the 1920's and the early 1930's. With industrial development and the emergence of manufacturing jobs, many African Americans moved north to work in industrial cities such as New York, Chicago and Detroit. With the settlement of African Americans in various parts of these cities, black neighbourhoods known as ghettos started to emerge.

The development of black neighbourhoods resulted in the revival of the KKK (the second movement) in 1915. It took its inspiration from D. W. Griffith's 1915 silent film *The Birth of a Nation*, which mythologized the founding of the first Klan. The KKK movement extended its campaign to include discrimination against Roman Catholics, Jews and Mexicans at a time of high emigration from the mostly Catholic nations of Central and Southern Europe. Its membership increased to over 100,000 in 1921 and to 5 million by the mid-1920s, but it started to decrease towards the late-1920s.

The above brief background provided in this section clearly illustrates why Shoghi Effendi refers to "engrained prejudice" as one of the maladies affecting North American society. There is strong evidence indicating that racial prejudice has continued to be prevalent in American society in spite of strict anti-discrimination legislations. Racial segregation in American cities, the biased negative attitudes of whites towards other ethnic and racial groups, social separation and isolation of racial groups, and many other factors, demonstrate that prejudice is deeply entrenched in American society and in the minds of many of its citizens.

6.8 Activities

6.8.1 Short answer questions

1. Briefly describe your understanding of the following challenges mentioned by Shoghi Effendi in paragraph 16:

   a) "relatively negligible in its numerical strength"

   _____

   _____

   _____

   _____

   b) "separated by vast distances from both the focal-Centre of its Faith and the land wherein the preponderating mass of its fellow-believers reside"

   _____

   _____

   _____

   _____

   c) "bereft in the main of material resources and lacking in experience and in prominence"

   _____

   _____

   _____

   _____

   d) "ignorant of the beliefs, concepts and habits of those peoples and races from which its spiritual Founders have sprung"

   _____

   _____

   _____

   _____

   e) "wholly unfamiliar with the languages in which its sacred Books were originally revealed"

   _____

   _____

   _____

   _____

f) "constrained to place its sole reliance upon an inadequate rendering of only a fragmentary portion of the literature embodying its laws, its tenets, and its history"

_____

_____

_____

_____

2. How did American Bahá'ís realize that what Dr K͟hayru'lláh taught was not a true representation of the Bahá'í scriptures?

_____

_____

_____

3. Why did Dr K͟hayru'lláh decide to break away from 'Abdu'l-Bahá and start his own sect?

_____

_____

_____

_____

4. What are the key points in the following statement from Shoghi Effendi?

"... the devastating crisis which the ambition of Dr K͟hayru'lláh had, upon his return from the Holy Land (December, 1899) precipitated; ... the agitation which he, working in collaboration with the arch-breaker of the Covenant and his messengers, had provoked; ... the attacks launched by him and his fellow-seceders, as well as by Christian ecclesiastics increasingly jealous of the rising power and extending influence of the Faith ...."[1]

_____

_____

_____

_____

_____

_____

_____

_____

---

[1] Shoghi Effendi, *God Passes By*, p. 259.

5.   What is your understanding from the following statement from Shoghi Effendi?

"... the greedy and conceited Ibráhím-i-Khayru'lláh, who had chosen to uphold the banner of his rebellion in America for no less than twenty years, and who had the temerity to denounce, in writing, 'Abdu'l-Bahá, His 'false teachings, His misrepresentations of Bahaism, His dissimulation,' and to stigmatize His visit to America as 'a death-blow' to the 'Cause of God,' ...."[1]

_____

_____

_____

_____

_____

_____

_____

_____

6.   Why did Ruth White oppose Shoghi Effendi?

_____

_____

_____

7.   Why were Aḥmad Suhráb and Mrs Julia Chanler expelled from the Faith?

_____

_____

_____

_____

8.   What is corruption?

_____

_____

_____

9.   Describe the nature of the following corrupt behaviours:

a)   Bribery:

_____

---

[1]   Shoghi Effendi, *God Passes By*, p. 319.

b) Extortion:

c) Cronyism:

d) Nepotism:

e) Patronage politics:

f) Influence peddling:

g) Graft:

h) Embezzlement:

i) Gerrymander:

10. Describe your understanding of the nature of corruption in the United States.

11. What were the major changes in American moral values and standards in the 1920's in the following contexts?

a) Family

_____

_____

_____

_____

b)   Attitude and behaviour of the lower class

_____

_____

_____

_____

c)   Sexual morality

_____

_____

_____

_____

_____

12.   What were the two objectives of the American Civil War?

_____

_____

_____

_____

13.   What was the Reconstruction period in the US history?

_____

_____

_____

_____

14.   What were the demands and beliefs of the Ku Klux Klan?

_____

_____

_____

_____

15.   What were the Jim Crow laws?

_____

_____

_____

_____

16.   Why was the KKK revived in 1915?

_____

_____

_____

_____

17.   What is your understanding of "engrained prejudice" as stated by Shoghi Effendi?

_____

_____

_____

_____

6.8.2   *Mini-project*

Conduct research on the nature of the forces of corruption, moral laxity and prejudice in the United States since the start of the 21st century. Organize your findings as a PowerPoint presentation and share it with your community.

7.
Matchless record of service

7.1 Introduction

This chapter is focused on paragraphs 17–18 of *The Advent of Divine Justice*. In these paragraphs Shoghi Effendi highlights the matchless record of service of the North American Bahá'í community. In paragraph 17, Shoghi Effendi spells out some of the major achievements of the North American Bahá'í community over the previous 20 years through a series of 11 rhetorical questions. He reiterates in paragraph 18, his conviction that "a community capable of showing forth such deeds, of evincing such a spirit, of rising to such heights," already has the potential to be eventually the chief creator and champion of the World Order of Bahá'u'lláh.

In this chapter, you need to reflect on and understand the following key points:

a) Shoghi Effendi praises "the resourcefulness, the discipline, the iron determination, the zeal and perseverance, the devotion and fidelity" of the North American Bahá'í community, so essential for building and extending the framework of the Bahá'í Administrative Order.

b) He also highlights the crucial role of that community in "fixing the pattern" and "imparting the original impulse" to the institutions leading the World Order of Bahá'u'lláh.

c) The framework of the Bahá'í Administrative Order are the institutions that are ordained by Bahá'u'lláh in His Writings and further expanded by 'Abdu'l-Bahá in His Will and Testament.

d) The "... birth and the primary stages in the erection of the framework of the Administrative Order of the Faith"[1] signalled the first epoch of the Formative Age.

e) In 1902, the governing board of the Bahá'ís of Chicago, known as the "House of Spirituality", asked 'Abdu'l-Bahá for permission to build a House of Worship in Chicago.

---

[1] Shoghi Effendi, *Citadel of Faith*, p. 5.

f) The "Royalty" referred to by Shoghi Effendi is Queen Marie of Romania and "one of its humble members" is a reference to Martha Root.

g) A major achievement of the early North American Bahá'í community was the development of Bahá'í Schools throughout the continent.

7.2 Paragraphs under study

17 What other community, it can confidently be asked, has been instrumental in fixing the pattern, and in imparting the original impulse, to those administrative institutions that constitute the vanguard of the World Order of Bahá'u'lláh? What other community has been capable of demonstrating, with such consistency, the resourcefulness, the discipline, the iron determination, the zeal and perseverance, the devotion and fidelity, so indispensable to the erection and the continued extension of the framework within which those nascent institutions can alone multiply and mature? What other community has proved itself to be fired by so noble a vision, or willing to rise to such heights of self-sacrifice, or ready to achieve so great a measure of solidarity, as to be able to raise, in so short a time and in the course of such crucial years, an edifice that can well deserve to be regarded as the greatest contribution ever made by the West to the Cause of Bahá'u'lláh? What other community can justifiably lay claim to have succeeded, through the unsupported efforts of one of its humble members, in securing the spontaneous allegiance of Royalty to its Cause, and in winning such marvellous and written testimonies to its truth? What other community has shown the foresight, the organizing ability, the enthusiastic eagerness, that have been responsible for the establishment and multiplication, throughout its territory, of those initial schools which, as time goes by, will, on the one hand, evolve into powerful centres of Bahá'í learning, and, on the other, provide a fertile recruiting ground for the enrichment and consolidation of its teaching force? What other community has produced pioneers combining to such a degree the essential qualities of audacity, of consecration, of tenacity, of self-renunciation, and unstinted devotion, that have prompted them to abandon their homes, and forsake their all, and scatter over the surface of the globe, and hoist in its uttermost corners the triumphant banner of Bahá'u'lláh? Who else but the members of this community have won the eternal distinction of being the first to raise the call of Yá Bahá'u'l-Abhá in such highly important and widely scattered centres and territories as the hearts of both the British and French empires, Germany, the Far East, the Balkan States, the Scandinavian countries, Latin America, the Islands of the Pacific, South Africa, Australia and New Zealand, and now more recently the Baltic States? Who else but those same pioneers have shown themselves ready to undertake the labour, to exercise the patience, and to provide the funds, required for the translation and publication, in no less than forty languages, of their sacred literature, the dissemination of which is an essential prerequisite to any effectively organized campaign of teaching? What other community can lay claim to have had a decisive share in the worldwide efforts that have been exerted for the safeguarding and the extension of the immediate surroundings of its holy shrines, as well as for the preliminary acquisition of the future sites of

its international institutions at its world Centre? What other community can to its eternal credit claim to have been the first to frame its national and local constitutions, thereby laying down the fundamental lines of the twin charters designed to regulate the activities, define the functions, and safeguard the rights, of its institutions? What other community can boast of having simultaneously acquired and legally secured the basis of its national endowments, thus paving the way for a similar action on the part of its local communities? What other community has achieved the supreme distinction of having obtained, long before any of its sister communities had envisaged such a possibility, the necessary documents assuring the recognition, by both the federal and state authorities, of its Spiritual Assemblies and national endowments?   And finally what other community has had the privilege, and been granted the means, to succour the needy, to plead the cause of the downtrodden, and to intervene so energetically for the safeguarding of Bahá'í edifices and institutions in countries such as Persia, Egypt, 'Iráq, Russia, and Germany, where, at various times, its fellow-believers have had to suffer the rigors of both religious and racial persecution?

18   Such a matchless and brilliant record of service, extending over a period of well-nigh twenty years, and so closely interwoven with the interest and fortunes of such a large section of the worldwide Bahá'í community, deserves to rank as a memorable chapter in the history of the Formative Period of the Faith of Bahá'u'lláh. Reinforced and enriched as it is by the memory of the American believers' earlier achievements, such a record is in itself convincing testimony to their ability to befittingly shoulder the responsibilities which any task may impose upon them in the future. To overrate the significance of these manifold services would be well-nigh impossible. To appraise correctly their value, and dilate on their merits and immediate consequences, is a task which only a future Bahá'í historian can properly discharge. I can only for the present place on record my profound conviction that a community capable of showing forth such deeds, of evincing such a spirit, of rising to such heights, cannot but be already possessed of such potentialities as will enable it to vindicate, in the fullness of time, its right to be acclaimed as the chief creator and champion of the World Order of Bahá'u'lláh.

7.3 Building a framework for nascent institutions

In paragraph 17, Shoghi Effendi highlights the major contribution of the North American Bahá'í community in the development of the Bahá'í Administrative Order through two rhetorical questions. In these questions, he initially praises "the resourcefulness, the discipline, the iron determination, the zeal and perseverance, the devotion and fidelity" of the North American Bahá'í community, so essential for building and extending the framework supporting the multiplication and the maturation of the Bahá'í institutions. He then highlights the crucial role of that community in "fixing the pattern" and "imparting the original impulse" to the institutions leading to the World Order of Bahá'u'lláh.

7.3.1 Nature of the framework

The framework of the Bahá'í Administrative Order is the institutions ordained by Bahá'u'lláh in His Writings and further expanded by 'Abdu'l-Bahá in His Will and Testament. They consist of the local, intermediary and Universal Houses of Justice.

Bahá'u'lláh has ordained the establishment of the elected councils of His future Administrative Order, and referred to them as "Houses of Justice". The context of the statements made by Bahá'u'lláh clearly shows that He is referring to two different entities, the Universal House of Justice and the Local Houses of Justice. In *The Kitáb-i-Aqdas*, Bahá'u'lláh ordains the establishment of the Local Houses of Justice: *"The Lord hath ordained that in every city a House of Justice be established wherein shall gather counselors to the number of Bahá, and should it exceed this number it doth not matter."*[1] The word Bahá in this statement has a numerical value of nine based on the abjad numbering system. The Local Houses of Justice are currently called Local Spiritual Assemblies.

Subsequent to the provisions revealed in *The Kitáb-i-Aqdas* (the Most Holy Book), Bahá'u'lláh revealed supplementary passages in a number of other Tablets. In the Tablet of Ishráqát, He states: *"This passage, now written by the Pen of Glory, is accounted as part of the Most Holy Book: The men of God's House of Justice have been charged with the affairs of the people. They, in truth, are the Trustees of God among His servants and the dayspringss of authority in His countries."*[2] This is a reference to the Universal House of Justice.

'Abdu'l-Bahá provides a more explicit explanation of the Houses of Justice in His Will and Testament. In addition He introduces the Secondary Houses of Justice and explicitly states: *"... in all countries a secondary House of Justice must be instituted."*[3] This institution is currently called the National Spiritual Assembly.

The *"... birth and the primary stages in the erection of the framework of the Administrative Order of the Faith"*[4] signalled the first epoch of the Formative Age starting with the ministry of Shoghi Effendi and completed in 1944–46, the closing of the first century after the Declaration of the Báb. The crowning institution of the framework, the Universal House of Justice, was elected in 1963, ending the second epoch of the Formative Age.

7.3.2 Building of the framework

The development of the Bahá'í institutions in the United states started as early as 1899 when a council board of seven officers administrating the North American continent was established in the city of Kenosha. In 1900, 'Abdu'l-Bahá instructed a number of Bahá'í teachers, including Hájí 'Abdu'l-Karím-i-Ṭihrání, Hájí Mírzá Ḥasan-i-Khurásání, Mírzá Asadu'lláh and Mírzá Abu'l-Faḍl, to travel to the United

---

[1]   Bahá'u'lláh, *The Kitáb-i-Aqdas*, para. 30, p. 29.

[2]   Bahá'u'lláh, *Tablets of Bahá'u'lláh*, p. 128.

[3]   'Abdu'l-Bahá, *The Will and Testament of 'Abdu'l-Bahá*, p. 14. Refer also to *The Kitáb-i-Aqdas*, Notes, No. 49, p. 188.

[4]   Shoghi Effendi, *Citadel of Faith*, p. 5.

States to restore the confidence of the community undermined by the defection of Ibráhím-i-<u>Kh</u>ayru'lláh. The consolidation work carried out by these travel teachers proved very effective. In a very short time they succeeded in dispelling the doubts implanted in the hearts of the Bahá'ís by <u>Kh</u>ayru'lláh, deepening their understanding of the fundamental verities of the Faith and giving an impulse to the formation of the nucleus of the Bahá'í institutions.

Consultative bodies were elected in Chicago, New York, and Northern New Jersey between 1900 and 1904. A Bahá'í Publishing Society was established in Chicago in 1902 and the *Bahá'í Bulletin* was initiated in New York to disseminate the teachings of the Faith. Another periodical, *Bahai News,* appeared in Chicago on 21 March 1910 and a year later was renamed the *Star of the West.* This period also witnessed the emergence of many American travel teachers who travelled in the United States as well as Europe, the Far East and the islands of the Pacific.

The major works of Bahá'u'lláh and 'Abdu'l-Bahá and various articles written by eastern Bahá'í scholars were translated, published and disseminated between 1904 and 1908. Further consultative bodies were formed in Washington, Boston and Spokane. During 1909–1911 various national initiatives emerged: the formation of the Bahá'í Temple Unity, the publication of *Star of the West*, and the commencement of the construction of the Bahá'í Temple in Chicago.

The visit of 'Abdu'l-Bahá to the United States and Canada for eight months in 1912 had a significant impact on the Bahá'í community, resulting in proclamation, consolidation and growth of the Bahá'í community.

In 1921, on assuming the Guardianship, Shoghi Effendi wrote to the American Bahá'í community that every locality should elect a Local Spiritual Assembly and the Bahá'í Temple Unity should evolve into a National Spiritual Assembly. The American Bahá'í community diligently followed the guidelines given by Shoghi Effendi. The evolution of the Bahá'í Temple Unity to the National Spiritual Assembly of the Bahá'ís of the United States and Canada was completed by 1925. There were 45 spiritual Assemblies in the United States by April 1928, increasing to 64 by 1936.

7.4 Construction of the Bahá'í House of Worship

In paragraph 17, Shoghi Effendi refers to the Bahá'í House of Worship in Wilmette, Chicago, by asking: "What other community has proved itself to be fired by so noble a vision, or willing to rise to such heights of self-sacrifice, or ready to achieve so great a measure of solidarity, as to be able to raise, in so short a time and in the course of such crucial years, an edifice that can well deserve to be regarded as the greatest contribution ever made by the West to the Cause of Bahá'u'lláh?"

In 1902, the governing board of the Bahá'ís of Chicago, known as "House of Spirituality", asked 'Abdu'l-Bahá for permission to build a House of Worship in Chicago. 'Abdu'l-Bahá responded by granting permission for the construction of the Bahá'í House of Worship in the following Tablet dated 7 June 1903:

> *O ye who are attracted! O ye who are firm! O ye who are zealous in the service of the Cause of God and are sacrificers of possessions and lives for the promotion*

of the Word of God!

I perused your recent letter, ... and my heart was filled with joy through its beautiful meanings and its eloquent contents. Truly they were suggested by the breaths of confirmation from the Glorious Lord.

O friends of 'Abdu'l-Bahá and his co-sharers and partners in the servitude of the Lord of Hosts! Verily the greatest affair and the most important matter today is to establish a Mashriqu'l-Adhkár and to found a Temple from which the voice of praise may rise to the Kingdom of the majestic Lord. Blessings be upon you for having thought to do so and intending to erect such an edifice, advancing all in devoting your wealth in this great purpose and in this splendid work. You will soon see the angels of confirmation following after you and the hosts of reinforcement crowding before you.

When the Mashriqu'l-Adhkár is accomplished, when the lights are emanating therefrom, the righteous ones are presenting themselves therein, the prayers are performed with supplication towards the mysterious Kingdom (of heaven), the voice of glorification is raised to the Lord, the Supreme, then the believers shall rejoice, the hearts shall be dilated and overflow with the love of the All-living and Self-existent (God). The people shall hasten to worship in that heavenly Temple, the fragrances of God will be elevated, the divine teachings will be established in the hearts like the establishment of the Spirit in mankind; the people will then stand firm in the Cause of your Lord, the Merciful. Praise and greetings be upon you.[1]

'Abdu'l-Bahá provided constant guidance on the design and architectural form of the Temple through various Tablets that He wrote to the American Bahá'í community as well as counsels He gave to the American pilgrims who visited Him in the Holy Land. In 1907, 'Abdu'l-Bahá highlighted the significance and importance of building the Mashriqu'l-Adhkár in Chicago and described how it would contribute to the unity and prosperity of the Cause. These messages resulted in a new surge of activity and increased contributions by Assemblies and individuals.

The House of Spirituality of Chicago invited representatives from various cities to attend a meeting on 27 November 1907 to consult on the project. A committee of nine people was appointed by the convention to co-ordinate and oversee the work of the Temple. On 9 April 1908 the first two building lots for the Temple were purchased. On 19 June, 'Abdu'l-Bahá directed the Bahá'ís in Chicago to hold another national convention for the Temple with one representative selected from each community around the country. This convention was held on 22–23 March 1909 in Chicago and the proceedings opened with the reading of a Tablet received from 'Abdu'l-Bahá. The convention created a Bahá'í Temple Unity committee to undertake the work of the construction of the Temple and other Bahá'í activities of national importance until the formation of the National Spiritual Assembly of the Bahá'ís of the United States and Canada.

---

[1]   'Abdu'l-Bahá, *Tablets of Abdul-Baha Abbas*, Vol. 1, p. 16.

On 1 May 1912 'Abdu'l-Bahá visited the Temple site and personally laid the corner stone of the building. The purchase of Temple land was completed in 1914 with contributions received from both within the United States and abroad. The architectural design of the Temple, developed by Louis J. Bourgeois, was presented to the Convention held in New York in 1920 as a large plaster model. The construction of caisson foundations began on 17 December 1920 with a contract given to Mr. Avery Brundage.

The Executive Board of the Bahá'í Temple Unity committee decided to seek the guidance of 'Abdu'l-Bahá on the design. Mr Bourgeois prepared some drawings of the design and in the middle of January 1921 sailed to the Holy Land to personally share the design with 'Abdu'l-Bahá.

After seeing the design, 'Abdu'l-Bahá indicated to Mrs Corinne True in a Tablet that the design was too large and too costly. Accordingly, Mr Bourgeois modified the plan and the construction of the Temple commenced. In 1925, Shoghi Effendi advised the American Bahá'í community not to start the next stage of the project until they had accumulated $400,000. The superstructure of the Temple was completed and handed over at the opening of the Convention in 1931. As mentioned before, Shoghi Effendi set the completion of the exterior of the Temple as one of the Goals of the North American Bahá'í community's first Seven Year Plan that started in 1937.[1]

7.5 Securing the allegiance of royalty

One of the questions asked by Shoghi Effendi in paragraph 17 is: "What other community can justifiably lay claim to have succeeded, through the unsupported efforts of one of its humble members, in securing the spontaneous allegiance of Royalty to its Cause, and in winning such marvellous and written testimonies to its truth?" The "Royalty" referred to Queen Marie of Romania and "one of its humble members" is a reference to Martha Root, the first American Bahá'í who arose to teach the Faith after meeting 'Abdu'l-Bahá in 1911 and 1912. She left the United States on January 1915 on her first travel-teaching trip to Europe. She responded to the call of 'Abdu'l-Bahá in the Tablets of the Divine Plan in the same year they were unveiled in the United States (1919) and embarked on the first of her world journeys, which were to span a total period of 20 years.[2]

Among the many great services that Martha Root rendered to the Cause, taking the Message of Bahá'u'lláh to Queen Marie of Romania is considered by Shoghi Effendi as "the most superb and by far the most momentous".[3] This was during her first tour of Europe between 1926 and 1929. In her first visit to the palace in Bucharest, Marth Root presented *Bahá'u'lláh and the New Era* by Esslemont to Queen Marie. Martha Root realized in an audience with the Queen the next day that she had stayed up all night to read the book. Martha Root met the Queen seven more times.

---

[1] The historical facts in this section were sourced from: National Spiritual Assembly of the Bahá'ís of the United States and Canada, *The Bahá'í Temple, House Worship of a World Faith*, Commemorating completion of exterior ornamentation, 1942.

[2] Shoghi Effendi, *God Passes By*, p. 386.

[3] Shoghi Effendi, *Gold Passes By*, p. 389.

Queen Marie was born in Kent, England. Her mother was the only surviving daughter of Tsar Alexander II of Russia, who had received a special Tablet from Bahá'u'lláh. Her father was the Duke of Edinburgh. She was the grand-daughter of Queen Victoria who also received a Tablet from Bahá'u'lláh. Queen Marie married Crown Prince Ferdinand I of Romania in 1893 and reigned with him from 1914 to 1927, and then as queen dowager from 1927 to 1938.

Queen Marie sent open letters to Canadian and American newspapers and publicly proclaimed her support for the Faith. Her letter in the *Toronto Star* 4 May 1926 reads:

> It is a wondrous Message that Bahá'u'lláh and his son 'Abdu'l-Bahá have given us. ...

> ... Love, the mainspring of every energy, tolerance towards each other, desire of understanding each other, knowing each other, helping each other, forgiving each other.

> It is Christ's Message taken up anew, in the same words almost, but adapted to the thousand years and more difference that lies between the year one and today ....

> ... If ever the name of Bahá'u'lláh or 'Abdu'l-Bahá comes to your attention, do not put their writings from you. Search out their Books, and let their glorious, peace-bringing, love-creating words and lessons sink into your hearts as they have into mine.

> ... Seek them, and be the happier.[1]

King Ferdinand died on 20 July 1927 and Martha Root had her second audience with the Queen on 9 October 1927. She was told that the Queen and her daughter Princess Ileana had been reading *The Kitáb-i-Íqán*, learning about life after death.

Queen Marie and her daughter Ileana planned to visit the Bahá'í holy places as part of a trip to the Near East. In anticipation of receiving the guests, the house of 'Abdu'l-Bahá was prepared. In March 1930, Shoghi Effendi sent a formal invitation to the Queen to visit the World Centre of the Faith. As there was no response to the invitation, Shoghi Effendi sent another cable on 26 March to her hotel in Cairo. Two days later came the response from the Romanian Minister in Cairo: "HER MAJESTY REGRETS THAT NOT PASSING THROUGH PALESTINE SHE WILL NOT BE ABLE TO VISIT YOU." This was a source of disappointment to the Queen and the holy family.[2]

7.6 Establishment of Bahá'í schools

Another major achievement of the North American Bahá'í community at the time, as mentioned by Shoghi Effendi in paragraph 17, was the development of Bahá'í schools throughout the continent. He raises this point by asking: "What other community has shown the foresight, the organizing ability, the enthusiastic

---

[1] *The Bahá'í World*, Vol. II, p. 174.

[2] Janet A. Khan, *Prophet's Daughter: The Life and Legacy of Bahíyyih Khánum, Outstanding Heroine of the Bahá'í Faith*, Bahá'í Publishing Wilmette, IL., 2005.

eagerness, that have been responsible for the establishment and multiplication, throughout its territory, of those initial schools…?" Three Bahá'í schools were established in the United States by 1938: Green Acre Bahá'í School, Bosch Bahá'í School and Louhelen Bahá'í School.

7.6.1 Green Acre Bahá'í School

The Farmer family moved to Eliot Maine in the mid-1880's. Sarah Farmer started a resort hotel in Eliot in 1990 and called it "Green-Acre-on-the Piscataqua". Sarah developed a vision for Green Acre as a centre for expression of various religions and philosophy, and she dedicated Green Acre to peace and unity of religions in 1894. She began to invite speakers from different backgrounds to Green Acre and encouraged them to participate in all the lectures without bias. The work at Green Acre became known around the world by the end of 1897.

Financial problems faced by Green Acre in the following years put a great deal of pressure on Sarah. Suffering from stress and ill health, Sarah left the United States for the Mediterranean in January 1900. She met two old friends on the ship who were travelling to 'Akká to meet 'Abdu'l-Bahá. Sarah cabled 'Abdu'l-Bahá in advance and asked for permission to join the party of pilgrims. The request was granted by 'Abdu'l-Bahá.

The visit resulted in a great bond between 'Abdu'l-Bahá and Sarah. On her return to Green Acre, Sarah started to offer private classes on "The Persian Revelation". The program of the school also started to give prominence to topics associated with the Bahá'í Faith. However, financial difficulties, opposition of some people to her new religion, and the burning of her family home to the ground placed so much stress on her that in 1904 she moved to Melrose, Massachusetts for rest and recovery. During this difficult period, she received Tablets from 'Abdu'l-Bahá encouraging her to stay steadfast and not to grieve.

In 1912, 'Abdu'l-Baha visited Green Acre, stayed for a week, gave many public talks and shared His vision of the future for Green Acre with Sarah and others. He stated: *"This is hallowed ground made so by your vision and sacrifice. Always remember this is hallowed ground which I am pointing out to you. This is where the first Bahá'í University will be built; this is where the second Bahá'í Temple in the United States will be raised."*[1]

In 1913, the Green Acre board of the directors consisted of six Bahá'ís. They influenced the program and attracted more Bahá'ís to participate in the programs. Sarah Farmer passed away in 1916 and, before her death, entrusted Harry Randal to look after Green Acre. Harry was urged by 'Abdu'l-Bahá to pursue the growth of the school to achieve its purpose.

Green Acre has continued its development and is closely associated with the progress of the Bahá'í Faith in the North America. Many Eastern and Western Bahá'í scholars have taught in the school. The first election of the National Spiritual Assembly of the Bahá'ís of the United States and Canada took place in

---

[1]   Anne Gordon Atkinson, "Introduction to Green Acre Bahá'í School", *Green Acre on Piscatqua: A Centennial Celebration*, Eliot, Maine: Green Acre Bahá'í School Council, 1990.

Green Acre, and it accommodated the first office of the National Spiritual Assembly and the residence of its secretary, Horace Holley. Green Acre now serves as an "all-year–round" Bahá'í school.

7.6.2   *Bosch Bahá'í School*

Bosch Bahá'í School was established in 1927 when two devoted Bahá'ís, John and Louise Bosch, donated their extensive property located in the village of Geyserville, California, to the Faith to be used as a Bahá'í school. It became known as "Geyserville Bahá'í School" and became a gathering place for the Bahá'ís to study and discuss various topics related to the Faith.

In 1973, with the news of the construction of a highway through the property, it was sold and the fund was used to acquire a property in the mountains above Santa Cruz. It was dedicated as the Bosch Bahá'í School on 13 July 1974 in honour of John and Louis.

Bosch Bahá'í School is now a fully functional Bahá'í school providing educational programs and seminars for around two thousand people annually from different backgrounds.[1]

7.6.3   *Louhelen Bahá'í School*

Mr Lewis (Lou) Eggleston, soon after becoming a Bahá'í in 1930, purchased a farm near Davison, Michigan with the intention of using it for Bahá'í Summer Schools. He married Helen Whitney in the same year, and together they started to plan for the first Summer School the year after.

The first Bahá'í Summer School at the farm in August 1931 was the inaugural event for Louhelen Bahá'í School. Sessions were held either in a lodge or in a nearby open-air amphitheatre. Louhelen School is now a fully functional Bahá'í School.[2]

7.7 Other major achievements

In the remainder of paragraph 18, Shoghi Effendi mentions other achievements of the North American Bahá'í community. In this section, a brief introduction to these victories is provided.

7.7.1   *International pioneering*

Shoghi Effendi praises the audacity, consecration, tenacity, self renunciation and unstinted devotion of the North American pioneers who scattered around the world to establish the Faith.

An early American pioneer was Agnes Alexander. She received a Tablet from 'Abdu'l-Bahá encouraging her to travel to Japan and teach the Faith. She moved to Japan in 1914 and stayed there for 23 years.

The North American Bahá'ís became aware of the significance of pioneering to distant parts of the globe as soon as the Tablets of the Divine Plan were unfolded

---

[1]   Cited at http://www.bosch.org/history.

[2]   Cited at http://www.louhelen.org/history.

in the United States in 1919, as mentioned in section 7.5. Miss Martha Root was the first one who responded to the call of 'Abdu'l-Bahá and embarked on her world travel teaching tour. Shoghi Effendi has referred to her as "that archetype of Bahá'í itinerant teachers and the foremost Hand raised by Bahá'u'lláh since 'Abdu'l-Bahá's passing", and giving her the title of "Leading Ambassadress of His Faith and Pride of Bahá'í teachers, whether men or women, in both the East and the West."[1]

John Henry Hyde Dunn and his wife, Clara Dunn, arose spontaneously to serve as soon as they read the Tablets of the Divine Plan. Mr Dunn resigned his position, and the Dunns left their home in San Francisco for Australia, arriving on 3 February 1920. They remained in Australia until their deaths in 1941 and 1960, respectively.

As mentioned in section 2.4, international pioneering became more systematic in 1936, when Shoghi Effendi sent a cable to the National Convention of the Bahá'ís of the United States and Canada and asked for their systematic action in realising 'Abdu'l-Bahá's vision as revealed in the Tablets of the Divine Plan. On 19th May, he sent another cable to the American Bahá'í community calling for permanent pioneers to all the countries of Latin America. The sessions of the 1937 National Convention were extended for the delegates to consult on plans to facilitate pioneering to Latin America. The National Assembly established the Inter-America committee and auxiliary Regional Teaching committees to facilitate and support pioneering.

As mentioned in section 2.3, establishing the Faith in every Latin American country formed one of the goals of the first Seven Year Plan of the North American Bahá'í community, a goal that was successfully achieved.

7.7.2   Translation and publication of Sacred writings

By 1938, the book by Dr J. E, Esslemont, *Bahá'u'lláh and the New Era*, was translated into 40 different languages and published in 33 languages. *The Kitáb-i-Íqán* was published in 13 different languages and work on its translation to eight other languages was under way. The *Hidden Words of Bahá'u'lláh* was published in 15 languages and translation into another four languages was in process. *Some Answered Questions* of 'Abdu'l-Bahá was published in six languages and work was in progress to translate it to another ten languages.[2] In paragraph 17, Shoghi Effendi indicates that such translations were resourced and undertaken by the American pioneers.

7.7.3   Endowments at the Bahá'í World Centre

Shoghi Effendi took critical steps regarding the ownership of all Bahá'í properties. According to Ugo Giachery "he [Shoghi Effendi] mentioned that after the reading of the Will and Testament of 'Abdu'l-Bahá, when he found himself appointed Guardian of the Cause of God, he told the assembled members of the whole family that he renounced, then and there, the ownership of any estate,

---

[1]   Shoghi Effendi, *God Passes By*, p. 386.

[2]   *The Bahá'í World*, Vol. VII, p. 100.

possessions and chattels that would be his rightful inheritance."[1] He also arranged for all assets to be held in trust in the names of the donors of those assets, and later "registered in the name of incorporated National Assemblies."[2]

In paragraph 17, Shoghi Effendi mentions the "decisive share" of the American Bahá'í community in the acquisition of properties in the immediate surroundings of the holy shrines and the preliminary purchase of land for future international institutions at the Bahá'í World Centre. For example, Amelia Collins, one of the Hands of the Cause, donated the entire sum required to purchase of the land on the Mt. Carmel, overlooking the Cave of Elijah, for the future Mashriqu'l-Adhkár of the Holy Land.[3] The Guardian transferred the ownership of these properties to the Palestine Branch of the National Spiritual Assembly of the Bahá'ís of the United States, as a legal entity registered in Palestine.[4]

According to Rúḥíyyih Khánum:

This was the first step in constituting Palestine Branches—which were later changed to Israel Branches—of various National Assemblies and registering in their names properties owned in the Holy Land. Although the power of disposing of these properties was entirely vested locally at the World Centre, the prestige of the Faith was greatly enhanced by this move, its Holy Places were buttressed and safeguarded, its world character emphasized in the eyes of the authorities, and national Bahá'í communities were encouraged and strengthened.[5]

By the time of his passing, Shoghi Effendi had effected similar negotiations to register ownership of properties on Mt Carmel to the Israel Branches of a total of nine Bahá'í Assemblies around the world in recognition of their donations. Not only did this emphasize the international character of the Faith but it was also part of his policy of owning nothing himself. This touches on the question why Shoghi Effendi left no will and testament. On the one hand, he had no possessions to bequeath while, on the other, he had no son to whom he could pass the office of the Guardianship, and all the male descendants of Bahá'u'lláh had broken the Covenant[6].

7.7.4   *Incorporation and endowment fund*

One of the objectives pursued by Shoghi Effendi during his ministry was to ensure that entities of the Bahá'í Administrative Order were legally recognized in each country at both national and local levels and that any assets were held by an endowment fund. The National Spiritual Assembly of the Bahá'ís of the United States and Canada was the first national institution that embarked on this task in

---

[1]   Ugo Giachery, *Shoghi Effendi: Recollections*, p. 27.
[2]   Shoghi Effendi, *God Passes By*, p. 338.
[3]   Shoghi Effendi, *Messages to the Bahá'í World: 1950–1957*, pp. 78–79.
[4]   Shoghi Effendi, *God Passes By*, p. 356.
[5]   Rúḥíyyih Khánum, *The Priceless Pearl*, p. 267.
[6]   The complexities around this issue are beyond the scope of this book. However this topic is covered elsewhere. See: Fazel Naghdy, *A Tutorial on the Dispensation of Bahá'u'lláh*, p. 296.

1926 by creating a legal entity known as Voluntary Trust, a type of corporation recognized under common law. The Declaration of Trust and its By-Laws reflect the administrative principles and elements defined by Shoghi Effendi.

The legal process of incorporation was later adopted by American Local Spiritual Assemblies and other National Spiritual Assemblies around the world. In 1932, the Local Spiritual Assembly of the Bahá'ís of New York was legally incorporated. The By-Laws developed by this assembly in 1931 served "as a pattern for every Bahá'í local Assembly in America and a model for every local community throughout the Bahá'í world."[1]

In parallel, with the incorporation process, the National Spiritual Assembly of the Bahá'ís of the United States and Canada established a series of Indentures of Trust that owned Bahá'í properties and assets. In *God Passes By*, Shoghi Effendi described this major achievement:

> In the United States of America the national endowments of the Faith, already representing one and three-quarter million dollars of assets, and established through a series of Indentures of Trust, created in 1928, 1929, 1935, 1938, 1939, 1941 and 1942 by the National Spiritual Assembly in that country, acting as Trustees of the American Bahá'í Community, now include the land and structure of the Mashriqu'l-Adhkár, and the caretaker's cottage in Wilmette, Ill.; the adjoining Ḥazíratu'l-Quds (Bahá'í National Headquarters) and its supplementary administrative office; the Inn, the Fellowship House, the Bahá'í Hall, the Arts and Crafts Studio, a farm, a number of cottages, several parcels of land, including the holding on Monsalvat, blessed by the footsteps of 'Abdu'l-Bahá, in Green Acre, in the state of Maine; Bosch House, the Bahá'í Hall, a fruit orchard, the Redwood Grove, a dormitory and Ranch Buildings in Geyserville, Calif.; Wilhelm House, Evergreen Cabin, a pine grove and seven lots with buildings at West Englewood, N.J., the scene of the memorable Unity Feast given by 'Abdu'l-Bahá, in June, 1912, to the Bahá'ís of the New York Metropolitan district; Wilson House, blessed by His presence, and land in Malden, Mass.; Mathews House and Ranch Buildings in Pine Valley, Colo.; land in Muskegon, Mich., and a cemetery lot in Portsmouth, N.H.[2]

This legal model was subsequently adopted by other national communities.

7.7.5   *International intervention*

Finally, in paragraph 17 Shoghi Effendi praises the North American Bahá'í community for their efforts in safeguarding the Bahá'í Faith and its institutions in countries where the community had been experiencing persecution. He mentions Persia, Egypt, 'Iráq, Russia and Germany as some examples.

In *God Passes By*, Shoghi Effendi identifies some specific authorities who were approached by the National Spiritual Assembly of the Bahá'ís of the United States and Canada:[3]

---

1   Shoghi Effendi, cited in *The Bahá'í World*, Vol. 13, p. 153.
2   Shoghi Effendi, *God Passes By*, p. 337.
3   Shoghi Effendi, *God Passes By*, pp. 343–344.

- The Palestine High Commissioner for the restitution of the keys of the Tomb of Bahá'u'lláh to its custodian.
- The S͟háh of Persia, on four occasions, pleading for justice on behalf of their persecuted brethren within his domains.
- The Persian Prime Minister on that same subject.
- The Heads of Islám in Persia, appealing for harmony and peace among religions.
- King Feisal of 'Iráq to ensure the security of the Most Great House in Ba͟g͟hdád.
- The Soviet authorities on behalf of the Bahá'í communities in Russia.
- The German authorities regarding the persecution suffered by their German brethren.
- The Egyptian Government concerning the emancipation of their co-religionists from the yoke of Islamic orthodoxy.
- Persian cabinet in connection with the closing of Persian Bahá'í educational institutions.
- The US State Department, the Turkish Ambassador in Washington and the Turkish Cabinet in Ankara, in defence of the interests of the Faith in Turkey.

7.8 Activities

7.8.1 Short answer questions

1. Consider the following statement from paragraph 18:

    "I can only for the present place on record my profound conviction that a community capable of showing forth such deeds, of evincing such a spirit, of rising to such heights, cannot but be already possessed of such potentialities as will enable it to vindicate, in the fullness of time, its right to be acclaimed as the chief creator and champion of the World Order of Bahá'u'lláh."

    a) Which community is Shoghi Effendi referring to?

    _____

    _____

    _____

    _____

    b) What are the qualities of the community mentioned by Shoghi Effendi?

    _____

    _____

    c) What is the conviction of Shoghi Effendi about this community?

    _____

    _____

2. What does Shoghi Effendi mean by the framework of the Bahá'í Administrative Order?

    _____

    _____

    _____

    _____

3. What was the role of the North American Bahá'í community in connection with the framework?

    _____

    _____

    _____

    _____

4. What were the major steps taken in the construction of the Bahá'í House of Worship in Chicago? Show them as bullet points.

    _____

    _____

5. What was the early background of Queen Marie?

6. Who introduced the Bahá'í Faith to Queen Marie?

7. Briefly describe the origin and background of the Green Acre Bahá'í School?

8. Briefly describe the origin and background of the Bosch Bahá'í School?

9. Briefly describe the origin and background of the Louhelen Bahá'í School?

10. Briefly describe each of the achievements of North American Bahá'í community as mentioned in section 7.7:

   a) International pioneering

   b) Translation and publication of Sacred Writings

_____

_____

   c)   Endowments at the Bahá'í World Centre

_____

_____

   d)   Incorporation and endowment fund

_____

_____

   e)   International intervention

_____

_____

7.8.2   *Mini-project*

Develop a timeline to illustrate the development of the Bahá'í institutions in the United States.

8.
Future missions

8.1 Introduction

This chapter covers paragraphs 19–27, in which Shoghi Effendi highlights the nature and significance of the future missions of the North American Bahá'í community. The undertakings of the community over the previous 50 years, as stated by Shoghi Effendi, would be infinitesimal compared to the future endeavours and achievements of the community. In this section, the Guardian also identifies some future developments in the worldwide Bahá'í community in which the North American Bahá'í community would potentially play major roles.

In this chapter, you need to reflect on and understand the following key points:

a) Shoghi Effendi identifies the early signs of the "catastrophic upheaval" proclaiming the death throes of the old world order and birth pains of the New World Order.

b) The messages of Shoghi Effendi indicate that the upheaval referred to by Bahá'u'lláh is not just a single event, but a series of crises that unfold over time.

c) The future turmoil will provide tremendous opportunities for the North American Bahá'í community.

d) The inaugural Universal House of Justice was elected at the first International Convention that was held in Haifa on 21–23 April 1963.

e) The first dependency of the Wilmette Bahá'í House of Worship was a home for the aged that opened on 1 February 1959.

f) The codification of the laws and ordinances of *The Kitáb-i-Aqdas* was one of the goals of the Ten Year Crusade that was started by Shoghi Effendi and completed by the Universal House of Justice during the Nine Year Plan.

g) There are references to Bahá'í courts in other writings of Shoghi Effendi in different contexts.

h) Construction of a Mashriqu'l-Adhkár in Ṭihrán was a goal that Shoghi Effendi had in mind as early as 1932, though it has not yet been realized due to the hostility towards the Persian Bahá'í community by the Islamic government in Írán.

i) The design of the Mashriqu'l-Adhkár on Mt Carmel is ready and the land has been acquired.

j) Bahá'í communities are still under various restrictions and constraints in Islamic countries.

k) The Faith has emerged from obscurity during the third epoch of the Formative Age that began in 1963 and ended in 1986.

8.2 Paragraphs under study

19 Magnificent as has been this record, reminiscent as it is, in some of its aspects, of the exploits with which the dawn-breakers of an heroic Age have proclaimed the birth of the Faith itself, the task associated with the name of this privileged community is, far from approaching its climax, only beginning to unfold. What the American believers have, within the space of almost fifty years, achieved is infinitesimal when compared to the magnitude of the tasks ahead of them. The rumblings of that catastrophic upheaval, which is to proclaim, at one and the same time, the death-pangs of the old order and the birth-pangs of the new, indicate both the steady approach, as well as the awe-inspiring character, of those tasks.

20 The virtual establishment of the Administrative Order of their Faith, the erection of its framework, the fashioning of its instruments, and the consolidation of its subsidiary institutions, was the first task committed to their charge, as an organized community called into being by the Will, and under the instructions, of 'Abdu'l-Bahá. Of this initial task they have acquitted themselves with marvellous promptitude, fidelity, and vigour. No sooner had they created and correlated the various and necessary agencies for the efficient conduct of any policy they might subsequently wish to initiate, than they addressed themselves, with equal zest and consecration, to the next more arduous task of erecting the superstructure of an edifice the cornerstone of which 'Abdu'l-Bahá Himself had laid. And when that feat was achieved, this community, alive to the passionate pleas, exhortations, and promises recorded in the Tablets of the Divine Plan, resolved to undertake yet another task, which in its scope and spiritual potentialities is sure to outshine any of the works they have already accomplished. Launching with unquenchable enthusiasm and dauntless courage the Seven Year Plan, as the first and practical step towards the fulfilment of the mission prescribed in those epoch-making Tablets, they entered, with a spirit of renewed consecration, upon their dual task, the consummation of which, it is hoped, will synchronize with the celebration of the centenary of the birth of the Faith of Bahá'u'lláh. Well aware that every advance made in the external ornamentation of their majestic edifice would directly react on the progress of the teaching campaign initiated by them in both the northern and southern American continents, and realizing that every victory gained in the teaching field would, in its turn, facilitate the work, and hasten the completion, of their Temple, they are now pressing on, with courage and faith, in their efforts to discharge, in both of its phases, their obligations under the Plan they have dedicated themselves to execute.

21   Let them not, however, imagine that the carrying out of the Seven Year Plan, coinciding as it does with the termination of the first century of the Bahá'í era, signifies either the termination of, or even an interruption in, the work which the unerring Hand of the Almighty is directing them to perform. The opening of the second century of the Bahá'í era must needs disclose greater vistas, usher in further stages, and witness the initiation of plans more far-reaching than any as yet conceived. The Plan on which is now focused the attention, the aspirations, and the resources of the entire community of the American believers should be viewed as a mere beginning, as a trial of strength, a stepping-stone to a crusade of still greater magnitude, if the duties and responsibilities with which the Author of the Divine Plan has invested them are to be honourably and entirely fulfilled.

22   For the consummation of the present Plan can result in no more than the formation of at least one Centre in each of the Republics of the Western Hemisphere, whereas the duties prescribed in those Tablets call for a wider diffusion, and imply the scattering of a far greater and more representative number of the members of the North American Bahá'í community over the entire surface of the New World. It is the undoubted mission of the American believers, therefore, to carry forward into the second century the glorious work initiated in the closing years of the first. Not until they have played their part in guiding the activities of these isolated and newly fledged centres, and in fostering their capacity to initiate in their turn institutions, both local and national, modelled on their own, can they be satisfied to have adequately discharged their immediate obligations under 'Abdu'l-Bahá's divinely revealed Plan.

23   Nor should it for a moment be supposed that the completion of a task which aims at the multiplication of Bahá'í centres and the provision of the assistance and guidance necessary for the establishment of the Administrative Order of the Bahá'í Faith in the countries of Latin America realizes in its entirety the scheme visualized for them by 'Abdu'l-Bahá. A perusal, however perfunctory, of those Tablets embodying His Plan will instantly reveal a scope for their activities that stretches far beyond the confines of the Western Hemisphere. With their inter-American tasks and responsibilities virtually discharged, their intercontinental mission enters upon its most glorious and decisive phase. *"The moment this Divine Message,"* 'Abdu'l-Bahá Himself has written, *"is carried forward by the American believers from the shores of America and is propagated through the continents of Europe, of Asia, of Africa, and of Australasia, and as far as the islands of the Pacific, this community will find itself securely established upon the throne of an everlasting dominion."*[A]

24   And who knows but that when this colossal task has been accomplished a greater, a still more superb mission, incomparable in its splendour, and foreordained for them by Bahá'u'lláh, may not be thrust upon them? The glories of such a mission are of such dazzling splendour, the circumstances attending it so remote, and the contemporary events with the culmination of which it is so closely knit in such a state of flux, that it would be premature to attempt, at the present time, any accurate delineation of its features.

Suffice it to say that out of the turmoil and tribulations of these "latter years" opportunities undreamt of will be born, and circumstances unpredictable created, that will enable, nay impel, the victorious prosecutors 'Abdu'l-Bahá Plan, to add, through the part they will play in the unrolling of the New World Order, fresh laurels to the crown of their servitude to the threshold of Bahá'u'lláh.

25 Nor should any of the manifold opportunities, of a totally different order, be allowed to pass unnoticed which the evolution of the Faith itself, whether at its world Centre, or in the North American continent, or even in the most outlying regions of the earth, must create, calling once again upon the American believers to play a part, no less conspicuous than the share they have previously had in their collective contributions to the propagation of the Cause of Bahá'u'lláh. I can only for the moment cite at random certain of these opportunities which stand out preeminently, in any attempt to survey the possibilities of the future: The election of the International House of Justice and its establishment in the Holy Land, the spiritual and administrative Centre of the Bahá'í world, together with the formation of its auxiliary branches and subsidiary institutions; the gradual erection of the various dependencies of the first Ma<u>sh</u>riqu'l-<u>A</u>dhkár of the West, and the intricate issues involving the establishment and the extension of the structural basis of Bahá'í community life; the codification and promulgation of the ordinances of the Most Holy Book, necessitating the formation, in certain countries of the East, of properly constituted and officially recognized courts of Bahá'í law; the building of the third Ma<u>sh</u>riqu'l-<u>A</u>dhkár of the Bahá'í world in the outskirts of the city of Ṭihrán, to be followed by the rise of a similar House of Worship in the Holy Land itself; the deliverance of Bahá'í communities from the fetters of religious orthodoxy in such Islamic countries as Persia, 'Iráq, and Egypt, and the consequent recognition, by the civil authorities in those states, of the independent status and religious character of Bahá'í National and Local Assemblies; the precautionary and defensive measures to be devised, coordinated, and carried out to counteract the full force of the inescapable attacks which the organized efforts of ecclesiastical organizations of various denominations will progressively launch and relentlessly pursue; and, last but not least, the multitudinous issues that must be faced, the obstacles that must be overcome, and the responsibilities that must be assumed, to enable a sore-tried Faith to pass through the successive stages of unmitigated obscurity, of active repression, and of complete emancipation, leading in turn to its being acknowledged as an independent Faith, enjoying the status of full equality with its sister religions, to be followed by its establishment and recognition as a State religion, which in turn must give way to its assumption of the rights and prerogatives associated with the Bahá'í state, functioning in the plenitude of its powers, a stage which must ultimately culminate in the emergence of the worldwide Bahá'í Commonwealth, animated wholly by the spirit, and operating solely in direct conformity with the laws and principles of Bahá'u'lláh.

26 The challenge offered by these opportunities the American believers, I feel confident, will, in addition to their answer to the teaching call voiced by

'Abdu'l-Bahá in His Tablets, unhesitatingly take up, and will, with their traditional fearlessness, tenacity, and efficiency, so respond to it as to confirm, before all the world, their title and rank as the champion-builders of the mightiest institutions of the Faith of Bahá'u'lláh.

27   Dearly beloved friends! Though the task be long and arduous, yet the prize which the All-Bountiful Bestower has chosen to confer upon you is of such preciousness that neither tongue nor pen can befittingly appraise it. Though the goal towards which you are now so strenuously striving be distant, and as yet undisclosed to men's eyes, yet its promise lies firmly embedded in the authoritative and unalterable utterances of Bahá'u'lláh. Though the course He has traced for you seems, at times, lost in the threatening shadows with which a stricken humanity is now enveloped, yet the unfailing light He has caused to shine continually upon you is of such brightness that no earthly dusk can ever eclipse its splendour.   Though small in numbers, and circumscribed as yet in your experiences, powers, and resources, yet the Force which energizes your mission is limitless in its range and incalculable in its potency. Though the enemies which every acceleration in the progress of your mission must raise up be fierce, numerous, and unrelenting, yet the invisible Hosts which, if you persevere, must, as promised, rush forth to your aid, will, in the end, enable you to vanquish their hopes and annihilate their forces. Though the ultimate blessings that must crown the consummation of your mission be undoubted, and the Divine promises given you firm and irrevocable, yet the measure of the goodly reward which every one of you is to reap must depend on the extent to which your daily exertions will have contributed to the expansion of that mission and the hastening of its triumph.

8.3 Catastrophic upheaval

In paragraph 19, Shoghi Effendi reminds the American believers that, despite the valiant deeds of the early heroes of the Faith, the Bahá'í community is only at the initial stages of what must yet be accomplished. The Guardian refers to the early signs of the "catastrophic upheaval" accompanying the destruction of the outdated social structures and the painful birth of the New World Order, as an indication of both the relentlessly approaching time and the stupendous quality of the future missions of the North American Bahá'í community.

The majority of the world's sacred scriptures predict various upheavals and catastrophes followed by world peace. Bahá'u'lláh, in some of His Writings, particularly *The Kitáb-i-Íqán*, interprets some of these references to be symbolic, representing the spiritual events that occur with the coming of a new Manifestation of God. At the same time, He anticipates upheavals and calamities that will be a prelude to the emergence of His New World Order.

The warnings of Bahá'u'lláh about impending upheavals clearly refer to incidents that occur in the physical world and cannot be interpreted as symbolic. In one Tablet, He states:

Witness how the world is being afflicted with a fresh calamity every day. Its tribulation is continually deepening. From the moment the Súriy-i-Ra'ís (Tablet to Ra'ís) was revealed until the present day, neither hath the world been tranquillized, nor have the hearts of its peoples been at rest. At one time it hath been agitated by contentions and disputes, at another it hath been convulsed by wars, and fallen a victim to inveterate diseases. Its sickness is approaching the stage of utter hopelessness, inasmuch as true Physician is debarred from administering the remedy, whilst unskilled practitioners are regarded with favour, and are accorded full freedom to act. ... The dust of sedition hath clouded the hearts of men, and blinded their eyes. Erelong, they will perceive the consequences of what their hands have wrought in the Day of God. Thus warneth you He Who is the All-Informed, as bidden by One Who is the Most Powerful, the Almighty.[1]

In another Tablet, Bahá'u'lláh warns the peoples of the world:

Know, verily, that an unforeseen calamity is following you, and that grievous retribution awaiteth you. Think not the deeds ye have committed have been blotted from My sight. By My beauty! All your doings hath My Pen graven with open characters upon tablets of chrysolite.[2]

In yet another Tablet, Bahá'u'lláh states:

The world is in travail, and its agitation waxeth day by day. Its face is turned towards waywardness and unbelief. Such shall be its plight, that to disclose it now would not be meet and seemly. Its perversity will long continue. And when the appointed hour is come, there shall suddenly appear that which shall cause the limbs of mankind to quake. Then, and only then, will the Divine Standard be unfurled, and the Nightingale of Paradise warble its melody.[3]

The messages of Shoghi Effendi indicate that such an upheaval is not just a single event but a series of crises that unfold over time. The Guardian has referred to the two great wars as the realization of different stages of the upheaval prophesied by Bahá'u'lláh. For example, he specifically observed World War I as "... the first stage in a titanic convulsion long predicted by Bahá'u'lláh."[4] In a message he wrote on 18 October 1927 he expresses his fear "... at the prospect of yet another deadly encounter, the inevitability of which" was "... becoming increasingly manifest."[5] The "rumblings of that catastrophic upheaval" mentioned in paragraph 19 is a reference to the World War II.

In a letter to the National Spiritual Assembly of the Bahá'ís of United States and Canada dated 5 July 1938, Shoghi Effendi mentions these rumblings once more:

Pregnant indeed are the years looming ahead of us all. The twin processes of internal disintegration and external chaos are being accelerated every day and are inexorably moving towards a climax. The rumblings that must precede

---

[1] Bahá'u'lláh, *Gleanings from the Writings of Bahá'u'lláh*, pp. 39–40.
[2] Bahá'u'lláh, *Gleanings from the Writings of Bahá'u'lláh*, pp. 209–210.
[3] Bahá'u'lláh, *Gleanings from the Writings of Bahá'u'lláh*, pp. 118–119.
[4] Shoghi Effendi, *God Passes By*, p. 305.
[5] Shoghi Effendi, *Bahá'í Administration*, p. 145.

the eruption of those forces that must cause "the limbs of humanity to quake" can already be heard. "The time of the end", "the latter years", as foretold in the Scriptures, are at long last upon us. The Pen of Bahá'u'lláh, the voice of 'Abdu'l-Bahá, have time and again, insistently and in terms unmistakable, warned an unheeding humanity of impending disaster.[1]

In a cablegram dated 8 December 1941, Shoghi Effendi, in reference to World War II, states that the "MOST GREAT CONVULSION ENVISAGED BY PROPHETS FROM ISAIAH TO BAHÁ'U'LLÁH CATACLYSMIC IN VIOLENCE PLANETARY IN RANGE ASSAILING AT LONG LAST PREDOMINANT NATIONS ASIATIC AMERICAN CONTINENTS."[2]

Three letters written to various individual believers on behalf of Shoghi Effendi in 1949, indicate that upheavals were not over with the two World Wars, and that other stages of the upheaval as foretold by Bahá'u'lláh were yet to happen. In the first letter, Shoghi Effendi states:

… that the great failure to respond to Bahá'u'lláh's instructions, appeals and warnings issued in the 19th Century, has now sent the world along a path, and released forces, which must culminate in a still more violent upheaval and agony. The thing is out of hand, so to speak, and it is too late to avert catastrophic trials.[3]

In the second message he affirms that we:

… do not know what form the immediate future will take, anywhere. Because the passions of mankind are so unregenerate, and it is so deaf to the voice of Bahá'u'lláh, no doubt great suffering will be experienced.[4]

Expressing a similar view in the third letter, he asserts:

We have no indication of exactly what nature the apocalyptic upheaval will be: it might be another war… but as students of our Bahá'í writings it is clear that the longer the 'Divine Physician' (i.e. Bahá'u'lláh) is withheld from healing the ill of the world, the more severe will be the crisis, and the more terrible the sufferings of the patient.[5]

8.4 A mere beginning

In paragraphs 20 to 24, Shoghi Effendi briefly reviews the tasks undertaken by the North American Bahá'í community since the Ministry of 'Abdu'l-Bahá and points out that all those achievements represent a mere beginning to much more important future undertakings destined for that community as envisioned by 'Abdu'l-Bahá.

In paragraph 20, Shoghi Effendi mentions the "virtual establishment of the Administrative Order of their Faith, the erection of its framework, the fashioning of its instruments, and the consolidation of its subsidiary institutions" as the first

---

[1] Shoghi Effendi, *This Decisive Hour*, p. 23.
[2] Shoghi Effendi, *This Decisive Hour*, p. 69.
[3] Shoghi Effendi, cited in *Lights of Guidance*, p. 129.
[4] Shoghi Effendi, cited in *Lights of Guidance*, p. 129.
[5] Shoghi Effendi, cited in *Lights of Guidance*, p. 131.

responsibility given to the North American Bahá'í community, and erecting the superstructure of the Bahá'í House of Worship in Chicago as the second task.

Having constructed, on the one hand, the institutions and agencies through which they could enact their policies, and, on the other hand, the concrete shell of their first edifice to the Glory of God, the North American Bahá'í community now set forth on the inauguration of the first Seven Year Plan. The Guardian refers to this as "yet another task, which in its scope and spiritual potentialities is sure to outshine any of the works they have already accomplished."

Thus, the first tangible step was taken towards the realization of the mandate given to the North American Bahá'í community by 'Abdu'l-Bahá in the Tablets of the Divine Plan. Shoghi Effendi describes every advance in the ornamentation of the exterior of the Temple in Wilmette and the progress of the teaching campaign in both the northern and southern American continents, as having a reciprocal effect upon each other.

The completion of the first Seven Year Plan in 1944 coincided with the termination of the first century of the Bahá'í era, i.e., one hundred years from the declaration of the Báb in 1844. The first 80 years of that century covered the Heroic, the Primitive, or the Apostolic Age of the Bahá'í Faith and the last 20 years represented the beginnings of the Formative, the Transitional or the Iron Age. In paragraph 21, Shoghi Effendi states that, for the North American Bahá'í community, the opening of the second century of the Bahá'í era would reveal "greater vistas, usher in further stages, and witness the initiation of plans more far-reaching than any as yet conceived."

In paragraphs 22 and 23, Shoghi Effendi points out that the Tablets of the Divine Plan call for a wider diffusion and scattering of a far greater and more representative number of the members of the North American Bahá'í community across all corners of the globe, compared to the goals of the first Seven Year Plan. The task would go beyond just opening new Bahá'í centres, requiring the fostering of capacity building in the new Bahá'í communities to a point that they could initiate their own local and national institutions. In discharging these responsibilities, the intercontinental mission of the North American Bahá'í community would enter upon "its most glorious and decisive phase."

In paragraph 24, Shoghi Effendi reveals that, with such changes that lie far ahead into the future, it is too early to foresee exactly what glorious deeds will be required from the American Bahá'í believers. However, he concludes that as yet unimagined opportunities would be born out of the future turmoils for the North American Bahá'í community to play their destined role in unrolling the New World Order.

8.5 Future opportunities

In paragraph 25, Shoghi Effendi surveys some of the future opportunities that would call forth the highest levels of prowess in the activities of the North American Bahá'í community. Some of these opportunities are explored in the following sections.

8.5.1   Election of the Universal House of Justice

The inaugural Universal House of Justice was elected on 21 April during the first International Convention that was held between 21–23 April 1963 at the house of 'Abdu'l-Bahá in Haifa. The members of all 56 National Spiritual Assemblies participated in the election. The nine elected members were:

Mr Hugh Chance	Dr Luṭfu'lláh Ḥakím
Mr 'Alí Nakhjavání	Mr Húshmand Fathe-Azam
Mr David Hofman	Mr Ian Semple
Mr Amos Gibson	Mr H. Borrah Kavelin
Mr Charles Wolcott	

The National Spiritual Assemblies, being the pillars of the Universal House of Justice, were formed as a result of the expansion and consolidations plans devised by Shoghi Effendi. As discussed in the previous sections, the North American Bahá'í communities played a major role in implementing these plans. Four members of the inaugural Universal House of Justice were Americans. Until 1996, seven out of the 14 members elected to the Universal House of Justice were either American by birth or had been members of the American National Spiritual Assembly.

8.5.2   Subsidiaries of Wilmette Bahá'í House of Worship

The institution of the Maṣhriqu'l-Aḏhkár ("the Dawning-place of the Praise of God") was established by Bahá'u'lláh in *The Kitáb-i-Aqdas*:

> *O people of the world! Build ye houses of worship throughout the lands in the name of Him Who is the Lord of all religions. Make them as perfect as is possible in the world of being, and adorn them with that which befitteth them, not with images and effigies. Then, with radiance and joy, celebrate therein the praise of your Lord, the Most Compassionate. Verily, by His remembrance the eye is cheered and the heart is filled with light.*[1]

The Maṣhriqu'l-Aḏhkár consists of a House of Worship as its central edifice and a number of dependencies. The dependencies of the Maṣhriqu'l-Aḏhkár are dedicated to social, humanitarian, educational and scientific pursuits. 'Abdu'l-Bahá refers to Maṣhriqu'l-Aḏhkár as *"one of the most vital institutions in the world."*[2] According to Shoghi Effendi, the dependencies of the Maṣhriqu'l-Aḏhkár that "shall afford relief to the suffering, sustenance to the poor, shelter to the wayfarer, solace to the bereaved, and education to the ignorant,"[3] should be considered as separate from the House of Worship, which is devoted solely to the worship of God.

One of the goals of the American Bahá'í community during the Ten Year Crusade was to establish a Home for the Aged as the first dependency of the Wilmette Bahá'í House of Worship. A suitable property was acquired near the House of Worship and the Home was opened on 1 February 1959. It operated until

---

[1]   Bahá'u'lláh, *The Kitáb-i-Aqdas*, pp. 29–30.

[2]   'Abdu'l-Bahá, cited in *Lights of Guidance*, p. 606.

[3]   Shoghi Effendi, *Bahá'í Administration*, p. 184.

2002, when the National Spiritual Assembly found it economically unviable to modernize it to conform to new building codes, and decided to close the Home.

8.5.3   *Most Holy Book codification & promulgation*

Shoghi Effendi adopted the codification of the laws and ordinances of *The Kitáb-i-Aqdas* as one of the goals of the Ten Year Crusade. He announced this decision in a message to the Bahá'í world, dated April 1955:

> In the Holy Land, the Centre and Pivot around which the institutions of a world-encompassing Administrative Order revolve, steps have been taken for the preparation of a Synopsis, and for the Codification of the Laws, of the Most Holy Book, *The Kitáb-i-Aqdas*, the Mother-Book of the Bahá'í Revelation, as an essential prelude to the eventual translation and publication of its entire text.[1]

Shoghi Effendi himself started to work on this project and left an outline of the synopsis and codification in English and notes in Persian. The Universal House of Justice set the completion of this task as a goal of the Nine Year Plan (1964–1973), using the work conducted by Shoghi Effendi as a major component. Thus, the goal was achieved according to the pattern set by Shoghi Effendi, and the synopsis and codification of *The Kitáb-i-Aqdas* was published in 1973.

The Guardian had envisaged that the codification of the Most Holy Book would be followed by a complete translation of the Book. *The Kitáb-i-Aqdas* is rich in allusion and makes references to the laws revealed in previous dispensations. Hence, Shoghi Effendi deemed it necessary that the translation of the Book into English would be completely annotated with detailed explanations to prevent any misunderstanding for those unfamiliar with the previous laws and ordinances, and the core teachings of the Bahá'í Faith.

In 1986, the Universal House of Justice decided that time had come for an English translation of the complete text of the Most Holy Book. This was set as a goal of the Six Year Plan (1986–1992). The annotations and explanations provided in the book draw on the many Tablets of Bahá'u'lláh, that supplement *The Kitáb-i-Aqdas,* and the interpretations made of some the passages by 'Abdu'l-Bahá and Shoghi Effendi, in order to clarify the religious, cultural and historical contexts of the laws.

The publication in 1992 of *The Kitáb-i-Aqdas* did not necessarily increase the number of laws binding upon Bahá'ís. Additional laws become binding when the Universal House of Justice deems it timely to apply them.

8.5.4   *Bahá'í courts*

The establishment of Bahá'í courts has not yet been realized. There are references to Bahá'í courts in other writings of Shoghi Effendi in different contexts. In *The World Order of Bahá'u'lláh,* he envisages that the

> ... day may not be far distant when in certain countries of the East, in which religious communities exercise jurisdiction in matters of personal status, Bahá'í Assemblies may be called upon to assume the duties and

---

[1]   Shoghi Effendi, *Messages to the Bahá'í World: 1950–1957*, p. 78.

responsibilities devolving upon officially constituted Bahá'í courts. They will be empowered, in such matters as marriage, divorce, and inheritance, to execute and apply, within their respective jurisdictions, and with the sanction of civil authorities, such laws and ordinances as have been expressly provided in their Most Holy Book.[1]

There are also references to the establishment of Bahá'í courts in the goals of the Ten Year Crusade. In the message to the Intercontinental Conference in New Delhi, in October 1953, Shoghi Effendi describes one goal of the plan as "the establishment of a national Bahá'í Court in the capital cities of Persia, of Iraq, of Pakistan and of Afghanistan—the leading Muslim centres in the Asiatic continent."[2]

In the message to the African Intercontinental Conference in Kampala, February 1953, Shoghi Effendi identified one goal as "the establishment, circumstances permitting, of a national Bahá'í Court in the capital city of Egypt, the recognized centre of both the Islamic and Arab worlds, officially empowered to apply, in matters of personal status, the laws and ordinances revealed in *The Kitáb-i-Aqdas*, the Mother-Book of the Bahá'í Revelation."[3]

The previous two goals cover primarily the countries in the East, where during the Ottoman rule religious courts had been established for Jews, Christians and Muslims.[4]

In addition, there are some references in the messages of Shoghi Effendi to the evolution of the International Bahá'í Council to a Bahá'í court before it becomes the Universal House of Justice. In a message dated 29 March 1951, he explains that

> ... these successive manifestations of the good will and support of the civil authorities will, if steadily maintained, greatly reinforce, and lend a tremendous impetus to this process of recognition which constitutes an historic landmark in the evolution of the World Center of the Faith of Bahá'u'lláh—a process which the newly formed Council [International Bahá'í Council], now established at its very heart [Bahá'í World Centre], is designed to foster, which will gather momentum, with the emergence in the course of time of a properly recognized and independently functioning Bahá'í court, which will attain its consummation in the institution of the Universal House of Justice and the emergence of the auxiliary administrative agencies, revolving around this highest legislative body ...[5]

The five main powers and duties of the Universal House of Justice are listed in the Declaration of Trust of the Constitution of the Universal House of Justice.[6] The future world tribunal operating under the guidance of the Universal House of Justice is to perform the fifth of the listed powers and duties:

---

[1] Shoghi Effendi, *The World Order of Bahá'u'lláh*, p. 199.

[2] Shoghi Effendi, *Dawn of a New Day*, p. 170.

[3] Shoghi Effendi, *Messages to the Bahá'í World: 1950–1957*, p. 139.

[4] 'Alí Nakhjavání, "Supreme Tribunal", *Lights of 'Irfán*, 13, 2012, pp. 423–424.

[5] Shoghi Effendi, *Citadel of Faith*, pp. 94–95.

[6] *The Constitution of the Universal House of Justice*, pp. 5–6.

To adjudicate disputes falling within its purview; to give judgement in cases of violation of the laws of the Faith and to pronounce sanctions for such violations; to provide for the enforcement of its decisions; to provide for the arbitration and settlement of disputes arising between peoples; and to be the exponent and guardian of that Divine Justice which can alone ensure the security of, and establish the reign of law and order in, the world.[1]

Shoghi Effendi stated the world tribunal "... will adjudicate and deliver its compulsory and final verdict in all and any disputes that may arise between the various elements constituting this universal system"[2] in the Bahá'í World Commonwealth.

8.5.5   *Bahá'í House of Worship in Ṭihrán*

Construction of a Mashriqu'l-Adhkár in Ṭihrán was a goal that Shoghi Effendi had in mind as early as 1932, when a Temple Committee was established in Írán to purchase land for the future Mashriqu'l-Adhkár near Ṭihrán. Shoghi Effendi provided 30,000 rials towards this fund.[3] On 4 May 1953 Shoghi Effendi reported to the Bahá'í world that the "area of land purchased on the slopes of the Elburz Mountains, overlooking the city of Ṭihrán, in anticipation of the construction of the first Mashriqu'l-Adhkár of Persia, has reached approximately four million square meters."[4]

Shoghi Effendi set the construction of the Mashriqu'l-Adhkár in Ṭihrán as one of the goals of the Ten Year Crusade. However, antagonism of the Iranian government toward "the Faith caused the plans for its construction to be held in abeyance."[5] In its Riḍván message of 1973, the Universal House of Justice informed the worldwide Bahá'í community that it "... has proved still impossible to begin work on the erection of the Mashriqu'l-Adhkár in Ṭihrán, but contracts have been signed for the preparation of detailed drawings, geological surveys are being made, and everything made ready for immediate action whenever the situation in Persia becomes propitious."[6]

The continued hostility of the Islamic government in Írán towards the Bahá'í community has prevented the realization of this goal to date.

8.5.6   *Bahá'í House of Worship in Holy Land*

On 4 May 1953, Shoghi Effendi announced that the "design for the Mashriqu'l-Adhkár on Mt. Carmel, conceived by the architect appointed by 'Abdu'l-Bahá, has been completed, and a model constructed, which is soon to be unveiled at the All-America Intercontinental Teaching Conference, in anticipation of the selection

---

[1]   *The Constitution of the Universal House of Justice*, pp. 5–6.

[2]   Shoghi Effendi, *The World Order of Bahá'u'lláh*, p. 203.

[3]   *Bahá'í World*, Vol. 6, p. 116.

[4]   Shoghi Effendi, *Messages to the Bahá'í World: 1950–1957*, p. 47.

[5]   The Universal House of Justice, *Messages from the Universal House of Justice 1963—1986*, p. 33.

[6]   The Universal House of Justice, *Messages from the Universal House of Justice 1968–1973*, pp. 118–119.

and the purchase of its future site, and of its ultimate construction in the neighbourhood of the Báb's Sepulchre."[1]

On 7 October 1953, he informed the Bahá'í community that:

... preliminary steps have been taken, aiming at the acquisition of an extensive area at the head of the holy mountain, scene of the revelation of the Tablet of Carmel, preparatory to the purchase of the site for the future Mother Mashriqu'l-Adhkár of the Holy Land, made possible by the munificent hundred thousand dollar donation of the Hand of the Cause, Amelia Collins, signalizing the opening of the second stage in the unfoldment of the mighty process set in motion by the Author of the Faith.[2]

In April 1954, Shoghi Effendi stated that the:

... site for the first Mashriqu'l-Adhkár of the Holy Land has been selected—an area of approximately twenty thousand square meters—situated at the head of the Mountain of God, in close proximity to the Spot hallowed by the footsteps of Bahá'u'lláh, near the time-honoured Cave of Elijah, and associated with the revelation of the Tablet of Carmel, the Charter of the World Spiritual and Administrative Centres of the Faith on that mountain. ... and negotiations have been initiated with the Israeli authorities for the purpose of effecting the immediate purchase of the selected site.[3]

On 19 July 1956 he announced that the site had been purchased.[4]

In a message dated 7 March 1967, while addressing the needs of the Faith at the Bahá'í World centre, the Universal House of Justice explained that:

... extensive beautification of the sacred endowments surrounding the holy shrines in Bahjí and Haifa, as well as the site of the future Mashriqu'l-Adhkár on Mount Carmel, must be undertaken, both for its own sake and for the protection of these lands which are situated within the boundaries of rapidly expanding cities ....[5]

Finally, on 13 December 1971, the Universal House of Justice announced:

"To all National Spiritual Assemblies

JOYOUSLY ANNOUNCE FURTHER DEVELOPMENTS WORLD CENTRE. AFTER MANY YEARS DIFFICULT NEGOTIATIONS ERECTION OBELISK MARKING SITE FUTURE MASHRIQU'L-ADHKÁR MOUNT CARMEL COMPLETED THUS FULFILLING PROJECT INITIATED BELOVED GUARDIAN EARLY YEARS CRUSADE.[6]

---

[1]   Shoghi Effendi, *Messages to the Bahá'í World: 1950–1957*, p. 149.

[2]   Shoghi Effendi, *Messages to the Bahá'í World: 1950–1957*, p. 170.

[3]   Shoghi Effendi, *Messages to the Bahá'í World: 1950–1957*, p. 63.

[4]   Shoghi Effendi, *Citadel of Faith*, p. 147.

[5]   The Universal House of Justice, *Messages from the Universal House of Justice 1963–1986*, p. 97.

[6]   The Universal House of Justice, *Messages from the Universal House of Justice 1963–1986*, p. 209.

8.5.7 *Emancipation of Bahá'ís in Islamic countries*

Bahá'í communities in Islamic countries are still under various restrictions and constraints, though the intensity of the persecution varies from one country to another. Under the Islamic Republic of Írán the persecution of Bahá'ís has become more systematic and intense, affecting all aspects of Bahá'í community life. Oppression and discrimination exist in Egypt and more recently in Yemen. In 2014, the Indonesian Religious Affairs Minister Lukman Haki Saifuddin recognized the Bahá'í Faith as a religion and stated that Bahá'í worshipers would be protected by the Constitution.[1] However, a more recent report states:

> Indonesia's Baha'i community still experiences government discrimination because of their faith. Despite Religious Affairs Minister Lukman's 2014 statement that the Baha'i faith should be recognized as a religion protected by the constitution, the government has not changed official policy. Baha'i followers are not able to obtain state recognition of civil marriages, have limited educational opportunities, and must state a faith other than their own on their ID cards.[2]

8.5.7 *World-wide Bahá'í Commonwealth emergence*

At the end of paragraph 25, Shoghi Effendi refers to two more potential future undertakings. The first is the development of precautionary and defensive measures to counteract attacks on the Faith. There has been significant development in this area including the development of the Bahá'í International Community and Offices of External Affairs in different countries, working closely with the United Nations and national governments to inform them of the nature the Bahá'í Faith and to draw on these relationships to protect the Faith. The work in this area is well advanced and explaining it is beyond the scope of this book.

The second task, as mentioned by Shoghi Effendi, is to pursue the development of Bahá'í communities across the globe to assist them to pass through the following stages:

a)   Unmitigated obscurity,
b)   Active repression,
c)   Complete emancipation,
d)   Recognition of the Faith as an independent religion,
e)   Recognition of the Faith as a state religion,
f)   Emergence of the worldwide Bahá'í Commonwealth.

According to the Universal House of Justice, the Faith emerged from obscurity during the third epoch of the Formative Age that began in 1963 and ended in 1986.[3] The active repression of the Faith has continued in some Islamic countries as explained above in section 8.5.7. In the West, there has not been any systematic

---

[1]   Cited at http://jakartaglobe.id/news/indonesias-bahai-community-grateful-long-awaited-state-recognition/.

[2]   USCIRF Annual Report 2016—Tier 2 countries—Indonesia. See https://www.refworld.org/docid/ 57307ce411.html.

[3]   The Universal House of Justice, *Messages from the Universal House of Justice 1963–1986*, p. 715.

and active repression of the Faith apart from the persecutions that occurred in Germany and the Soviet Union as explained in Chapter 3. However, there has been random opposition to the Faith.

The independence of the Faith is formally recognized in many countries around the globe, with some exceptions, particularly in Islamic countries. The Faith has not yet been recognized as the state religion in any nation.

8.6 Activities

8.6.1 Short answer questions

1. The following questions relate to the first sentence of paragraph 19:

    a) What is the reference to "the dawn-breakers of an heroic Age"?

    _____

    _____

    _____

    _____

    b) What is your understanding of the statement?

    _____

    _____

    _____

    _____

2. What was the "catastrophic upheaval" mentioned by Shoghi Effendi in paragraph 19?

    _____

    _____

    _____

    _____

3. Consider paragraph 20.

    a) What was the first task committed to the charge of the North American Bahá'í community?

    _____

    _____

    _____

    _____

    b) What was the second task committed to the charge of the North American Bahá'í community?

    _____

    _____

    _____

    _____

c)   What was the third task committed to the charge of the North American Bahá'í community?

_____

_____

_____

_____

4.   What is your understanding of the last sentence in paragraph 21?

_____

_____

_____

_____

5.   Under what conditions would the North American Bahá'í community have adequately discharged their obligations as described in paragraph 22?

_____

_____

_____

_____

6.   What were the implications for the North American Bahá'í community of quote 23:A by 'Abdu'l-Bahá?

_____

_____

_____

_____

7.   What is you understanding of paragraph 24?

_____

_____

_____

_____

8.   Briefly comment on the following future opportunities mentioned in paragraph 25.

a)   Election of the Universal House of Justice

_____

_____

_____

b)   Subsidiaries of the Wilmette Bahá'í House of Worship

_____

_____

_____

_____

c)   Codification and promulgation of the Most Holy Book

_____

_____

_____

_____

d)   Bahá'í Courts

_____

_____

_____

_____

e)   Bahá'í House of Worship in Ṭihrán

_____

_____

_____

_____

f)   Bahá'í House of Worship in Holy Land

_____

_____

_____

_____

9.   What are the different stages of the development of the Bahá'í community as envisaged by Shoghi Effendi in paragraph 25?

_____

_____

_____

10.   What are the key points in paragraph 26?

_____

_____

_____

_____

11.   What are the key points in paragraph 27?

_____

_____

_____

_____

8.6.2   Mini-project

In connection with the Tablets of the Divine Plan, Shoghi Effendi states in paragraph 23 that a "... perusal, however perfunctory, of those Tablets embodying His Plan will instantly reveal a scope for their activities that stretches far beyond the confines of the Western Hemisphere. With their inter-American tasks and responsibilities virtually discharged, their intercontinental mission enters upon its most glorious and decisive phase." Identify in the Tablets of the Divine Plan (see Appendix) the scope of international activities involving the North American Bahá'í community, as mentioned by Shoghi Effendi.

9.
A word of warning

9.1 Introduction

This chapter covers paragraphs 28–33, in which Shoghi Effendi warns that the capacity, the spirit, the conduct and high rank of the American believers, either individually or as a community, are not the typical characteristics of the people from which God has raised them. Such a distinction demonstrates the impact of the transmuting power of the Revelation of Bahá'u'lláh on the lives and standards of those who have come under His banner. North America has been chosen as the cradle for the Bahá'í Administrative Order to demonstrate this power.

In this chapter, you need to reflect on and understand the following key points:

a) The Manifestations of God always appear among people and races at the lowest depths of moral and spiritual degradation.

b) The Manifestations of God transform the selected people and societies to create the most advanced civilizations that then influence other races and nations.

c) *"Moses came during a time of darkness, when ignorance and childishness prevailed amongst the people, and they were waverers."*[1]

d) When the Israelites lost the spirit of Judaism and became fanatical and disunited, Jesus Christ appeared.

e) Muḥammad appeared among the savage tribes of Arabia and transformed them into a nation that became a great civilization.

f) At the time of the advent of the Báb and Bahá'u'lláh, Persia was a feeble and backward nation.

g) The distinction conferred by Bahá'u'lláh on America is to demonstrate the transforming power of His revelation.

---

[1] 'Abdu'l-Bahá, *'Abdu'l-Bahá in London*, p. 44.

h)   During His travels to Europe and the United States, 'Abdu'l-Bahá repeatedly talked about the excessive materialism affecting the world and its harmful consequences.

i)   Lawlessness and violence are dominant characteristics of American society.

9.2 Paragraphs under study

28   Dearly beloved friends!   Great as is my love and admiration for you, convinced as I am of the paramount share which you can, and will, undoubtedly have in both the continental and international spheres of future Bahá'í activity and service, I feel it nevertheless incumbent upon me to utter, at this juncture, a word of warning. The glowing tributes, so repeatedly and deservedly paid to the capacity, the spirit, the conduct, and the high rank, of the American believers, both individually and as an organic community, must, under no circumstances, be confounded with the characteristics and nature of the people from which God has raised them up. A sharp distinction between that community and that people must be made, and resolutely and fearlessly upheld, if we wish to give due recognition to the transmuting power of the Faith of Bahá'u'lláh, in its impact on the lives and standards of those who have chosen to enlist under His banner. Otherwise, the supreme and distinguishing function of His Revelation, which is none other than the calling into being of a new race of men, will remain wholly unrecognized and completely obscured.

29   How often have the Prophets of God, not excepting Bahá'u'lláh Himself, chosen to appear, and deliver their Message in countries and amidst peoples and races, at a time when they were either fast declining, or had already touched the lowest depths of moral and spiritual degradation. The appalling misery and wretchedness to which the Israelites had sunk, under the debasing and tyrannical rule of the Pharaohs, in the days preceding their exodus from Egypt under the leadership of Moses; the decline that had set in the religious, the spiritual, the cultural, and the moral life of the Jewish people, at the time of the appearance of Jesus Christ; the barbarous cruelty, the gross idolatry and immorality, which had for so long been the most distressing features of the tribes of Arabia and brought such shame upon them when Muḥammad arose to proclaim His Message in their midst; the indescribable state of decadence, with its attendant corruption, confusion, intolerance, and oppression, in both the civil and religious life of Persia, so graphically portrayed by the pen of a considerable number of scholars, diplomats, and travellers, at the hour of the Revelation of Bahá'u'lláh—all demonstrate this basic and inescapable fact. To contend that the innate worthiness, the high moral standard, the political aptitude, and social attainments of any race or nation is the reason for the appearance in its midst of any of these Divine Luminaries would be an absolute perversion of historical facts, and would amount to a complete repudiation of the undoubted interpretation placed upon them, so clearly and emphatically, by both Bahá'u'lláh and 'Abdu'l-Bahá.

30   How great, then, must be the challenge to those who, belonging to such races and nations, and having responded to the call which these Prophets have

raised, to unreservedly recognize and courageously testify to this indubitable truth, that not by reason of any racial superiority, political capacity, or spiritual virtue which a race or nation might possess, but rather as a direct consequence of its crying needs, its lamentable degeneracy, and irremediable perversity, has the Prophet of God chosen to appear in its midst, and with it as a lever has lifted the entire human race to a higher and nobler plane of life and conduct. For it is precisely under such circumstances, and by such means that the Prophets have, from time immemorial, chosen and were able to demonstrate their redemptive power to raise from the depths of abasement and of misery, the people of their own race and nation, empowering them to transmit in turn to other races and nations the saving grace and the energizing influence of their Revelation.

31   In the light of this fundamental principle it should always be borne in mind, nor can it be sufficiently emphasized, that the primary reason why the Báb and Bahá'u'lláh chose to appear in Persia, and to make it the first repository of their Revelation, was because, of all the peoples and nations of the civilized world, that race and nation had, as so often depicted by 'Abdu'l-Bahá, sunk to such ignominious depths, and manifested so great a perversity, as to find no parallel among its contemporaries. For no more convincing proof could be adduced demonstrating the regenerating spirit animating the Revelations proclaimed by the Báb and Bahá'u'lláh than their power to transform what can be truly regarded as one of the most backward, the most cowardly, and perverse of peoples into a race of heroes, fit to effect in turn a similar revolution in the life of mankind. To have appeared among a race or nation which by its intrinsic worth and high attainments seemed to warrant the inestimable privilege of being made the receptacle of such a Revelation would in the eyes of an unbelieving world greatly reduce the efficacy of that Message, and detract from the self-sufficiency of its omnipotent power. The contrast so strikingly presented in the pages of Nabíl's Narrative between the heroism that immortalized the life and deeds of the Dawn-Breakers and the degeneracy and cowardice of their defamers and persecutors is in itself a most impressive testimony to the truth of the Message of Him Who had instilled such a spirit into the breasts of His disciples. For any believer of that race to maintain that the excellence of his country and the innate nobility of its people were the fundamental reasons for its being singled out as the primary receptacle of the Revelations of the Báb and Bahá'u'lláh would be untenable in the face of the overwhelming evidence afforded so convincingly by that Narrative.

32   To a lesser degree this principle must of necessity apply to the country which has vindicated its right to be regarded as the cradle of the World Order of Bahá'u'lláh. So great a function, so noble a role, can be regarded as no less inferior to the part played by those immortal souls who, through their sublime renunciation and unparalleled deeds, have been responsible for the birth of the Faith itself. Let not, therefore, those who are to participate so predominantly in the birth of that world civilization, which is the direct offspring of their Faith, imagine for a moment that for some mysterious purpose or by any reason of inherent excellence or special merit Bahá'u'lláh has chosen to confer upon their country and people so great and lasting a

distinction. It is precisely by reason of the patent evils which, notwithstanding its other admittedly great characteristics and achievements, an excessive and binding materialism has unfortunately engendered within it that the Author of their Faith and the Centre of His Covenant have singled it out to become the standard-bearer of the New World Order envisaged in their writings. It is by such means as this that Bahá'u'lláh can best demonstrate to a heedless generation His almighty power to raise up from the very midst of a people, immersed in a sea of materialism, a prey to one of the most virulent and long-standing forms of racial prejudice, and notorious for its political corruption, lawlessness and laxity in moral standards, men and women who, as time goes by, will increasingly exemplify those essential virtues of self-renunciation, of moral rectitude, of chastity, of indiscriminating fellowship, of holy discipline, and of spiritual insight that will fit them for the preponderating share they will have in calling into being that World Order and that World Civilization of which their country, no less than the entire human race, stands in desperate need. Theirs will be the duty and privilege, in their capacity first as the establishers of one of the most powerful pillars sustaining the edifice of the Universal House of Justice, and then as the champion-builders of that New World Order of which that House is to be the nucleus and forerunner, to inculcate, demonstrate, and apply those twin and sorely needed principles of Divine justice and order—principles to which the political corruption and the moral license, increasingly staining the society to which they belong, offer so sad and striking a contrast.

33 Observations such as these, however distasteful and depressing they may be, should not, in the least, blind us to those virtues and qualities of high intelligence, of youthfulness, of unbounded initiative, and enterprise which the nation as a whole so conspicuously displays, and which are being increasingly reflected by the community of the believers within it. Upon these virtues and qualities, no less than upon the elimination of the evils referred to, must depend, to a very great extent, the ability of that community to lay a firm foundation for the country's future role in ushering in the Golden Age of the Cause of Bahá'u'lláh.

9.3 Appearance of the Manifestations of God

In paragraphs 29–31, the Guardian explains that the Manifestations of God always appear among peoples and races at their lowest depths of moral and spiritual degradation. Through their divine power, they transform the selected people and societies to create the most advanced civilizations of the time, which then influence other races and nations. In order to illustrate this concept, Shoghi Effendi briefly refers to the conditions of people amidst whom Moses, Christ, Muḥammad, the Báb and Bahá'u'lláh appeared.

Particularly in paragraph 31, Shoghi Effendi emphasizes that the Báb and Bahá'u'lláh chose to appear in Persia "because, of all the peoples and nations of the civilized world, that race and nation had, as so often depicted by 'Abdu'l-Bahá, sunk to such ignominious depths, and manifested so great a perversity, as to find no parallel among its contemporaries." The power of the revelations of the Báb and Bahá'u'lláh transformed the most backward, cowardly and perverse people into a new race of heroes.

In the following sections, some background on the state of the people among whom each one of the revelations mentioned by the Guardian is provided.

9.3.1 Moses

The term Israelite is a reference to the descendants of the Patriarch Jacob. The Patriarchs of the Bible are Abraham, his son Isaac and the son of Isaac, Jacob. Jacob had 13 children, 12 sons and one daughter. Through a chain of events in connection with one of his sons, Joseph, Jacob moved the entire family to Egypt where the descendants settled and multiplied significantly. Threatened by the number of Israelites, the Pharaoh decided to deal with them harshly. Initially, he ordered the enslavement of the Israelites under extremely harsh conditions. According to Exodus, the Egyptian masters treated the Israelites ruthlessly and made their lives bitter and miserable. Since the numbers of the Israelites continued to grow even under oppression, the Pharaoh ordered that every newly born Hebrew boy be thrown into the river Nile.[1]

'Abdu'l-Bahá explains:

At a time when the Israelites had multiplied in Egypt and were spread throughout the whole country, the Coptic Pharaohs of Egypt determined to strengthen and favour their own Coptic peoples and to degrade and dishonour the children of Israel, whom they regarded as foreigners. Over a long period, the Israelites, divided and scattered, were captive in the hands of the tyrannical Copts, and were scorned and despised by all, so that the meanest of the Copts would freely persecute and lord it over the noblest of the Israelites. The enslavement, wretchedness and helplessness of the Hebrews reached such a pitch that they were never, day or night, secure in their own persons nor able to provide any defence for their wives and families against the tyranny of their Pharaohic captors. Then their food was the fragments of their own broken hearts, and their drink a river of tears.[2]

The misery of Israelites continued

... until suddenly Moses, the All-Beauteous, beheld the Divine Light streaming out of the blessed Vale, the place that was holy ground, and heard the quickening voice of God as it spoke from the flame of that Tree 'neither of the East nor of the West,'[3] and He stood up in the full panoply of His universal prophethood. In the midst of the Israelites, He blazed out like a lamp of Divine guidance, and by the light of salvation He led that lost people out of the shadows of ignorance into knowledge and perfection. He gathered Israel's scattered tribes into the shelter of the unifying and universal Word of God, and over the heights of union He raised up the banner of harmony, so that within a brief interval those benighted souls became spiritually educated, and they who had been strangers to the truth, rallied to the cause of the oneness of God, and were delivered out of their

---

[1] Exodus 1:8–14.

[2] 'Abdu'l-Bahá, *The Secret of Divine Civilization*, p. 75.

[3] Qur'án, 24:35.

wretchedness, their indigence, their incomprehension and captivity and achieved a supreme degree of happiness and honour.[1]

'Abdu'l-Bahá explains that

Moses came during a time of darkness, when ignorance and childishness prevailed amongst the people, and they were waverers. Moses was the teacher of God; He gave the teachings of holiness and educated the Israelites. He raised up the people from their degradation and caused them to be highly honoured. He taught them Sciences and Arts, trained them in civilization and increased their human virtues.[2]

In another talk, 'Abdu'l-Bahá states that

... Moses through the influence of His great mission was instrumental in releasing the Israelites from a low state of debasement and humiliation, establishing them in a station of prestige and glorification, disciplining and educating them, ...[3]

9.3.2 Jesus Christ

Under the guidance received through the revelation of Moses, the Israelites made significant progress in all aspects of civilization to the point that they inspired the great philosophers of Greece, such as Pythagoras and Socrates, who developed many of their profoundest theories from the concepts of Israel's scholars and theologians.[4] However, after reaching the peak of their civilization, the Israelites *"... began little by little to forget the root-principles of the Mosaic Law and Faith, to busy themselves with rites and ceremonials and to show forth unbecoming conduct."*[5]

'Abdu'l-Bahá then states that the Israelites

... forgot the meaning of the Law of God that they became involved in ignorant fanaticism and blameworthy practices such as insurgence and sedition. Their divines, having concluded that all those essential qualifications of humankind set forth in the Holy Book were by then a dead letter, began to think only of furthering their own selfish interests, and afflicted the people by allowing them to sink into the lowest depths of heedlessness and ignorance. And the fruit of their wrong doing was this, that the old-time glory which had endured so long now changed to degradation, and the rulers of Persia, of Greece, and of Rome, took them over. The banners of their sovereignty were reversed; the ignorance, foolishness, abasement and self-love of their religious leaders and their scholars were brought to light in the coming of Nebuchadnezzar, King of Babylon, who destroyed them. After a general massacre, and the sacking and razing of their houses and even the uprooting of their trees, he took captive whatever remnants his sword had spared and carried them off to Babylon. Seventy years later the descendants of these captives were released and went back to Jerusalem. Then

---

[1] 'Abdu'l-Bahá, *The Secret of Divine Civilization*, pp. 75–76.

[2] 'Abdu'l-Bahá, *'Abdu'l-Bahá in London*, p. 44.

[3] 'Abdu'l-Bahá, *The Promulgation of Universal Peace*, p. 406.

[4] 'Abdu'l-Bahá, *The Secret of Divine Civilization*, p. 76.

[5] 'Abdu'l-Bahá, *The Secret of Divine Civilization*, p. 77.

Hezekiah and Ezra reestablished in their midst the fundamental principles of the Holy Book, and day by day the Israelites advanced, and the morning-brightness of their earlier ages dawned again. In a short time, however, great dissensions as to belief and conduct broke out anew, and again the one concern of the Jewish doctors became the promotion of their own selfish purposes, and the reforms that had obtained in Ezra's time were changed to perversity and corruption. The situation worsened to such a degree that time and again, the armies of the republic of Rome and of its rulers conquered Israelite territory. Finally the warlike Titus, commander of the Roman forces, trampled the Jewish homeland into dust, putting every man to the sword, taking the women and children captive, flattening their houses, tearing out their trees, burning their books, looting their treasures, and reducing Jerusalem and the Temple to an ash heap.[1]

At this time Jesus Christ appeared and

... through an extraordinary power abrogated the ancient Mosaic Law and undertook to reform the morals of the people. He once again laid the foundation of eternal honour for the Israelites—nay, He undertook to rehabilitate the fortunes of the entire human race—and spread abroad teachings that were not reserved for Israel alone but formed the basis for the universal happiness of human society.[2]

9.3.3   Muḥammad

The pre-Islamic period in Arabia is usually known as the era of Jáhilíyyih[3]. Although, Arabs were descendent from Ismá'íl, the son of Abraham, polytheism and idolatry dominated their religious beliefs. During this period there was no political organization of any form in the Arabian Peninsula. There were a number of Arab tribes, and the chief of each tribe had ultimate authority. Since there was no government, there was no law or order. Continuous war between tribes was the core feature of Arabian society. Usury was widespread and sometimes interest of 200–400 per cent was charged. Drinking and gambling were major pastimes. Arabia was a male-dominated society and women had no status. A man could marry any number of women.

In *Some Answered Questions*, 'Abdu'l-Bahá briefly describes the state of pre-Islamic Arabia:

These Arab tribes were most barbarous and rapacious, and in comparison with them the wild and fierce natives of America were the Platos of the age, for they did not bury their children alive as these Arabs did their daughters, claiming this to be an act of honour and taking pride therein. Thus many of the men would threaten their wives, saying, 'If a daughter is born to you, I will kill you.' Even to the present day the Arabs dread having daughters.

Moreover, one man could take a thousand wives, and most husbands had more than ten wives in their household. When these tribes waged war against each

---

[1]   'Abdu'l-Bahá, *The Secret of Divine Civilization*, pp. 78–79.

[2]   'Abdu'l-Bahá, *Some Answered Questions*, 2nd Edition, 2014, pp. 20–21.

[3]   Transcribed from the Persian, "State of ignorance; pre-Islamic paganism". The dark age of ignorance among the Arabs before the appearance of Muḥammad.

other, the victors would take captive the women and children of the vanquished, regard them as slaves, and engage in buying and selling them.

If a man died and left behind ten wives, the sons of these women would rush at each other's mothers, and as soon as one of them had thrown his mantle over the head of one of his stepmothers and claimed her as his lawful property, that unfortunate woman would become the captive and slave of her stepson and the latter could do with her as he pleased.[1]

Muḥammad appeared among the savage tribes of Arabia, who

... were in the utmost ignorance and barbarism. ... They lived in bondage and serfdom under the Persian and Roman governments and were scattered throughout the desert, engaged in continual strife and bloodshed. When the light of Muḥammad dawned, the darkness of ignorance was dispelled from the deserts of Arabia. In a short period of time those barbarous peoples attained a superlative degree of civilization which, with Baghdád as its centre, extended as far westward as Spain and afterward influenced the greater part of Europe.[2]

9.3.4   The Báb and Bahá'u'lláh

In paragraph 29, Shoghi Effendi labels the state of decadence in Persia in the 19th century and the "corruption, confusion, intolerance, and oppression, in both the civil and religious life of Persia" associated with that moral decay as "indescribable". 'Abdu'l-Bahá identifies the cause of the state of decadence in Persia as "*... the interference of the ignorant and fanatical leaders ....*"[3]

In the introduction to *The Dawn-Breakers*, while referring to the literature about Persia in the 19th century, Shoghi Effendi states that all

... observers agree in representing Persia as a feeble and backward nation divided against itself by corrupt practices and ferocious bigotries. Inefficiency and wretchedness, the fruit of moral decay, filled the land. From the highest to the lowest there appeared neither the capacity to carry out methods of reform nor even the will seriously to institute them National conceit preached a grandiose self-content. A pall of immobility lay over all things, and a general paralysis of mind made any development impossible.[4]

Shoghi Effendi also includes extracts from Lord Curzon's *Persia and the Persian Question* at the beginning of *The Dawn Breakers* that provides some details about the decadence and corruption that surrounded the Qájár sovereigns, the Persian government and the people in the 19th century.

In *The Secret of Divine Civilization*, 'Abdu'l-Bahá sheds more light on the nature of the degeneracy that afflicted Persia at that time. In different parts of the book, He compares the glorious past of Persia with the sad state of its affairs in those

[1]   'Abdu'l-Bahá, *Some Answered Questions*, 2nd Edition, 2014, pp. 23.
[2]   'Abdu'l-Bahá, *The Promulgation of universal Peace*, p. 368.
[3]   'Abdu'l-Bahá, *Tablets of Abdul-Baha Abbas*, Vol. 2, p. 403.
[4]   Shoghi Effendi, *The Dawn-Breakers*, p. xxiv.

days. In one section, He calls on the people of Persia to wake up from their drunken sleep and lethargy, and then poses a number of questions to them:

... will the dictates of honour permit this holy land, once the wellspring of world civilization, the source of glory and joy for all mankind, the envy of East and West, to remain an object of pity, deplored by all nations? She was once the noblest of peoples: will you let contemporary history register for the ages her now degenerate state? Will you complacently accept her present wretchedness, when she was once the land of all mankind's desire? Must she now, for this contemptible sloth, this failure to struggle, this utter ignorance, be accounted the most backward of nations?

Were not the people of Persia, in days long gone, the head and front of intellect and wisdom? Did they not, by God's grace, shine out like the daystar from the horizons of Divine knowledge? How is it that we are satisfied today with this miserable condition, are engrossed in our licentious passions, have blinded ourselves to supreme happiness, to that which is pleasing in God's sight, and have all become absorbed in our selfish concerns and the search for ignoble, personal advantage?

'Abdu'l-Bahá then continues by explaining why the light of Persia has turned to darkness:

This fairest of lands was once a lamp, streaming with the rays of Divine knowledge, of science and art, of nobility and high achievement, of wisdom and valour. Today, because of the idleness and lethargy of her people, their torpor, their undisciplined way of life, their lack of pride, lack of ambition—her bright fortune has been totally eclipsed, her light has turned to darkness. 'The seven heavens and the seven earths weep over the mighty when he is brought low.'[1]

9.4 Maladies afflicting American society

In paragraph 32, Shoghi Effendi explains that the principles governing the birthplace of a revelation apply to a lesser degree to the country chosen to be the cradle of the New World Order. Such distinction conferred by Bahá'u'lláh on America and its people is not because of "some mysterious purpose or by any reason of inherent excellence or special merit". Rather, this is how Bahá'u'lláh demonstrates the transforming power of His revelation in bringing forth a new generation of people with high moral standards from "a people immersed in a sea of materialism", involved in the most violent and long standing racial prejudice, and a society "notorious for its political corruption, lawlessness and laxity in moral standards".

Thus commissioned, the American Bahá'í community was privileged to become the champion-builders of the new Divine civilization, with its National Assembly as one of foundational supports of the future Universal House of Justice, the nucleus and forerunner of the New World Order. The National Spiritual Assembly of the Bahá'ís of the United States and Canada would instil and exemplify the core values of Divine justice and order that would be in such

---

[1] 'Abdu'l-Bahá, *The Secret of Divine Civilization*, pp. 8–9.

contrast to the corruption and low moral standards that were increasingly affecting America.

Shoghi Effendi particularly emphasizes in paragraph 32 that "political corruption and the moral license" are "increasingly staining" American society. Later writings of Shoghi Effendi reflect the pace at which that society is sinking into these maladies. In a message he wrote to the American Bahá'ís on 28 July 1954 he states:

> The steady and alarming deterioration in the standard of morality as exemplified by the appalling increase of crime, by political corruption in ever widening and ever higher circles, by the loosening of the sacred ties of marriage, by the inordinate craving for pleasure and diversion, and by the marked and progressive slackening of parental control, is no doubt the most arresting and distressing aspect of the decline that has set in, and can be clearly perceived, in the fortunes of the entire nation.[1]

Shoghi Effendi points out in paragraph 33 that his observations of the maladies afflicting American society have no bearing on the qualities of "high intelligence, youthfulness, unbounded initiative, and enterprise" of the United States of American—a country that had only relatively recently achieved nationhood. However, if the high moral standards expected in the Faith are added to the above-named qualities, the result will be a community that will lay the foundation for its future role of establishing the Golden Age of the Cause of Bahá'u'lláh.

Issues of corruption, moral laxity and racial prejudice in America were studied in sections 6.5, 6.6 and 6.7. In the following sections, some background information is provided on the excessive materialism and lawlessness dominating the American society.

9.4.1   Sea of materialism

The term "materialism" is used in the English language within two contexts. In the first sense, materialism is a philosophical ideology proposing matter as the main substance of all living and non-living entities, referred to as philosophical materialism. In its other context, materialism represents a set of attitudes and behaviours primarily concerned with the production and acquisition of income and worldly goods.[2] In a materialistic society, people base their sense of themselves, their happiness, well-being, and social standing on the accumulation of material possessions. Hence, materialism becomes part of the culture and it can be referred to as social materialism.

Although, philosophical materialism may directly or indirectly justify social materialism, many people influenced by social materialism are not aware of or relate to philosophical materialism. Consumerism, the ideology that encourages the acquisition of goods in ever-increasing quantities for personal satisfaction and economic stimulation, is usually the main driving force behind social

---

1   Shoghi Effendi, *Citadel of Faith*, p. 124.
2   Raymond Williams, *A Vocabulary of Culture and Society*, New York: Oxford University Press, 1975, p. 163.

materialism. Consumerism is able to flourish in affluent and prosperous societies as people have disposable resources to spend on excessive goods and services.

The unprecedented prosperity of many middle-class Americans in the 1920's as a result of rising earnings meant more disposable income was available to American families to purchase consumer goods. This led to new patterns of consumption that included the acquisition of continually updated manufactured goods, such as clothing, beauty products, cars and home appliances, resulting from technological innovations. In this process, advertising became a central institution to promote the purchase of new goods and services. Over time, as the machinery driving consumerism grew stronger, the United States sank deeper into materialism.

The capitalist system dominant in the United States was a fertile ground for the rise and growth of materialism. 'Abdu'l-Bahá had seen the signs and perceived its spread to other parts of the world well before the prosperous years of the 1920's. During his travels to Europe and the United States, 'Abdu'l-Bahá repeatedly talked about the excessive materialism affecting the world and its harmful consequences. In a talk given on 4 April 1912 in New York, He warned that the *"world of humanity is submerged in a sea of materialism. The rays of the Sun of Reality are seen but dimly and darkly through opaque glasses. The penetrative power of the divine bounty is not fully manifest."*[1]

In another talk 'Abdu'l-Baha gave in Green Acre, on 17 August 1912, He stated:

In cities like New York the people are submerged in the sea of materialism. Their sensibilities are attuned to material forces, their perceptions purely physical. The animal energies predominate in their activities; all their thoughts are directed to material things; day and night they are devoted to the attractions of this world, without aspiration beyond the life that is vanishing and mortal. In schools and temples of learning knowledge of the sciences acquired is based upon material observations only; there is no realization of Divinity in their methods and conclusions—all have reference to the world of matter. They are not interested in attaining knowledge of the mysteries of God or understanding the secrets of the heavenly Kingdom; what they acquire is based altogether upon visible and tangible evidences. Beyond these evidences they are without susceptibilities; they have no idea of the world of inner significances and are utterly out of touch with God, considering this an indication of reasonable attitude and philosophical judgement whereof they are self-sufficient and proud.[2]

The economic materialism that infected the United States, where the whole machinery of consumerism proliferated, spread throughout the developed world and is now afflicting many different nations. Shoghi Effendi gives us a snapshot of the influence of materialism on the United States and the rest of the world in a message dated 28 July 1954. In the paragraph prior to the following extract, he refers to the deterioration of the standard of morality in America. He then states:

---

[1] 'Abdu'l-Bahá, *The Promulgation of Universal Peace*, p. 10.
[2] 'Abdu'l-Bahá, *The Promulgation of Universal Peace*, pp. 261–262.

Parallel with this, and pervading all departments of life—an evil which the nation, and indeed all those within the capitalist system, though to a lesser degree, share with that state and its satellites regarded as the sworn enemies of that system—is the crass materialism, which lays excessive and ever-increasing emphasis on material well-being, forgetful of those things of the spirit on which alone a sure and stable foundation can be laid for human society. It is this same cancerous materialism, born originally in Europe, carried to excess in the North American continent, contaminating the Asiatic peoples and nations, spreading its ominous tentacles to the borders of Africa, and now invading its very heart, which Bahá'u'lláh in unequivocal and emphatic language denounced in His Writings, comparing it to a devouring flame and regarding it as the chief factor in precipitating the dire ordeals and world-shaking crises that must necessarily involve the burning of cities and the spread of terror and consternation in the hearts of men. Indeed a foretaste of the devastation which this consuming fire will wreak upon the world, and with which it will lay waste the cities of the nations participating in this tragic world-engulfing contest, has been afforded by the last World War, marking the second stage in the global havoc which humanity, forgetful of its God and heedless of the clear warnings uttered by His appointed Messenger for this day, must, alas, inevitably experience. It is this same all-pervasive, pernicious materialism against which the voice of the Centre of Bahá'u'lláh's Covenant was raised, with pathetic persistence, from platform and pulpit, in His addresses to the heedless multitudes, which, on the morrow of His fateful visit to both Europe and America, found themselves suddenly swept into the vortex of a tempest which in its range and severity was unsurpassed in the world's history.[1]

9.4.2   Lawlessness

Lawlessness and violence are dominant characteristics of American society. Grimshaw categorises lawlessness and violence in the United States into two groups. He refers to the first group as ethnic violence based on religion and nativity, including Black-White social violence and conflict.[2]

In the 19th century, particularly the period before the American Civil War, an anti-Catholic tradition was responsible for recurrent violence. This manifested itself as street fights and riots, attacks on religious edifices, and constant vilification of and occasional assault on Catholics. Hostility was also directed at other religious groups such as Jews and Mormons. Attacks on indigenous American Indians were commonplace.

Nearly all immigrant groups have been the target of hostility, especially if they could be distinguished from the larger population by their physical characteristics. Resentment towards the Chinese resulted in anti-Chinese riots in the final decades of the 19th century. Mexican-Americans were as poorly treated

---

[1]   Shoghi Effendi, *Citadel of Faith*, pp. 124–125.

[2]   Allen D. Grimshaw, "Lawlessness and Violence in America and their Special Manifestations in Changing Negro-White Relationships", *The Journal of Negro History*, Vol. 44, No. 1, Jan. 1959, pp. 52–72.

A Tutorial on The Advent of Divine Justice

in the Southwest as Black-Americans were in the South. During the 1940's, there were assaults against the persons and properties of Mexican-Americans, Japanese-Americans and Black-Americans.

Grimshaw identifies the second category of lawlessness and violence afflicting the American nation as the result of politics, the relations of the populace to the government and economic competition. In fact, the birth of the United States as a republic and other major changes, such as the abolition of slavery, were achieved through violence and war. According to Grimshaw, there were "spectacular election riots" in the 19th century and the 20th century elections were "often characterized by sharp violations of the law". This situation continues today. There has also been violence in economic conflicts over unionisation, often resulting in big labour strikes. Grimshaw concludes:

> America has been, then, a land of lawlessness and violence, ranging from spontaneous brawls between servicemen of different branches and schoolboys from different schools, through the 'blood feud' and gangster warfare, to the full-fledged military campaigns which have occurred in struggles between class and class and between adherents of different religious faiths. The tradition of lawlessness includes both a contempt of parking regulations and an admiration of gangster heroes and, on the other hand, an excess zeal in the administration of 'vigilante justice,' 'lynch law,' and 'six-shooter law' on the frontier. ... there is practically no section of the United States which has not, at one time or another, been a centre of lawlessness and violence. If there is less actual participation in violence today, and if Americans must sublimate their propensities to violence by watching television, the potentiality still remains.[1]

---

[1] Allen D. Grimshaw, "Lawlessness and Violence in America and their Special Manifestations in Changing Negro-White Relationships", *The Journal of Negro History*, Vol. 44, No. 1, Jan. 1959, p. 55.

9.5 Activities

9.5.1 *Short answer questions*

1. What is the "sharp distinction" Shoghi Effendi mentions in paragraph 28?

    _____

    _____

    _____

    _____

2. Why do the Manifestations of God appear among peoples and races at the lowest depths of moral and spiritual degradation?

    _____

    _____

    _____

    _____

3. Expand on the following statements made by Shoghi Effendi in paragraph 29.

    a) "The appalling misery and wretchedness to which the Israelites had sunk, under the debasing and tyrannical rule of the Pharaohs, in the days preceding their exodus from Egypt under the leadership of Moses;"

        _____

        _____

        _____

        _____

    b) "the decline that had set in the religious, the spiritual, the cultural, and the moral life of the Jewish people, at the time of the appearance of Jesus Christ;"

        _____

        _____

        _____

        _____

    c) "the barbarous cruelty, the gross idolatry and immorality, which had for so long been the most distressing features of the tribes of Arabia and brought such shame upon them when Muḥammad arose to proclaim His Message in their midst;"

        _____

        _____

_____

_____

    d)   "the indescribable state of decadence, with its attendant corruption, confusion, intolerance, and oppression, in both the civil and religious life of Persia, so graphically portrayed by the pen of a considerable number of scholars, diplomats, and travellers, at the hour of the Revelation of Bahá'u'lláh"

_____

_____

_____

_____

    e)   What is the spiritual principle underlying all the above events?

_____

_____

_____

_____

4.   What is your understanding of paragraph 30?

_____

_____

_____

_____

5.   What is the nature of materialism in American society as described by Shoghi Effendi in paragraph 32?

_____

_____

_____

_____

6.   What is the nature of lawlessness in American society as described by Shoghi Effendi in paragraph 32?

_____

_____

_____

_____

7.   What is your understanding of the last sentence in paragraph 32?

_____

_____

_____

_____

8. The following questions relate to the first sentence in paragraph 33 regarding the American nation:

    Describe your understanding of the following qualities mentioned by Shoghi Effendi for American people and give an example for each:

    a) High intelligence

    _____

    _____

    _____

    _____

    b) Youthfulness

    _____

    _____

    _____

    _____

    c) Unbounded initiative

    _____

    _____

    _____

    _____

    d) Enterprise

    _____

    _____

    _____

    _____

9.5.2   Mini-project

Consider the quotation cited from Grimshaw in section 9.4.2. In this statement reference is made to "vigilante justice", "lynch law" and "six-shooter law". Conduct some research on the nature of these violent practices.

10.
Rectitude of conduct

10.1   Introduction

This lesson covers paragraphs 34–41. In these paragraphs the Guardian counsels the North American Bahá'í community to cleanse their lives of the shortcomings and erroneous inclinations that reflect the faults imbedded within their society, while cultivating the qualities crucial for success in their Bahá'í endeavours. He then identifies the spiritual pre-requisites that are the bedrock of their undertakings and instrumental in attracting the divine blessings, categorizing them as rectitude of conduct, absolute chastity, and complete freedom from prejudice. In paragraphs 36–41, he focusses on rectitude of conduct.

In this chapter, you need to reflect on and understand the following key points:

a) The American believers should weed out the "faults, habits, and tendencies" that they have inherited from their nation.

b) The New World Order cannot be reared unless and until the generality of people in America are purified from the social and political evils currently inflicting them.

c) Shoghi Effendi identifies "rectitude of conduct" as one of the first spiritual pre-requisites.

d) The implications of "rectitude of conduct" are justice, equity, truthfulness, honesty, fairmindedness, reliability and trustworthiness.

e) Equity has a broad meaning and refers to a range of values such as fairness, justice and impartiality.

f) Truthfulness is a virtue that ensures our thoughts, words and actions reflect the truth.

g) Honesty is a quality that governs the attitudes, words and deeds of an individual and ensures that they are truthful and sincere, morally correct or virtuous, and free from deceit.

h) Fair-mindedness is a virtue that governs the attitude, words and deeds of an individual.

i) As a virtue, reliability is a character trait and indicates that an individual is dependable, trustworthy, honest and responsible.

j) Trustworthiness is a virtue indicating that an individual can be relied on as being honest, truthful and reliable.

k) Shoghi Effendi describes the specific aspects of the life of a Bahá'í where rectitude of conduct and its associated virtues must be applied.

10.2 Paragraphs under study

34 How great, therefore, how staggering the responsibility that must weigh upon the present generation of the American believers, at this early stage in their spiritual and administrative evolution, to weed out, by every means in their power, those faults, habits, and tendencies which they have inherited from their own nation, and to cultivate, patiently and prayerfully, those distinctive qualities and characteristics that are so indispensable to their effective participation in the great redemptive work of their Faith. Incapable as yet, in view of the restricted size of their community and the limited influence it now wields, of producing any marked effect on the great mass of their countrymen, let them focus their attention, for the present, on their own selves, their own individual needs, their own personal deficiencies and weaknesses, ever mindful that every intensification of effort on their part will better equip them for the time when they will be called upon to eradicate in their turn such evil tendencies from the lives and the hearts of the entire body of their fellow-citizens. Nor must they overlook the fact that the World Order, whose basis they, as the advance-guard of the future Bahá'í generations of their countrymen, are now labouring to establish, can never be reared unless and until the generality of the people to which they belong has been already purged from the divers ills, whether social or political, that now so severely afflict it.

35 Surveying as a whole the most pressing needs of this community, attempting to estimate the more serious deficiencies by which it is being handicapped in the discharge of its task, and ever bearing in mind the nature of that still greater task with which it will be forced to wrestle in the future, I feel it my duty to lay special stress upon, and draw the special and urgent attention of the entire body of the American believers, be they young or old, white or coloured, teachers or administrators, veterans or newcomers, to what I firmly believe are the essential requirements for the success of the tasks which are now claiming their undivided attention. Great as is the importance of fashioning the outward instruments, and of perfecting the administrative agencies, which they can utilize for the prosecution of their dual task under the Seven Year Plan; vital and urgent as are the campaigns which they are initiating, the schemes and projects which they are devising, and the funds which they are raising, for the efficient conduct of both the Teaching and Temple work, the imponderable, the spiritual, factors, which are bound up with their own individual and inner lives, and with which are associated their human and social relationships, are no less urgent and vital, and demand constant scrutiny, continual self-examination and heart-searching on their part, lest their value be impaired or their vital necessity be obscured or forgotten.

36   Of these spiritual prerequisites of success, which constitute the bedrock on which the security of all teaching plans, Temple projects, and financial schemes, must ultimately rest, the following stand out as preeminent and vital, which the members of the American Bahá'í community will do well to ponder. Upon the extent to which these basic requirements are met, and the manner in which the American believers fulfil them in their individual lives, administrative activities, and social relationships, must depend the measure of the manifold blessings which the All-Bountiful Possessor can vouchsafe to them all. These requirements are none other than a high sense of moral rectitude in their social and administrative activities, absolute chastity in their individual lives, and complete freedom from prejudice in their dealings with peoples of a different race, class, creed, or colour.

37   The first is specially, though not exclusively, directed to their elected representatives, whether local, regional, or national, who, in their capacity as the custodians and members of the nascent institutions of the Faith of Bahá'u'lláh, are shouldering the chief responsibility in laying an unassailable foundation for that Universal House of Justice which, as its title implies, is to be the exponent and guardian of that Divine Justice which can alone insure the security of, and establish the reign of law and order in, a strangely disordered world. The second is mainly and directly concerned with the Bahá'í youth, who can contribute so decisively to the virility, the purity, and the driving force of the life of the Bahá'í community, and upon whom must depend the future orientation of its destiny, and the complete unfoldment of the potentialities with which God has endowed it. The third should be the immediate, the universal, and the chief concern of all and sundry members of the Bahá'í community, of whatever age, rank, experience, class, or colour, as all, with no exception, must face its challenging implications, and none can claim, however much he may have progressed along this line, to have completely discharged the stern responsibilities which it inculcates.

38   A rectitude of conduct, an abiding sense of undeviating justice, unobscured by the demoralizing influences which a corruption-ridden political life so strikingly manifests; a chaste, pure, and holy life, unsullied and unclouded by the indecencies, the vices, the false standards, which an inherently deficient moral code tolerates, perpetuates, and fosters; a fraternity freed from that cancerous growth of racial prejudice, which is eating into the vitals of an already debilitated society—these are the ideals which the American believers must, from now on, individually and through concerted action, strive to promote, in both their private and public lives, ideals which are the chief propelling forces that can most effectively accelerate the march of their institutions, plans, and enterprises, that can guard the honour and integrity of their Faith, and subdue any obstacles that may confront it in the future.

39   This rectitude of conduct, with its implications of justice, equity, truthfulness, honesty, fair-mindedness, reliability, and trustworthiness, must distinguish every phase of the life of the Bahá'í community. *"The companions of God,"* Bahá'u'lláh Himself has declared, *"are, in this day, the lump that must leaven the peoples of the world. They must show forth such trustworthiness, such truthfulness and perseverance, such deeds and character*

that all mankind may profit by their example."[A] "I swear by Him Who is the Most Great Ocean!" He again affirms, "Within the very breath of such souls as are pure and sanctified far-reaching potentialities are hidden. So great are these potentialities that they exercise their influence upon all created things."[B] "He is the true servant of God," He, in another passage has written, "who, in this day, were he to pass through cities of silver and gold, would not deign to look upon them, and whose heart would remain pure and undefiled from whatever things can be seen in this world, be they its goods or its treasures. I swear by the Sun of Truth! The breath of such a man is endowed with potency, and his words with attraction."[C] "By Him Who shineth above the Dayspring of sanctity!" He, still more emphatically, has revealed, "If the whole earth were to be converted into silver and gold, no man who can be said to have truly ascended into the heaven of faith and certitude would deign to regard it, much less to seize and keep it. They who dwell within the Tabernacle of God, and are established upon the seats of everlasting glory, will refuse, though they be dying of hunger, to stretch their hands, and seize unlawfully the property of their neighbour, however vile and worthless he may be. The purpose of the one true God in manifesting Himself is to summon all mankind to truthfulness and sincerity, to piety and trustworthiness, to resignation and submissiveness to the will of God, to forbearance and kindliness, to uprightness and wisdom. His object is to array every man with the mantle of a saintly character, and to adorn him with the ornament of holy and goodly deeds."[D] "We have admonished all the loved ones of God," He insists, "to take heed lest the hem of Our sacred vesture be smirched with the mire of unlawful deeds, or be stained with the dust of reprehensible conduct."[E] "Cleave unto righteousness, O people of Bahá," He thus exhorts them, "This, verily, is the commandment which this wronged One hath given unto you, and the first choice of His unrestrained will for every one of you."[F] "A good character," He explains, "is, verily, the best mantle for men from God. With it He adorneth the temples of His loved ones. By My life! The light of a good character surpasseth the light of the sun and the radiance thereof."[G] "One righteous act," He, again, has written, "is endowed with a potency that can so elevate the dust as to cause it to pass beyond the heaven of heavens. It can tear every bond asunder, and hath the power to restore the force that hath spent itself and vanished. ... Be pure, O people of God, be pure; be righteous, be righteous .... Say: O people of God! That which can insure the victory of Him Who is the Eternal Truth, His hosts and helpers on earth, have been set down in the sacred Books and Scriptures, and are as clear and manifest as the sun. These hosts are such righteous deeds, such conduct and character, as are acceptable in His sight. Whoso ariseth, in this Day, to aid Our Cause, and summoneth to his assistance the hosts of a praiseworthy character and upright conduct, the influence from such an action will, most certainly, be diffused throughout the whole world."[H] "The betterment of the world," is yet another statement, "can be accomplished through pure and goodly deeds, through commendable and seemly conduct."[I] "Be fair to yourselves and to others," He thus counselleth them, "that the evidences of justice may be revealed through your deeds among Our faithful servants."[J] "Equity," He also has written, "is the most fundamental among human virtues. The evaluation of all things must needs depend upon it."[K] And again, *"Observe equity in your judgement, ye men of understanding heart! He that is unjust in his judgement is destitute of the characteristics that distinguish man's station."*[L] *"Beautify your tongues, O people,"* He further admonishes them, *"with truthfulness, and adorn your souls with the ornament of honesty. Beware, O people, that ye deal not treacherously with anyone. Be ye the trustees of God amongst His creatures, and the emblems of His generosity amidst His people."*[M] *"Let your eye be chaste,"* is yet another counsel, *"your hand faithful, your tongue truthful, and your heart enlightened."*[N] *"Be an ornament to the countenance of truth,"* is yet another admonition, *"a crown to the brow of fidelity, a pillar of the temple of righteousness, a breath of life to the body of mankind, an ensign of the hosts of justice, a luminary above the horizon of virtue."*[O] *"Let truthfulness and courtesy be your adorning,"* is still another admonition; *"suffer not yourselves to be deprived of the robe of forbearance and justice, that the sweet savers of holiness may be wafted from your hearts upon all created things. Say: Beware, O people of Bahá, lest ye walk in the ways of them whose words differ from their deeds. Strive that ye may be enabled to manifest to the peoples of the earth the signs of God, and to mirror forth His commandments. Let your acts be a guide unto all mankind, for the professions of most men, be they high or low, differ from their conduct. It is through your deeds that ye can distinguish yourselves from others. Through them the brightness of your light can be shed upon the whole earth. Happy is the man that heedeth My counsel, and keepeth the precepts prescribed by Him Who is the All-Knowing, the All-Wise."*[P]

40   *"O army of God!"* writes 'Abdu'l-Bahá, *"Through the protection and help vouchsafed by the Blessed Beauty—may my life be a sacrifice to His loved ones—ye must conduct yourselves in such a manner that ye may stand out distinguished and brilliant as the sun among other souls. Should any one of you enter a city, he should become a Centre of attraction by reason of his sincerity, his faithfulness and love, his honesty and fidelity, his truthfulness and loving-kindness towards all the peoples of the world, so that the people of that city may cry out and say: 'This man is unquestionably a Bahá'í, for his manners, his behaviour, his conduct, his morals, his nature, and disposition reflect the attributes of the Bahá'ís.' Not until ye attain this station can ye be said to have been faithful to the Covenant and Testament of God."*[A] *"The most vital duty, in this day,"* He, moreover, has written, *"is to purify your characters, to correct your manners, and improve your conduct. The beloved of the Merciful must show forth such character and conduct among His creatures, that the fragrance of their holiness may be shed upon the whole world, and may quicken the dead, inasmuch as the purpose of the Manifestation of God and the dawning of the limitless lights of the Invisible is to educate the souls of men, and refine the character of every living man. ..."*[B] *"Truthfulness,"* He asserts, *"is the foundation of all human virtues. Without truthfulness progress and success, in all the worlds of God, are impossible for any soul. When this holy attribute is established in man, all the divine qualities will also be acquired."*[C]

41   Such a rectitude of conduct must manifest itself, with ever-increasing potency, in every verdict which the elected representatives of the Bahá'í community, in whatever capacity they may find themselves, may be called

upon to pronounce. It must be constantly reflected in the business dealings of all its members, in their domestic lives, in all manner of employment, and in any service they may, in the future, render their government or people. It must be exemplified in the conduct of all Bahá'í electors, when exercising their sacred rights and functions. It must characterize the attitude of every loyal believer towards nonacceptance of political posts, nonidentification with political parties, nonparticipation in political controversies, and nonmembership in political organizations and ecclesiastical institutions. It must reveal itself in the uncompromising adherence of all, whether young or old, to the clearly enunciated and fundamental principles laid down by 'Abdu'l-Bahá in His addresses, and to the laws and ordinances revealed by Bahá'u'lláh in His Most Holy Book. It must be demonstrated in the impartiality of every defender of the Faith against its enemies, in his fair-mindedness in recognizing any merits that enemy may possess, and in his honesty in discharging any obligations he may have towards him. It must constitute the brightest ornament of the life, the pursuits, the exertions, and the utterances of every Bahá'í teacher, whether labouring at home or abroad, whether in the front ranks of the teaching force, or occupying a less active and responsible position. It must be made the hallmark of that numerically small, yet intensely dynamic and highly responsible body of the elected national representatives of every Bahá'í community, which constitutes the sustaining pillar, and the sole instrument for the election, in every community, of that Universal House whose very name and title, as ordained by Bahá'u'lláh, symbolizes that rectitude of conduct which is its highest mission to safeguard and enforce.

10.3 Spiritual pre-requisites

Shoghi Effendi starts his analysis of the "spiritual pre-requisites" from paragraph 34. In this paragraph, he points out that the American believers should weed out the "faults, habit, and tendencies" that they have inherited from their nation. They must cultivate in themselves the qualities and tools needed for their effective engagement in eradicating the evils of their society.

They should initially focus their attention on addressing their own deficiencies as due to their small number, their influence on their countrymen is limited at present. Thus, when they are eventually summoned to strive for the moral betterment of the wider community, they will be well prepared for the task. Not until American society has been sufficiently purged of its present social and political ills, will the foundations of the New World Order, towards the erection of which the North American Bahá'ís are toiling, be established.

In paragraph 35, the Guardian emphasizes that the urgency of fostering the spiritual factors governing the inner lives of the Bahá'ís and their social relationships with others are no less important than that of developing plans, raising funds and constructing the temple. In regards to the significance of spiritual pre-requisites, he describes them in paragraph 36 as "the bedrock on which the security of all teaching plans, Temple projects, and financial schemes, must ultimately rest." The blessing vouchsafed to the community in their endeavours is proportional to the extent that the American believers realize these spiritual pre-requisites in their lives. He then identifies these spiritual pre-requisites as

a) A high sense of moral rectitude in their individual lives, administrative activities and social relationships with others.
b) Absolute chastity in their individual lives.
c) Complete freedom from prejudice in dealing with peoples of a different race, class, creed or colour.

In paragraph 37, Shoghi Effendi clarifies that the "high sense of moral rectitude" is directed specially but not exclusively at the elected representatives—whether local, regional or national—who are the custodians of the Faith and have the chief responsibility to lay the foundation for the Universal House of Justice. The "chaste and holy life" is mainly directed to the youth who can contribute to the vigour, the purity and the driving force of the life of the Bahá'í community and upon whom the future of the Faith depends. The freedom from prejudices should be "the immediate, the universal, and the chief concern" of all community members of any age, rank, experience, class or colour. Everyone must face the challenges imposed by these requirements and no one can claim to have completely discharged the responsibilities associated with them.

In paragraph 38, Shoghi Effendi further clarifies the nature and scope of each one of the spiritual pre-requisites:

a) "A rectitude of conduct, an abiding sense of undeviating justice, unobscured by the demoralizing influences which a corruption-ridden political life so strikingly manifests."
b) A "chaste, pure, and holy life, unsullied and unclouded by the indecencies, the vices, the false standards, which an inherently deficient moral code tolerates, perpetuates, and fosters."
c) A "fraternity freed from that cancerous growth of racial prejudice, which is eating into the vitals of an already debilitated society."

10.4   Implications of "rectitude of conduct"

Shoghi Effendi deals with the first spiritual pre-requisite, "rectitude of conduct", in paragraphs 39–41. In paragraph 39, he initially clarifies that the implications of "rectitude of conduct" in the life of an individual are:

- Justice
- Equity
- Truthfulness
- Honesty
- Fair-mindedness
- Reliability
- Trustworthiness

He then cites 19 statements from Bahá'u'lláh and 'Abdu'l-Bahá highlighting the significance of the qualities associated with "rectitude of conduct". In the following sections, some background on the above attributes, except justice (it is covered in the next chapter), is provided, together with appropriate quotations from Bahá'u'lláh and 'Abdu'l-Bahá.

10.4.1 Equity

Equity has a broad meaning and refers to a range of values such as fairness, justice and impartiality, particularly in the way people are treated.

Bahá'u'lláh identifies justice and equity as "... *twin Guardians that watch over men. From them are revealed such blessed and perspicuous words as are the cause of the well-being of the world and the protection of the nations.*"[1] In another Tablet, He refers to equity as *"the most fundamental among human virtues. The evaluation of all things must needs depend upon it."*[2] In the same Tablet, He warns people: *"Observe equity in your judgement, ye men of understanding heart! He that is unjust in his judgement is destitute of the characteristics that distinguish man's station."*[3] Referring to the oppression afflicting the world, Bahá'u'lláh states that *"Justice is, in this day, bewailing its plight, and Equity groaneth beneath the yoke of oppression. The thick clouds of tyranny have darkened the face of the earth, and enveloped its peoples."*[4]

The economic and legal aspects of equity have been the centre of attention and discussion since the time of Plato who defined equity as "giving every man his due".[5] In the context of social justice, this statement has been interpreted to mean that the rewards given to an individual should address their basic needs as well as their contributions to society. This makes equity different from equality in which everyone gets an equal share independent of their contribution.

According to Falk et. al., "Equity derives from a concept of social justice. It represents a belief that there are some things which people should have, that there are basic needs that should be fulfilled, that burdens and rewards should not be spread too divergently across the community, and that policy should be directed with impartiality, fairness and justice towards these ends."[6]

It is also recognized that equity as a concept is fundamental to sustainable development.

> Poverty is not only an evil in itself, but sustainable development requires meeting the basic needs of all and extending to all the opportunity to fulfil their aspirations for a better life .... Meeting essential needs requires not only a new era of economic growth for nations in which the majority are poor, but an assurance that those poor get their fair share of the resources required to sustain that growth.[7]

---

[1] Bahá'u'lláh, *Epistle to the Son of the Wolf*, p. 12.

[2] Bahá'u'lláh, *Gleanings from the Writings of Bahá'u'lláh*, p. 202.

[3] Bahá'u'lláh, *Gleanings from the Writings of Bahá'u'lláh*, p. 203.

[4] Bahá'u'lláh, *Gleanings from the Writings of Bahá'u'lláh*, p. 92.

[5] Plato, *Republic*, Book 1, p. 335.

[6] Falk, Jim, Hampton, Greg, Hodgkinson, Ann, Parker, Kevin and Rorris, Arthur, *Social Equity and the Urban Environment, Report to the Commonwealth Environment Protection Agency*, AGPS, Canberra, 1993, p. 2.

[7] WCED (World Commission on Environment and Development), *Our common future*, 1987, Oxford: Oxford University Press, p. 8.

Quotes 39:K and 39:L explicitly refer to the importance of equity.

10.4.2 Truthfulness

Truthfulness is a virtue that ensures our thoughts, words and actions reflect the truth. When we are truthful, we do our utmost to find truth in every matter and distinguish truth from fantasy. We do not believe, misrepresent or promote something as the truth when we know it is not true. We do not tell lies even to protect ourselves or others. We do not exaggerate about who and what we are to impress others.

Bahá'u'lláh identifies truthfulness as one of the fruits of the tree of life.[1] He counsels people to adorn and beautify their *"tongues with absolute truthfulness."*[2]

'Abdu'l-Bahá recognizes truthfulness as *"the foundation of all the virtues of the world of humanity."* He stresses that without *"truthfulness, progress and success in all of the worlds of God are impossible for a soul. When this holy attribute is established in man, all the divine qualities will also become realized."*[3]

Quotes 39:A, 39:D, 39:M, 39:O, 39:P, 40:A and 40:C explicitly refer to the importance of truthfulness.

10.4.3 Honesty

Honesty is a quality that governs the attitudes, words and deeds of an individual and ensures that they are truthful and sincere, morally correct or virtuous, and free from deceit. Bahá'u'lláh distinguishes between honesty and truthfulness. He states: *"Beautify your tongues, O people, with truthfulness, and adorn your souls with the ornament of honesty."*[4] Hence, while truthfulness governs what we verbally express, honesty is the quality of our soul and controls our attitudes and deeds. Honesty and truthfulness are closely linked as a dishonest person can easily lie to deceive and mislead.

Bahá'u'lláh identifies honesty and piety as the cause of happiness and exaltation. He states:

> *O ye friends of God in His cities and His loved ones in His lands! This Wronged One enjoineth on you honesty and piety. Blessed the city that shineth by their light. Through them man is exalted, and the door of security is unlocked before the face of all creation. Happy the man that cleaveth fast unto them, and recognizeth their virtue, and woe betide him that denieth their station.*[5]

In another Tablet He asserts: *"Say: Honesty, virtue, wisdom and a saintly character redound to the exaltation of man, while dishonesty, imposture, ignorance and hypocrisy lead to his abasement."*[6]

---

[1] Bahá'u'lláh, cited in *Lights of Guidance*, p. 228.

[2] Bahá'u'lláh, *The Kitáb-i-Aqdas*, p. 62.

[3] 'Abdu'l-Bahá, *Bahá'í World Faith*, p. 384.

[4] Bahá'u'lláh, *Gleanings from the Writings of Bahá'u'lláh*, p. 296.

[5] Bahá'u'lláh, *Epistle to the Son of the Wolf*, p. 23.

[6] Bahá'u'lláh, *Tablets of Bahá'u'lláh*, p. 57.

Quotes 39:M and 40:A explicitly refer to the importance of honesty.

10.4.4 Fair-mindedness

Fair-mindedness is a virtue that governs the attitude, words and deeds of an individual. A fair-minded person is impartial, even-handed and reasonable. Bahá'u'lláh makes many references in His Writings to fair-mindedness and being fair-minded. He considers fairmindedness as one of the expressions of justice. In the same Tablet He beseeches God *"... to graciously adorn the world of humanity with justice and fair-mindedness."*[1]

In another Tablet, Bahá'u'lláh states:

If a man would seek distinction he should suffice himself with a frugal provision, seek to better the lot of the realm, choose the way of justice and fair mindedness, and tread the path of high-spirited service. Such a one, needy though he be, shall win imperishable riches and attain unto everlasting honour.[2]

Bahá'u'lláh repeatedly admires people who are fair-minded in different contexts, and clarifies the meaning of this attribute in the context of Bahá'í moral standards. Here are some examples:

- *"Blessed are the fair-minded, and woe betide them that have turned aside."*[3]
- *"Happy are the fair-minded."*[4]
- *"O concourse of the fair-minded! Observe and reflect upon the billows of the ocean of the utterance and knowledge of God, so that ye may testify with your inner and outer tongues that with Him is the knowledge of all that is in the Book. Nothing escapeth His knowledge. He, verily, hath manifested that which was hidden, when He, upon His return, mounted the throne of the Bayan. All that hath been sent down hath and will come to pass, word for word, upon earth. No possibility is left for anyone either to turn aside or protest. As fairness, however, is disgraced and concealed, most men speak as prompted by their own idle fancies."*[5]
- *"These passages stand in need of no commentary. They are shining and manifest as the sun, and glowing and luminous as light itself. Every fair-minded person is led, by the fragrance of these words, unto the garden of understanding, and attaineth unto that from which most men are veiled and debarred."*[6]
- *"Where is the fair-minded person who will equitably consider what hath been perpetrated against Us without any clear token or proof?"*[7]

---

[1] Bahá'u'lláh, *Tabernacle of Unity*, paragraph 2.60, cited at http://www.bahai.org/library/.

[2] Bahá'u'lláh, *Lights of Guidance*, p. 453.

[3] Bahá'u'lláh, *Epistle to the Son of the Wolf*, p. 161.

[4] Bahá'u'lláh, *Epistle to the Son of the Wolf*, p. 162.

[5] Bahá'u'lláh, *Epistle to the Son of the Wolf*, pp. 151–152.

[6] Bahá'u'lláh, *Epistle to the Son of the Wolf*, p. 146.

[7] Bahá'u'lláh, *Epistle to the Son of the Wolf*, p. 126.

- *"Well is it with every fair-minded person that hath judged fairly Him Who is the Most Great Remembrance, and woe betide him that hath erred and doubted."*[1]
- *"We pray to God to graciously assist them that have been led astray to be just and fair-minded, and to make them aware of that whereof they have been heedless."*[2]
- *"And there befell Me at the hands of both of them that which made every man of understanding to cry out, and he who is endued with insight to groan aloud, and the tears of the fair-minded to flow."*[3]
- *"In these days there are some who, far from being just and fair-minded, have assaulted Me with the sword of hatred and the spear of enmity, forgetting that it behoveth every fair-minded person to succour Him Whom the world hath cast away and the nations abandoned, and to lay hold on piety and righteousness."*[4]

In paragraph, Shoghi Effendi cites a statement from Bahá'u'lláh (quote 39:J) that explicitly refers to the importance of fair-mindedness.

10.4.5   Reliability

People or things that are reliable can be trusted to work well or behave as expected. A reliable person can usually be depended on in an undertaking in both cognitive and practical realms. In this context, reliability is more a capability than a virtue as the degree of reliability can vary depending on the match between the task against the training, experience and skills of the individual.

As a virtue, reliability is a character trait and indicates that an individual is dependable, trustworthy, honest, and responsible. This is a stable characteristic of the individual and does not significantly vary according to the nature of the task. A reliable person is genuine and authentic, has pure motivations, adheres to all commitments and ensures that they are achieved.

The significance of this virtue is implicitly highlighted in some of the quotations in paragraphs 39 and 40 as part of other virtues.

10.4.6   Trustworthiness

Trustworthiness is a virtue indicating that an individual can be relied upon as honest, truthful and reliable. This is the impression that is developed by others of the words and deeds of an honest and truthful person.

Bahá'u'lláh has given a great deal of importance to trustworthiness and refers to this virtue in many of His Tablets. Counselling His followers, He states:

O people of Bahá! Trustworthiness is in truth the best of vestures for your temples and the most glorious crown for your heads. Take ye fast hold of it at

---

[1]   Bahá'u'lláh, *Epistle to the Son of the Wolf*, p. 79.
[2]   Bahá'u'lláh, *Epistle to the Son of the Wolf*, p. 70.
[3]   Bahá'u'lláh, *Epistle to the Son of the Wolf*, p. 70.
[4]   Bahá'u'lláh, *Epistle to the Son of the Wolf*, p. 36.

the behest of Him Who is the Ordainer, the All-Informed.[1]

Bahá'u'lláh states: *"Say, O friends! Strive that haply the tribulations suffered by this Wronged One and by you, in the path of God, may not prove to have been in vain. Cling ye to the hem of virtue, and hold fast to the cord of trustworthiness and piety."*[2] In the same book, He further refers to the two virtues of trustworthiness and piety: *"Say: O people of God! Adorn your temples with the adornment of trustworthiness and piety. Help, then, your Lord with the hosts of goodly deeds and a praiseworthy character."*[3]

In the *Tablet of Ṭarázát* (Ornaments) that was revealed after *The Kitáb-i-Aqdas*, the fourth Ṭaráz is dedicated to trustworthiness:

> *Verily it is the door of security for all that dwell on earth and a token of glory on the part of the All-Merciful. He who partaketh thereof hath indeed partaken of the treasures of wealth and prosperity. Trustworthiness is the greatest portal leading unto the tranquillity and security of the people. In truth the stability of every affair hath depended and doth depend upon it. All the domains of power, of grandeur and of wealth are illumined by its light.*

Bahá'u'lláh then quotes His own words from another Tablet, describing the station of trustworthiness:

> 'We will now mention unto thee Trustworthiness and the station thereof in the estimation of God, thy Lord, the Lord of the Mighty Throne. One day of days We repaired unto Our Green Island. Upon Our arrival, We beheld its streams flowing, and its trees luxuriant, and the sunlight playing in their midst. Turning Our face to the right, We beheld what the pen is powerless to describe; nor can it set forth that which the eye of the Lord of Mankind witnessed in that most sanctified, that most sublime, that blest, and most exalted Spot. Turning, then, to the left We gazed on one of the Beauties of the Most Sublime Paradise, standing on a pillar of light, and calling aloud saying: 'O inmates of earth and heaven! Behold ye My beauty, and My radiance, and My revelation, and My effulgence. By God, the True One! I am Trustworthiness and the revelation thereof, and the beauty thereof. I will recompense whosoever will cleave unto Me, and recognize My rank and station, and hold fast unto My hem. I am the most great ornament of the people of Bahá, and the vesture of glory unto all who are in the kingdom of creation. I am the supreme instrument for the prosperity of the world, and the horizon of assurance unto all beings.' Thus have We sent down for thee that which will draw men nigh unto the Lord of creation.'[4]

Bahá'u'lláh continues the *Tablet of Ṭarázát* by emphasizing the importance of trustworthiness: *"O people of Bahá! Trustworthiness is in truth the best of vestures*

[1] Bahá'u'lláh, *Tablets of Bahá'u'lláh*, p. 37.
[2] Bahá'u'lláh, *Epistle to the Son of the Wolf*, p. 29.
[3] Bahá'u'lláh, *Epistle to the Son of the Wolf*, p. 135.
[4] Bahá'u'lláh, *Tablets of Bahá'u'lláh*, pp 121–122.

for your temples and the most glorious crown for your heads. Take ye fast hold of it at the behest of Him Who is the Ordainer, the All-Informed."[1]

The significance of this virtue is implicitly highlighted in some of the quotations in paragraphs 39 and 40 as part of other virtues.

10.5   Application and scope of attributes

In paragraph 41, Shoghi Effendi describes the specific aspects of the life of a Bahá'í where rectitude of conduct and its associated virtues, as identified in paragraph 39, must be applied. Such traits must manifest themselves in:

- Every judgement that the elected body of the Bahá'í community may make.
- The business dealings of all members of the community.
- Domestic lives of every Bahá'í.
- The employment and services through which Bahá'ís serve their people and their government.
- The Bahá'í electors when exercising their rights and functions.
- The attitudes of the believers towards non-acceptance of political posts, non-identification with political parties, non-involvement in political controversies, and non-membership in political organizations and ecclesiastical institutions.
- Adherence to all the fundamental principles laid down by 'Abdu'l-Bahá and the laws revealed by Bahá'u'lláh.
- The impartiality of the defenders of the Faith against its enemies, recognizing the merits of the enemy with fairmindedness, and discharging any obligation towards them with honesty.
- The adornment of every Bahá'í teacher.
- The distinctive characteristics of elected members of national institutions.

The moral decay that is currently eating into the political, commercial and social systems in many countries is in direct contrast to the rectitude of conduct described by Shoghi Effendi in this section as the moral standard expected from the followers of Bahá'u'lláh. The manifestation of such moral decay in various aspects of American society must have been relatively subtle at the time of Shoghi Effendi compared to the current climate in which corruption, indecency, dishonesty, unreliability, injustice, and violence are publicly portrayed at all levels of society, from grassroots to high ranking political figures. Maintaining such a rectitude of conduct is perhaps more urgent for the Bahá'í community while it might be much more challenging.

---

[1]   Bahá'u'lláh, *Tablets of Bahá'u'lláh*, p. 38.

10.6 Activities

10.6.1 Short answer questions

1. Identify some of the faults, habits and tendencies that Shoghi Effendi asks the American believers to remove from their character and behaviour.

    _____

    _____

    _____

    _____

2. What is your understanding of the following statement from paragraph 34?

    "... let them focus their attention, for the present, on their own selves, their own individual needs, their own personal deficiencies and weaknesses, ever mindful that every intensification of effort on their part will better equip them for the time when they will be called upon to eradicate in their turn such evil tendencies from the lives and the hearts of the entire body of their fellow-citizens."

    _____

    _____

    _____

    _____

3. What is your understanding of the following statement from paragraph 34?

    "... the World Order, ... can never be reared unless and until the generality of the people to which they belong has been already purged from the divers ills, whether social or political, that now so severely afflict it."

    _____

    _____

    _____

    _____

4. Consider the following statement from paragraph 35:

    "... the spiritual, factors, which are bound up with their own individual and inner lives, and with which are associated their human and social relationships, are no less urgent and vital, and demand constant scrutiny, continual self-examination and heart-searching on their part, lest their value be impaired or their vital necessity be obscured or forgotten."

    a) What is the "inner life"?

    _____

    _____

_____

_____

    b)   What is meant by "human and social relationships"?

_____

_____

_____

_____

    c)   What is your understanding of this statement?

_____

_____

_____

_____

5.   What are the three spiritual pre-requisites mentioned in paragraph 36?

_____

_____

_____

_____

6.   In paragraph 37, Shoghi Effendi identifies a specific cohort of the American Bahá'í community that should be particularly conscious of each spiritual pre-requisite. Describe the spiritual pre-requisites that apply to them.

_____

_____

_____

_____

_____

_____

_____

7.   In paragraph 38, Shoghi Effendi expands on the implications of each of the spiritual pre-requisites. Share your understanding of this paragraph.

_____

_____

_____

8. What are different manifestations of the rectitude of conduct?

_____

_____

_____

_____

9. Briefly describe:

a) Equity

_____

_____

b) Truthfulness

_____

_____

c) Honesty

_____

_____

d) Fair-mindedness

_____

_____

e) Reliability

_____

_____

f) Trustworthiness

_____

10. Briefly identify the key points in the quotations that Shoghi Effendi has given from Bahá'u'lláh and 'Abdu'l-Bahá in paragraphs 39 and 40.

a) Quote 39:A

_____

_____

b) Quote 39:B

_____

_____

c) Quote 39:C

_____

_____

d) Quote 39:D

_____

_____

e) Quote 39:E

_____

_____

f) Quote 39:F

_____

_____

g) Quote 39:G

_____

_____

h) Quote 39:H

_____

_____

i) Quote 39:I

_____

_____

j) Quote 39:J

_____

_____

k) Quote 39:K

_____

_____

l) Quote 39:L

_____

_____

m) Quote 39:M

_____

n) Quote 39:N

o) Quote 39:O

p) Quote 39:P

q) Quote 40:A

r) Quote 40:B

s) Quote 40:C

11. In paragraph 41, Shoghi Effendi describes the application and scope of the attributes manifested through rectitude of conduct. For each case given below, provide one possible scenario and identify virtues that should be deployed to demonstrate rectitude of conduct.

a) Elected body of the Bahá'í community

b) Business dealings

c)   Domestic lives

_____

_____

_____

_____

d)   Employment and service

_____

_____

_____

_____

e)   Bahá'í electors

_____

_____

_____

_____

f)   Abstaining from involvement in partisan politics

_____

_____

_____

_____

g)   Obedience to laws and principles pronounced by Bahá'u'lláh and 'Abdu'l-Bahá

_____

_____

_____

_____

h)   Treatment of enemies of the Faith

_____

_____

_____

_____

i)   Bahá'í teachers

_____

_____

_____

_____

10.6.2 Mini-project

Identify a real example of political corruption in the United States through research on the internet. Conduct an analysis on how the virtues Shoghi Effendi has defined as the manifestation of rectitude of conduct would have prevented it.

11.
Justice

11.1   Introduction

This chapter covers paragraphs 42–44 in which the Guardian expands on justice as one of the important qualities of a rectitude of conduct. He cites a number of statements from Bahá'u'lláh and 'Abdu'l-Bahá in paragraphs 42 and 43 to illustrate the nature of Divine justice, referred to by Bahá'u'lláh as "*the Most Great Justice*", to be established through the Revelation of Bahá'u'lláh. During the course of this chapter, injustice and its root causes are explored, some theories of justice proposed in Western philosophy are studied, and the nature of Divine justice is investigated.

In this chapter, you need to reflect on and understand the following key points:

a)   Over the last 10,000 years, humanity has persistently experienced various systematic injustices.
b)   Human nature has the potential to commit good and evil and there is evidence in human history demonstrating both behaviours.
c)   A weak spiritual reality can result in the dominance of physical reality and its agent ego to determine the moral choices we make.
d)   An authentic relation is the presence of unconditional love or altruism in a relationship.
e)   Authenticity is the essence of our spiritual reality and creates a need that drives us to achieve authenticity, and, if unsuccessful, it results in a dilemma of authenticity.
f)   In general, the dilemma of authenticity is dealt with by creating abstract ideologies and enforcing them at any cost.
g)   Failure to establish an authentic relationship often results in replacing it with a pursuit of power over others in order to control and dominate them.
h)   In Western philosophy, justice is generally considered as the most fundamental of all virtues governing the relationship between people and ensuring the stability of society.

i) If we use our powers to establish love and an authentic relationship with others, then justice prevails.

j) The justice established through a revelation from God is referred to as Divine justice.

k) Divine justice, not forgiveness, is the shelter of the world of existence and a foundation of the life of mankind.

l) The American nation was established on an ideal of justice or "fairness to all", although in practice justice has proved a challenging concept to realize.

11.2   Paragraphs under study

42   So great and transcendental is this principle of Divine justice, a principle that must be regarded as the crowning distinction of all Local and National Assemblies, in their capacity as forerunners of the Universal House of Justice, that Bahá'u'lláh Himself subordinates His personal inclination and wish to the all-compelling force of its demands and implications. *"God is My witness!"* He thus explains, *"were it not contrary to the Law of God, I would have kissed the hand of My would-be murderer, and would cause him to inherit My earthly goods. I am restrained, however, by the binding Law laid down in the Book, and am Myself bereft of all worldly possessions."*[A] *"Know thou, of a truth,"* He significantly affirms, *"these great oppressions that have befallen the world are preparing it for the advent of the Most Great Justice."*[B] *"Say,"* He again asserts, *"He hath appeared with that Justice wherewith mankind hath been adorned, and yet the people are, for the most part, asleep."*[C] *"The light of men is Justice,"* He moreover states, *"Quench it not with the contrary winds of oppression and tyranny. The purpose of justice is the appearance of unity among men."*[D] *"No radiance,"* He declares, *"can compare with that of justice. The organization of the world and the tranquillity of mankind depend upon it."*[E] *"O people of God!"* He exclaims, *"That which traineth the world is Justice, for it is upheld by two pillars, reward and punishment. These two pillars are the sources of life to the world."*[F] *"Justice and equity,"* is yet another assertion, *"are two guardians for the protection of man. They have appeared arrayed in their mighty and sacred names to maintain the world in uprightness and protect the nations."*[G] *"Bestir yourselves, O people,"* is His emphatic warning, *"in anticipation of the days of Divine justice, for the promised hour is now come. Beware lest ye fail to apprehend its import, and be accounted among the erring."*[H] *"The day is approaching,"* He similarly has written, *"when the faithful will behold the daystar of justice shining in its full splendour from the dayspring of glory."*[I] *"The shame I was made to bear,"* He significantly remarks, *"hath uncovered the glory with which the whole of creation had been invested, and through the cruelties I have endured, the daystar of justice hath manifested itself, and shed its splendour upon men."*[J] *"The world,"* He again has written, *"is in great turmoil, and the minds of its people are in a state of utter confusion. We entreat the Almighty that He may graciously illuminate them with the glory of His Justice, and enable them to discover that which will be profitable unto them at all times and under all conditions."*[K] And again, *"There can be no doubt whatever that if the daystar*

of justice, which the clouds of tyranny have obscured, were to shed its light upon men, the face of the earth would be completely transformed."[L]

43   "*God be praised!*" 'Abdu'l-Bahá, in His turn, exclaims, "*The sun of justice hath risen above the horizon of Bahá'u'lláh. For in His Tablets the foundations of such a justice have been laid as no mind hath, from the beginning of creation, conceived.*"[A] "*The canopy of existence,*" He further explains, "*resteth upon the pole of justice, and not of forgiveness, and the life of mankind dependeth on justice and not on forgiveness.*"[B]

44   Small wonder, therefore, that the Author of the Bahá'í Revelation should have chosen to associate the name and title of that House, which is to be the crowning glory of His administrative institutions, not with forgiveness but with justice, to have made justice the only basis and the permanent foundation of His Most Great Peace, and to have proclaimed it in His Hidden Words as "*the best beloved of all things*" in His sight. It is to the American believers, particularly, that I feel urged to direct this fervent plea to ponder in their hearts the implications of this moral rectitude, and to uphold, with heart and soul and uncompromisingly, both individually and collectively, this sublime standard—a standard of which justice is so essential and potent an element.

11.3   Injustice

Over the last 10,000 years, humanity has persistently experienced various systematic injustices such as slavery, genocide, torture, forced conversions, and domination of women by men. Nations have often directly or subtly abused a particular religious, ethical or racial minority. The aggression and violation of human rights resulting from these injustices have been woeful and even tragic. There are different theories proposed on the reasons for such human behaviour.

11.3.1   Root causes of injustice

David Gil considers the imbalanced and inegalitarian modes of work, division of labour and exchange of products applied forcefully in different societies as the causes of the atrocities committed by man.[1] He refers to this systematic obstruction of the growth of human potentialities as a social violence. While such conceptions explain the dynamics observed in the societies under oppression, it ignores the spiritual causes that result in such behaviour.

Another ideology suggests that injustices committed by human beings and violence committed throughout human history originate from human nature and are biologically driven and, therefore, inevitable.[2] There is no doubt that human nature has the potential to commit good and evil and there is evidence in human history demonstrating both behaviours. The model suggested by 'Abdu'l-Bahá for human reality clearly describes how the ability to do both good and evil are

---

[1]   David G. Gil, "Work, Violence, Injustice and War", *The Journal of Sociology & Social Welfare*, Vol. 16, Iss. 1, March 1989, article 5, available at htp://scholarworks.wmich.edu/jssw/vol16/iss1/5.

[2]   Steven Pinker, *The Better Angels of Our Nature*, Penguin Random House, 2012.

associated with human nature. He states that there are three realities embedded in man: physical reality, intellectual reality and spiritual reality. In one of his talks, He describes these three realities:

a) *"Man is endowed with an outer or physical reality. It belongs to the material realm, the animal kingdom, because it has sprung from the material world. This animalistic reality of man he shares in common with the animals."*

b) *"… man is endowed with a second reality, the rational or intellectual reality; and the intellectual reality of man predominates over nature …. All these sciences which we enjoy were the hidden and recondite secrets of nature, unknowable to nature, but man was enabled to discover these mysteries, and out of the plane of the unseen he brought them into the plane of the seen."*

c) Spiritual reality is *"… an eternal reality, an indestructible reality, a reality belonging to the divine, supernatural kingdom; a reality whereby the world is illumined, a reality which grants unto man eternal life."*[1]

The attitudes, words and deeds manifested by a human being are dictated by the degrees to which these three realities are developed and the balance between these realities in an individual. A weak spiritual reality can result in the dominance of the physical reality and its agent ego to determine the moral choices we make.

11.3.2 *Authenticity and injustice*

William Hatcher provides an explanation for the root causes of injustice by drawing on the concept of authentic relationships. He describes an authentic relationship between two people "as mutual recognition of the universal value which they each share as human beings and which is inherent in their essential nature."[2] The sign of authenticity is the existence of unconditional love or altruism in the relationship. This reflects the authenticity of our relationship with God and is dependent on it. Hatcher refers to the former as the lateral authenticity and the latter as vertical authenticity.

Lateral authenticity is more than our words and deeds towards others; it also represents our spiritual and moral happiness, and status. It reflects the essence of our spiritual reality and the purpose of our existence as a human being. This creates a need that drives us to achieve authenticity, and, if unsuccessful, it results in the frustration of the will to achieve authenticity, referred to as a "dilemma of authenticity".

Human history shows various attempts to deal with the dilemma of authenticity. Bolshevism in Russia based on Marxism tried to achieve authenticity by creating an egalitarian society but without an altruistic motivation. In the United States, as an action-oriented, individualistic and pragmatic society, the dilemma of authenticity is addressed by faking or pretending authenticity, a condition that looks like authenticity but has no

---

1   'Abdu'l-Bahá, *Foundations of World Unity*, pp. 50–51. Bullets are added for emphasis.
2   William Hatcher, "Love, Power, and Justice", *Journal of Bahá'í Studies*, Vol. 9, number 3, 1994, p. 1.

substance. This has been interwoven within American entertainment such as Hollywood movies and TV soap operas.

In general, the dilemma of authenticity is dealt with by creating abstract ideologies and enforcing them at any cost. Such ideologies have given moral justification to inauthentic behaviour, such as perpetrating injustice and cruelty to others. Such a phenomenon is apparent in all the atrocities that have been committed in the past, particularly during the 19th and 20th centuries and in our contemporary world. In principle, ideologies should assist human beings in building a more authentic world rather than being a justification for injustice and oppression.

This point is clearly highlighted by Shoghi Effendi:

The call of Bahá'u'lláh is primarily directed against all forms of provincialism, all insularities and prejudices. If long-cherished ideals and time-honoured institutions, if certain social assumptions and religious formulae have ceased to promote the welfare of the generality of mankind, if they no longer minister to the needs of a continually evolving humanity, let them be swept away and relegated to the limbo of obsolescent and forgotten doctrines. ... For legal standards, political and economic theories are solely designed to safeguard the interests of humanity as a whole, and not humanity to be crucified for the preservation of the integrity of any particular law or doctrine.[1]

11.3.3   Power-seeking and injustice

Hatcher explores the relationship between ego-driven power-seeking tendencies and injustice. He argues that failure in establishing an authentic relationship often results in replacing it by pursuing power over others in order to control and dominate them.[2] Bahá'u'lláh identifies the pursuit of power as the root cause of many injustices committed over human history. He states:

And amongst the realms of unity is the unity of rank and station. It redoundeth to the exaltation of the Cause, glorifying it among all peoples. Ever since the seeking of preference and distinction came into play, the world hath been laid waste. It hath become desolate. Those who have quaffed from the ocean of divine utterance and fixed their gaze upon the Realm of Glory should regard themselves as being on the same level as the others and in the same station. Were this matter to be definitely established and conclusively demonstrated through the power and might of God, the world would become as the Abhá Paradise.

Indeed, man is noble, inasmuch as each one is a repository of the sign of God. Nevertheless, to regard oneself as superior in knowledge, learning or virtue, or to exalt oneself or seek preference, is a grievous transgression. Great is the blessedness of those who are adorned with the ornament of this unity and have

---

[1]   Shoghi Effendi, *The World Order of Bahá'u'lláh*, p. 42.
[2]   William Hatcher, "Love, Power, and Justice", *Journal of Bahá'í Studies*, Vol. 9, number 3, 1994.

been graciously confirmed by God.[1]

Power can be sought through physical force or in more subtle ways such as occupying roles in society that provide an opportunity to dominate others. Competition is another widespread means of seeking power in which one strives to outperform another with the aim of achieving superiority and dominance. Currently, the materialistic culture—intensively promoted through the entertainment industry and social media—encourages competition in nearly all facets of life, whether in accumulation of wealth, achieving positions of power and status, or generally gaining popularity and prestige in society. Under such intensive social pressure, people are prepared to win at any cost, not hesitating to use unfair and unjust practices; and even unethical and corrupt strategies when considered necessary.

11.4   Theories of justice

The word justice originates from the Latin *jus*, meaning right or law. According to the *Oxford English Dictionary*, a "just" person typically "does what is morally right" and is inclined to "giving everyone his or her due". In general, justice can convey different meanings in different practical contexts. The most common understanding of justice is when a criminal receives his due punishment. This is usually known as legal justice. There is also the concept of social justice advocating basic rights to shelter, education and healthcare for everyone. Social justice usually represents qualities such as equity, fairness, equality and opportunity.

11.4.1   Justice in Western philosophy

In Western philosophy, justice has generally been considered as the most fundamental of all virtues governing the relationship between people and ensuring the stability of a society. Theories on justice have included its application in areas such as politics, governance and social relationships. There have also been opposite views that suggest acquiring an objective knowledge of justice as a moral or political absolute value would be impossible.

The complexity of the concept of justice has meant it has been the focus of philosophers from at least as early as the ancient Greeks. There are references to the concept of *dikaios* (δίκαιος), describing a just person, in the writings of Homer from which the general concept of justice (*dikaiosyni*, δικαιοσύνη) has emerged as a virtue governing a society. Plato's *Republic* provides a careful analysis of justice as a virtue that establishes rational order. This concept is conveyed through a dialogue with his teacher, Socrates, describing justice as an essential virtue of both a good political state and a good individual. Plato considers the four qualities of wisdom, fortitude or courage, temperance and justice as central or core virtues. Aristotle deals with justice in Book V of his best-known work on ethics, *Nicomachean Ethics*, and he defines justice as what is lawful and fair, while describing fairness as an equitable distribution of wealth and the correction of what is not equitable.

---

[1]   Bahá'u'lláh, quoted by the Universal House of Justice, *Messages from the Universal House of Justice 1963 to 1986*, pp. 376–377.

Christian thinkers started to develop their own philosophy in the Middle Ages. Aurelius Augustine (354–430) adopted Platonic philosophy as much as it could be reconciled with Christian core concepts. He embraced the four core virtues defined by Plato, defining justice as "the virtue by which all people are given their due"[1] and maintaining that "an unjust law is no law at all."[2]

A few centuries later, Thomas Aquinas (1225–1274) combined Christian thoughts, the works by Augustinian and Aristotelian philosophy to develop some new philosophical ideologies, compatible with Augustine's theory of justice. He also incorporated Plato's four core virtues in his views on justice, and described it as a proportional equality or equity rather than numerical equality. He also identified justice as a natural law stemming from the will of God.[3]

With the emergence of modernity and the Enlightenment, empiricist philosophers, such as Thomas Hobbes (1588–1679) and later David Hume (1771–1776), rejected the platonic view of justice and insisted that developing an objective knowledge of justice as a moral or political absolute value was impossible. Hobbes defined justice simply as a social construct developed to satisfy certain human needs and passions. This was later reiterated by Hume, who argued that we should be just because it was agreeable and useful. In recent modernity, Immanuel Kant (1724–1804) considered justice as a moral and political virtue and suggested that we should practice justice because it was the right thing to do, not because it produced good consequences.

Among the contemporary philosophers, John Rawls (1921–2002) and his 1971 book, *A Theory of Justice*, is strikingly unique. Rawls referred to justice as fairness, and argued that the concepts of freedom and equality were not mutually exclusive. True justice should ensure that everyone was given the same rights under the law. To illustrate the concept of equality, Rawls asked about the type of justice system that people would prefer to experience if everyone were made absolutely equal by stripping them of their privileges and social status. He suggested that the only logical choice was a justice system that treats people equally regardless of their race, colour, ethical background, religion, etc.

Rawls offered two fundamental principles as the basis of his theory of justice that would guarantee a just and morally acceptable society. The "first requires equality in the assignment of basic rights and duties, while the second holds that social and economic inequalities, for example inequalities of wealth and authority, are just only if they result in compensating benefits for everyone, and in particular for the least advantaged members of society."[4]

[1] Augustine, *On Free Choice of Will*, tr. Thomas Williams, Indianapolis: Hackett Publishing Company, 1993, p. 20.

[2] Augustine, *On Free Choice of Will*, tr. Thomas Williams, Indianapolis: Hackett Publishing Company, 1993, p. 5.

[3] Thomas Aquinas, *Summa Theologica*, originally published in Latin, 1485.

[4] John Rawls, *A Theory of Justice*, Harvard University Press, revised edition 1999, p. 13.

11.4.2 *Justice and love*

William Hatcher describes justice as a spiritual condition under which love is born and developed.[1] Injustice emerges when we seek power to dominate and control others. However, if we use our power to establish love and an authentic relationship with others then justice prevails. Hence, an authentic application of power results in the establishment of justice.

Love is a unique human relationship through which both giver and receiver of love feel good and are satisfied. This is a win-win transaction with no trade-offs. This is the love that 'Abdu'l-Bahá describes as:

- *"... the secret of God's holy Dispensation, the manifestation of the All-Merciful, the fountain of spiritual outpourings."*
- *"... heaven's kindly light, the Holy Spirit's eternal breath that vivifieth the human soul."*
- *"... the cause of God's revelation unto man, the vital bond inherent, in accordance with the divine creation, in the realities of things."*
- *"... the one means that ensureth true felicity both in this world and the next."*
- *"... the light that guideth in darkness, the living link that uniteth God with man, that assureth the progress of every illumined soul."*
- *"... the most great law that ruleth this mighty and heavenly cycle, the unique power that bindeth together the divers elements of this material world, the supreme magnetic force that directeth the movements of the spheres in the celestial realms."*
- *"... revealeth with unfailing and limitless power the mysteries latent in the universe."*
- *"... the spirit of life unto the adorned body of mankind, the establisher of true civilization in this mortal world, and the shedder of imperishable glory upon every high-aiming race and nation."*[2]

11.5 Divine justice

Justice has a lofty rank in the Bahá'í Teachings to the extent that Bahá'u'lláh refers to it as *"the best beloved of all things"* in His sight.[3] He counsels His followers:

... turn not away therefrom if thou desirest Me, and neglect it not that I may confide in thee. By its aid thou shall see with thine own eyes and not through the eyes of others, and shalt know of thine own knowledge and not through the knowledge of thy neighbour. Ponder this in thy heart; how it behoveth thee to be. Verily justice is My gift to thee and the sign of My loving-kindness. Set it then before thine eyes.[4]

---

[1] William Hatcher, "Love, Power, and Justice", *Journal of Bahá'í Studies*, Vol. 9, number 3, 1994.
[2] 'Abdu'l-Bahá, *Selections from the Writings of 'Abdu'l-Bahá*, p. 27. Bullets are added for emphasis.
[3] Bahá'u'lláh, *Hidden Words*, Arabic no. 2.
[4] Bahá'u'lláh, *Hidden Words*, Arabic no. 2.

The justice established through a revelation from God is referred to in the Bahá'í writings as Divine justice. Bahá'u'lláh speaks of the Manifestations of God as the *"Manifestations of Divine justice"*.[1] Divine justice represents the Will of God for a particular age revealed to humanity through the laws, ordinances and teachings of a new religion destined for a particular period of human history. Through Divine justice, an authentic relationship is established between people through love and upholding the standards of justice through the enforcement of Divine laws.

In paragraphs 42 and 43, Shoghi Effendi cites a number of statements from Bahá'u'lláh and 'Abdu'l-Bahá to illustrate the nature of Divine justice, referred to by Bahá'u'lláh as *"the Most Great Justice"*, to be established through the Revelation of Bahá'u'lláh. He emphasizes that the principle of Divine justice "... must be regarded as the crowning distinction of all Local and National Assemblies, in their capacity as forerunners of the Universal House of Justice." Here are some of the major points raised in these quotations:

- Divine justice, not forgiveness, is the shelter of the world of existence and the foundation of the life of mankind (quotes 42:A and 43:B).
- The great oppression experienced by humanity is preparing it for the coming of the *"the Most Great Justice"* through the Revelation of Bahá'u'lláh (quote 42:B).
- The purpose of justice is to create unity and to establish tranquillity (quotes 42:D and 42:E).
- Reward and punishment are the two pillars of justice (quote 42:F).
- Divine justice and equity are the two guardians protecting humanity (quote 42:G).
- Divine justice was manifested as a result of the shame and cruelties inflicted on Bahá'u'lláh (quote 42:J).
- Divine justice illuminates humanity and clears the confusions in the minds of people (quote 42:K).
- The face of the earth will be completely transformed through Divine justice (quote 42:L).
- The foundations of Divine justice have been laid in the Tablets of Bahá'u'lláh (quote 43:A).

In order to highlight the significance of justice and distinguish it from forgiveness as the foundation of the New World Order, Shoghi Effendi mentions in paragraph 44 that the crowning institution of the Bahá'í Administrative Order is referred to by Bahá'u'lláh as the House of Justice, not the house of forgiveness.

11.6 Justice in America

Towards the end of paragraph 44, Shoghi Effendi urges the American Bahá'í community, collectively and individually, to uphold with their hearts and souls the standard of moral rectitude, "... of which justice is so essential and potent an element." The great emphasis given by Shoghi Effendi to the issue of justice in *The Advent of Divine Justice* is not surprising in light of the injustices embedded in

---

[1]   Bahá'u'lláh, *Gleanings from the Writings of Bahá'u'lláh*, p. 71.

many aspects of American society. This is despite the focus of American political thought on justice ever since the founding of that nation.

One of the goals included in the Preamble to the American Constitution was to "establish justice". In 1788, the founding father of the nation, James Madison, wrote in *The Federalist Papers*[1] that justice should be the goal of all governments and of all civil societies, that people must be willing to risk even liberty in the pursuit of justice. The foundational idea of the United States Constitution is that all men are created equal. The aim was to ensure a democratic government and to prevent any type of dictatorship. American schoolchildren memorize and recite the *Pledge of Allegiance*: "I pledge allegiance to the Flag of the United States of America, and the Republic for which it stands, one Nation and under God indivisible, with liberty and justice for all."

Hence, justice is the ideal on which the American nation was established and has been the driving force behind political thoughts and concepts. However, achieving justice in practice has proved very challenging due to the prevalence of prejudices, corruption and violence in the American society. The legal system is harsh towards the poor and lenient towards the rich—white-collar criminals receive mild sentences for serious offences whilst the poor are severely punished for minor wrongdoings.[2] As mentioned in section 11.3.2, the absence of true authenticity in relationships between people has maintained an indifference to injustice at all levels of society.

The unjust treatment of African Americans will be studied in later chapters of the book.

---

[1] A collection of 85 articles written by Alexander Hamilton, James Madison and John Jay to promote the ratification of the United States Constitution.

[2] Matt Taibbi, *The Divide: American Injustice in the Age of the Wealth Gap*, Spiegel & Grau, July 2014.

11.7   Activities

11.7.1   Short answer questions

1.   What is your understanding of the first sentence in paragraph 42?

_____

_____

_____

_____

2.   Refute the suggestion that injustices committed by human beings originate from human nature?

_____

_____

_____

_____

3.   Describe your understanding of the following concepts:

  a)   Authenticity

_____

_____

_____

_____

  b)   Lateral and vertical authenticity

_____

_____

_____

_____

  c)   Dilemma of authenticity

_____

_____

_____

_____

4.   How was the dilemma of authenticity dealt with in Bolshevik Russia?

_____

_____

5. How is the dilemma of authenticity dealt with in American society?

_____

_____

_____

_____

6. What is the relationship between authenticity, power seeking and injustice?

_____

_____

_____

_____

7. How is justice interpreted in the Western philosophy?

_____

_____

_____

_____

8. What is Divine justice?

_____

_____

_____

_____

9. Briefly identify the key points in the quotations Shoghi Effendi used from Bahá'u'lláh and 'Abdu'l-Bahá in paragraphs 42 and 43.

   a) Quote 42:A

_____

_____

   b) Quote 42:B

_____

_____

   c) Quote 42:C

_____

_____

d)   Quote 42:D

_____

_____

e)   Quote 42:E

_____

_____

f)   Quote 42:F

_____

_____

g)   Quote 42:G

_____

_____

h)   Quote 42:H

_____

_____

i)   Quote 42:I

_____

_____

j)   Quote 42:J

_____

_____

k)   Quote 42:K

_____

_____

l)   Quote 42:L

_____

_____

m)   Quote 43:A

_____

_____

n)   Quote 43:B

_____

10. What is the purpose of justice as described by Bahá'u'lláh?

11. What are the two pillars of justice? Explain.

12. What are the two guardians for the protection of humanity?

13. How is justice interpreted in American political thought?

14. What are the barriers to justice in American society?

11.7.2 Mini-project

Identify some of the theories in the 20th century that resulted in major injustices and violence. Prepare a PowerPoint presentation of your research and share it with your friends.

12.
A chaste and holy life—I

12.1   Introduction

The topic of "a chaste and holy life" will be covered in two chapters. In this chapter, the focus will be on the contents of paragraphs 45–46 and the beginning of paragraph 47. These paragraphs highlight the importance of a chaste and holy life in strengthening and vitalizing a Bahá'í community as well as ensuring the success of Bahá'í plans. In these paragraphs, Shoghi Effendi emphasizes that moral standards should be the controlling principles in the life of every individual Bahá'í, both within and without the Bahá'í community. He identifies the attributes of a chaste and holy life as modesty, purity, temperance, decency and clean-mindedness.

In this chapter, you need to reflect on and understand the following key points:

a)   All members of the Bahá'í community must examine their conduct to remove every trace of moral laxity that might stain the name of the Faith.

b)   Chastity in the strict sense means no sexual intimacy before marriage.

c)   A holy life in the Bahá'í teachings is one of attachment to God, His Precepts and His Will.

d)   The moral standards of a chaste and holy life in the Bahá'í Faith is not meant to reject or condemn the sexual impulse but to control and regulate it.

e)   The moral standards defined in the Bahá'í teachings should be the controlling principles in the life of every individual Bahá'í.

f)   Modesty is reflected by a mode of dress and behaviour that do not arouse others sexually.

g)   Purity is freedom from contamination, but as a quality of an individual it implies freedom from sexual immorality and a rejection of harmful substances.

h)   Temperance is a voluntary self-restraint in controlling an excess of emotions and impulses (anger, vanity and sexual desire) originating from one's character.

i) Decency is a behaviour that is good, moral and acceptable in a moral society.
j) Clean-mindedness is a quality of our inner life based on how noble our thoughts and feelings are in response to what we see, hear or experience.

12.2   Paragraphs under study

45   As to a chaste and holy life, it should be regarded as no less essential a factor that must contribute its proper share to the strengthening and vitalisation of the Bahá'í community, upon which must in turn depend the success of any Bahá'í plan or enterprise. In these days when the forces of irreligion are weakening the moral fibre, and undermining the foundations of individual morality, the obligation of chastity and holiness must claim an increasing share of the attention of the American believers, both in their individual capacities and as the responsible custodians of the interests of the Faith of Bahá'u'lláh. In the discharge of such an obligation, to which the special circumstances resulting from an excessive and enervating materialism now prevailing in their country lend particular significance, they must play a conspicuous and predominant role. All of them, be they men or women, must, at this threatening hour when the lights of religion are fading out, and its restraints are one by one being abolished, pause to examine themselves, scrutinize their conduct, and with characteristic resolution arise to purge the life of their community of every trace of moral laxity that might stain the name, or impair the integrity, of so holy and precious a Faith.

46   A chaste and holy life must be made the controlling principle in the behaviour and conduct of all Bahá'ís, both in their social relations with the members of their own community, and in their contact with the world at large. It must adorn and reinforce the ceaseless labours and meritorious exertions of those whose enviable position is to propagate the Message, and to administer the affairs, of the Faith of Bahá'u'lláh. It must be upheld, in all its integrity and implications, in every phase of the life of those who fill the ranks of that Faith, whether in their homes, their travels, their clubs, their societies, their entertainments, their schools, and their universities. It must be accorded special consideration in the conduct of the social activities of every Bahá'í summer school and any other occasions on which Bahá'í community life is organized and fostered. It must be closely and continually identified with the mission of the Bahá'í youth, both as an element in the life of the Bahá'í community, and as a factor in the future progress and orientation of the youth of their own country.

47   Such a chaste and holy life, with its implications of modesty, purity, temperance, decency, and clean-mindedness, ...

12.3   Chastity and holiness

In paragraph 45, Shoghi Effendi highlights the importance of a chaste and holy life in strengthening and vitalizing the Bahá'í community and, thus, leading to the success of activities undertaken for the Faith. He stresses that the community should be especially conscious of the need for chastity in light of the weakening of moral standards by the forces of irreligion. All members of a community, regardless of gender, must take time to evaluate their conduct and strive to remove any hint of sexual immorality that might sully the name of the Faith.

Chastity and holiness as mentioned by Shoghi Effendi together reflect a unique pattern of life. In this regard, the Universal House of Justice explains that in *The Advent of Divine Justice*, "the beloved Guardian is describing the requirements not only of chastity, but of 'a chaste and holy life'—both the adjectives are important."[1]

12.3.1 Chastity

The root of the words "chaste" and "chastity" comes from the Latin adjective "*castus*" meaning pure, holy, pious and godly. The word "chaste" was introduced into the English language in about the 13th century. Initially, as an adjective, it conveyed the concept of virtue or purity from unlawful sexual intercourse, though the meaning changed over time. In the 14th century, chaste as a noun meant a "virgin person" and, by the 15th century, it implied the sense of "sexually pure". In the 1620s, chaste was used to suggest a language "free from obscenity" and in 1753 it represented a literary style that was "severely simple, unadorned".[2]

In traditional religions, the concept of chastity implies that sexual relationships are acceptable when performed within the framework of marriage between wife and husband. All sexual acts outside marriage are explicitly condemned. In Catholicism, chastity is considered the opposite of lust, which is classified as one of the seven deadly sins—pride, greed, lust, envy, gluttony, wrath and sloth.[3] In marriage, wife and husband are expected to commit to a lifelong relationship with fidelity, excluding sexual intimacy with other people.

In Islám, chastity is binding on both men and women, and both genders are subject to legal punishment if they break this law. However, in many Muslim countries the standard applied to the unchaste behaviour of men is more lenient than that applied to women. In some communities, there is an implicit acceptance or disregard of adultery and promiscuity by men.

In response to an individual, Shoghi Effendi states "chastity in the strict sense means not to have sexual intercourse, or sexual intimacies, before marriage." He then explains:

> In the general sense it [chastity] means not to be licentious. This does not mean we Bahá'ís believe sexual relations to be impure or wrong. On the contrary they are natural and should be considered one of God's many blessings.[4]

Elucidating on the meaning of chastity, the Universal House of Justice explains:

Concerning the positive aspects of chastity the Universal House of Justice

1 Letter dated 8 May 1979 written on behalf of the Universal House of Justice to an individual believer, cited in *The Compilation of Compilations*, Vol. I, p. 53.
2 *Online Etymology Dictionary*, available at https://www.etymonline.com.
3 Thomas Aquinas, *Summa Theologica*, Benziger Bros. Edition, 1947.
4 Shoghi Effendi, *The Light of Divine Guidance*, Vol. II, p. 69.

states that the Bahá'í Faith recognizes the value of the sex impulse and holds that the institution of marriage has been established as the channel of its rightful expression. Bahá'ís do not believe that the sex impulse should be suppressed but that it should be regulated and controlled.

Chastity in no way implies withdrawal from human relationships. It liberates people from the tyranny of the ubiquity of sex. A person who is in control of his sexual impulses is enabled to have profound and enduring friendships with many people, both men and women, without ever sullying that unique and priceless bond that should unite man and wife.[1]

In another letter written on behalf of the Universal House of Justice to a National Spiritual Assembly, it is explained how to approach an individual who has blatantly broken the law of chastity in the Bahá'í Faith:

As you readily understand, Bahá'ís are exhorted to lead a chaste and holy life, and, according to Bahá'í Law, sexual intercourse is permissible only between a man and the woman who is his wife. In sexual morality, as in other realms of behaviour, people often stumble and fall short of the ideal. It is the task of Spiritual Assemblies to ensure that the friends are deepened in their understanding of the teachings, and are exhorted to apply them in their lives. In caring for its community, a Spiritual Assembly should act as a loving father rather than as a stern judge in such matters. Nevertheless, if a believer's behaviour is blatantly and flagrantly immoral and, therefore, is harmful to the good name of the Faith, the Assembly must counsel him (or her), urge him to reform his conduct, warn him of the consequences if he does not mend his ways and, ultimately, if the believer persists in misbehaviour, the Assembly must deprive him of his administrative rights. This deprivation remains in force until such time that he has rectified his behaviour.[2]

12.3.2   A holy life

Holiness represents perfect purity and integrity of moral character. Shoghi Effendi defines a holy life in the Bahá'í teachings as "attachment to God, His Precepts and His Will." He then continues by clarifying that:

We are not ascetics in any sense of the word. On the contrary, Bahá'u'lláh says God has created all the good things in the world for us to enjoy and partake. But we must not become attached to them and put them before the spiritual things.[3]

'Abdu'l-Bahá further clarifies the nature of attachment to God and its practical implications:

All that has been created is for man who is at the apex of creation and who must be thankful for the divine bestowals, so that through his gratitude he may learn

---

1   Written on behalf the Universal House of Justice to an individual believer, dated May 8, 1979, cited in *The Compilation of Compilations*, Vol. I, p. 50.

2   Written on behalf the Universal House of Justice to a National Spiritual Assembly dated 5 June 1986, cited in *Lights of Guidance*, p. 362.

3   Shoghi Effendi, *The Lights of Divine Guidance*, Vol. II, p. 69.

to understand life as a divine benefit. If we hold enmity with life, we are ingrates, for our material and spiritual existence is the outward evidences of the divine mercy. Therefore we must be happy and pass our time in praises, appreciating all things. But there is something else: detachment. We can appreciate without attaching ourselves to the things of this world. It sometimes happens that if a man loses his fortune he is so disheartened that he dies or becomes insane. While enjoying the things of this world we must remember that one day we shall have to do without them.

Attach not thyself to anything unless in it thou seest the reality of God - this is the first step into the court of eternity. The earth life lasts but a short time, even its benefits are transitory; that which is temporary does not deserve our heart's attachment.

... Detachment does not consist in setting fire to one's house, or becoming bankrupt or throwing one's fortune out of the window, or even giving away all of one's possessions. Detachment consists in refraining from letting our possessions possess us. A prosperous merchant who is not absorbed in his business knows severance. A banker whose occupation does not prevent him from serving humanity is severed. A poor man can be attached to a small thing.[1]

The holiness of our moral character must manifest itself in our deeds. In a letter written on his behalf, Shoghi Effendi counsels the youth to "... constantly and determinedly strive to exemplify a Bahá'í life." He then explains what he means by a Bahá'í life:

In the world around us we see moral decay, promiscuity, indecency, vulgarity, bad manners—the Bahá'í young people must be the opposite of these things, and, by their chastity, their uprightness, their decency, their consideration and good manners, attract others, old and young, to the Faith. The world is tired of words; it wants example, and it is up to the Bahá'í youth to furnish it.[2]

12.4   Moral standards for a chaste and holy life

The moral standard of a chaste and holy life in the Bahá'í Faith is not meant to reject or condemn the sex impulse, but to control and regulate it. This is clearly explained in a letter dated 13 December 1940 written on behalf of Shoghi Effendi to an individual believer:

Concerning your question whether there are any legitimate forms of expression of the sex instinct outside of marriage; according to the Bahá'í Teachings no sexual act can be considered lawful unless performed between lawfully married persons. Outside of marital life there can be no lawful or healthy use of the sex impulse.[3]

The letter then continues by explaining how the Bahá'í youth should respond to the sex impulse:

---

[1]   'Abdu'l-Bahá, *Divine Philosophy*, pp. 135–136.

[2]   Letter writing on behalf of Shoghi Effendi to Green Acre Summer School, dated 19 September, 1946, cited in *The Compilation of Compilations*, Vol. II, p. 17.

[3]   Shoghi Effendi, cited in *The Compilation of Compilations,* Vol. I, p. 56.

The Bahá'í youth should, on the one hand, be taught the lesson of self-control which, when exercised, undoubtedly has a salutary effect on the development of character and of personality in general, and on the other should be advised, nay even encouraged, to contract marriage while still young and in full possession of their physical vigour. Economic factors, no doubt, are often a serious hindrance to early marriage, but in most cases are only an excuse, and as such should not be overstressed.

In another letter dated 5 September 1938 written on behalf of Shoghi Effendi to an individual, he explains the Bahá'í conception of sex:

Briefly stated the Bahá'í conception of sex is based on the belief that chastity should be strictly practiced by both sexes, not only because it is in itself highly commendable ethically, but also due to its being the only way to a happy and successful marital life. Sex relationships of any form, outside marriage, are not permissible therefore, and whoso violates this rule will not only be responsible to God, but will incur the necessary punishment from society.[1]

Shoghi Effendi stated that the punishment for violations of chastity will be both physical and spiritual. For example, Bahá'u'lláh has explicitly specified that adultery retards the progress of the soul in the next world.[2] Bahá'u'lláh has left the Universal House of Justice to set the details of the penalties to be applied for breaking the Bahá'í law of chastity.

Overall, the moral standards associated with a chaste and holy life in the Bahá'í Faith go far beyond governing the sexual relationship between individuals. Being chaste and holy together represent a pattern of living.

In paragraph 46, Shoghi Effendi emphasizes that moral standards should be the controlling principles in the life of every individual Bahá'í, both within and without the Bahá'í community. They should be upheld:

- In the behaviour of the teachers of the Faith and its administrators.
- By the rank of the believers in every aspect of their lives.
- In the social activities of Bahá'í Summer-schools and on any other occasion that forms a part of Bahá'í community life.
- As part of the mission of the Bahá'í youth, both in their Bahá'í life and during their future progress and development.

12.5   Implications of a chaste and holy life

Shoghi Efendi opens paragraph 47, with the virtues that constitute a chaste and holy life, summarizing them as modesty, purity, temperance, decency and clean-mindedness—these will be studied in the following sections. The rest of paragraph 47, which details how these virtues are practiced in our lives in the face of the decadence of the present age, will be reviewed in the next chapter.

---

[1]   Shoghi Effendi, cited in *Lights of Guidance*, pp. 344–345.

[2]   Mentioned by Shoghi Effendi in a letter date September 30, 1949 written on behalf of Shoghi Effendi to an individual believer, cited in *Lights of Guidance*, p. 345.

12.5.1 Modesty

The word "modesty" conveys different meanings according to the context in which it is used. As a virtue, this is the quality of not being proud or boastful about oneself or one's abilities. For example, 'Abdu'l-Bahá states: *"Act ye in such wise, showing forth pure and goodly deeds, and modesty and humility, that ye will cause others to be awakened."*[1] In this context, *"modesty"* strengthens the emphasis of 'Abdu'l-Bahá on the virtue of humility.

In another context, modesty reflects a mode of dress and behaviour that does not arouse others sexually. For example, Shoghi Effendi states that "In the teaching there is nothing against dancing, but the friends should remember that the standard of Bahá'u'lláh is modesty and chastity."[2] It is more reasonable to suggest that in paragraph 47 Shoghi Effendi implies "modesty" in the context of a chaste and holy life.

The defined and accepted standards of modesty may vary from one culture to another. Such standards determine how the appearance, behaviour and clothing of an individual is interpreted by others as modest or otherwise. However, the modesty expected in the teachings of the Faith seems rather different as it reflects the intention of an individual to avoid being sexually titillating in one's behaviour and appearance.

Nevertheless, one should take into consideration the stricter standard of dress in some societies, so as not to offend. When asked whether Bahá'í women go without veils in the East, 'Abdu'l-Bahá answered: *"It is not possible for them to do so universally yet, but the conditions are not nearly so restrictive as they were. The Bahá'í men and women meet together. This is the beginning of woman's emancipation from the thralldom of centuries."*[3]

12.5.2 Purity

The word "purity" is also used in different contexts with different meanings. In principle, purity is freedom from contamination but, as a virtue, it implies freedom from sexual immorality and the avoidance of harmful substances. 'Abdu'l-Bahá describes the characteristics of a pure individual in one of His Tablets:

> *Cleanliness and sanctity in all conditions are characteristics of pure beings and necessities of free souls. The first perfection consists in cleanliness and sanctity and in purity from every defect. When man in all conditions is pure and immaculate, he will become the centre of the reflection of the manifest Light. In all his actions and conduct there must first be purity, then beauty and independence. The channel must be cleansed before it is filled with sweet water. The pure eye comprehendeth the sight and the meeting of God; the pure nostril inhaleth the perfumes of the rose-garden of bounty; the pure heart becometh the mirror of the beauty of truth. This is why, in the heavenly Books, the divine*

---

[1] 'Abdu'l-Bahá, *Selections from the Writings of 'Abdu'l-Bahá*, p. 203.
[2] Shoghi Effendi, cited in *Lights of Guidance*, p. 98.
[3] 'Abdu'l-Baha, *Promulgation of Universal Peace*, pp. 251–252.

counsels and commands have been compared to water. So, in the Qur'án it is said, 'and we have caused a pure water to descend from heaven;' and in the Gospel, 'Except a man hath received the baptism of water and of the spirit, he cannot enter into the Kingdom of God.' Then it is evident that the divine teachings are the heavenly grace and the showers of the mercy of God, which purify the hearts of men.

The meaning is, in all conditions, cleanliness and sanctity, purity and delicacy exalt humanity and make the contingent beings progress. Even when applied to physical things, delicacy causeth the attainment of spirituality, as it is established in the Holy Scriptures.[1]

12.5.3 Temperance

Temperance is a voluntary self-restraint in controlling an excess of emotions and impulses, such as anger, vanity and sexual desire, originating from one's character. Traditionally, temperance has been recognized as a virtue in the sacred writings of religions and the writings of philosophers. It has been one of the cardinal virtues in Greek philosophy, Christianity, Buddhism and Hinduism.

In modern times, temperance is used as one of the six virtues discussed in positive psychology along with wisdom, courage, humanity, justice and transcendence. These six virtues are part of an assessment method known as Values in Action Inventory–Inventory of Strength (VIA–IS), and designed to measure the character strength of an individual.[2]

'Abdu'l-Bahá refers to temperance as one of the inward perfections:

The spiritually learned must be characterized by both inward and outward perfections; they must possess a good character, an enlightened nature, a pure intent, as well as intellectual power, brilliance and discernment, intuition, discretion and foresight, temperance, reverence, and a heartfelt fear of God. For an unlit candle, however great in diameter and tall, is no better than a barren palm tree or a pile of dead wood.[3]

12.5.4 Decency

Decency is a behaviour that is good, moral and acceptable in a moral society. In the Bahá'í Faith, decent behaviour complies with the universal principles and norms as well as with the moral standards set in the Writings. There are many references to the virtue of decency in the Bahá'í writings. In a Tablet, Bahá'u'lláh states: *"We have permitted you to listen to music and singing. Beware lest such listening cause you to transgress the bounds of decency and dignity."*[4]

In one of his messages, Shoghi Effendi refers to the obscuration of the sense of decency when the light of religion is quenched in men's hearts:

---

[1]   'Abdu'l-Bahá, *Bahá'í World Faith*, pp. 333–334.

[2]   Peterson and Seligman, *Character strengths and virtues: a handbook and classification*, 2004, Washington, DC: APA Press.

[3]   'Abdu'l-Bahá, *The Secret of Divine Civilization*, pp. 33–34.

[4]   Bahá'u'lláh, *The Compilation of Compilations*, Vol. I, p. 51.

No wonder, therefore, that when, as a result of human perversity, the light of religion is quenched in men's hearts, and the divinely appointed Robe, designed to adorn the human temple, is deliberately discarded, a deplorable decline in the fortunes of humanity immediately sets in, bringing in its wake all the evils which a wayward soul is capable of revealing. The perversion of human nature, the degradation of human conduct, the corruption and dissolution of human institutions, reveal themselves, under such circumstances, in their worst and most revolting aspects. Human character is debased, confidence is shaken, the nerves of discipline are relaxed, the voice of human conscience is stilled, the sense of decency and shame is obscured, conceptions of duty, of solidarity, of reciprocity and loyalty are distorted, and the very feeling of peacefulness, of joy and of hope is gradually extinguished.[1]

In one of its messages to the youth, the Universal House of Justice, emphasizes that:

The life of a Bahá'í will be characterized by truthfulness and decency; he will walk uprightly among his fellowmen, dependent upon none save God, yet linked by bonds of love and brotherhood with all mankind; he will be entirely detached from the loose standards, the decadent theories, the frenetic experimentation, the desperation of present-day society, will look upon his neighbours with a bright and friendly face, and be a beacon light and a haven for all those who would emulate his strength of character and assurance of soul.[2]

In another message, the Universal House of Justice counsels the Bahá'í community that it

... must demonstrate in ever-increasing measure its ability to redeem the disorderliness, the lack of cohesion, the permissiveness, the godlessness of modern society; the laws, the religious obligations, the observances of Bahá'í life, Bahá'í moral principles and standards of dignity, decency and reverence, must become deeply implanted in Bahá'í consciousness and increasingly inform and characterize this community.[3]

12.5.5 Clean-mindedness

Clean-mindedness is the quality of our inner life and indicates how noble our thoughts and feelings are in response to what we see, hear or experience. Its opposite is dirty-mindedness, which applies to an individual who entertains indecent, obscene or lewd thoughts, interpretations and feelings.

The quality of our inner life plays a key role in the outcome of our Bahá'í endeavours and the advancement of the Cause. Shoghi Effendi states:

Not by the force of numbers, not by the mere exposition of a set of new and

---

[1] Shoghi Effendi, *The World Order of Bahá'u'lláh*, p. 187.
[2] The Universal House of Justice, *Messages from the Universal House of Justice 1963–1968*, pp. 93–94.
[3] The Universal House of Justice, *Messages from the Universal House of Justice 1968–1973*, p. 90.

noble principles, not by an organized campaign of teaching—no matter how worldwide and elaborate in its character—not even by the staunchness of our faith or the exaltation of our enthusiasm, can we ultimately hope to vindicate in the eyes of a critical and sceptical age the supreme claim of the Abhá Revelation. One thing and only one thing will unfailingly and alone secure the undoubted triumph of this sacred Cause, namely, the extent to which our own inner life and private character mirror forth in their manifold aspects the splendour of those eternal principles proclaimed by Bahá'u'lláh.[1]

---

[1] Shoghi Effendi, quoted in a letter written on behalf of the Universal House of Justice, dated January 9, 1977, cited in *Lights of Guidance*, p. 366.

12.6   Activities

12.6.1   Short answer questions

1. What is the overall significance of a chaste and holy life for a Bahá'í and a Bahá'í community?

_____

_____

_____

_____

2. What are the special circumstances in American society that require the American believers to place greater attention to chastity and holiness?

_____

_____

_____

_____

3. What is your understanding of the last sentence in paragraph 45?

_____

_____

_____

_____

4. In paragraph 46, Shoghi Effendi mentions specific cohorts in the American Bahá'í community that must control their behaviour and conduct through the standards of a chaste and holy life. Who are these cohorts?

_____

_____

_____

_____

5. What are the implications of a chaste and holy life mentioned in paragraph 47?

_____

_____

_____

_____

6. What is chastity according to the Bahá'í teachings?

_____

_____

_____

_____

7. What is the nature of a holy life according to the Bahá'í teachings?

_____

_____

_____

_____

8. How does Shoghi Effendi define the Bahá'í life?

_____

_____

_____

_____

9. What is the Bahá'í conception of sex?

_____

_____

_____

_____

10. What are the meanings of the following qualities in the context of a chaste and holy life?

    a) Modesty

_____

_____

_____

_____

    b) Purity

_____

_____

_____

_____

    c) Temperance

_____

_____

---

d)   Decency

---

e)   Clean-mindedness

12.6.2   *Mini-project*

Conduct research to determine whether the moral laxity is further deteriorated in the present American society compared to the 1930s.

13.
A chaste and holy life—II

13.1   Introduction

This chapter covers paragraphs 47–50 in which the Guardian addresses in more detail the requirements of a chaste and holy life, and describes specific applications of the moral standards of modesty, purity, temperance, decency and clean-mindedness. He also cites a number of statements from Bahá'u'lláh and 'Abdu'l-Bahá on the nature and implications of a chaste and holy life. In paragraph 50, Shoghi Effendi emphasizes that the high moral standards expected in the teachings of the Faith should not be confused with "any form of asceticism, or of excessive and bigoted puritanism."

In this chapter, you need to reflect on and understand the following key points:

a)   The moral standards defined in the Bahá'í Faith include guidelines for their application to one's life.

b)   Frivolous conduct is a lack of seriousness in one's behaviour.

c)   Any form of creative work produced to promote and sell sexual pleasure and immorality represents the "prostitution of arts and literature".

d)   According to one definition, companionate marriage is a trial marriage in which the partners postpone having children until a decision is made to stay married, otherwise they can be divorced by mutual consent.

e)   Infidelity in a marriage means that one of the partners engages in an intimate and sexual relationship with someone outside the marriage.

f)   Promiscuity represents the practice of engaging in indiscriminate intimate and sexual relationships with different partners.

g)   Easy familiarity in the form of "indiscriminate kissing and embracing involving unrelated people of opposite sexes is not desirable and is discouraged."

h)   Sexual vices are habits that are considered diversions to a natural expression of the sex impulse.

i) Bahá'u'lláh explicitly states that *"Living in seclusion or practising asceticism is not acceptable in the presence of God."*[1]

13.2 Paragraphs under study

47 Such a chaste and holy life … involves no less than the exercise of moderation in all that pertains to dress, language, amusements, and all artistic and literary avocations. It demands daily vigilance in the control of one's carnal desires and corrupt inclinations. It calls for the abandonment of a frivolous conduct, with its excessive attachment to trivial and often misdirected pleasures. It requires total abstinence from all alcoholic drinks, from opium, and from similar habit-forming drugs. It condemns the prostitution of art and of literature, the practices of nudism and of companionate marriage, infidelity in marital relationships, and all manner of promiscuity, of easy familiarity, and of sexual vices. It can tolerate no compromise with the theories, the standards, the habits, and the excesses of a decadent age. Nay rather it seeks to demonstrate, through the dynamic force of its example, the pernicious character of such theories, the falsity of such standards, the hollowness of such claims, the perversity of such habits, and the sacrilegious character of such excesses.

48 *"By the righteousness of God!"* writes Bahá'u'lláh, *"The world, its vanities and its glory, and whatever delights it can offer, are all, in the sight of God, as worthless as, nay even more contemptible than, dust and ashes. Would that the hearts of men could comprehend it. Wash yourselves thoroughly, O people of Bahá, from the defilement of the world, and of all that pertaineth unto it. God Himself beareth Me witness! The things of the earth ill beseem you. Cast them away unto such as may desire them, and fasten your eyes upon this most holy and effulgent Vision."*[A] *"O ye My loved ones!"* He thus exhorts His followers, *"Suffer not the hem of My sacred vesture to be smirched and mired with the things of this world, and follow not the promptings of your evil and corrupt desires."*[B] And again, *"O ye the beloved of the one true God! Pass beyond the narrow retreats of your evil and corrupt desires, and advance into the vast immensity of the realm of God, and abide ye in the meads of sanctity and of detachment, that the fragrance of your deeds may lead the whole of mankind to the ocean of God's unfading glory."*[C] *"Disencumber yourselves,"* He thus commands them, *"of all attachment to this world and the vanities thereof. Beware that ye approach them not, inasmuch as they prompt you to walk after your own lusts and covetous desires, and hinder you from entering the straight and glorious Path."*[D] *"Eschew all manner of wickedness,"* is His commandment, *"for such things are forbidden unto you in the Book which none touch except such as God hath cleansed from every taint of guilt, and numbered among the purified."*[E] *"A race of men,"* is His written promise, *"incomparable in character, shall be raised up which, with the feet of detachment, will tread under all who are in heaven and on earth, and will cast the sleeve of holiness over all that hath been created from water and clay."*[F] *"The civilization,"* is His grave warning, *"so often vaunted by the learned exponents of arts and*

---

1 Bahá'u'lláh, *The Tablets of Bahá'u'lláh*, p. 71.

sciences, will, if allowed to overleap the bounds of moderation, bring great evil upon men .... If carried to excess, civilization will prove as prolific a source of evil as it had been of goodness when kept within the restraints of moderation."[G] "He hath chosen out of the whole world the hearts of His servants," He explains, "and made them each a seat for the revelation of His glory. Wherefore, sanctify them from every defilement, that the things for which they were created may be engraven upon them. This indeed is a token of God's bountiful favour."[H] "Say," He proclaims, "He is not to be numbered with the people of Bahá who followeth his mundane desires, or fixeth his heart on things of the earth. He is My true follower who, if he come to a valley of pure gold will pass straight through it aloof as a cloud, and will neither turn back, nor pause. Such a man is assuredly of Me. From his garment the Concourse on high can inhale the fragrance of sanctity .... And if he met the fairest and most comely of women, he would not feel his heart seduced by the least shadow of desire for her beauty. Such an one indeed is the creation of spotless chastity. Thus instructeth you the Pen of the Ancient of Days, as bidden by your Lord, the Almighty, the All-Bountiful."[I] "They that follow their lusts and corrupt inclinations," is yet another warning, "have erred and dissipated their efforts. They indeed are of the lost."[J] "It behoveth the people of Bahá," He also has written, "to die to the world and all that is therein, to be so detached from all earthly things that the inmates of Paradise may inhale from their garment the sweet smelling savour of sanctity .... They that have tarnished the fair name of the Cause of God by following the things of the flesh—these are in palpable error!"[K] "Purity and chastity," He particularly admonishes, "have been, and still are, the most great ornaments for the handmaidens of God. God is My Witness! The brightness of the light of chastity sheddeth its illumination upon the worlds of the spirit, and its fragrance is wafted even unto the Most Exalted Paradise."[L] "God," He again affirms, "hath verily made chastity to be a crown for the heads of His handmaidens. Great is the blessedness of that handmaiden that hath attained unto this great station."[M] "We, verily, have decreed in Our Book," is His assurance, "a goodly and bountiful reward to whosoever will turn away from wickedness, and lead a chaste and godly life. He, in truth, is the Great Giver, the All-Bountiful."[N] "We have sustained the weight of all calamities," He testifies, "to sanctify you from all earthly corruption and ye are yet indifferent .... We, verily, behold your actions. If We perceive from them the sweet smelling savour of purity and holiness, We will most certainly bless you. Then will the tongues of the inmates of Paradise utter your praise and magnify your names amidst them who have drawn nigh unto God."[O]

49 "The drinking of wine," writes 'Abdu'l-Bahá, "is, according to the text of the Most Holy Book, forbidden; for it is the cause of chronic diseases, weakeneth the nerves, and consumeth the mind."[A] "Drink ye, O handmaidens of God," Bahá'u'lláh Himself has affirmed, "the Mystic Wine from the cup of My words. Cast away, then, from you that which your minds abhor, for it hath been forbidden unto you in His Tablets and His Scriptures. Beware lest ye barter away the River that is life indeed for that which the souls of the pure-hearted detest. Become ye intoxicated with the wine of the love of God, and not with that which deadeneth your minds, O ye that adore Him! Verily, it hath been

forbidden unto every believer, whether man or woman. Thus hath the sun of My commandment shone forth above the horizon of My utterance, that the handmaidens who believe in Me may be illumined."[B]

50 It must be remembered, however, that the maintenance of such a high standard of moral conduct is not to be associated or confused with any form of asceticism, or of excessive and bigoted puritanism. The standard inculcated by Bahá'u'lláh seeks, under no circumstances, to deny anyone the legitimate right and privilege to derive the fullest advantage and benefit from the manifold joys, beauties, and pleasures with which the world has been so plentifully enriched by an All-Loving Creator. *"Should a man,"* Bahá'u'lláh Himself reassures us, *"wish to adorn himself with the ornaments of the earth, to wear its apparels, or partake of the benefits it can bestow, no harm can befall him, if he alloweth nothing whatever to intervene between him and God, for God hath ordained every good thing, whether created in the heavens or in the earth, for such of His servants as truly believe in Him. Eat ye, O people, of the good things which God hath allowed you, and deprive not yourselves from His wondrous bounties. Render thanks and praise unto Him, and be of them that are truly thankful."*[A]

13.3 Application of moral standards

In the remainder of paragraph 47 not included in Chapter 12, Shoghi Effendi describes specific applications of the moral standards of modesty, purity, temperance, decency and clean-mindedness. This should be understood against the background of the increasing forces of irreligion and the acceleration of moral decay, with their impact on all facets of human life. This is best described by Shoghi Effendi in one of his letters:

> The recrudescence of religious intolerance, of racial animosity, and of patriotic arrogance; the increasing evidences of selfishness, of suspicion, of fear and of fraud; the spread of terrorism, of lawlessness, of drunkenness and of crime; the unquenchable thirst for, and the feverish pursuit after, earthly vanities, riches and pleasures; the weakening of family solidarity; the laxity in parental control; the lapse into luxurious indulgence; the irresponsible attitude towards marriage and the consequent rising tide of divorce; the degeneracy of art and music, the infection of literature, and the corruption of the press; the extension of the influence and activities of those 'prophets of decadence' who advocate companionate marriage, who preach the philosophy of nudism, who call modesty an intellectual fiction, who refuse to regard the procreation of children as the sacred and primary purpose of marriage, who denounce religion as an opiate of the people, who would, if given free rein, lead back the human race to barbarism, chaos, and ultimate extinction—these appear as the outstanding characteristics of a decadent society, a society that must either be reborn or perish.[1]

It is not difficult to observe that on a global scale our society today is much more decadent in every respect than that mentioned in the above quotation.

---

[1] Shoghi Effendi, *The World Order of Bahá'u'lláh: Selected Letters*, Wilmette Bahá'í Publishing Trust, 1982, pp. 187–188.

Here are the specific requirements of a chaste and holy life as described by Shoghi Effendi:

- Moderation in dress, language, amusements, artistic and literary works.
- Daily vigilance in the control of one's carnal desires and corrupt inclinations.
- The abandonment of a frivolous conduct, with its excessive attachment to trivial and often misdirected pleasures.
- Total abstinence from all alcoholic drinks, from opium, and from similar habit-forming drugs.
- Condemnation of the prostitution of art and of literature, the practices of nudism and of companionate marriage, infidelity in marital relationships, and all manner of promiscuity, of easy familiarity, and of sexual vices.
- No compromise with the theories, the standards, the habits, and the excesses of a decadent age.
- Demonstrating "... through the dynamic force of its example, the pernicious character of such theories, the falsity of such standards, the hollowness of such claims, the perversity of such habits, and the sacrilegious character of such excesses."

It is important to stress that the moral standards defined in the Bahá'í Faith are a set of guidelines. Individuals are expected to determine how the defined standards should be applied to their lives. This is explained in a letter by the Universal House of Justice to an individual believer, dated 17 October 1968:

> It is neither possible nor desirable for the Universal House of Justice to set forth a set of rules covering every situation. Rather it is the task of the individual believer to determine, according to his own prayerful understanding of the Writings, precisely what his course of conduct should be in relation to situations which he encounters in his daily life. If he is to fulfil his true mission in life as a follower of the Blessed Perfection, he will pattern his life according to the Teachings. The believer cannot attain this objective merely by living according to a set of rigid regulations. When his life is oriented toward service to Bahá'u'lláh, and when every conscious act is performed within this frame of reference, he will not fail to achieve the true purpose of his life.

> Therefore, every believer must continually study the sacred Writings and the instructions of the beloved Guardian, striving always to attain a new and better understanding of their import to him and to his society. He should pray fervently for Divine Guidance, wisdom and strength to do what is pleasing to God, and to serve Him at all times and to the best of his ability.[1]

In paragraphs 48 and 49, Shoghi Effendi cites a number of statements from Bahá'u'lláh and 'Abdu'l-Bahá on the nature and implications of a chaste and holy life.

The following sections review some of the less obvious issues raised by Shoghi Effendi.

---

[1] The Universal House of Justice, cited in *Lights of Guidance*, p. 359.

13.4   Frivolous conduct

Something is frivolous when it has no serious purpose or value. A frivolous person is someone who is self-indulgently carefree and superficial. Frivolous conduct is lack of seriousness in one's behaviour. Shoghi Effendi specially associates frivolous conduct with trivial and inappropriate pleasures. In response to a question asked by a believer on the meaning of "a frivolous conduct" in paragraph 47, the following elucidation is provided on behalf of the Universal House of Justice:

> One of the signs of a decadent society, a sign which is very evident in the world today, is an almost frenetic devotion to pleasure and diversion, an insatiable thirst for amusement, a fanatical devotion to games and sport, a reluctance to treat any matter seriously, and a scornful, derisory attitude towards virtue and solid worth. Abandonment of 'a frivolous conduct' does not imply that a Bahá'í must be sour-faced or perpetually solemn. Humour, happiness, joy are characteristics of a true Bahá'í life. Frivolity palls and eventually leads to boredom and emptiness, but true happiness and joy and humour that are parts of a balanced life that includes serious thought, compassion and humble servitude to God, are characteristics that enrich life and add to its radiance.

Shoghi Effendi's choice of words was always significant, and each one is important in understanding his guidance. In this particular passage, he does not forbid "trivial" pleasures, but he does warn against "excessive attachment" to them and indicates that they can often be "misdirected". One is reminded of 'Abdu'l-Bahá's caution that we should not let a pastime become a waste of time.[1]

13.5   Prostitution of arts and literature

Art represents various branches of human creative activities expressed through written, visual or performing channels to share the experiences, thoughts and emotions of an artist. Over human history, the arts have fulfilled various roles and have contributed significantly to the evolution of human civilization. The purpose of works of art has varied from communicating spiritual, philosophical or political ideas, to creating a sense of beauty and generating strong emotions.

As to the role of arts, Bahá'u'lláh states that "*Arts, crafts and sciences uplift the world of being, and are conducive to its exaltation.*"[2] In another Tablet He states that:

> *The source of crafts, sciences and arts is the power of reflection. Make ye every effort that out of this ideal mine there may gleam forth such pearls of wisdom and utterance as will promote the well-being and harmony of all the kindreds of the earth.*[3]

Lady Blomfield cites an utterance from 'Abdu'l-Bahá in which He states:

---

1   Letter dated 8 May 1979 written on behalf of the Universal House of Justice to an individual believer, cited in *The Compilation of Compilations*, Vol, I, pp. 53–54.

2   Bahá'u'lláh, *Epistle to the Son of the Wolf*, p. 26.

3   Bahá'u'lláh, *Tablets of Bahá'u'lláh*, p. 72.

All Art is a gift of the Holy Spirit. When this light shines through the mind of a musician, it manifests itself in beautiful harmonies. Again, shining through the mind of a poet, it is seen in fine poetry and poetic prose. When the light of the Sun of Truth inspires the mind of a painter, he produces marvellous pictures. These gifts are fulfilling their highest purpose when showing forth the praise of God.[1]

The statement of Shoghi Effendi regarding the "prostitution of arts and literature" in paragraph 47 reflects the immoral exploitation of the arts as a commodity. Prostitution is the practice of engaging in sexual activity with someone for payment. Hence, arts and literature produced to promote and sell sexual pleasure and immorality can represent the "prostitution of arts and literature". In a letter dated 15 March 1972 written on behalf of the Universal House of Justice, a brief elucidation on this statement of Shoghi Effendi is provided: "As to your question about the 'prostitution of arts and literature' we understand by this, using art and literature for debased ends."[2] The word 'debased' has a variety of meanings, though in this context, the most relevant are immoral, vile or corrupt.

13.6   Practice of nudism

Covering the body in social settings has always been a common practice in human society. In pre-historic times, animal skins and vegetable materials were used. With the evolution of human consciousness and guidance received from the divine religions, wearing clothing became an intrinsic part of being human and a sign of respect and dignity.

Nudism is a philosophical and political movement practicing, promoting and defending personal and social nudity. Supporters of the movement consider nudity as the authentic human-nature state with benefits of achieving and maintaining physical, mental and spiritual health. As a social practice, both male and female nudists generally interact freely without engaging in sexual activities.

The nudism movement started in the early 20th century in Germany as a response to the rigid moral attitudes of the late 19th century. The first nudist club known as Freilichtpark ("Free-Light Park") emerged around 1903 near Hamburg. It was followed by a network of over 200 private clubs in Germany, known as Nacktkultur ("Naturalism"), practicing and promoting nudism. A popular book by Richard Ungewitter, *Die Nacktheit* (Nakedness), was published in 1906.[3] Nudism spread throughout Europe after World War I and achieved prominence in the 1920s.

Some groups refer to the nudism movement as naturism, though naturism itself has a vastly different meaning in philosophy and literature.

---

[1] 'Abdu'l-Bahá, cited by Lady Blomfield, *The Chosen Highway*, Wilmette: Bahá'u'lláh publishing Trust, 1986, p. 167.

[2] The Universal House of Justice, cited in *The Importance of the Arts in Promoting the Faith*, p. 4.

[3] *Encyclopaedia Britannica*, Nudism, available at https://www.britannica.com/topic/nudism.

13.7   Companionate marriage

The concept of companionate marriage was developed in the 1920's by social scientists and "sex radicals" to adapt marriage to an emerging youth culture and women's independence. Judge Benjamin Barr Lindsey (25 November 1869–2 March 1943), an American judge and social reformer, wrote a controversial book, *Companionate Marriage*, in which he suggested that young men and women should be able to live together in a trial marriage for a year to evaluate whether they match. If the relationship was not sustainable the couple could dissolve the marriage, otherwise they could change the marriage to a traditionally understood marriage. The couple should avoid having children during the trial period.

There are different understandings about the meaning and implications of a companionate marriage. One dictionary defines the companionate marriage as a trial marriage in which the partners postpone having children until a decision is made to stay married, otherwise they can be divorced by mutual consent.[1] According to another definition, the companionate marriage is a form of marriage in which the partners decide not to have children through birth control. In this marriage, divorce can occur by mutual agreement of the partners and there is no legal responsibility for financial support.[2]

In a letter written on behalf of the Universal House of Justice to the national Spiritual Assembly of the Bahá'ís of Paraguay, dated 21 November 1967, a companionate marriage is compared with a traditional marriage, known as "common law marriage":

> The basic difference between the two categories of relationship is that common law marriage is considered by the parties concerned as a solemn contract with the sole intention of establishing a family but which, because of legal complications, cannot be duly registered, whereas in companionate marriage and the like the parties concerned initiate and maintain their relationship either on a trial basis or on other immoral grounds, both of which are condemned in our Teachings.

> We feel that by applying these principles in each of the cases you cite in your letter, with wisdom, kindness and love you will be able gradually to educate the friends in the fundamentals of our Teachings and enable them to overcome their moral difficulties.[3]

In another letter written on behalf of the Universal House of Justice in response to an individual, dated 3 November 1982, the Bahá'í views on three different definitions of "companionate marriage" are clarified:

> Concerning the three definitions of 'companionate marriage' which you give in your letter, the first, which is defined as living together without being married, on either a trial or immoral basis, is obviously unacceptable in Bahá'í teachings and is, moreover, an offence which, if persisted in, could call for

1   *Webster's New World College Dictionary*, 4th Edition.
2   "Companionate Marriage", *Merriam-Webster.com*, n.d. Web. 14 June 2018.
3   Written on behalf of the Universal House of Justice, cited in *Lights of Guidance*, p. 380.

deprivation of voting rights. The second and third, namely (2) a marriage where the couple agree ahead of time that they will not have children, ever, and (3) a marriage in which the couple would not have children until they are sure that they wish to stay married, divorce by mutual consent being envisaged before children are born, are private situations which would be undetectable by anyone who has not been confided in by either the husband or the wife. Thus, unlike the first type of 'companionate marriage' they do not constitute blatant immorality and no question of removal of voting rights would arise. Nevertheless they are also both contrary to the spirit of Bahá'í Law. The Bahá'í teachings do not contemplate any form of 'trial marriage'. A couple should study each other's character and spend time getting to know each other before they decide to marry, and when they do marry it should be with the intention of establishing an eternal bond. They should realize, moreover, that the primary purpose of marriage is the procreation of children. A couple who are physically incapable of having children may, of course, marry, since the procreation of children is not the only purpose of marriage. However, it would be contrary to the spirit of the Teachings for a couple to decide voluntarily never to have any children.[1]

In a letter written on behalf of Shoghi Effendi, to the National Spiritual Assembly of the Bahá'ís of Argentina, Bolivia, Chile, Paraguay and Uruguay, dated 26 September 1957, he also refers to companionate marriage as a couple living together without marriage and states that "companionate marriage, where there is no legal or religious marriage, is an immoral relationship and we cannot accept as believers those who are openly behaving in this way."[2]

13.8   Infidelity

The word infidelity in general means being unfaithful and disloyal, and can convey more specific meanings in particular contexts. Infidelity in a marriage means that one of the partners engages in an intimate and sexual relationship with someone outside the marriage. In a religious context, it reflects disbelief in a religion. In some religions, the term "infidel" refers to those who are accused of rejecting the fundamentals of their own religion, followers of other religions, or those who do not believe in any religion or deny God. In paragraph 47, Shoghi Effendi is referring to infidelity in marriage.

In the Bahá'í teachings, fidelity and faithfulness are critical characteristic of a chaste and holy life. In a letter written on behalf of Shoghi Effendi to an individual, dated 28 September 1941, this point is emphasized:

> The question you raise as to the place in one's life that a deep bond of love with someone we meet other than our husband or wife can have is easily defined in view of the teachings. Chastity implies both before and after marriage an unsullied, chaste sex life. Before marriage absolutely chaste, after marriage absolutely faithful to one's chosen companion. Faithful in all sexual acts,

---

[1]   Written on behalf of the Universal House of Justice, cited in *Lights of Guidance*, p. 379.

[2]   Shoghi Effendi, cited in *Lights of Guidance*, p. 381.

faithful in word and in deed.[1]

13.9   Promiscuity

Promiscuity represents the indiscriminate practice of engaging in intimate and sexual relationships with different partners. What distinguishes promiscuity from other sexual behaviours is its casual nature. A promiscuous individual is characterized by transient, unselective and indiscriminate sexual behaviour. Promiscuous behaviour is very common today and there are places and opportunities to meet others for such transient relationships.

In a letter written on behalf of the Guardian to the National Spiritual Assembly of India, reference is made to modern dance halls where promiscuity takes place:

> In the teaching there is nothing against dancing, but the friends should remember that the standard of Bahá'u'lláh is modesty and chastity. The atmosphere of modern dance halls, where so much smoking and drinking and promiscuity goes on, is very bad, but decent dances are not harmful in themselves. There is certainly no harm in classical dancing or learning dancing in school. There is also no harm in taking part in dramas. Likewise in cinema acting. The harmful thing, nowadays, is not the art itself but the unfortunate corruption which often surrounds these arts. As Bahá'ís we need to avoid none of the arts, but acts and the atmosphere that sometimes go with these professions we should avoid.[2]

13.10   Easy familiarity

In modern English, one of the meanings of 'familiarity" is relaxed, friendly, informal and intimate behaviour. In Middle English,[3] the word "familiarity" conveyed sexual intimacy and close relationship. This seems to be the context in which Shoghi Effendi has used this term in paragraph 47. As far as the Bahá'í writings are concerned, this is the only reference made to the specific term "easy familiarity" in the published authoritative works. Although, there are other explanations and elucidations on relationships such as the display of affection through embracing and kissing between members of the opposite sex that might highlight what Shoghi Effendi meant by "easy familiarity".

In a letter written to the Guardian, dated 21 September 1947, John B. Cornell asks the following question:

> Although the principle of chastity has been strongly emphasized, I have been unable to find any authoritative writings that explain clearly enough what it means for Bahá'ís. English dictionaries define chastity as freedom from unlawful sexual intercourse, and no believer doubts this requirement, so that free love, companionate marriage, etc., are regarded as wrong. However, not all can agree on whether any of the forms of sexual activity which stop short of intercourse are forbidden. A pilgrim's note by Ann Boylan reports the

---

[1]   Shoghi Effendi, cited by the Universal House of Justice, *Messages from the Universal House of Justice 1968–1973*, p. 108.

[2]   Shoghi Effendi, cited in *Lights of Guidance*, pp. 98–99.

[3]   c. 1150 to c. 1470

Master as saying: 'Women and men must not embrace each other when not married, or not about to be married. They must not kiss each other .... If they wish to greet each other, or comfort each other, they may take each other by the hand.' Many believers do not know this or do not believe it. The term, 'easy familiarity,' is thought by many to mean simply rudeness and not applicable to invited or accepted demonstrations. Even some of the most unquestionably loyal follow the Christian custom of 'kissing the bride' at Bahá'í weddings. Would you explain for us what our conduct should be in order to uphold the Bahá'í concept of chastity?[1]

The following is the response by written by Rúḥíyyih Khánum on behalf of Shoghi Effendi, dated 19 October 1947:

What Bahá'u'lláh means by chastity certainly does not include the kissing that goes on in modern society. It is detrimental to the morals of young people, and often leads them to go too far, or arouses appetites which they cannot perhaps at the time satisfy legitimately through marriage, and the suppression of which is a strain on them. The Bahá'í standard is very high, more particularly when compared with the thoroughly rotten morals of the present world. But this standard of ours will produce healthier, happier, nobler people, and induce stabler marriages. The Master's words to Ann Boylan, which you quoted, can certainly be taken as the true spirit of the teachings on the subject of sex. We must strive to achieve this exalted standard.[2]

An unpublished letter to an individual, written on behalf of the Universal House of Justice and dated 5 February 1992, provides some elucidation on "easy familiarity":

As you know, in *The Advent of Divine Justice* [Shoghi Effendi] has stated the principles of Bahá'í conduct which apply and he has condemned easy familiarity and frivolous conduct. Certainly the practice of indiscriminate kissing and embracing involving unrelated people of opposite sexes is not desirable and is discouraged. Particularly in these days when restraints are being abolished one by one, the Bahá'ís should make great efforts to uphold, in their personal lives and in their relationships to each other, the standards of conduct set forth in the teachings.[3]

13.11 Sexual vices

Vice is a behaviour that is immoral and wicked. It can include criminal activities such as prostitution, pornography, or drugs; or habits that are not criminal but immoral and unacceptable. Vice more specifically reflects a practice that is engrained in an individual as a habit. Sexual vices are habits that are considered diversions to a natural expression of the sex impulse. Sexual vices such as masturbation may be personal and affect the spiritual health of an

---

[1] Cited at https://bahai-library.com/guardian_easy_familiarity.

[2] Shoghi Effendi, cited in *Lights of Guidance*, p. 360.

[3] The Universal House of Justice, cited by in Susanne M. Alexander and Johanna Merritt Wu, *Marriage Can Be Forever–Preparation Counts!, Walking a Path to a Spiritually-Based Marriage*, A Workbook, p. 19.

individual without any impact on others. There are other sexual vices such as sexual violence and paedophilia that can harm others, and society treats them as criminal acts.

The spiritual principles covered in previous sections of this chapter show the importance of dealing with sexual vices and overcoming the challenges caused by them. A more detailed discussion of this topic is beyond the scope of this book.

13.12 Denouncing asceticism

In paragraph 50, Shoghi Effendi emphasizes that the high moral standards laid down in the teachings of the Faith should not be confused with "any form of asceticism, or of excessive and bigoted puritanism." In fact, the standards set by Bahá'u'lláh do not deny anyone the full right to enjoy the pleasures of this physical life.

In asceticism, an individual abstains from physical pleasures in the belief that he will grow spiritually and attain salvation. There are different degrees of asceticism. In extreme cases, the individual completely withdraws from society and lives in isolation. In other forms, the ascetic remains in a community, but renounces material possessions and physical pleasures, while being primarily preoccupied with spiritual matters. Historically, asceticism has been practiced by minority groups in all traditional religions such as Buddhism, Hinduism, Christianity, Judaism and Islám.

Bahá'u'lláh explicitly states that:

Living in seclusion or practising asceticism is not acceptable in the presence of God. It behoveth them that are endued with insight and understanding to observe that which will cause joy and radiance. Such practices as are sprung from the loins of idle fancy or are begotten of the womb of superstition ill beseem men of knowledge. In former times and more recently some people have been taking up their abodes in the caves of the mountains while others have repaired to graveyards at night. Say, give ear unto the counsels of this Wronged One. Abandon the things current amongst you and adopt that which the faithful Counsellor biddeth you. Deprive not yourselves of the bounties which have been created for your sake.[1]

In one of His talks, 'Abdu'l-Bahá explains that the teachings of the Faith do not imply:

... that one should give up avocation and attainment to livelihood. On the contrary, in the Cause of Bahá'u'lláh monasticism and asceticism are not sanctioned. In this great Cause the light of guidance is shining and radiant. Bahá'u'lláh has even said that occupation and labour are devotion. All humanity must obtain a livelihood by sweat of the brow and bodily exertion, at the same time seeking to lift the burden of others, striving to be the source of comfort to souls and facilitating the means of living. This in itself is devotion to God. Bahá'u'lláh has thereby encouraged action and stimulated service. But the energies of the heart must not be attached to these things; the soul must not be

---

[1] Bahá'u'lláh, *The Tablets of Bahá'u'lláh*, p. 71.

completely occupied with them. Though the mind is busy, the heart must be attracted toward the Kingdom of God in order that the virtues of humanity may be attained from every direction and source.[1]

The term *"excessive and bigoted puritanism"* is a reference to unwarranted and biased admonishment.

---

[1]   'Abdu'l-Bahá, *The promulgation of Universal Peace*, p. 187.

13.13 Activities

13.13.1 Short answer questions

1. What is your understanding of the following statements by Shoghi Effendi in paragraph 47?

    a) "moderation in all that pertains to dress, language, amusements, and all artistic and literary avocations."

    _____

    _____

    _____

    _____

    b) "daily vigilance in the control of one's carnal desires and corrupt inclinations"

    _____

    _____

    _____

    _____

    c) "the abandonment of a frivolous conduct, with its excessive attachment to trivial and often misdirected pleasures"

    _____

    _____

    _____

    _____

    d) "abstinence from all alcoholic drinks, from opium, and from similar habit-forming drugs"

    _____

    _____

    _____

    _____

    e) Condemnation of the prostitution of art and of literature"

    _____

    _____

    _____

    _____

    f) Condemnation of the practice of nudism

_____

_____

_____

_____

g)   Condemnation of the practice of companionate marriage

_____

_____

_____

h)   Condemnation of the practice of infidelity in marital relationships

_____

_____

_____

i)   Condemnation of all manner of promiscuity

_____

_____

_____

j)   Condemnation of all manner of easy familiarity

_____

_____

_____

k)   Condemnation of all manner of sexual vices

_____

_____

_____

2.   Give some examples of the theories, the standards, the habits, and the excesses of a decadent age.

_____

_____

_____

_____

_____

_____

_____

_____

3. Briefly identify the key points in the following quotes from Bahá'u'lláh and 'Abdu'l-Bahá that Shoghi Effendi used in paragraphs 48–50.

   a) Quote 48:A

_____

_____

   b) Quote 48:B

_____

_____

   c) Quote 48:C

_____

_____

   d) Quote 48:D

_____

_____

   e) Quote 48:E

_____

_____

   f) Quote 48:F

_____

_____

   g) Quote 48:G

_____

_____

   h) Quote 48:H

_____

_____

   i) Quote 48:I

j) Quote 48:J

k) Quote 48:K

l) Quote 48:L

m) Quote 48:M

n) Quote 48:N

l) Quote 48:O

p) Quote 49:A

q) Quote 49:B

r) Quote 50:A

4. What is your understanding of the first sentence in paragraph 50?

13.13.2 *Mini-project*

Identify at least two contemporary theories dominant in our society that are directly against the standards of a chaste and holy life explained by Shoghi Effendi.

14.
Race and racism

14.1   Introduction

This chapter covers paragraphs 51–52 and represents the first chapter on the issue of race and the expectations of Shoghi Effendi about racial relationships in the American Bahá'í community.   The concept of race and its historical background is first studied. It is shown that the term "race", meaning a nation or a group of people with common descent, was first used between the 16ᵗʰ and 19ᵗʰ century.   In the mid-19ᵗʰ century, it acquired its contemporary meaning of categorizing people according to their colour, ethnicity and origin and was used as a political tool to promote hate and cultural animosity.

In this chapter, you need to reflect on and understand the following key points:

a)   Racial prejudice is referred to as the most vital and challenging issue confronting the American Bahá'í community.
b)   The modern concept of race assumes that a race can be characterized by a biological foundation, whether Aristotelian essences or modern genes.
c)   While ancient cultures were conscious of physical variations in humans, much more importance was given to family or tribal affiliation than race.
d)   In the Middle Ages, a combination of ancient beliefs and the Bible description of human origin formed the dominant view on race.
e)   The subject of race emerged as a field of study during European expeditions when explorers discovered very different groups of people living in different continents.
f)   Houston Stewart Chamberlain moved the topic of race to the political domain when he argued that Christianity, ancient Greek philosophy and art all emerged from the Aryan race.
g)   Chamberlain's views formed the underlying intellectual framework for 20ᵗʰ century German anti-Semitism, and the crimes committed by Adolf Hitler and the Nazis.

h) A similar intellectual framework of racial prejudice against African Americans and American Indians developed in the United States.

i) The historical reason for slavery was economic, but in modern times, and in some countries such as the United States, biological racism has been used to justify slavery.

j) The concept of race has been challenged scientifically and philosophically since the Second World War.

k) The talks and behaviour of 'Abdu'l-Bahá while travelling in North America can be used as a model in dealing with racial prejudice.

14.2 Paragraphs under study

51 As to racial prejudice, the corrosion of which, for well-nigh a century, has bitten into the fibre, and attacked the whole social structure of American society, it should be regarded as constituting the most vital and challenging issue confronting the Bahá'í community at the present stage of its evolution. The ceaseless exertions which this issue of paramount importance calls for, the sacrifices it must impose, the care and vigilance it demands, the moral courage and fortitude it requires, the tact and sympathy it necessitates, invest this problem, which the American believers are still far from having satisfactorily resolved, with an urgency and importance that cannot be overestimated.   White and Negro, high and low, young and old, whether newly converted to the Faith or not, all who stand identified with it must participate in, and lend their assistance, each according to his or her capacity, experience, and opportunities, to the common task of fulfilling the instructions, realizing the hopes, and following the example, of 'Abdu'l-Bahá. Whether coloured or noncoloured, neither race has the right, or can conscientiously claim, to be regarded as absolved from such an obligation, as having realized such hopes, or having faithfully followed such an example. A long and thorny road, beset with pitfalls, still remains untraveled, both by the white and the Negro exponents of the redeeming Faith of Bahá'u'lláh. On the distance they cover, and the manner in which they travel that road, must depend, to an extent which few among them can imagine, the operation of those intangible influences which are indispensable to the spiritual triumph of the American believers and the material success of their newly launched enterprise.

52 Let them call to mind, fearlessly and determinedly, the example and conduct of 'Abdu'l-Bahá while in their midst. Let them remember His courage, His genuine love, His informal and indiscriminating fellowship, His contempt for and impatience of criticism, tempered by His tact and wisdom. Let them revive and perpetuate the memory of those unforgettable and historic episodes and occasions on which He so strikingly demonstrated His keen sense of justice, His spontaneous sympathy for the downtrodden, His ever-abiding sense of the oneness of the human race, His overflowing love for its members, and His displeasure with those who dared to flout His wishes, to deride His methods, to challenge His principles, or to nullify His acts.

14.3   Challenge of racial prejudice

In paragraph 51, Shoghi Effendi asserts that the corrosion of racial prejudice, "for well-nigh a century, has bitten into the fibre, and attacked the whole social structure of American society." He considers racial prejudice as the "most vital and challenging issue" confronting the American Bahá'í community at that stage of its evolution. Since racial prejudice is still deep rooted in American society, it probably remains a major challenge for the community today. This important issue requires the attention of the whole community to fulfil the instructions given by 'Abdu'l-Bahá on this matter, to realize His hopes and to follow Him as an example.

The term "race" meaning a nation or a group of people with common descent was first used during the 16th to the 19th century. In the mid-19th century it acquired its contemporary meaning of categorizing people according to their colour, ethnicity and origin, and was used as a political tool to promote hate and cultural animosity. Such views influenced major political crises in the early 20th century such as the rise of anti-Semitism in Germany, institutionalized racism in the United States and Apartheid in South Africa. The modern concept of race is based on five assumptions:

a) A race is characterized by a biological foundation, whether consisting of Aristotelian essences or modern genes.
b) Discrete racial groupings that share the same biological characteristics form a racial group.
c) The biological characteristics of each racial group are passed from one generation to the next, allowing the race of an individual to be classified through ancestry.
d) A study of genealogy should determine the geographic origin of a race, typically in Africa, Europe, Asia, or North and South America.
e) The biological characteristics manifest themselves in physical phenotypes (such as skin colour, eye shape, hair texture, and bone structure) and behavioural phenotypes (such as intelligence or delinquency).[1]

The concept of race has been challenged scientifically and philosophically since the Second World War. In particular, genetic discoveries have shown that genes do not identify the ethnic roots of an individual and there are no specific genes associated exclusively with one cultural group.

In the following sections, various aspects of the issue of race are studied in order to develop a better appreciation of the racial prejudice challenge highlighted by Shoghi Effendi.

14.4   History of race

While ancient cultures were conscious of physical variations in humans, much more importance was given to family or tribal affiliation than race. In Ancient Greece and Rome, human diversity was believed to be caused by environmental

---

[1]   Michael James, "Race", The Stanford Encyclopaedia of Philosophy (Spring 2017 Edition), Edward N. Zalta (ed.), https://plato.stanford.edu/archives/spr2017/entries/race/.

factors such as climate and geographical location. For example, Hippocrates of Kos (c. 460–c. 370 BC), a Greek Physician, believed that the physical form and inherent qualities of people were determined by environmental factors dominant in the region in which they lived.[1]

The first recorded attempt at systematic grouping of humans was made in ancient Egypt. In the *Book of Gates*, an ancient Egyptian funerary text dating to the New Kingdom,[2] different cultural groups known to Egyptians were divided into the four categories of Reth (Egyptians), Aamu (Asiatics), Themehu (Libyans) and Nehsu (Nubians) based on both physical and geographical characteristics.[3]

In the Middle Ages, a combination of ancient beliefs and the Bible description of human origin formed the dominant view on race. According to the Babylonian Talmud, humanity descended from the three sons of Noah: Shem, Ham and Japheth, resulting in the three distinct groups of Semitic (Asiatic) people, Hamitic (African) people and Japhetic (Indo-European) people. This reflected a monogenesis concept of race maintaining that all humans descended from a common ancestor. The modern race concepts assert that human races descended from different ancestors, a theory known as polygenesis.

The subject of race emerged as a field of study during European expeditions when explorers discovered very different groups of people living in different continents.[4] In 1684, François Bernier (1625–1688) introduced the first articulation of race in *A New Division of the Earth,* based on his visits to Egypt, Persia and India. He grouped humans into four race types—or possibly five, if American Indians were considered—of people who were so different that they could serve as the basis of a new division of the earth.[5]

In 1779, Carl Linnaeus (23 May 1707–10 January 1778), a Swedish botanist, physician and zoologist, organized humans into four primary races of Americanus, Europaeus, Asiaticus and Afer. His classification was primarily based on geographic location and skin colour, though he identified for each race some subjective attributes based on the four temperaments of ancient Greek philosophy.[6]

In 1795, Johann Friedrich Blumenbach (11 May 1752–22 January 1840), a German naturalist, advanced the science of race by grouping humans into five races: Caucasian or white race; the Malay or brown race, including Southeast Asian and

---

[1]   Hippocrates, *On Airs, Waters, and Places,* cited at
http://classics.mit.edu/Hippocrates/airwatpl.24.24.html.

[2]   This is also known as Egyptian Empire, is the period in the ancient Egyptian history between the 16th century BC and the 11th century BC.

[3]   E. A. Wallis Budge and E. A. Thomson Wallis Budge, *The Book of Gates,* Library of Alexandria, eBook.

[4]   Jonathan Marks, "Race: Past, present and future," in Barbara Koenig, Sandra Soo-Jin Lee, and Sarah S. Richardson, *Revisiting Race in a Genomic Age,* 2008, Rutgers University Press.

[5]   See https://www.jstor.org/stable/4289731?seq=1#page_scan_tab_contents

[6]   Stacie R. Chismark, M. S. Sheets, Kayla Mandel, M.S., "Race", *Salem Press Encyclopaedia of Health,* 2015.

Pacific Islanders; the Ethiopian or black race, including sub-Saharan Africans; the American or red race, including American Indians; and the Mongolian or yellow race, including all East Asians and some Central Asians.[1] Blumenbach was a monogenist who argued that variation in humans was caused by a biological reaction to environmental factors.

Many variations of the taxonomies of Linnaeus and Blumenbach were later proposed by monogenist and polygenist philosophers. Some naturalists attempted to change race from a taxonomy to a biological concept. With the success of the Darwin's theory of evolution, polygenesis basis of race declined since humans were considered to be descendants of animals who have emerged through natural selection.[2]

In his book, *The Foundations of the Nineteenth Century*, Houston Stewart Chamberlain (1855–1927), the son-in-law of German Composer Richard Wagner, moved the concept of race to the political domain by arguing that Christianity, ancient Greek philosophy and art emerged from the Aryan race. Even Jesus was assumed to be of the Aryan race despite His Jewish background. Chamberlain believed that during the Reformation, the union of Greek and Christian strands resulted in freeing the Teutonic strain of the Aryan race from Roman Catholic cultural constraints. Jews, the manifestation of Semitic Race, were considered to be diametrically opposite to the Teutonic Germans.[3] Chamberlain's views became the underlying intellectual framework of 20th century German anti-Semitism, and the crimes committed by Adolf Hitler and the Nazis.

A similar intellectual framework for racial prejudice against African Americans and American Indians developed in the United States after the publication in 1916 of *The Passing of the Great Race* by Madison Grant (1865–1937). Grant advocated strict segregation of the different races and prohibition of interbreeding between them (miscegenation).[4] Grant's views influenced public policy and this resulted in racist constraints on immigration and anti-miscegenation laws in 30 American states, which remained in force until 1967 when they were overturned by the United States Supreme Court.

At the same time as Chamberlain and Grant, assumptions about the biological nature of race, as discussed in the introduction, started to be discredited through the work of anthropologists and experimental genetics scientists. Their studies demonstrated that the observed differences between different groups of humans are the result of environmental and cultural factors, not inherent biological parameters. It then proved problematic to divide humans into groups based on geographical regions. Overall, the fundamental unity of human species, irrespective of physical traits, has been scientifically proven.

---

[1] *Encyclopaedia Britannica*, cited at https://www.britannica.com/biography/Johann-Friedrich-Blumenbach.

[2] C. L. Brace, *Race is a Four-Letter Word*, New York: Oxford University Press, p. 124, 2005.

[3] I. Hannaford, *Race: The History of an Idea in the West*, Baltimore, MD: The Johns Hopkins University Press, 1996.

[4] I. Hannaford, *Race: The History of an Idea in the West*, Baltimore, MD: The Johns Hopkins University Press, 1996.

14.5 UNESCO declarations on race

After World War II and the racism advocated and practiced by the Nazi regime, the United National Educational, Scientific and Cultural organization (UNESCO) released a series of statements on the question of race. The first statement, titled "The Race Question", was issued on 18 July 1950. It was aimed at combating racial prejudice and making the scientific facts about race known. It covered three topics:

a) Biological aspects of the race question
b) Social aspects of the race question
c) Statement on race

"The Race Question" asserts that:

National, religious, geographic, linguistic and cultural groups do not necessarily coincide with racial groups and the cultural traits of such groups have no demonstrated genetic connection with racial traits. Because serious errors of this kind are habitually committed when the term 'race' is used in popular parlance, it would be better when speaking of human races to drop the term 'race' altogether and speak of ethnic groups.[1]

A second statement was released in June 1951 on the nature of race and racial differences. It refutes the major assumptions of the biological concept of race by confirming that *Homo sapiens* is one species and:

The concept of race is unanimously regarded by anthropologists as a classificatory device providing a zoological frame within which the various groups of mankind may be arranged and by means of which studies of evolutionary processes can be facilitated. In its anthropological sense, the word 'race' should be reserved for groups of mankind possessing well-developed and primarily heritable physical differences from other groups.[2]

According to these statements, differences are the result of isolation, geography and culture. Scientific observations indicate that "pure races" do not exist and there is no scientific justification to discourage reproduction between people of different races.

A third statement, released in August 1964, titled "Proposals on the biological aspects of race" asserted that:

The peoples of the world today appear to possess equal biological potentialities for attaining any civilizational level. Differences in the achievements of different peoples must be attributed solely to their cultural history.[3]

---

[1] UNESCO, *Four Statements on Race Question*, p. 31, available at http://unesdoc. unesco.org/images/0012/001229/122962eo.pdf.

[2] UNESCO, *Four Statements on Race Question*, p. 38, available at http://unesdoc. unesco.org/images/0012/001229/122962eo.pdf.

[3] UNESCO, *Four Statements on Race Question*, p. 47, available at http://unesdoc. unesco.org/images/0012/001229/122962eo.pdf.

In a fourth statement released in August 1964, titled "Statement on Race and Racial Prejudice", the concept of racism is analyzed and its root causes are identified. It asserted:

> Racism has historical roots. It has not been a universal phenomenon. Many contemporary societies and cultures show little trace of it. It was not evident for long periods in world history. Many forms of racism have arisen out of the conditions of conquest, out of the justification of Negro Slavery and its aftermath of racial inequality in the West, and out of the colonial relationship. Among other examples is that of anti-Semitism, which has played a particular role in history, with Jews being the chosen scapegoat to take the blame for problems and crises met by many societies."[1]

UNESCO has released similar statements since 1964. For example, in a statement issued in 1978 titled "The UNESCO Declaration on Race and Racial Prejudice", it is confirmed that "All peoples of the world possess equal faculties for attaining the highest level in intellectual, technical, social, economic, cultural and political development ...," and "The differences between the achievements of the different peoples are entirely attributable to geographical, historical, political, economic, social and cultural factors."[2]

14.6   Slavery and racism

Slavery is any system in which individuals are allowed to own, buy and sell other individuals. A slave is treated as property, works without remuneration, and is deprived of basic human rights. The slave status is imposed on the children of the enslaved at birth. Scholars describe this as "chattel slavery".[3] Slavery has not been exclusive to a particular culture or society. There are indications that slavery existed in prehistoric times. Chattel slavery is now legally outlawed and banned in all nations of world, though millions of people are still exploited under modern forms of slavery.

Some scholars believe that slavery started in farming communities when there was a shortage of labour and an abundance of land. Otherwise, economically it would have been a better option to hire labour than to set up an infrastructure to manage and guard the slaves.[4] For example, slavery declined in Europe as populations increased, but it was forcefully pursued in the Americas and Russia when large areas of land were discovered and there were not enough people to farm them.[5]

---

[1]   UNESCO, *Four Statements on Race Question*, p. 51, available at http://unesdoc.unesco.org/images/0012/ 001229/122962eo.pdf.

[2]   Available at http://portal.unesco.org/en/ev.php-URL_ID=13161&URL_DO=DO_TOPIC&URL_SECTION=201.html.

[3]   Dan Frost, "Chattel Slavery". In P. Junius Rodriguez, *Slavery in the Modern World*, 1. ABC-CLIO, 2011, p. 182.

[4]   Douglass C. North, Thomas Paul Robert, "The Rise and Fall of the Manorial System: A Theoretical Model". *The Journal of Economic History*, 31 (4), 1971, pp. 777–803.

[5]   Evsey D. Domar, (March 1970). "The Causes of Slavery or Serfdom: A Hypothesis", *The Journal of Economic History*. 30 (1), March 1970, pp. 18–32.

While the historical reason for slavery has been economic, in modern times, and in some countries such as the United States where the nation has been founded on liberal values, biological racism has been used to justify slavery. However, the legal liberation of slaves in the United States has largely not addressed the conscious and unconscious racism of white Americans against black and red Americans. This is primarily the phenomenon Shoghi Effendi refers to as "ingrained prejudice".

Slavery began in America when African slaves were taken to the British colony of Jamestown, Virginia in 1619. The African slaves proved more cost effective and abundant than poor European servants. As a result, enslaving Africans became an acceptable and attractive practice during the 17th and 18th centuries. According to some estimates, around 6 to 7 million black slaves where imported into North America during this period. Most of them worked on the tobacco, rice and indigo plantations of the southern coast of America.[1]

The movement to abolish slavery began in the North after the American Revolution (1775-1783). The advocates of abolition linked the oppression of African Americans to the oppression they suffered under British rule. Some abolition activists considered slavery as a sin while others argued against its cost effectiveness. The movement against slavery gained momentum from the 1830s to the 1860s.

Following the presidential election in 1860 of Abraham Lincoln, with his anti-slavery views, 11 southern states declared their independence from the United States and formed the Confederate States of America. This resulted in the American Civil war, whose initial primary goal was that of preserving the unity of the Unites States, though abolition of slavery gained momentum as the war progressed.

On 1 January 1863, Abraham Lincoln issued an order to end slavery and to free millions of slaves. The emancipation occurred with the adoption of the 13th Amendment and the end of the Civil war in 1865. Former slaves were recognized as citizens of the United States. In the 14th Amendment they received constitutional protection and in the 15th Amendment the right to vote. However, significant political changes did not change racism and discrimination towards African Americans. The white supremacy movement opposing the rights of the blacks was covered in section 6.7. The civil rights movement of the 1960s secured more civil rights for the African Americans.

At the beginning of paragraph 51, Shoghi Effendi refers to a period of a hundred years of racial prejudice in the United States. This is probably a reference to the start of the anti-slavery movement in the 1830's.

14.7   The model of 'Abdu'l-Bahá

In dealing with racial prejudice, Shoghi Effendi counsels the North American Bahá'ís in paragraph 52 to remember the example and conduct of 'Abdu'l-Bahá when He visited them, in particular "His courage, His genuine love, His informal

---

[1]   *Slavery in America*, retrieved from https://www.history.com/topics/black-history/slavery.

and indiscriminating fellowship, His contempt for and impatience of criticism, tempered by His tact and wisdom." He then asks the Bahá'ís to revive and perpetuate the events in which He demonstrated:

- His keen sense of justice.
- His spontaneous sympathy for the downtrodden.
- His sense of the oneness of the human race.
- His overflowing love for its members.
- His displeasure with those who dared to flout His wishes, deride His methods, to challenge His principles, or to nullify His acts.

'Abdu'l-Bahá addressed the issue of race unity in the American Bahá'í community at a time when the number of enrolments started to increase in the United States. The following three stories illustrate some of the thoughts of 'Abdu'l-Bahá in relation to racial harmony.

14.7.1   Louis Gregory

In 1911, 'Abdu'l-Bahá invited a well-known African American Bahá'í, Louis Gregory, to visit Him. During this visit 'Abdu'l-Bahá stressed to Louis Gregory the significance of race unity and of bringing together white and black Americans. Gregory travelled to Egypt where 'Abdu'l-Bahá was staying at the time. He then visited the Bahá'í holy places in Palestine. Gregory recalls: "'Abdu'l-Bahá said many wonderful things during my brief contact with him in Egypt, which lasted less than a fortnight. But more than anything else his discourse was about the American race problem."[1] After the pilgrimage, 'Abdu'l-Bahá continued to urge Gregory to work for unity and harmony between the races.[2]

'Abdu'l-Bahá also encouraged the marriage of Gregory and a white English Bahá'í, Louisa (Louise) A. M. Mathew, who visited 'Abdu'l-Bahá in 1911 at the same time as Gregory. She also travelled with 'Abdu'l-Bahá to America on His invitation. When Gregory and Louisa met again in America, 'Abdu'l-Bahá urged them to consider their relationship in a new light. This transformed their friendship into love and they married on 27 September 1912 in New York City. They became the first interracial Bahá'í couple at a time when there were scientific arguments against mixing races (miscegenation) through marriage. There were even anti-miscegenation laws enforced in over half of the American states.[3]

14.7.2   'Abdu'l-Bahá in New York

'Abdu'l-Bahá deplored the racial segregation prevalent in the United States and He strongly urged the friends to associate with each other in the utmost joy and happiness. He called for such a gathering, and it took place

---

[1] Gregory, *"Racial Unity"*, Chap. 18: "Reminiscent."

[2] Louis G. Gregory, *A Heavenly Vista: The Pilgrimage of Louis G. Gregory*, Washington: n.p., n.d., p. 10.

[3] *The Bahá'í Encyclopaedia Project*, George Louis, retrieved at http://www.bahai-encyclopedia-project.org/index.php?option=com_content&view=article&id=63:gregory-louis-george&catid=37:biography.

Wednesday, April 17, at the home of Mr and Mrs Kinney, where Bahá'ís and their friends of both the black and white races met in unity. He prepared and served the meal Himself, speaking of the human family as 'a garden of flowers of various hues.' The Master was most happy and the spirit of the friends was high. It was felt that this was a landmark in the city. This memorable event was followed by a public address at the hotel.[1]

14.7.3 'Abdu'l-Bahá in Washington

Racial prejudice was in its heyday in the Washington of 1912. Even the Washington Bahá'í community of that day was not immune to its deadly virus. 'Abdu'l-Bahá openly challenged the status quo in words and deeds. Speaking at Howard University—an all-black institution—He said, 'If the heart is pure, white or black or any colour makes no difference. God does not look at colours; He looks at the hearts.'

At an all-whites luncheon, where many of the glitterati of Washington society were present, 'Abdu'l-Bahá suddenly stood up, looked all around, and said to His host: 'Where is Mr Gregory? Bring Mr Gregory!' The host rushed to get Louis Gregory (1874–1951), a distinguished black Bahá'í who was no doubt thought to be one of the blacks serving those present at the table. Mr Gregory was brought to the head of the table and seated in the place of honour at 'Abdu'l-Bahá's right.

In Washington, 'Abdu'l-Bahá asserted that harmony between the black and white races would be an assurance of the world's peace.[2]

---

[1]   Eliane Lacroix-Hopson, 'Abdu'l-Bahá in New York: The City of the Covenant, retrieved from https://bahai-library.com/hopson_abdulbaha_new_york.

[2]   'Abdu'l-Bahá in America 1912–2012, retrieved from https://centenary.bahai.us/cities/washington-dc.

14.8 Activities

14.8.1 Short answer questions

1. The following questions relate to the first sentence of paragraph 51.

   a) What period does "well-nigh a century" refer to?

   _____

   _____

   _____

   _____

   b) What is the key point of this statement?

   _____

   _____

   _____

   _____

2. The following questions relate to the second sentence of paragraph 51:

   a) What are the specific qualities and actions that are required to deal with racial prejudice?

   _____

   _____

   _____

   _____

   b) What is your understanding of the above statement?

   _____

   _____

   _____

   _____

3. The following questions relate to the last two sentences of paragraph 51:

   a) What could be the pitfalls referred to by Shoghi Effendi?

   _____

   _____

   _____

   _____

   b) What are the "intangible influences"?

_____

_____

_____

_____

    c)   What is the enterprise mentioned in this statement?

_____

_____

_____

    d)   What does Shoghi Effendi mean by "material success"?

_____

_____

_____

4.   Briefly describe the assumptions made by the biological theories on race?

_____

_____

_____

5.   What are the monogenist and polygenist concepts of race?

_____

_____

_____

6.   What was the underlying racist concept of Nazism?

_____

_____

_____

7.   What was the racist conceptual framework that emerged in the United States in the early 20th century?

_____

_____

_____

_____

8. What were the major steps taken to abolish slavery in the United States?

_____

_____

_____

_____

_____

_____

_____

9. In paragraph 52, Shoghi Effendi describes 'Abdu'l-Bahá's approach to race unity by the following qualities: courage, genuine love, informal and indiscriminating fellowship, contempt for and impatience of criticism, tact and wisdom, keen sense of justice, spontaneous sympathy for the downtrodden, His ever-abiding sense of the oneness of the human race.

Which qualities do the three stories described in the section 14.7.1–3 demonstrate?

a) Louis Gregory

_____

_____

_____

b) 'Abdu'l-Bahá in New York

_____

_____

_____

c) 'Abdu'l-Bahá in Washington

_____

_____

_____

_____

14.8.2 *Mini-project*

At the time of writing *The Advent of Divine Justice*, the Guardian believed that the American Bahá'ís were still far from having satisfactorily resolved the problem of racial prejudice within their community. Conduct some research to identify how the situation has changed since then.

15.
Abandoning racial prejudice

15.1 Introduction

This chapter covers paragraphs 53–58 in which Shoghi Effendi explains the Bahá'í perspective on the issue of racism in light of the core teachings of Bahá'u'lláh—the unity of mankind. He also provides a strategy for both the black and white races to abandon racial prejudice and achieve race unity. He cites a number of statements from Bahá'u'lláh and 'Abdu'l-Bahá on the unity of mankind and abandonment of all types of prejudices.

In this chapter, you need to reflect on and understand the following key points:

a)   'Abdu'l-Bahá acknowledges that physical diversity of human beings is caused by environmental factors.

b)   Any form of discrimination based on race is strongly condemned in the Bahá'í teachings.

c)   'Abdu'l-Bahá rejects the biological concept of race and confirms that the concept of race is a social reality constructed, promoted and accepted by the human mind.

d)   According to the Bahá'í teachings

- There is only one human species.
- While the construct of race is based on some physical differences in human beings, it has no reality.
- Discriminating against a particular group of people because of physical characteristics, such as skin colour, is unacceptable.

e)   Shoghi Effendi explains that discrimination based on race is only acceptable if it is in the form of positive discrimination in favour of minorities.

f)   Tremendous effort is required by both white and black races in their relationship with each other to reflect the spirit and teachings of the Faith, abandoning forever the false doctrine of racial superiority.

g) Although universally condemned in principle, racism has survived as a social attitude.

15.2 Paragraphs under study

53 To discriminate against any race, on the ground of its being socially backward, politically immature, and numerically in a minority, is a flagrant violation of the spirit that animates the Faith of Bahá'u'lláh. The consciousness of any division or cleavage in its ranks is alien to its very purpose, principles, and ideals. Once its members have fully recognized the claim of its Author, and, by identifying themselves with its Administrative Order, accepted unreservedly the principles and laws embodied in its teachings, every differentiation of class, creed, or colour must automatically be obliterated, and never be allowed, under any pretext, and however great the pressure of events or of public opinion, to reassert itself. If any discrimination is at all to be tolerated, it should be a discrimination not against, but rather in favour of the minority, be it racial or otherwise. Unlike the nations and peoples of the earth, be they of the East or of the West, democratic or authoritarian, communist or capitalist, whether belonging to the Old World or the New, who either ignore, trample upon, or extirpate, the racial, religious, or political minorities within the sphere of their jurisdiction, every organized community enlisted under the banner of Bahá'u'lláh should feel it to be its first and inescapable obligation to nurture, encourage, and safeguard every minority belonging to any faith, race, class, or nation within it. So great and vital is this principle that in such circumstances, as when an equal number of ballots have been cast in an election, or where the qualifications for any office are balanced as between the various races, faiths or nationalities within the community, priority should unhesitatingly be accorded the party representing the minority, and this for no other reason except to stimulate and encourage it, and afford it an opportunity to further the interests of the community. In the light of this principle, and bearing in mind the extreme desirability of having the minority elements participate and share responsibility in the conduct of Bahá'í activity, it should be the duty of every Bahá'í community so to arrange its affairs that in cases where individuals belonging to the divers minority elements within it are already qualified and fulfil the necessary requirements, Bahá'í representative institutions, be they Assemblies, conventions, conferences, or committees, may have represented on them as many of these divers elements, racial or otherwise, as possible. The adoption of such a course, and faithful adherence to it, would not only be a source of inspiration and encouragement to those elements that are numerically small and inadequately represented, but would demonstrate to the world at large the universality and representative character of the Faith of Bahá'u'lláh, and the freedom of His followers from the taint of those prejudices which have already wrought such havoc in the domestic affairs, as well as the foreign relationships, of the nations.

54 Freedom from racial prejudice, in any of its forms, should, at such a time as this when an increasingly large section of the human race is falling a victim to its devastating ferocity, be adopted as the watchword of the entire body of the American believers, in whichever state they reside, in whatever circles

they move, whatever their age, traditions, tastes, and habits. It should be consistently demonstrated in every phase of their activity and life, whether in the Bahá'í community or outside it, in public or in private, formally as well as informally, individually as well as in their official capacity as organized groups, committees and Assemblies. It should be deliberately cultivated through the various and everyday opportunities, no matter how insignificant, that present themselves, whether in their homes, their business offices, their schools and colleges, their social parties and recreation grounds, their Bahá'í meetings, conferences, conventions, summer schools and Assemblies. It should, above all else, become the keynote of the policy of that august body which, in its capacity as the national representative, and the director and coordinator of the affairs of the community, must set the example, and facilitate the application of such a vital principle to the lives and activities of those whose interests it safeguards and represents.

55   *"O ye discerning ones!"* Bahá'u'lláh has written, *"Verily, the words which have descended from the heaven of the Will of God are the source of unity and harmony for the world. Close your eyes to racial differences, and welcome all with the light of oneness."*[A] *"We desire but the good of the world and the happiness of the nations,"* He proclaims, *"... that all nations should become one in faith and all men as brothers; that the bonds of affection and unity between the sons of men should be strengthened; that diversity of religion should cease, and differences of race be annulled."*[B] *"Bahá'u'lláh hath said,"* writes 'Abdu'l-Bahá, *"that the various races of humankind lend a composite harmony and beauty of colour to the whole. Let all associate, therefore, in this great human garden even as flowers grow and blend together side by side without discord or disagreement between them."*[C] *"Bahá'u'lláh,"* 'Abdu'l-Bahá moreover has said, *"once compared the coloured people to the black pupil of the eye surrounded by the white. In this black pupil is seen the reflection of that which is before it, and through it the light of the spirit shineth forth."*[D]

56   *"God,"* 'Abdu'l-Bahá Himself declares, *"maketh no distinction between the white and the black. If the hearts are pure both are acceptable unto Him. God is no respecter of persons on account of either colour or race. All colours are acceptable unto Him, be they white, black, or yellow. Inasmuch as all were created in the image of God, we must bring ourselves to realize that all embody divine possibilities."*[A] *"In the estimation of God,"* He states, *"all men are equal. There is no distinction or preference for any soul, in the realm of His justice and equity."*[B] *"God did not make these divisions,"* He affirms; *"these divisions have had their origin in man himself. Therefore, as they are against the plan and purpose of God they are false and imaginary."*[C] *"In the estimation of God,"* He again affirms, *"there is no distinction of colour; all are one in the colour and beauty of servitude to Him. Colour is not important; the heart is all-important. It mattereth not what the exterior may be if the heart is pure and white within. God doth not behold differences of hue and complexion. He looketh at the hearts. He whose morals and virtues are praiseworthy is preferred in the presence of God; he who is devoted to the Kingdom is most beloved. In the realm of genesis and creation the question of colour is of least importance."*[D]

"Throughout the animal kingdom," He explains, *"we do not find the creatures separated because of colour. They recognize unity of species and oneness of kind. If we do not find colour distinction drawn in a kingdom of lower intelligence and reason, how can it be justified among human beings, especially when we know that all have come from the same source and belong to the same household? In origin and intention of creation mankind is one. Distinctions of race and colour have arisen afterward."*[E] *"Man is endowed with superior reasoning power and the faculty of perception"*; He further explains, *"he is the manifestation of divine bestowals. Shall racial ideas prevail and obscure the creative purpose of unity in his kingdom?"*[F] *"One of the important questions,"* He significantly remarks, *"which affect the unity and the solidarity of mankind is the fellowship and equality of the white and coloured races. Between these two races certain points of agreement and points of distinction exist which warrant just and mutual consideration. The points of contact are many .... In this country, the United States of America, patriotism is common to both races; all have equal rights to citizenship, speak one language, receive the blessings of the same civilization, and follow the precepts of the same religion. In fact numerous points of partnership and agreement exist between the two races, whereas the one point of distinction is that of colour. Shall this, the least of all distinctions, be allowed to separate you as races and individuals?"*[G] *"This variety in forms and colouring,"* He stresses, *"which is manifest in all the kingdoms is according to creative Wisdom and hath a divine purpose."*[H] *"The diversity in the human family,"* He claims, *"should be the cause of love and harmony, as it is in music where many different notes blend together in the making of a perfect chord."*[I] *"If you meet,"* is His admonition, *"those of a different race and colour from yourself, do not mistrust them, and withdraw yourself into your shell of conventionality, but rather be glad and show them kindness."*[J] *"In the world of being,"* He testifies, *"the meeting is blessed when the white and coloured races meet together with infinite spiritual love and heavenly harmony. When such meetings are established, and the participants associate with each other with perfect love, unity and kindness, the angels of the Kingdom praise them, and the Beauty of Bahá'u'lláh addresseth them, 'Blessed are ye! Blessed are ye!'"*[K] *"When a gathering of these two races is brought about,"* He likewise asserts, *"that assemblage will become the magnet of the Concourse on high, and the confirmation of the Blessed Beauty will surround it."*[L] *"Strive earnestly,"* He again exhorts both races, *"and put forth your greatest endeavour toward the accomplishment of this fellowship and the cementing of this bond of brotherhood between you. Such an attainment is not possible without will and effort on the part of each; from one, expressions of gratitude and appreciation; from the other, kindliness and recognition of equality. Each one should endeavour to develop and assist the other toward mutual advancement .... Love and unity will be fostered between you, thereby bringing about the oneness of mankind. For the accomplishment of unity between the coloured and white will be an assurance of the world's peace."*[M] *"I hope,"* He thus addresses members of the white race, *"that ye may cause that downtrodden race to become glorious, and to be joined with the white race, to serve the world of man with the utmost sincerity, faithfulness, love, and purity. This opposition, enmity, and prejudice among the white race and the*

coloured cannot be effaced except through faith, assurance, and the teachings of the Blessed Beauty."[N] *"This question of the union of the white and the black is very important,"* He warns, *"for if it is not realized, erelong great difficulties will arise, and harmful results will follow."*[O] *"If this matter remaineth without change,"* is yet another warning, *"enmity will be increased day by day, and the final result will be hardship and may end in bloodshed."*[P]

57   A tremendous effort is required by both races if their outlook, their manners, and conduct are to reflect, in this darkened age, the spirit and teachings of the Faith of Bahá'u'lláh. Casting away once and for all the fallacious doctrine of racial superiority, with all its attendant evils, confusion, and miseries, and welcoming and encouraging the intermixture of races, and tearing down the barriers that now divide them, they should each endeavour, day and night, to fulfil their particular responsibilities in the common task which so urgently faces them. Let them, while each is attempting to contribute its share to the solution of this perplexing problem, call to mind the warnings of 'Abdu'l-Bahá, and visualize, while there is yet time, the dire consequences that must follow if this challenging and unhappy situation that faces the entire American nation is not definitely remedied.

58   Let the white make a supreme effort in their resolve to contribute their share to the solution of this problem, to abandon once for all their usually inherent and at times subconscious sense of superiority, to correct their tendency towards revealing a patronizing attitude towards the members of the other race, to persuade them through their intimate, spontaneous and informal association with them of the genuineness of their friendship and the sincerity of their intentions, and to master their impatience of any lack of responsiveness on the part of a people who have received, for so long a period, such grievous and slow-healing wounds. Let the Negroes, through a corresponding effort on their part, show by every means in their power the warmth of their response, their readiness to forget the past, and their ability to wipe out every trace of suspicion that may still linger in their hearts and minds. Let neither think that the solution of so vast a problem is a matter that exclusively concerns the other. Let neither think that such a problem can either easily or immediately be resolved. Let neither think that they can wait confidently for the solution of this problem until the initiative has been taken, and the favourable circumstances created, by agencies that stand outside the orbit of their Faith. Let neither think that anything short of genuine love, extreme patience, true humility, consummate tact, sound initiative, mature wisdom, and deliberate, persistent, and prayerful effort, can succeed in blotting out the stain which this patent evil has left on the fair name of their common country. Let them rather believe, and be firmly convinced, that on their mutual understanding, their amity, and sustained cooperation, must depend, more than on any other force or organization operating outside the circle of their Faith, the deflection of that dangerous course so greatly feared by 'Abdu'l-Bahá, and the materialization of the hopes He cherished for their joint contribution to the fulfilment of that country's glorious destiny.

15.3 Bahá'í perspective on race

In paragraph 53, Shoghi Effendi explains the Bahá'í perspective on the issue of racism. While human diversity is acknowledged in the Bahá'í Faith as being desirable, any form of discrimination based on race is strongly condemned. The principle of the unity of mankind that embraces human diversity is the core teaching of the revelation of Bahá'u'lláh and reflects its opposition to any type of racism. In a letter written on his behalf to an individual believer, Shoghi Effendi explicitly highlights this important teaching of the Faith:

> In regard to your question concerning the Bahá'í attitude towards the Coloured Race. It is only evident that the principle of the oneness of Mankind—which is the main pivot round which all the Teachings of Bahá'u'lláh revolves—precludes the possibility of considering race as a bar to any intercourse, be it social or otherwise. The Faith, indeed, by its very nature and purpose transcends all racial limitations and differences, and proclaims the basic essential unity of the entire human race. Racial prejudice, of whatever nature and character, is therefore severely condemned, and as such should be wiped out by the friends in all their relations, whether private or social.[1]

For this reason, Shoghi Effendi strongly asserts in paragraph 53 that discrimination "... against any race, on the ground of its being socially backward, politically immature, and numerically in a minority, is a flagrant violation of the spirit that animates the Faith of Bahá'u'lláh."

During the same period that the biological concept of race was being promoted and becoming a core hypothesis of a number of political movements, the concept of the oneness of mankind enshrined in the revelation of Bahá'u'lláh was being promoted by 'Abdu'l-Bahá in His Tablets and later during His trips and talks in Europe and the United States. 'Abdu'l-Bahá was fully aware of the assumptions of the biological theories on race, as discussed in the previous chapter, and therefore His analyses, reasoning and articulations of the concepts were primarily targeted at refuting them.

15.3.1 *Acknowledging human diversity*

'Abdu'l-Bahá acknowledges that physical diversity of human beings is caused by environmental factors, resulting in different colours of skin, facial features, heights and other physical characteristics. In a talk given at Hull House, Chicago, the United States, He states that such differences, though observed between individuals should be treated as being less important than the similarities:

> *In the human kingdom itself there are points of contact, properties common to all mankind; likewise, there are points of distinction which separate race from race, individual from individual. If the points of contact, which are the common properties of humanity, overcome the peculiar points of distinction, unity is assured. On the other hand, if the points of differentiation overcome the points*

---

[1]   Letter written on behalf of Shoghi Effendi, 16 February 1935, cited in *Lights of Guidance*, p. 527.

of agreement, disunion and weakness result.[1]

In the next part of His talk, 'Abdu'l-Bahá applies his analysis of the similarities and differences among different groups of people to racism and the racial discrimination that He witnessed in America:

One of the important questions which affect the unity and the solidarity of mankind is the fellowship and equality of the white and coloured races. Between these two races certain points of agreement and points of distinction exist which warrant just and mutual consideration. The points of contact are many; for in the material or physical plane of being, both are constituted alike and exist under the same law of growth and bodily development. Furthermore, both live and move in the plane of the senses and are endowed with human intelligence. There are many other mutual qualifications. In this country, the United States of America, patriotism is common to both races; all have equal rights to citizenship, speak one language, receive the blessings of the same civilization, and follow the precepts of the same religion. In fact numerous points of partnership and agreement exist between the two races; whereas the one point of distinction is that of colour. Shall this, the least of all distinctions, be allowed to separate you as races and individuals? In physical bodies, in the law of growth, in sense endowment, intelligence, patriotism, language, citizenship, civilization and religion you are one and the same. A single point of distinction exists—that of racial colour. God is not pleased with—neither should any reasonable or intelligent man be willing to recognize—inequality in the races because of this distinction.[2]

In another Tablet, 'Abdu'l-Bahá refers to the diverse groups of people in the world as "races and tribes":

The century has come when all the races and tribes of the world shall do away with racial prejudice and associate fully. The century has arrived when all the nativities of the world shall prove to be one home of the human family. Thus may mankind, in its entirety, rest comfortably and in peace under the great and broad tabernacle of the one Lord.[3]

15.3.2 *Refuting biological concept of race*

While 'Abdu'l-Bahá acknowledges human diversity and the translation uses the term "race" to refer to different groups of people with similar physical characteristics, He rejects the biological concept of race and confirms that the concept of race is a social reality constructed, promoted and accepted by the human mind. In a talk given in Paris, 'Abdu'l-Bahá, highlights that the apparent multiplicity of "*Religions, races, and nations are all divisions of man's making only, and are necessary only in his thought; ....*"[4]

---

[1] 'Abdu'l-Bahá, *The Promulgation of Universal Peace*, pp. 67–68. By "the points of contact", 'Abdu'l-Bahá means similarities.
[2] 'Abdu'l-Bahá, *The Promulgation of Universal Peace*, p. 68.
[3] 'Abdu'l-Bahá, *Bahá'í Scriptures*, p. 399.
[4] 'Abdu'l-Baha, *Paris Talks*, p. 131.

In another talk delivered at the Church of the Messiah in Montréal, Canada, 'Abdu'l-Bahá states:

All humanity are the children of God; they belong to the same family, to the same original race. There can be no multiplicity of races, since all are the descendants of Adam. This signifies that racial assumption and distinction are nothing but superstition. In the estimate of God there are no English, French, Germans, Turkish or Persians. All these in the presence of God are equal; they are of one race and creation; God did not make these divisions. These distinctions have had their origin in man himself. Therefore, as they are against the plan and purpose of reality, they are false and imaginary. We are of one physical race, even as we are of one physical plan of material body—each endowed with two eyes, two ears, one head, two feet.[1]

In another talk given in Paris, 'Abdu'l-Bahá states:

Concerning the prejudice of race: it is an illusion, a superstition pure and simple! For God created us all of one race. There were no differences in the beginning, for we are all descendants of Adam. In the beginning, also, there were no limits and boundaries between the different lands; no part of the earth belonged more to one people than to another. In the sight of God there is no difference between the various races. Why should man invent such a prejudice? How can we uphold war caused by an illusion?[2]

In conclusion, there are a number of important principles that form the core Bahá'í perspective on race:

- There is only one human species
- While the construct of race may represent some physical differences in humans, it has no basis in reality.
- Therefore, discriminating against a particular group of people because of their physical characteristics, such as skin colour, and depriving them of their basic human rights is unacceptable.

15.3.3 Positive discrimination against minorities

Shoghi Effendi explains in paragraph 53 that the only acceptable discrimination based on race is that of positive discrimination in favour of minorities. The first obligation of any Bahá'í community is to nurture, encourage and safeguard any minority within it regardless of which faith, race, class or nation they belong. Shoghi Effendi then highlights a number of specific outcomes that should result from this significant principle:

a) If an equal number of ballots are cast in an election for people from different races, faiths or nationalities, then priority should be given to the person representing the minority.
b) It is the duty of every Bahá'í community to arrange its affairs so that its diverse minority elements are represented in its Assemblies, conventions, conferences and committees.

---

1   'Abdu'l-Bahá, *The Promulgation of Universal Peace*, p. 298.
2   'Abdu'l-Bahá, *Paris Talks*, p. 148.

c) Adoption of this principle will not only be a source of encouragement for minority groups, but it would demonstrate the universality of the Faith of Bahá'u'lláh and its freedom from any type of prejudice.

The principle of positive discrimination was built into the by-laws that govern Bahá'í institutions in the United States and subsequently into other national Bahá'í communities. The application of this principle is illustrated in a message sent by the Universal House of Justice to the National Spiritual Assembly of the Bahá'í of United States, dated 25 January 1967:

> Since the Guardian's instruction on this point is unequivocal where it is obvious that one of the persons involved represents a minority, that person should be accorded the priority without question. Where there is doubt further balloting will allow every voter present to participate.

> With reference to the provision in article V of the National By-Laws governing the situation where two or more members have received the same highest number of votes, if one of those members represents a minority that individual should be given priority as if selected by lot.[1]

In another letter written on behalf of the Universal House of Justice to the National Spiritual Assembly of the United Kingdom, dated 5 March 1986, some clarification is provided on the definition of a minority:

> ... the definition of a minority in any locality is in the discretion of the National Spiritual Assembly. It is clear that pioneers from other lands should not be regarded as belonging to a minority, neither do the categories quoted by the Guardian in *The Advent of Divine Justice*, namely, 'faith race, class or nation', include sex. The overriding principle is always that if there is any doubt as to whether the minority principle should be invoked, then a further ballot should be taken.[2]

15.4   Freedom from racial prejudice

In paragraph 54, Shoghi Effendi observes that an increasingly large section of the human race was a victim of the brutality of racial prejudice at that time. Hence, he asserts that freedom from racial prejudice should be a core aim of the Bahá'í community. It should be practiced in all aspects of their lives and be a keynote policy of the National Spiritual Assembly to facilitate its application to the community. In paragraphs 55 and 56, Shoghi Effendi cites some statements from Bahá'u'lláh and 'Abdu'l-Bahá regarding the unity of mankind and the abandonment of racial prejudice.

In paragraphs 57 and 58, Shoghi Effendi states that tremendous effort is required by both races in their relationship with each other to reflect the spirit and teachings of the Faith. They should abandon forever the false doctrine of racial superiority. He then provides a strategy for both white and black races to achieve freedom from engrained prejudices.

---

[1]   The Universal House of Justice, cited in *Lights of Guidance*, p. 24.

[2]   Letter written on behalf of the Universal House of Justice, cited in *Lights of Guidance*, p. 24.

According to paragraph 58, the white race should make a supreme effort to:

- Contribute their share to the solution of this problem
- Abandon their usually inherent and at times sub-conscious sense of superiority.
- Correct their patronising attitudes towards members of other races.
- Persuade the black race of their genuine friendship and the sincerity of their intentions.
- Show patience if no response is received from the black race.

Exerting similar efforts, the black race should demonstrate by every means in their power:

- The warmness of their response.
- Their readiness to forget the past.
- Their ability to wipe out every trace of suspicion that may still be in their hearts and minds.

Let neither race think:

- That the solution to the problem exclusively concerns the other.
- That such a problem can either be easily or immediately resolved.
- That they can wait confidently for the solution until the initiative is taken.
- That "anything short of genuine love, extreme patience, true humility, consummate tact, sound initiative, mature wisdom, and deliberate, persistent, and prayerful effort, can succeed in blotting out the stain which this patent evil has left on the fair name of their common country."

'Abdu'l-Bahá warns (quote 56:O) that if the union of the white and black is not realized, "*... erelong great difficulties will arise, and harmful results will follow.*" This warning is then reiterated (quote 56:P). Towards the end of paragraph 58, Shoghi Effendi asks both races to

> ... believe, and be firmly convinced, that on their mutual understanding, their amity, and sustained cooperation, must depend, more than on any other force or organization operating outside the circle of their Faith, the deflection of that dangerous course so greatly feared by 'Abdu'l-Bahá, and the materialization of the hopes He cherished for their joint contribution to the fulfilment of that country's glorious destiny.

15.5   Progress on race unity

Progress on race unity in the United States has been slow. Although the black Americans have been given legal equality and can potentially benefit from all the opportunities open to white Americans, racial prejudice is still ingrained in the society and there is segregation between white and black as well as other races. A review of the letters of Shoghi Effendi on the race issue in America written after *The Advent of Divine Justice,* and the messages of the Universal House of Justice, shed some light on the status of the race issue in America and in other parts of the world.

In a letter written on behalf of Shoghi Effendi to an individual believer dated 30 January 1941, it is mentioned:

In America, where racial prejudice is still so widely prevalent, it is the responsibility of the believers to combat and uproot it with all their force, first by endeavouring to introduce into the Cause as many racial and minority groups as they can approach and teach, and second by, stimulating close fellowship and intercourse between them and the rest of the Community.

It should be the paramount concern of your Committee to foster this aim through every means available. Not only the coloured people, who because of the increasing receptivity they are evincing to the Message and truly deserve special attention, but all other minorities, whether racial or religious, Jews, Red Indians, all alike should be contacted and confirmed. The greater the receptivity of a particular class or group, the stronger should wax the desire and determination of the believers to attract and teach its members. At a time when the whole world is steeped in prejudices of race, class, and nation, the Bahá'í, by upholding, firmly and loyally, this cardinal principle of their Faith, can best hope to vindicate its truth, and establish its right to bring order and peace out of the chaos and strife of this war-torn world.[1]

In a message dated 28 July 1954 to the American Bahá'í community, after addressing various challenges faced by the American nation such as materialism, moral laxity, and political crises, Shoghi Effendi states:

No less serious is the stress and strain imposed on the fabric of American society through the fundamental and persistent neglect, by the governed and governors alike, of the supreme, the inescapable and urgent duty—so repeatedly and graphically represented and stressed by 'Abdu'l-Bahá in His arraignment of the basic weaknesses in the social fabric of the nation—of remedying, while there is yet time, through a revolutionary change in the concept and attitude of the average white American toward his Negro fellow citizen, a situation which, if allowed to drift, will, in the words of 'Abdu'l-Bahá, cause the streets of American cities to run with blood, aggravating thereby the havoc which the fearful weapons of destruction, raining from the air, and amassed by a ruthless, a vigilant, a powerful and inveterate enemy, will wreak upon those same cities.[2]

Finally, in a letter to the World's religious leaders, dated April 2002, the Universal House of Justice explains:

Racial and ethnic prejudices have been subjected to equally summary treatment by historical processes that have little patience left for such pretensions. Here, rejection of the past has been especially decisive. Racism is now tainted by its association with the horrors of the twentieth century to the degree that it has taken on something of the character of a spiritual disease. While surviving as a social attitude in many parts of the world—and as a blight on the lives of a significant segment of humankind—racial prejudice has become so universally condemned in principle that no body of people can any longer safely allow themselves to be identified with it.

---

[1] Written on behalf of Shoghi Effendi, cited in *Lights of Guidance*, pp. 531–532.
[2] Shoghi Effendi, *Citadel of Faith*, p. 126.

It is not that a dark past has been erased and a new world of light has suddenly been born. Vast numbers of people continue to endure the effects of ingrained prejudices of ethnicity, gender, nation, caste and class. All the evidence indicates that such injustices will long persist as the institutions and standards that humanity is devising only slowly become empowered to construct a new order of relationships and to bring relief to the oppressed. The point, rather, is that a threshold has been crossed from which there is no credible possibility of return. Fundamental principles have been identified, articulated, accorded broad publicity and are becoming progressively incarnated in institutions capable of imposing them on public behaviour. There is no doubt that, however protracted and painful the struggle, the outcome will be to revolutionize relationships among all peoples, at the grassroots level.[1]

---

[1] The Universal House of Justice, Letter to the World's Religious Leaders, April 2002, p. 1.

15.6 Activities

15.6.1 Short answer questions

1. What is your understanding of the first two sentences of paragraph 53?

_____

_____

_____

_____

2. Answer the following questions based on the first two sentences of paragraph 53:

   a) What is the nature of discrimination against minorities and the rationale behind it?

   _____

   _____

   _____

   _____

   b) Give an example of discrimination in favour of minorities in the Bahá'í administration.

   _____

   _____

   _____

   _____

3. Answer the following questions based on the first two sentences of paragraph 54:

   a) What does Shoghi Effendi mean by "an increasingly large section of the human race is falling a victim to its devastating ferocity"?

   _____

   _____

   _____

   b) What are the implications of the statement "whichever state they reside, in whatever circles they move, whatever their age, traditions, tastes, and habits" on freedom of prejudice in the context of the American Bahá'í community?

   _____

   _____

_____

_____

4. What is your understanding of the last sentence of paragraph 54?

_____

_____

_____

_____

5. Briefly identify the key points in the quotations that Shoghi Effendi has used from Bahá'u'lláh and 'Abdu'l-Bahá in paragraphs 55–56.

   a) Quote 55:A

_____

_____

   b) Quote 55:B

_____

_____

   c) Quote 55:C

_____

_____

   d) Quote 55:D

_____

_____

   e) Quote 56:A

_____

_____

   f) Quote 56:B

_____

_____

   g) Quote 56:C

_____

_____

   h) Quote 56:D

_____

_____

i) Quote 56:E

_____

_____

j) Quote 56:F

_____

_____

k) Quote 56:G

_____

_____

l) Quote 56:H

_____

_____

m) Quote 56:I

_____

_____

n) Quote 56:J

_____

_____

o) Quote 56:K

_____

_____

p) Quote 56:L

_____

_____

q) Quote 56:M

_____

_____

r) Quote 56:N

_____

_____

s) Quote 56:O

_____

t) Quote 56:P

5. What are the major principles of the Bahá'í perspective on the issue of race?

6. What is your understanding of the first sentence of paragraph 57?

7. Answer the following questions based on the last sentence of paragraph 57:

   a) What were the warnings (see paragraph 56) of 'Abdu'l-Bahá?

   b) What does Shoghi Effendi mean by "while there is yet time"?

   c) What would be the dire consequences referred to in this statement?

8. What are the major steps of the strategy recommended by Shoghi Effendi to establish race unity between the white and the black people?

_____

_____

_____

_____

_____

_____

15.6.2   Mini-project

Conduct research on the current state of racism in the United States and its implications on various races and ethnic groups forming the American society. Organize your findings as a paper for publication in a Bahá'í journal.

16.
Twofold crusade

16.1 Introduction

This chapter covers paragraphs 59-62, in which Shoghi Effendi identifies rectitude of conduct, a chaste and holy life, and freedom from racial prejudices, as three weapons that the American Bahá'í community must possess in their twofold crusade: first to regenerate the inner life of their own community and next to fight the evils that have been engraved in the life of the American society. In conducting the twofold crusade, the American Bahá'í community would experience tests and tribulations. This chapter explores the concept of the inner life of an individual and a community, together with the nature of tests that the American Bahá'í community have to face.

In this chapter, you need to reflect on and understand the following key points:

a)   The twofold crusade of the American Bahá'í community consists of first regenerating the inner life of their own community and then fighting the evils that have been imbedded in the life of American society.

b)   A community, like an individual, has a life that represents the dynamics and activities associated with it.

c)   The inner life of a community constitutes the collective beliefs and values of the community.

d)   In general, the collective transformation of a community depends to a great extent on the spiritual transformation of the individual.

e)   The deepening of the inner life of an individual is mentioned as being a direct consequence of recognition of the Manifestation of God and the resulting process of spiritual transformation.

f)   The tests that an American Bahá'í community would experience are both intellectual and mental.

g)   Mental tests are different from physical tests where an individual may be threatened, imprisoned, tortured and even killed to recant his/her faith.

h)   A mental test differs from a physical test in that its main aim is to undermine the faith of the believer and cause doubt in his heart.

16.2   Paragraphs under study

59   Dearly beloved friends!   A rectitude of conduct which, in all its manifestations, offers a striking contrast to the deceitfulness and corruption that characterize the political life of the nation and of the parties and factions that compose it; a holiness and chastity that are diametrically opposed to the moral laxity and licentiousness which defile the character of a not inconsiderable proportion of its citizens; an interracial fellowship completely purged from the curse of racial prejudice which stigmatizes the vast majority of its people—these are the weapons which the American believers can and must wield in their double crusade, first to regenerate the inward life of their own community, and next to assail the long-standing evils that have entrenched themselves in the life of their nation.   The perfection of such weapons, the wise and effective utilization of every one of them, more than the furtherance of any particular plan, or the devising of any special scheme, or the accumulation of any amount of material resources, can prepare them for the time when the Hand of Destiny will have directed them to assist in creating and in bringing into operation that World Order which is now incubating within the worldwide administrative institutions of their Faith.

60   In the conduct of this twofold crusade the valiant warriors struggling in the name and for the Cause of Bahá'u'lláh must, of necessity, encounter stiff resistance, and suffer many a setback.   Their own instincts, no less than the fury of conservative forces, the opposition of vested interests, and the objections of a corrupt and pleasure-seeking generation, must be reckoned with, resolutely resisted, and completely overcome.   As their defensive measures for the impending struggle are organized and extended, storms of abuse and ridicule, and campaigns of condemnation and misrepresentation, may be unloosed against them.   Their Faith, they may soon find, has been assaulted, their motives misconstrued, their aims defamed, their aspirations derided, their institutions scorned, their influence belittled, their authority undermined, and their Cause, at times, deserted by a few who will either be incapable of appreciating the nature of their ideals, or unwilling to bear the brunt of the mounting criticisms which such a contest is sure to involve.   *"Because of 'Abdu'l-Bahá,"* the beloved Master has prophesied, *"many a test will be visited upon you.   Troubles will befall you, and suffering afflict you."*[A]

61   Let not, however, the invincible army of Bahá'u'lláh, who in the West, and at one of its potential storm centres is to fight, in His name and for His sake, one of its fiercest and most glorious battles, be afraid of any criticism that might be directed against it.   Let it not be deterred by any condemnation with which the tongue of the slanderer may seek to debase its motives.   Let it not recoil before the threatening advance of the forces of fanaticism, of orthodoxy, of corruption, and of prejudice that may be leagued against it. The voice of criticism is a voice that indirectly reinforces the proclamation of its Cause.   Unpopularity but serves to throw into greater relief the contrast

between it and its adversaries, while ostracism is itself the magnetic power that must eventually win over to its camp the most vociferous and inveterate amongst its foes. Already in the land where the greatest battles of the Faith have been fought, and its most rapacious enemies have lived, the march of events, the slow yet steady infiltration of its ideals, and the fulfilment of its prophecies, have resulted not only in disarming and in transforming the character of some of its most redoubtable enemies, but also in securing their firm and unreserved allegiance to its Founders. So complete a transformation, so startling a reversal of attitude, can only be effected if that chosen vehicle which is designed to carry the Message of Bahá'u'lláh to the hungry, the restless, and unshepherded multitudes is itself thoroughly cleansed from the defilements which it seeks to remove.

62 It is upon you, therefore, my best-beloved friends, that I wish to impress not only the urgency and imperative necessity of your holy task, but also the limitless possibilities which it possesses of raising to such an exalted level not only the life and activities of your own community, but the motives and standards that govern the relationships existing among the people to which you belong. Undismayed by the formidable nature of this task, you will, I am confident, meet as befits you the challenge of these times, so fraught with peril, so full of corruption, and yet so pregnant with the promise of a future so bright that no previous age in the annals of mankind can rival its glory.

16.3 Regeneration of community's inner life

In paragraph 59, Shoghi Effendi refers to rectitude of conduct, a chaste and holy life, and freedom from racial prejudices—explained in detail in previous paragraphs—as three weapons that the American Bahá'ís must use in their double crusade: firstly to regenerate the inner life of their own community and next to fight the evils that have taken root in American society. The perfection of these weapons and the wise utilization of them will prepare the community more than any other plan or material resources to help initiate the World Order of Bahá'u'lláh when the right time has arrived.

16.3.1 *Inner life of community*

The life of a community is influenced by the dynamics of the relationships of the individuals within it and the activities associated with it. The social cohesion of a community is determined by a willingness of the members to set and strive for common goals. The degree of social cohesion within a community is determined by the historical background of the community, the quality of the relationships between the members, its social structure, its cultural values and how it governs itself. Observable community processes and characteristics represent the outer life of the community and those that are internal and hidden (such as love and compassion between the members) characterize the inner life of the community. The inner life of the community constitutes the collective beliefs and values of the community. Regenerating the inner life of a community requires the development of high ideals and values, such as the three standards defined by Shoghi Effendi: rectitude of conduct, a chaste and holy life and freedom from prejudice.

In general, the collective transformation of a community depends to a great extent on the spiritual transformation of the individuals. The Universal House of Justice explicitly states that "... the fate of the entire community depends upon the individual believers. Without the wholehearted support of each and every one of the friends, every measure adopted, no matter how well thought out, is foredoomed to failure."[1] In another message, the Universal House of Justice refers to the role of the individual as of unique importance in the work of the Cause: "It is the individual who manifests the vitality of faith upon which the success of the teaching work and the development of the community depend."[2]

As regards the community, the Universal House of Justice states that it

... assumes its own character and identity as it grows in size. ... A community is of course more than the sum of its membership; it is a comprehensive unit of civilization composed of individuals, families and institutions that are originators and encouragers of systems, agencies and organizations working together with a common purpose for the welfare of people both within and beyond its own borders; it is a composition of diverse, interacting participants that are achieving unity in an unremitting quest for spiritual and social progress.[3]

In the same message, the Universal House of Justice asserts that

... the flourishing of the community, especially at the local level, demands a significant enhancement in patterns of behaviour: those patterns by which the collective expression of the virtues of the individual members and the functioning of the Spiritual Assembly are manifest in the unity and fellowship of the community and the dynamism of its activity and growth.[4]

Hence, the three spiritual pre-requisites of rectitude of conduct, a chaste and holy life, and freedom from racial prejudices, while enhancing the patterns of behaviour of the individual, result in the collective transformation of a community. In other words, the deepening of the inner life of an individual within a community results in the regeneration of the inner life of the whole community.

16.3.2   *Inner life of individual*

In the Bahá'í writings, the deepening of the inner life of the individual is mentioned as the direct consequence of the recognition of the Manifestation of God followed by a process of spiritual transformation. Bahá'u'lláh identifies the primary purpose of every revelation from God as the transformation of the character of mankind that will affect its inner life. In *The Kitáb-i-Íqán* He states:

---

[1]   The Universal House of Justice, *Messages of the Universal House of Justice 1968–1973*, p. 16.

[2]   The Universal House of Justice, Riḍván message 153 (1996), *Messages from the Universal House of Justice 1986–2001*, p. 486.

[3]   The Universal House of Justice, Riḍván message 153 (1996), *Messages from the Universal House of Justice 1986–2001*, p. 488.

[4]   The Universal House of Justice, Riḍván message 153 (1996), *Messages from the Universal House of Justice 1986–2001*, p. 488.

... is not the object of every Revelation to effect a transformation in the whole character of mankind, a transformation that shall manifest itself both outwardly and inwardly, that shall affect both its inner life and external conditions? For if the character of mankind be not changed, the futility of God's universal Manifestations would be apparent.[1]

Regarding the significance of an enhanced inner life, Shoghi Effendi attests that

If people only realized it, the inner life of the spirit is that which counts, but they are so blinded by desires and so misled that they have brought upon themselves all the suffering we see at present in the world.[2]

Shoghi Effendi then highlights that the duty of the Bahá'ís is "... to lead people back to a knowledge of their true selves and the purpose for which they were created, and thus to their greatest happiness and highest good."[3]

A letter written on behalf of Shoghi Effendi, dated 12 December 1942, highlights various aspects of the revelation of Bahá'u'lláh that affect the inner life of the individual:

The Teachings of Bahá'u'lláh are so great, and deal with so many aspects of both the inner life of man and his communal life, that it takes years to really plumb them to the depths. He has brought spiritual food for the soul of the individual, to help each one to find himself and become a finer and better developed personality; and also He has brought the laws and principles needed to enable all men to live in harmony together in a great, united world. The Guardian hopes you ... will do all in your power to help the believers to understand both aspects of the teachings, and to develop both as individuals and as a community, an ever higher, finer, way of life.[4]

At the end of paragraph 59, Shoghi Effendi emphasizes that the perfection and wise utilization of the three spiritual pre-requisites ("weapons") will prepare the community more than any other plan or material resources to help to bring into operation the World Order of Bahá'u'lláh when the right time has arrived.

In summary, the revelation of Bahá'u'lláh should be assimilated into our inner being and reflected in our thoughts, attitudes and deeds. This is the process of spiritual transformation through which we acquire and develop the "weapons" we need to fight the evils that beset our own community and, thereafter, expunge them from the lives of people in the wider society.

16.4   Tribulations and tests

In paragraph 60, Shoghi Effendi describes the tribulations and tests that the American Bahá'ís would experience in conducting the twofold crusade against the evils within and outside of the community of believers. The nature of the turmoil

---

[1]   Bahá'u'lláh, *The Kitáb-i-Íqán*, pp. 240–241.
[2]   Shoghi Effendi, *High Endeavours: Messages to Alaska*, p. 7.
[3]   Shoghi Effendi, *High Endeavours: Messages to Alaska*, p. 7.
[4]   Shoghi Effendi cited in *Lights of Guidance*, p. 559.

and persecutions described by Shoghi Effendi is intellectual and psychological rather than the physical persecutions that were inflicted on the Persian Bahá'ís in the Cradle of the Faith.

In a Tablet addressed to Mr and Mrs Howard McNutt, 'Abdu'l-Bahá, while generalizing about the susceptibility of westerners, implies that some of the Bahá'ís of America would succumb to tests and compares this to the steadfastness of the Bahá'ís in Persia, none of whom recanted their faith even under torture:

> *In brief, my purpose is to show that whatever call is raised or proclaimed in America, a group will doubtless gather around it; while, on the other hand, the Oriental Friends (Bahá'ís) are firm like unto the immovable mountains. For thirty years have the violators striven to undermine the Cause, but they have failed even to attract to their side their own kindred and relatives. That is why, undoubtedly, in Persia, twenty thousand Bahá'ís have been martyred and severe tests have been brought about. Yet, praise be to God! not even a single soul among the Friends wavered.*[1]

16.4.1 Physical tests

The Bahá'í community is very familiar with the nature of physical tests. The Persian Bahá'ís have been subjected to physical tests since the time of the Báb. Enemies of the Faith, determined to stop the progress of the Faith and its numerical expansion, have used physical means to intimidate the followers of Bahá'u'lláh, to force them to abandon practicing their religion or to convince them to recant their faith.

Despite being the victims of numerous physical trials and tribulations, Persian Bahá'ís have remained firm in their belief. Their possessions have been confiscated. They have been arrested and jailed. They have been beaten by mobs. As many as 20,000 followers have been killed because they would not recant their faith.

Since the 1979 Islamic Revolution in Írán, the physical persecution of the Bahá'ís has become systematic and built into government policies and laws. During the first decade after the Revolution, more than 200 Bahá'ís were murdered or executed, and hundreds were imprisoned and tortured. Physical persecution has been extended to include dismissal from employment, denial of access to education, and other basic human rights.

The Islamic government is misusing its power and authority to force Bahá'ís to recant their faith. For example, Bahá'ís have been subjected to economic and educational discrimination, to the loss of their rights to assemble and to work. The government has given mobs free rein to attack Bahá'ís and their properties.

16.4.2 Mental tests

A mental test is different from a physical test in that its main aim is to undermine the faith of the believer and cause doubt in his heart. From the earliest years of his ministry, Shoghi Effendi referred to the inevitable mental tests that

---

[1] 'Abdu'l-Bahá cited in *Star of the West*, Vol. 11, no. 14, p. 241.

would be experienced by the Bahá'ís of the West, particularly in North America. In a message sent to the American believers, dated 21 January 1922, he stated:

> How dearly all the Holy Leaves cherish that memory of the departed Master, as He commented upon the fresh tidings that poured in from that continent, admiring the untiring activity of the friends, the complete subordination of their material interests to those of the Cause, the remarkable spread of the Movement in their midst and their staunch firmness in the Covenant of Bahá'u'lláh. It is these encouraging reflections of the Master about His loved ones in America and the tests intellectual rather than physical which He said He would send to them to purify and make them ever brighter than before— it is these comments and promises of His that make of the Movement in that land such a potential force in the world today. The Beloved Master's cable to the friends in that region is a clear indication of the presence of those counteracting forces that may usher in those storms of tests that the Master Himself has said will ultimately be for the good of the Cause in that land.[1]

A document prepared by the Research Department on behalf of the Universal House of Justice,[2] suggests that the "cable" mentioned above by the Guardian may be the following: *"He who sits with a leper catches leprosy. He who is with Christ shuns Pharisees and abhors Judas Iscariots. Certainly shun violators."*[3]

In another message dated 14 November 1923, Shoghi Effendi pointed out:

> And yet, how often we seem to forget the clear and repeated warnings of Our beloved Master, Who, in particular during the concluding years of His mission on earth, laid stress on the 'severe mental tests' that would inevitably sweep over His loved ones of the West—tests that would purge, purify and prepare them for their noble mission in life.[4]

The Iranian Bahá'í community has also been subjected to mental tests. The Iranian authorities have used official media to conduct a systematic campaign to demoralize and humiliate the Bahá'í community. The media spreads false information about the Bahá'í community and disseminates anti-Bahá'í propaganda.

16.4.3 *Tests, obstacles and inner life*

In paragraphs 60–62, Shoghi Effendi states that in conducting the twofold crusade, the American Bahá'í community will encounter stiff resistance and suffer many setbacks, which should be resisted. They include:

* Storms of abuse and ridicule.
* Campaigns of condemnation and misrepresentation.
* An assault on their Faith.

---

[1] Shoghi Effendi, *Bahá'í Administration: Selected Messages 1922–1932*, pp. 16–17.
[2] Prepared by the Research Department on behalf of the Universal House of Justice, *Mental Tests*, 12 March 1995, retrieved from https://bahai-library.com/uhj_mental_tests.
[3] *Star of the West*, Vol. 12, no. 14, p. 232.
[4] Shoghi Effendi, *Bahá'í Administration: Selected Messages 1922–1932*, p. 50.

- Defamation of their aims.
- Derision towards their aspirations.
- Scorn of their institutions.
- Undermining of their authority.
- Resignation from the Faith by a few.

The community will be called upon to fight one of its fiercest battles to overcome the resistance to the Faith. If the Bahá'í community is fully cleansed from the defilements it tries to remove, then the result will be a transformation and a complete reversal of attitude of the enemies of the Faith.

In his other messages, Shoghi Effendi sheds additional light on the obstacles faced by the American Bahá'í community in their twofold crusade, and how they can protect themselves against the inevitable mental tests. For example, in a message he wrote to the American Bahá'í community dated 19 July 1956, Shoghi Effendi identified the following obstacles:

> The gross materialism that engulfs the entire nation at the present hour; the attachment to worldly things that enshrouds the souls of men; the fear and anxieties that distract their minds; the pleasure and dissipations that fill their time, the prejudices and animosities that darken their outlook, the apathy and lethargy that paralyze their spiritual faculties—these are among the formidable obstacles that stand in the path of every world-be warrior in the service of Bahá'u'lláh, obstacles which he must battle against the surmount in his crusade for the redemption of his own countrymen.[1]

In another letter written on behalf of Shoghi Effendi to an individual believer dated 14 February 1925 it is stated:

> There is no need to fear opposition from without if the life within be sound and vigorous. Our Heavenly Father will always give us the strength to meet and overcome tests if we turn with all our hearts to Him, and difficulties if they are met in the right spirit only make us rely on God more firmly and completely.[2]

Hence, while conducting the twofold crusade incurs tests and tribulations for the American Bahá'í community, building a stronger inner life will be a protection against those tests.

---

[1] Shoghi Effendi, *Citadel of Faith*, p. 149.
[2] Shoghi Effendi, cited in *Lights of Guidance*, p. 417.

16.5   Activities

16.5.1   Short answer questions

1.   Consider paragraph 59 and answer the following questions.

a)   What are the three "weapons" mentioned by Shoghi Effendi?

_____

_____

_____

_____

b)   What is the twofold crusade?

_____

_____

_____

_____

c)   Why is the perfection of the three "weapons" important?

_____

_____

_____

_____

2.   What is inner life of an individual?

_____

_____

_____

_____

3.   What is the inner life of a community?

_____

_____

_____

_____

4.   What is the relationship between individual and community inner lives?

_____

_____

_____

5. What is a physical test?

6. What is a mental test?

7. What is the difference between the aims of physical and mental tests?

8. Identify different mental tests mentioned by Shoghi Effendi in paragraph 60.

9. What is your understanding of 'Abdu'l-Bahá's quote 60:A to the American believers?

10. What is your understanding of the first five sentences of paragraph 61?

_____

_____

_____

11.   What is your understanding of paragraph 62?

_____

_____

_____

_____

16.5.2   *Mini-project*

Conduct research to learn whether the American Bahá'í community has experienced any mental tests, as mentioned by Shoghi Effendi, since the time he wrote *The Advent of Divine Justice*. Prepare your findings as a presentation and share it with your community.

17.
Pondering on teaching

17.1   Introduction

This chapter covers paragraphs 63-73, in which Shoghi Effendi raises a number of important issues. Initially, he provides an outline of the content of the book so far and what he is going to address in the remainder. He then highlights the significance of teaching the Faith and how it is a duty for every individual Bahá'í. Finally, he describes the nature and impact of the Force released through the revelations of the Báb and Bahá'u'lláh. A force that acts as a two-edged sword, on one hand breaking apart the ties that have been holding together the fabric of human civilization, and on the other unloosing the bonds that have been restraining the advancement of the Faith of Bahá'u'lláh.

In this chapter, you need to reflect on and understand the following key points:

a)   The Bahá'í House of Worship in Wilmette is no more than an instrument for the more effective propagation of the Cause and should be viewed in the same light as the Administrative Order of the Cause.
b)   Teaching of the Cause is an obligation of every Bahá'í.
c)   Teaching the Faith is sharing the heat generated by the fire of the love of God in us.
d)   The receipt of divine confirmation is dependent on active teaching of the Cause.
e)   As shown by the early history of the Faith, many unschooled and inexperienced believers have won great victories for the Cause.
f)   The Force released through the revelations of the Báb and Bahá'u'lláh is creating unprecedented opportunities for the American Bahá'ís to arise and to exploit them for the advancement of the Cause.
g)   With the coming of any new revelation, this Force is released to achieve the purpose of that revelation in the world of creation.
h)   In the revelation of Bahá'u'lláh, this Force has been producing sweeping changes in the world since its release.

17.2   Paragraphs under study

63   Dearly beloved friends! I have attempted, in the beginning of these pages, to convey an idea of the glorious opportunities as well as the tremendous responsibilities which, as a result of the persecution of the far-flung Faith of Bahá'u'lláh, now face the community of the American believers, at so critical a stage in the Formative Period of their Faith, and in so crucial an epoch in the world's history. I have dwelt sufficiently upon the character of the mission which in a not too distant future that community must, through the impelling force of circumstances, to arise and carry out. I have uttered the warning which I felt would be necessary to a clearer understanding, and a better discharge, of the tasks lying ahead of it. I have set forth, and stressed as far as it was in my power, those exalted and dynamic virtues, those lofty standards, which, difficult as they are to attain, constitute nonetheless the essential requirements for the success of those tasks. A word, I believe, should now be said in connection with the material aspect of their immediate task, upon the termination of which, at its appointed time, must depend not only the unfoldment of the subsequent stages in the Divine Plan envisaged by 'Abdu'l-Bahá, but also the acquisition of those capacities which will qualify them to discharge, in the fullness of time, the duties and responsibilities demanded by that greater mission which it is their privilege to perform.

64   The Seven Year Plan, with its twofold aspects of Temple ornamentation and extension of teaching activity, embracing both the Northern and Southern American continents, is now well advanced into its second year, and offers to anyone who has observed its progress in recent months signs that are extremely heartening and which augur well for the attainment of its objectives within the allotted time. The successive steps designed to facilitate, and covering the entire field of, the work to be achieved in connection with the exterior ornamentation of the Temple have for the most part been taken. The final phase which is to mark the triumphant conclusion of a thirty-year old enterprise has at long last been entered. The initial contract connected with the first and main story of that historic edifice has been signed. The Fund associated with the beloved name of the Greatest Holy Leaf has been launched. The uninterrupted continuation to its very end of so laudable an enterprise is now assured. The poignant memories of one whose heart so greatly rejoiced at the rearing of the superstructure of this sacred House will so energize the final exertions required to complete it as to dissipate any doubt that may yet linger in any mind as to the capacity of its builders to worthily consummate their task.

65   The teaching aspect of the Plan must now be pondered. Its challenge must be met, and its requirements studied, weighed, and fulfilled. Superb and irresistible as is the beauty of the first Mashriqu'l-Adhkár of the West, majestic as are its dimensions, unique as is its architecture, and priceless as are the ideals and the aspirations which it symbolizes, it should be regarded, at the present time, as no more than an instrument for a more effective propagation of the Cause and a wider diffusion of its teachings. In this respect it should be viewed in the same light as the administrative

institutions of the Faith which are designed as vehicles for the proper dissemination of its ideals, its tenets, and its verities.

66 It is, therefore, to the teaching requirements of the Seven Year Plan that the community of the American believers must henceforth direct their careful and sustained attention. The entire community must, as one man, arise to fulfil them. To teach the Cause of God, to proclaim its truths, to defend its interests, to demonstrate, by words as well as by deeds, its indispensability, its potency, and universality, should at no time be regarded as the exclusive concern or sole privilege of Bahá'í administrative institutions, be they Assemblies, or committees. All must participate, however humble their origin, however limited their experience, however restricted their means, however deficient their education, however pressing their cares and preoccupations, however unfavourable the environment in which they live. "*God*," Bahá'u'lláh, Himself, has unmistakably revealed, "*hath prescribed unto everyone the duty of teaching His Cause.*"[A] "*Say*," He further has written, "*Teach ye the Cause of God, O people of Bahá, for God hath prescribed unto everyone the duty of proclaiming His Message, and regardeth it as the most meritorious of all deeds.*"[B]

67 A high and exalted position in the ranks of the community, conferring as it does on its holder certain privileges and prerogatives, no doubt invests him with a responsibility that he cannot honourably shirk in his duty to teach and promote the Faith of God. It may, at times, though not invariably, create greater opportunities and furnish better facilities to spread the knowledge of that Faith, and to win supporters to its institutions. It does not, however, under any circumstances, necessarily carry with it the power of exercising greater influence on the minds and hearts of those to whom that Faith is presented. How often—and the early history of the Faith in the land of its birth offers many a striking testimony—have the lowliest adherents of the Faith, unschooled and utterly inexperienced, and with no standing whatever, and in some cases devoid of intelligence, been capable of winning victories for their Cause, before which the most brilliant achievements of the learned, the wise, and the experienced have paled.

68 "*Peter*," 'Abdu'l-Bahá has testified, "*according to the history of the Church, was also incapable of keeping count of the days of the week. Whenever he decided to go fishing, he would tie up his weekly food into seven parcels, and every day he would eat one of them, and when he had reached the seventh, he would know that the Sabbath had arrived, and thereupon would observe it.*"[A] If the Son of Man was capable of infusing into apparently so crude and helpless an instrument such potency as to cause, in the words of Bahá'u'lláh, "*the mysteries of wisdom and of utterance to flow out of his mouth,*" and to exalt him above the rest of His disciples, and render him fit to become His successor and the founder of His Church, how much more can the Father, Who is Bahá'u'lláh, empower the most puny and insignificant among His followers to achieve, for the execution of His purpose, such wonders as would dwarf the mightiest achievements of even the first apostle of Jesus Christ!

69   *"The Báb,"* 'Abdu'l-Bahá, moreover, has written, *"hath said: 'Should a tiny ant desire, in this day, to be possessed of such power as to be able to unravel the abstrusest and most bewildering passages of the Qur'án, its wish will no doubt be fulfilled, inasmuch as the mystery of eternal might vibrates within the innermost being of all created things.' If so helpless a creature can be endowed with so subtle a capacity, how much more efficacious must be the power released through the liberal effusions of the grace of Bahá'u'lláh!"*[A]

70   The field is indeed so immense, the period so critical, the Cause so great, the workers so few, the time so short, the privilege so priceless, that no follower of the Faith of Bahá'u'lláh, worthy to bear His name, can afford a moment's hesitation. That God-born Force, irresistible in its sweeping power, incalculable in its potency, unpredictable in its course, mysterious in its workings, and awe-inspiring in its manifestations—a Force which, as the Báb has written, *"vibrates within the innermost being of all created things,"* and which, according to Bahá'u'lláh, has through its *"vibrating influence,"* *"upset the equilibrium of the world and revolutionized its ordered life"*—such a Force, acting even as a two-edged sword, is, under our very eyes, sundering, on the one hand, the age-old ties which for centuries have held together the fabric of civilized society, and is unloosing, on the other, the bonds that still fetter the infant and as yet unemancipated Faith of Bahá'u'lláh. The undreamt-of opportunities offered through the operation of this Force—the American believers must now rise, and fully and courageously exploit them. *"The holy realities of the Concourse on high,"* writes 'Abdu'l-Bahá, *"yearn, in this day, in the Most Exalted Paradise, to return unto this world, so that they may be aided to render some service to the threshold of the Abhá Beauty, and arise to demonstrate their servitude to His sacred Threshold."*[A]

71   A world, dimmed by the steadily dying-out light of religion, heaving with the explosive forces of a blind and triumphant nationalism; scorched with the fires of pitiless persecution, whether racial or religious; deluded by the false theories and doctrines that threaten to supplant the worship of God and the sanctification of His laws; enervated by a rampant and brutal materialism; disintegrating through the corrosive influence of moral and spiritual decadence; and enmeshed in the coils of economic anarchy and strife—such is the spectacle presented to men's eyes, as a result of the sweeping changes which this revolutionizing Force, as yet in the initial stage of its operation, is now producing in the life of the entire planet.

72   So sad and moving a spectacle, bewildering as it must be to every observer unaware of the purposes, the prophecies, and promises of Bahá'u'lláh, far from casting dismay into the hearts of His followers, or paralyzing their efforts, cannot but deepen their faith, and excite their enthusiastic eagerness to arise and display, in the vast field traced for them by the pen of 'Abdu'l-Bahá, their capacity to play their part in the work of universal redemption proclaimed by Bahá'u'lláh. Every instrument in the administrative machinery which, in the course of several years, they have so laboriously erected must be fully utilized, and subordinated to the end for which it was created. The Temple, that proud embodiment of so rare a spirit of self-

sacrifice, must likewise be made to play its part, and contribute its share to the teaching campaign designed to embrace the entire Western Hemisphere.

73   The opportunities which the turmoil of the present age presents, with all the sorrows which it evokes, the fears which it excites, the disillusionment which it produces, the perplexities which it creates, the indignation which it arouses, the revolt which it provokes, the grievances it engenders, the spirit of restless search which it awakens, must, in like manner, be exploited for the purpose of spreading far and wide the knowledge of the redemptive power of the Faith of Bahá'u'lláh, and for enlisting fresh recruits in the ever-swelling army of His followers. So precious an opportunity, so rare a conjunction of favourable circumstances, may never again recur. Now is the time, the appointed time, for the American believers, the vanguard of the hosts of the Most Great Name, to proclaim, through the agencies and channels of a specially designed Administrative Order, their capacity and readiness to rescue a fallen and sore-tried generation that has rebelled against its God and ignored His warnings, and to offer it that complete security which only the strongholds of their Faith can provide.

17.3   Overview of the book

In paragraph 63, Shoghi Effendi gives an outline of *The Advent of Divine Justice* up to this point and briefly previews future tasks emphasized in the rest of the book. So far, Shoghi Effendi has addressed the following issues:

a)   The opportunities and responsibilities that face the American Bahá'í community emerged as a result of the persecution of the Faith of Bahá'u'lláh.
b)   The characteristics of the mission that the American Bahá'í community should embark on in the future.
c)   A warning to ensure a better understanding of and to discharge the tasks associated with the mission.
d)   The moral standards that are essential for the success of those tasks.

The remainder of *The Advent of Divine Justice* concentrates on the material aspects of the community's immediate task. The completion of this task would not only unfold the subsequent stages of the Divine plan revealed by 'Abdu'l-Bahá, but would provide opportunities for the American Bahá'í community to acquire those capacities that will enable them to discharge the mission they are destined to complete.

In paragraph 64, Shoghi Effendi describes the progress made on one of the major goals of the first Seven Year Plan of the American Bahá'í community—the completion of the exterior of the Bahá'í House of Worship in Wilmette, Illinois (see section 7.4).

17.4   Duty and significance of teaching

In paragraph 65, Shoghi Effendi addresses the second major objective of the first Seven-Year Plan of the North American Bahá'í community: extension of the teaching activities in both the Northern and Southern Continents of America. In highlighting the significance of the expansion of the Faith, Shoghi Effendi notes that the Temple is no more than an instrument for the more effective propagation of the Cause and should be viewed in the same light as the Administrative Order of the Cause. The American believers should direct their careful and sustained attention to the teaching requirements of the Seven-Year Plan.

The importance of teaching as a duty for every individual is emphasized in paragraph 66. Shoghi Effendi cites statements from Bahá'u'lláh (quotes 66:A and 66:B) to demonstrate that teaching of the Cause is an obligation prescribed on everyone. The Universal House of Justice refers to teaching as "[t]he corner-stone of the foundation of all Bahá'í activity".[1]

Teaching the Faith is sharing the heat generated in us by the fire of the love of God. In a Tablet, Bahá'u'lláh exhorts His followers:

> *O Friends! You must all be so ablaze in this day with the fire of the love of God that the heat thereof may be manifest in all your veins, your limbs and members of your body, and the peoples of the world may be ignited by this heat and turn to the horizon of the Beloved.*[2]

In His Will and Testament, 'Abdu'l-Bahá identifies "*... the guidance of the nations and peoples of the world*" as "*the most important of all things*" and gives teaching the Cause "*... utmost importance for it is the head corner-stone of the foundation itself.*"[3] In a Tablet, 'Abdu'l-Bahá warns that the receipt of divine confirmation is dependent on active teaching of the Cause:

> *It is known and clear that today the unseen divine assistance encompasseth those who deliver the Message. And if the work of delivering the Message be neglected, the assistance shall be entirely cut off, for it is impossible that the friends of God could receive assistance unless they be engaged in delivering the Message.*[4]

In another Tablet, 'Abdu'l-Bahá emphasizes the connection between teaching and divine confirmations:

> *When the friends do not endeavour to spread the message, they fail to remember God befittingly, and will not witness the tokens of assistance and confirmation from the Abhá Kingdom nor comprehend the divine mysteries. However, when the tongue of the teacher is engaged in teaching, he will naturally himself be stimulated, will become a magnet attracting the divine aid and bounty of the Kingdom, and will be like unto the bird at the hour of dawn, which itself becometh exhilarated by its own singing, its warbling and its melody.*[5]

Reliance of divine confirmations on teaching is reiterated in another Tablet of 'Abdu'l-Bahá:

> *The teaching work should under all conditions be actively pursued by the*

---

[1]   The Universal House of Justice, *Messages from the Universal House of Justice 1963–1986*, p. 357.

[2]   Bahá'u'lláh, cited in *The Compilation of Compilations*, Vol. II, p. 293.

[3]   'Abdu'l-Bahá, *The Will and Testament of 'Abdu'l-Bahá*, p. 10.

[4]   'Abdu'l-Bahá, *Tablets of Abdul Abbas*, Vol. 3, pp. 390–391.

[5]   'Abdu'l-Bahá, *Selections from the Writings of 'Abdu'l-Bahá*, pp. 267–268.

believers because divine confirmations are dependent upon it. Should a Bahá'í refrain from being fully, vigorously and wholeheartedly involved in the teaching work he will undoubtedly be deprived of the blessings of the Abhá Kingdom. Even so, this activity should be tempered with wisdom—not that wisdom which requireth one to be silent and forgetful of such an obligation, but rather that which requireth one to display divine tolerance, love, kindness, patience, a goodly character, and holy deeds. In brief, encourage the friends individually to teach the Cause of God and draw their attention to this meaning of wisdom mentioned in the Writings, which is itself the essence of teaching the Faith—but all this to be done with the greatest tolerance, so that heavenly assistance and divine confirmation may aid the friends.[1]

17.5   Transforming power of Bahá'u'lláh

In paragraph 67, Shoghi Effendi explains that if a member of the community reaches a high rank, then that brings with it the responsibility to teach and propagate the Faith. Such a high rank may on some occasions provide better means and opportunities to spread knowledge of the Faith and to attract others to its institutions. However, a higher rank does not always exert a greater influence on the hearts and minds of people who are attracted to the Faith. The early history of the Faith contains stories of many unschooled and inexperienced believers who have won great victories for the Cause.

In paragraph 68, Shoghi Effendi gives the example of Peter, the unlettered disciple of Christ, who under the transforming power of the Son of Man (Jesus Christ) became the foremost disciple of Christ, His successor and the founder of His church. Shoghi Effendi then exclaims that, if that was the power of the Son, then how much more can Bahá'u'lláh, the Father, empower His insignificant followers to execute His purpose.

There are a number of stories about how Mírzá Abu'l-Faḍl-i-Gulpáygání (1844–1914) came across the Bahá'í Faith through his encounter with unlettered Bahá'ís. Abu'l-Faḍl became a foremost Bahá'í scholar who played a major role in spreading the Faith in Egypt and the United States. He was one of the few Apostles of Bahá'u'lláh who never met Him.

At the beginning of 1876, during his time in Ṭihrán, Abu'l-Faḍl met an uneducated cloth-seller named Áqá 'Abdu'l-Karím, and had discussions with him about religious issues. As Abu'l-Faḍl got to know Áqá 'Abdu'l-Karím over time, he was impressed by the qualities and insight of this unassuming man. Abu'l-Faḍl eventually learnt that Áqá 'Abdu'l-Karím was a Bahá'í and that his views primarily reflected the Bahá'í teachings. This made Abu'l-Faḍl curious about the Faith.

In another story, Mírzá Abu'l-Faḍl meets a Bahá'í blacksmith who asks him some questions. This was before Abu'l-Faḍl had recognized Bahá'u'lláh:

It so happened that on the way out one of the donkeys lost a shoe, so the party called at the nearest blacksmith for help. Noticing the long beard and large turban of Mírzá Abu'l-Faḍl—indications of his vast knowledge—the blacksmith Ustád Ḥusayn-i-Na'l-Band (shoeing smith), who was illiterate, was

---

[1]   'Abdu'l-Bahá, *Selections from the Writings of 'Abdu'l-*Bahá, p. 268.

tempted to enter into conversation with the learned man. He said to Mírzá that since he had honoured him with his presence, it would be a great privilege for him if he could be allowed to ask a question which had perplexed his mind for some time. When permission was granted he said, 'Is it true that in the Traditions of Shí'í Islám it is stated that each drop of rain is accompanied by an angel from heaven? And that this angel brings down the rain to the ground?' 'This is true,' Mírzá Abu'l-Faḍl responded. A pause, the blacksmith begged to be allowed to ask another question to which Mírzá gave his assent. 'Is it true', the blacksmith asked, 'that if there is a dog in a house no angel will ever visit that house?' Before thinking of the connection between the two questions, Mírzá Abu'l-Faḍl responded in the affirmative. 'In that case', commented the blacksmith, 'no rain should ever fall in a house where a dog is kept.' Mírzá Abu'l-Faḍl, the noted learned man of Islám, was now confounded by an illiterate blacksmith. His rage knew no bounds, and his companions noticed that he was filled with shame. They whispered to him, 'This blacksmith is a Bahá'í!'[1]

In paragraph 69, Shoghi Effendi cites another statement from 'Abdu'l-Bahá (quote 69:A) that emphasizes the transforming power of Bahá'u'lláh.

17.6   Revolutionizing *Force*

In paragraph 70, Shoghi Effendi explains the nature and impact of the "God-born Force" released through the revelations of the Báb and Bahá'u'lláh. He describes the characteristics of the Force as:

- "Irresistible in its sweeping power,
- Incalculable in its potency,
- Unpredictable in its course,
- Mysterious in its workings, and
- Awe-inspiring in its manifestation."[2]

The Force acts as a two-edged sword: on one hand the Force is breaking apart the ties that have been holding the fabric of human civilization together and, on the other hand, it loosens the bonds that have been restraining the advancement of the Faith of Bahá'u'lláh. Through these two processes, the Force is creating unprecedented opportunities for the American Bahá'ís to arise and to exploit them for the advancement of the Cause.

There are a number of references in the Writings of Bahá'u'lláh and 'Abdu'l-Bahá to the nature and impact of the Force mentioned by Shoghi Effendi in this paragraph. 'Abdu'l-Bahá explains that this Force is released with the coming of any new revelation. The Force operates within the world of creation to realize the purpose of that revelation. 'Abdu'l-Bahá highlights the dynamics of its manifestation and impact:

... it must of necessity express itself through the vehicle of a human temple, and the objective expression of this force manifests itself in thoughts of different

---

[1]   A. Taherzadeh, *The Revelation of Bahá'u'lláh*, Vol. 3, George Ronald, 1984, p. 93.

[2]   Bullets added for emphasis.

grades and degrees according to the capacity of the people.[1]

In one of His prayers Bahá'u'lláh states that the revolutionizing Force released in every revelation is embedded in the Word of God and has such a power that it transforms the realities of the entire world of being:

I testify that no sooner had the First Word proceeded, through the potency of Thy will and purpose, out of His mouth, and the First Call gone forth from His lips than the whole creation was revolutionized, and all that are in the heavens and all that are on earth were stirred to the depths. Through that Word the realities of all created things were shaken, were divided, separated, scattered, combined and reunited, disclosing, in both the contingent world and the heavenly kingdom, entities of a new creation, and revealing, in the unseen realms, the signs and tokens of Thy unity and oneness.[2]

In one of his messages, Shoghi Effendi cites an utterance by Bahá'u'lláh on the forces latent in His Revelation:

Through the movement of Our Pen of glory We have, at the bidding of the omnipotent Ordainer, breathed a new life into every human frame and instilled into every word a fresh potency. All created things proclaim the evidences of this world-wide regeneration. This is, the most great, the most joyful tidings imparted by the pen of this wronged One to mankind.[3]

Shoghi Effendi describes the impact of the Force in creating and developing the Bahá'í institutions:

The onrushing forces so miraculously released through the agency of two independent and swiftly successive Manifestations are now under our very eyes and through the care of the chosen stewards of a far-flung Faith being gradually mustered and disciplined. They are slowly crystallizing into institutions that will come to be regarded as the hall-mark and glory of the age we are called upon to establish and by our deeds immortalize.[4]

According to the Báb, as asserted by Shoghi Effendi in paragraph 70, this Force vibrates within the innermost being of all created things. Bahá'u'lláh has stated that the equilibrium of the world is upset and its ordered life is revolutionized by the vibrating influence of this Force.

In paragraph 71–73, Shoghi Effendi describes the impact of the Force released through the Revelations of the Báb and Bahá'u'lláh and what should be the reaction and response of the American believers. In its initial stage, the Force is upsetting the equilibrium of a world that is:

- Dimmed by the steadily dying-out of the light of religion.
- Afflicted with the explosive forces of a blind and triumphant nationalism.

---

[1]   'Abdu'l-Bahá, *Divine Philosophy*, p. 8.
[2]   Bahá'u'lláh, *Prayers and Meditation of Bahá'u'lláh*, p. 107.
[3]   Bahá'u'lláh, cited in *World Order of Bahá'u'lláh*, p. 107.
[4]   Shoghi Effendi, *The World Order of Bahá'u'lláh*, p. 98.

- Scorched with the false theories and doctrines that threaten to replace the worship of God.
- Weakened by a rampant and brutal materialism.
- Disintegrating through the corrosive influence of moral and spiritual decadence.
- Entangled in the coils of economic anarchy and strife.

Such conditions will only deepen the faith of the believers of Bahá'u'lláh, as they are aware of the prophecies and promises of Bahá'u'lláh. This is the time that the American believers should proclaim the Faith through the channels of the Administrative Order, and to increase their capacity and readiness to rescue a generation that has rebelled against its God and ignored His warnings.

17.7   Activities

17.7.1   Short answer questions

1.   Briefly describe the issues covered by the Guardian in the first part of the book.

_____

_____

_____

_____

2.   What are the topics that Shoghi Effendi will address in the remainder of the book?

_____

_____

_____

_____

3.   What is your understanding of the first two sentences of paragraph 66?

_____

_____

_____

_____

4.   What are the implications of teaching being a duty for everyone?

_____

_____

_____

_____

5.   What is the connection between teaching and divine confirmations?

_____

_____

_____

_____

6.   What is your understanding of the first three sentences of paragraph 67?

_____

_____

_____

7. What is your understanding of quote 68:A?

8. What is your understanding of the last sentence of paragraph 68:

9. Describe the key points of quote 69:A.

10. What are the characteristics of the God-born Force described by Shoghi Effendi in paragraph 70?

11. What is the impact of the Force on the world as described by the Báb, as cited in paragraph 70?

12. Why does Shoghi Effendi refer to this force as a two-edged sword?

13. What is your understanding of quote 70:A?

_____

_____

_____

_____

14. What are the sweeping changes the force is producing in the world in the initial stage of its operation?

_____

_____

_____

_____

15. Describe your understanding of how the force released through the revelations of the Báb and Bahá'u'lláh has changed the realities of all things.

_____

_____

_____

_____

16. What is the connection between the force and Bahá'í institutions?

_____

_____

_____

_____

17. What is your understanding of the last two sentences of paragraph 73?

_____

_____

_____

_____

17.7.2 Mini-project

As explained in section 17.5, many unschooled and inexperienced believers have won great victories for the Cause. As an example, the encounter of Mírzá Abu'l-Faḍl-i-Gulpáygání with the blacksmith Ustád Ḥusayn-i-Na'l-Band was described. Conduct some research to identify two more stories of how unschooled an unlettered Bahá'ís have been successful in advancing the Cause.

18.
Effective conduct of teaching

18.1   Introduction

This chapter covers paragraphs 74–80, in which the Guardian provides principles for conducting the teaching campaigns that had started in North America as part of the first Seven Year Plan. The guidance provided by Shoghi Effendi describes both the preparation for teaching and effective execution of teaching plans.

In this chapter, you need to reflect on and understand the following key points:

a)   A teaching campaign should be planned, have clear objectives and be carried out systematically.

b)   Those preparing for a teaching campaign, should initially study the history, teachings and administration of the Faith and be aware of all events associated with it.

c)   They should learn the language and culture of the region where they are planning to pioneer and teach.

d)   Everyone should use his/her initiative to find the most efficient approach for the proposed teaching plan. They should not wait for instructions from the Administrative Order.

e)   The believer who wishes to pioneer should not be deterred by lack of experience or resources, the opposition of family and friends, or by the volatility of world events.

f)   When a teacher places his whole trust in God, and is adorned with virtues, kindled with the love of Bahá'u'lláh, and detached, his words will influence others.

g)   A teacher should be as "unrestrained as the wind".

h)   A teacher of the Faith should "… consider the degree of his hearer's receptivity, and decide for himself the suitability of either the direct or indirect method of teaching."

i)   The obligation to teach should be the all-pervading concern of the lives of those who participate in teaching campaigns.

18.2   Paragraphs under study

74   The teaching campaign, inaugurated throughout the states of the North American Republic and the Dominion of Canada, acquires, therefore, an importance, and is invested with an urgency, that cannot be overestimated. Launched on its course through the creative energies released by the Will of 'Abdu'l-Bahá, and sweeping across the Western Hemisphere through the propelling force which it is generating, it must, I feel, be carried out in conformity with certain principles, designed to insure its efficient conduct, and to hasten the attainment of its objective.

75   Those who participate in such a campaign, whether in an organizing capacity, or as workers to whose care the execution of the task itself has been committed, must, as an essential preliminary to the discharge of their duties, thoroughly familiarize themselves with the various aspects of the history and teachings of their Faith. In their efforts to achieve this purpose they must study for themselves, conscientiously and painstakingly, the literature of their Faith, delve into its teachings, assimilate its laws and principles, ponder its admonitions, tenets and purposes, commit to memory certain of its exhortations and prayers, master the essentials of its administration, and keep abreast of its current affairs and latest developments. They must strive to obtain, from sources that are authoritative and unbiased, a sound knowledge of the history and tenets of Islám—the source and background of their Faith—and approach reverently and with a mind purged from preconceived ideas the study of the Qur'án which, apart from the sacred Scriptures of the Bábí and Bahá'í Revelations, constitutes the only Book which can be regarded as an absolutely authenticated Repository of the Word of God. They must devote special attention to the investigation of those institutions and circumstances that are directly connected with the origin and birth of their Faith, with the station claimed by its Forerunner, and with the laws revealed by its Author.

76   Having acquired, in their essentials, these prerequisites of success in the teaching field, they must, whenever they contemplate undertaking any specific mission in the countries of Latin America, endeavour, whenever feasible, to acquire a certain proficiency in the languages spoken by the inhabitants of those countries, and a knowledge of their customs, habits, and outlook. *"The teachers going to those parts,"* 'Abdu'l-Bahá, referring in one of the Tablets of the Divine Plan to the Central American Republics, has written, *"must also be familiar with the Spanish language."*[A] *"A party speaking their languages ...,"* He, in another Tablet, has written, *"must turn their faces to and travel through the three great Island groups of the Pacific Ocean."*[B] *"The teachers traveling in different directions,"* He further states, *"must know the language of the country in which they will enter. For example, a person being proficient in the Japanese language may travel to Japan, or a person knowing the Chinese language may hasten to China, and so forth."*[C]

77   No participator in this inter-American campaign of teaching must feel that the initiative for any particular activity connected with this work must rest solely with those agencies, whether Assemblies or committees, whose special concern is to promote and facilitate the attainment of this vital objective of the Seven Year Plan. It is the bounden duty of every American believer, as the faithful trustee of 'Abdu'l-Bahá's Divine Plan, to initiate, promote, and consolidate, within the limits fixed by the administrative principles of the Faith, any activity he or she deems fit to undertake for the furtherance of the Plan. Neither the threatening world situation, nor any consideration of lack of material resources, of mental equipment, of knowledge, or of experience—desirable as they are—should deter any prospective pioneer teacher from arising independently, and from setting in motion the forces which, 'Abdu'l-Bahá has repeatedly assured us, will, once released, attract even as a magnet the promised and infallible aid of Bahá'u'lláh. Let him not wait for any directions, or expect any special encouragement, from the elected representatives of his community, nor be deterred by any obstacles which his relatives, or fellow-citizens may be inclined to place in his path, nor mind the censure of his critics or enemies. *"Be unrestrained as the wind,"* is Bahá'u'lláh's counsel to every would-be teacher of His Cause, *"while carrying the Message of Him Who hath caused the dawn of Divine Guidance to break. Consider how the wind, faithful to that which God hath ordained, bloweth upon all regions of the earth, be they inhabited or desolate. Neither the sight of desolation, nor the evidences of prosperity, can either pain or please it. It bloweth in every direction, as bidden by its Creator."*[A] *"And when he determineth to leave his home, for the sake of the Cause of his Lord,"* Bahá'u'lláh, in another passage, referring to such a teacher, has revealed, *"let him put his whole trust in God, as the best provision for his journey, and array himself with the robe of virtue .... If he be kindled with the fire of His love, if he forgoeth all created things, the words he uttereth shall set on fire them that hear him."*[B]

78   Having on his own initiative, and undaunted by any hindrances with which either friend or foe may, unwittingly or deliberately, obstruct his path, resolved to arise and respond to the call of teaching, let him carefully consider every avenue of approach which he might utilize in his personal attempts to capture the attention, maintain the interest, and deepen the faith, of those whom he seeks to bring into the fold of his Faith. Let him survey the possibilities which the particular circumstances in which he lives offer him, evaluate their advantages, and proceed intelligently and systematically to utilize them for the achievement of the object he has in mind. Let him also attempt to devise such methods as association with clubs, exhibitions, and societies, lectures on subjects akin to the teachings and ideals of his Cause such as temperance, morality, social welfare, religious and racial tolerance, economic cooperation, Islám, and Comparative Religion, or participation in social, cultural, humanitarian, charitable, and educational organizations and enterprises which, while safeguarding the integrity of his Faith, will open up to him a multitude of ways and means whereby he can enlist successively the sympathy, the support, and ultimately the allegiance of those with whom he comes in contact. Let him, while such contacts are

being made, bear in mind the claims which his Faith is constantly making upon him to preserve its dignity, and station, to safeguard the integrity of its laws and principles, to demonstrate its comprehensiveness and universality, and to defend fearlessly its manifold and vital interests. Let him consider the degree of his hearer's receptivity, and decide for himself the suitability of either the direct or indirect method of teaching, whereby he can impress upon the seeker the vital importance of the Divine Message, and persuade him to throw in his lot with those who have already embraced it. Let him remember the example set by 'Abdu'l-Bahá, and His constant admonition to shower such kindness upon the seeker, and exemplify to such a degree the spirit of the teachings he hopes to instil into him, that the recipient will be spontaneously impelled to identify himself with the Cause embodying such teachings. Let him refrain, at the outset, from insisting on such laws and observances as might impose too severe a strain on the seeker's newly awakened faith, and endeavour to nurse him, patiently, tactfully, and yet determinedly, into full maturity, and aid him to proclaim his unqualified acceptance of whatever has been ordained by Bahá'u'lláh. Let him, as soon as that stage has been attained, introduce him to the body of his fellow-believers, and seek, through constant fellowship and active participation in the local activities of his community, to enable him to contribute his share to the enrichment of its life, the furtherance of its tasks, the consolidations of its interests, and the coordination of its activities with those of its sister communities. Let him not be content until he has infused into his spiritual child so deep a longing as to impel him to arise independently, in his turn, and devote his energies to the quickening of other souls, and the upholding of the laws and principles laid down by his newly adopted Faith.

79 Let every participator in the continent-wide campaign initiated by the American believers, and particularly those engaged in pioneer work in virgin territories, bear in mind the necessity of keeping in close and constant touch with those responsible agencies designed to direct, coordinate, and facilitate the teaching activities of the entire community. Whether it be the body of their elected national representatives, or its chief auxiliary institution, the National Teaching Committee, or its subsidiary organs, the regional teaching committees, or the local Spiritual Assemblies and their respective teaching committees, they who labour for the spread of the Cause of Bahá'u'lláh should, through constant interchange of ideas, through letters, circulars, reports, bulletins and other means of communication with these established instruments designed for the propagation of the Faith, insure the smooth and speedy functioning of the teaching machinery of their Administrative Order. Confusion, delay, duplication of efforts, dissipation of energy will, thereby, be completely avoided, and the mighty flood of the grace of Bahá'u'lláh, flowing abundantly and without the least obstruction through these essential channels will so inundate the hearts and souls of men as to enable them to bring forth the harvest repeatedly predicted by 'Abdu'l-Bahá.

80 Upon every participator in this concerted effort, unprecedented in the annals of the American Bahá'í community, rests the spiritual obligation to make of the mandate of teaching, so vitally binding upon all, the all-pervading concern of his life. In his daily activities and contacts, in all his

journeys, whether for business or otherwise, on his holidays and outings, and on any mission he may be called upon to undertake, every bearer of the Message of Bahá'u'lláh should consider it not only an obligation but a privilege to scatter far and wide the seeds of His Faith, and to rest content in the abiding knowledge that whatever be the immediate response to that Message, and however inadequate the vehicle that conveyed it, the power of its Author will, as He sees fit, enable those seeds to germinate, and in circumstances which no one can foresee enrich the harvest which the labour of His followers will gather. If he be member of any Spiritual Assembly let him encourage his Assembly to consecrate a certain part of its time, at each of its sessions, to the earnest and prayerful consideration of such ways and means as may foster the campaign of teaching, or may furnish whatever resources are available for its progress, extension, and consolidation. If he attends his summer school—and everyone without exception is urged to take advantage of attending it—let him consider such an occasion as a welcome and precious opportunity so to enrich, through lectures, study, and discussion, his knowledge of the fundamentals of his Faith as to be able to transmit, with greater confidence and effectiveness, the Message that has been entrusted to his care. Let him, moreover, seek, whenever feasible, through intercommunity visits to stimulate the zeal for teaching, and to demonstrate to outsiders the zest and alertness of the promoters of his Cause and the organic unity of its institutions.

18.3   Preparation for teaching

In paragraphs 74–76, Shoghi Effendi highlights some of the important preparations that teachers of the Faith should make.

18.3.1   Deepening

Shoghi Effendi asserts in paragraph 75 that, at the essential preliminary stage in preparation for teaching, the friends should familiarize themselves with the history and teachings of the Faith. Teaching is a duty for everyone, not just for a special group or category of friends. In a letter dated 21 September 1957 written on his behalf to the National Spiritual Assembly of the United States, he clarifies:

> It is not enough for the friends to make the excuse that their best teachers and their exemplary believers have arisen and answered the call to pioneer. A 'best teacher' and an 'exemplary believer' is ultimately neither more nor less than an ordinary Bahá'í who has consecrated himself to the work of the Faith, deepened his knowledge and understanding of its Teachings, placed his confidence in Bahá'u'lláh, and arisen to serve Him to the best of his ability. This door is one which we are assured will open before the face of every follower of the Faith who knocks hard enough, so to speak. When the will and the desire are strong enough, the means will be found and the way opened either to do more work locally, to go to a new goal town within the United States, or to enter the foreign pioneer field.[1]

---

[1]   A letter written on behalf of Shoghi Effendi, cited in *The Compilation of Compilations*, Vol. II, p. 27.

In paragraph 75, Shoghi Effendi identifies specific areas of deepening that should be considered during the preparation process. Those who participate in teaching campaigns:

- "... must study for themselves, conscientiously and painstakingly, the literature of their Faith,
- delve into its teachings,
- assimilate its laws and principles,
- ponder its admonitions, tenets and purposes,
- commit to memory certain of its exhortations and prayers,
- master the essentials of its administration, and
- keep abreast of its current affairs and latest developments."[1]

The process of deepening continues during active teaching as "... the friends must themselves be taught and deepened in the spirit of the Faith, which brings love and unity."[2]

18.3.2 Study of Islám and the Qur'án

Shoghi Effendi emphasizes the need to study Islám and the Qur'án, particularly from authoritative and unbiased sources, as "... Western historians have for many centuries distorted the facts to suit their religious and ancestral prejudices ..."[3], as highlighted by Shoghi Effendi in a letter written on his behalf to an individual believer, dated 27 April 1936.

In another letter written on behalf of the Guardian to an individual believer, dated 2 December 1935, he urges

> ... the friends to make a thorough study of the Qur'án as the knowledge of this Sacred Scripture is absolutely indispensable for every believer who wishes to adequately understand and intelligently read the Writings of Bahá'u'lláh.[4]

Shoghi Effendi refers to the Qur'án as "the only Book which can be regarded as an absolutely authenticated Repository of the Word of God." The Qur'án was gradually revealed to Muḥammad over the 23 years of His Ministry in Mecca and Medina. It started in AD 610 when He was 40 years old and continued until His ascension in Medina in AD 632. According to a ḥadíth, Muḥammad memorized the verses of *the Qur'án* and recited them to the learned among His followers.

The Qur'án consists of 114 Súrahs (chapters), which are divided into numbered verses. Muḥammad was given guidance as to the order of the Súrahs so that, in the traditional order, the Meccan Súrahs are interspersed with the Medinan Súrahs rather than being in the order in which they were revealed.

---

[1] Bullets added for emphasis.
[2] A letter written on behalf of Shoghi Effendi dated 17 July 1951, cited in *The Compilation of Compilations*, Vol. II, p. 317.
[3] A letter written on behalf of Shoghi Effendi, cited in *Lights of Guidance*, p. 496.
[4] A letter written on behalf of Shoghi Effendi, cited in *Lights of Guidance*, p. 561.

Verses 96:1–5 of the Qur'án were revealed to Muḥammad when he was approaching the age of 40.[1] He used to visit a cave on Mt. Ḥirá' to meditate. One day an angel called Gabriel appeared to Muḥammad and told Him: *"Read!"* Muḥammad responded: *"I cannot read!"* The angel cried again, *"Read!"* On the third call, Muḥammad asked: *"What shall I read?"* The angel said: *"Read, in the name of thy Lord who created; Created man from clots of blood …. Thy Lord is the most Beneficent, Who hath taught the use of the pen; Hath taught man that which he knoweth not."*

The Revelation of Muḥammad, including its laws and teachings, is contained in the Qur'án. It also includes stories similar to the ones found in the Christian and the Jewish Scriptures. For this reason, Muḥammad has been accused of copying the Qur'án from the Bible and the Gospels.[2] However, this accusation is not justified. The only language that Muḥammad knew was Arabic. The first formal translations of the Old and New Testaments into Arabic were not made until centuries after Muḥammad's death.[3]

18.3.3 Learning the language

In paragraph 76, the Guardian highlights the importance of acquiring some proficiency in the languages spoken in the countries of Latin America, if the American friends decide to pioneer to those countries to teach the Faith. He then cites three statements from the Tablets of the Divine Plan in which 'Abdu'l-Bahá specifically mentions that pioneers should know the language of the country they enter.

18.4 Conduct of teaching campaigns

In paragraphs 77–79, the Guardian provides guidance on how an effective teaching campaign can be conducted. In this section we briefly study some of the salient points in these paragraphs.

18.4.1 Unrestrained as the wind

In paragraph 77, Shoghi Effendi explains that the agencies of the Faith are not solely responsible for facilitating or promoting teaching. Every American Bahá'í has the duty to "to initiate, promote, and consolidate" any activity envisaged to expand the Faith, within the constraints set by the Bahá'í institutions. They should not be deterred by any obstacle since 'Abdu'l-Bahá promised they will receive the infallible aid of Bahá'u'lláh.

Shoghi Effendi then cites some guidance from Bahá'u'lláh for teachers of the Cause. In the first quotation, Bahá'u'lláh counsels teachers of His Faith to be like the wind and take His message in any direction destined by God, and not be diverted by misery or prosperity (quote 77:A). In the next statement, Bahá'u'lláh urges the teacher to place his trust in Him, adorn himself with virtues and be kindled with the fire of His love (quote 77:B).

---

[1]   Muḥammad was aged 39 (in Gregorian years).
[2]   M. Gail, *Six Lessons on Islám*, p. 17.
[3]   R. V. C. Bodley, *The Messenger*, p. 86.

18.4.2   *Personal initiative*

In paragraph 78, Shoghi Effendi discusses the importance of personal initiative and the resolve of teachers in effectively capturing "... the attention, maintain the interest, and deepen the faith, of those whom he seeks to bring into the fold of his Faith." Teachers should use their personal initiative to explore all possibilities and opportunities, identify their advantages, and systematically and intelligently exploit them to attain the goals set to advance the Cause.

Shoghi Effendi then suggests some tangible and practical suggestions that can be used by the teacher:

a)   The teacher should examine every option and find the most appropriate means of gaining the attention and interest of the people he meets.

b)   The teacher should contact like-minded organizations and offer to present lectures on topics that are likely to be of interest to them.

c)   The teacher should maintain the dignity and station of the Faith, safeguard the integrity of its laws and principles, demonstrate its universality and defend its interests.

d)   The teacher should wisely decide on the best way to approach every individual seeker.

e)   The teacher should introduce a seeker to the community and get him involved in local activities.

f)   The task of teaching a soul is not complete until the latter arises independently to teach other people, and follows the laws and teachings of the Faith.

18.4.3   *Direct or indirect teaching*

Shoghi Effendi counsels teachers of the Faith to "... consider the degree of his hearer's receptivity, and decide for himself the suitability of either the direct or indirect method of teaching." Shoghi Effendi provides some clarification in other messages on what he means by direct and indirect teaching, as well as deficiencies and advantages associated with each approach.

In a letter written on behalf of Shoghi Effendi to an individual believer, dated 28 May 1937, he explains that indirect teaching

"... essentially consists in presenting some of the humanitarian or social teachings of the Cause which are shared by those whom we are teaching, as a means of attracting them to those aspects of the Faith which are more challenging in character, and are specifically and solely Bahá'í. The teaching of Esperanto, for instance, has been a very useful way of presenting the Cause indirectly to many people. It has opened many doors of contact for the believers, and has lately proved to be of tremendous help in introducing the Teachings into important social and intellectual circles."[1]

Direct teaching, on the other hand, is the process of sharing with people the life and revelation of Bahá'u'lláh as the latest Manifestation of God, the Promise of all ages and the latest stage in the unfoldment of the eternal covenant. Social

---

[1]   Written on behalf of Shoghi Effendi, *Lights of Guidance*, p. 598.

teachings might be mentioned during direct teaching but they are described as intrinsic elements of the revelation of Bahá'u'lláh that can be used for indirect teaching or learnt after acceptance of the Faith.

Shoghi Effendi believed that the time was too short for indirect teaching. In response to an individual believer, he states:

> The time is too short to spend years preparing yourself to teach by the indirect approach. The world is ready for the direct Message, and it would be much better to equip yourself to do direct Bahá'í teaching.[1]

In another letter written on his behalf to Mrs Orpha Daugherty of Honolulu dated 24 April 1949, he explains:

> He approves of your desire to teach the principles of the Faith through radio. But he urges you to do all you can to always, however small the reference you are able to make to it may be, clearly identify or associate what you are giving out with Baha'u'llah. The time is too short now for us Baha'is to be able to first educate humanity and then tell it that the Source is this new World Faith. For their own spiritual protection people must hear of the name Baha'i—then, if they turn blindly away, they cannot excuse themselves by saying they never even knew it existed! For dark days seem still ahead of the world, and outside of this Divine Refuge the people will not, we firmly believe, find inner conviction, peace and security. So they have a right to at least hear of the Cause as such.[2]

18.4.4 *Communications with agencies*

In paragraph 79, Shoghi Effendi urges those who are involved in teaching campaigns initiated by the American Bahá'ís or have pioneered to virgin territories to maintain close and constant communication with the agencies responsible for the teaching activities. The teachers and pioneers should use any available communication channels with those agencies to ensure that the teaching machinery of the Faith is working effectively and efficiently.

18.5   Mandate of teaching

In paragraph 80, Shoghi Effendi asks all those participating in the Seven Year Plan, to make on every available occasion the mandate of teaching the all-pervading concern of their lives:

- Daily activities and contacts.
- Journeys, whether for business or otherwise.
- Holidays and outings.
- Every mission they may be called upon to undertake.

They should not be concerned about their inadequacy to deliver the message or the response they receive when teaching the Faith. Bahá'u'lláh Himself will germinate the seeds they sow.

---

[1] Shoghi Effendi, *Japan Will Turn Ablaze*, p. 102.
[2] Shoghi Effendi, cited in *The Compilation of Compilations*, Vol. II, p. 283.

Shoghi Effendi identifies opportunities that the teachers of the Faith should seize in order to become more competent teachers and to encourage others:

- If they are members of a Spiritual Assembly, they should encourage their Assembly members.
- If they attend summer schools, they should deepen their knowledge of the fundamentals of the Faith to develop better confidence in teaching.
- Make inter-community visits to stimulate a zeal for teaching.

Such diverse settings for teaching the Faith require different methods and styles of teaching, which should be determined through personal initiative and diligence.

18.6 Activities

18.6.1 Short answer questions

1. Answer the following questions based on the first two sentences of paragraph 75:

    a) How does deepening assist with participating in teaching campaigns?

    _____

    _____

    _____

    _____

    b) Identify the specific areas of deepening mentioned in the above statement?

    _____

    _____

    _____

    _____

2. Why does Shoghi Effendi mention in paragraph 75 that a sound knowledge of the history and tenets of Islám should be obtained from unbiased sources?

    _____

    _____

    _____

    _____

3. What is your understanding of the last sentence of paragraph 75?

    _____

    _____

    _____

    _____

4. Answer the following questions using the second sentence of paragraph 77:

    a) What is your understanding of this statement?

    _____

    _____

    _____

    _____

b) What is meant by "the limits fixed by the administrative principles of the Faith"?

_____

_____

_____

_____

5. Explain your understanding of quote 77:A.

_____

_____

_____

_____

6. Consider quote 77:B.

a) What are the two major key points in this quote?

_____

_____

_____

_____

b) What is meant by forgetting all created things?

_____

_____

_____

_____

7. In paragraph 78, Shoghi Effendi provides a set of guidelines on how teaching can be more effective through personal initiative. Identify the key points.

_____

_____

_____

_____

_____

_____

_____

8. In paragraph 78, Shoghi Effendi explains how to look after the seekers of the Faith. Identify the key points of his counsels.

_____

_____

_____

_____

9. What is your understanding of the last sentence of paragraph 79?

_____

_____

_____

_____

10. What is the "mandate of teaching" as explained in paragraph 80?

_____

_____

_____

_____

18.6.2 Mini-project

Analyze the guidance provided by Shoghi Effendi on teaching in this chapter along with the framework defined by the Universal House of Justice in the consecutive Five Year Plans unfolded since 1996. Identify the coherence and differences between the two frameworks. Write up your finding as a paper for presentation at a Bahá'í conference.

19.
Winning virgin territories

19.1   Introduction

This chapter covers paragraphs 81–86, in which the Guardian explains how the American Bahá'í community should open the virgin territories in North, Central and South America to the Faith. He also emphasizes the importance of increasing the diversity of the American community, supporting groups formed in different parts of North America to assist them to achieve administrative maturity, and opening virgin territories in Latin America.

In this chapter, you should reflect on and understand the following key points:

a)   Shoghi Effendi stresses the importance of increasing the diversity of the American Bahá'í community by attracting other ethnic groups into the Faith.

b)   The first African American who accepted Bahá'u'lláh, as attested by Shoghi Effendi in *God Passes By*, was Robert Turner.

c)   An African American Bahá'í who played a major role in race relations was Louis Gregory, who joined the Bahá'í community in 1909.

d)   Since the 1940's, an increasing number of Native Americans have been attracted to the Bahá'í Faith.

e)   Shoghi Effendi emphasizes that the Bahá'í groups formed in various states of North American must be strengthened and supported to evolve into fully functioning Assemblies.

f)   At the end of the first Seven Year Plan, Shoghi Effendi announced that the structural basis of the Administrative Order of the Faith of Bahá'u'lláh was firmly established in every state of America and every Province of the Dominion of Canada.

g)   The second phase of the first Seven Year Plan was "... the awaking of the nations of Latin America to the Call of Bahá'u'lláh."

19.2 Paragraphs under study

81   Let anyone who feels the urge among the participators in this crusade, which embraces all the races, all the republics, classes and denominations of the entire Western Hemisphere, arise, and, circumstances permitting, direct in particular the attention, and win eventually the unqualified adherence, of the Negro, the Indian, the Eskimo, and Jewish races to his Faith. No more laudable and meritorious service can be rendered the Cause of God, at the present hour, than a successful effort to enhance the diversity of the members of the American Bahá'í community by swelling the ranks of the Faith through the enrolment of the members of these races. A blending of these highly differentiated elements of the human race, harmoniously interwoven into the fabric of an all-embracing Bahá'í fraternity, and assimilated through the dynamic processes of a divinely appointed Administrative Order, and contributing each its share to the enrichment and glory of Bahá'í community life, is surely an achievement the contemplation of which must warm and thrill every Bahá'í heart. *"Consider the flowers of a garden"*, 'Abdu'l-Bahá has written, *"though differing in kind, colour, form, and shape, yet, inasmuch as they are refreshed by the waters of one spring, revived by the breath of one wind, invigorated by the rays of one sun, this diversity increaseth their charm, and addeth unto their beauty. How unpleasing to the eye if all the flowers and plants, the leaves and blossoms, the fruits, the branches and the trees of that garden were all of the same shape and colour! Diversity of hues, form and shape, enricheth and adorneth the garden, and heighteneth the effect thereof. In like manner, when divers shades of thought, temperament and character, are brought together under the power and influence of one central agency, the beauty and glory of human perfection will be revealed and made manifest. Naught but the celestial potency of the Word of God, which ruleth and transcendeth the realities of all things, is capable of harmonizing the divergent thoughts, sentiments, ideas, and convictions of the children of men."*[A] *"I hope,"* is the wish expressed by 'Abdu'l-Bahá, *"that ye may cause that downtrodden race [Negro] to become glorious, and to be joined with the white race to serve the world of man with the utmost sincerity, faithfulness, love and purity."*[B] *"One of the important questions,"* He also has written, *"which affect the unity and the solidarity of mankind is the fellowship and equality of the white and coloured races."*[C] *"You must attach great importance,"* writes 'Abdu'l-Bahá in the Tablets of the Divine Plan, *"to the Indians, the original inhabitants of America. For these souls may be likened unto the ancient inhabitants of the Arabian Peninsula, who, prior to the Revelation of Muḥammad, were like savages. When the Muhammadan Light shone forth in their midst, they became so enkindled that they shed illumination upon the world. Likewise, should these Indians be educated and properly guided, there can be no doubt that through the Divine teachings they will become so enlightened that the whole earth will be illumined."*[D] *"If it is possible,"* 'Abdu'l-Bahá has also written, *"send ye teachers to other portions of Canada; likewise, dispatch ye teachers to Greenland and the home of the Eskimos."*[E] *"God willing,"* He further has written in those same Tablets, *"the call of the Kingdom may reach the ears of the Eskimos .... Should you display an effort, so that the fragrances of God may be diffused among the Eskimos, its*

effect will be very great and far-reaching."[F] *"Praise be to God,"* writes 'Abdu'l-Bahá, *"that whatsoever hath been announced in the Blessed Tablets unto the Israelites, and the things explicitly written in the letters of 'Abdu'l-Bahá, are all being fulfilled. Some have come to pass; others will be revealed in the future. The Ancient Beauty hath in His sacred Tablets explicitly written that the day of their abasement is over. His bounty will overshadow them, and this race will day by day progress, and be delivered from its age-long obscurity and degradation.*"[G]

82   Let those who are holding administrative positions in their capacity as members of either the National Spiritual Assembly, or of the national, the regional, or local teaching committees, continually bear in mind the vital and urgent necessity of insuring, within as short a time as possible, the formation, in the few remaining states of the North American Republic and the provinces of the Dominion of Canada, of groups, however small and rudimentary, and of providing every facility within their power to enable these newly formed nuclei to evolve, swiftly and along sound lines, into properly functioning, self-sufficient, and recognized Assemblies. To the laying of such foundations, the erection of such outposts—a work admittedly arduous, yet sorely needed and highly inspiring—the individual members of the American Bahá'í community must lend their unstinted, continual, and enthusiastic support. Wise as may be the measures which their elected representatives may devise, however practical and well conceived the plans they formulate, such measures and plans can never yield any satisfactory results unless a sufficient number of pioneers have determined to make the necessary sacrifices, and to volunteer to carry these projects into effect. To implant, once and for all, the banner of Bahá'u'lláh in the heart of these virgin territories, to erect the structural basis of His Administrative Order in their cities and villages, and to establish a firm and permanent anchorage for its institutions in the minds and hearts of their inhabitants, constitute, I firmly believe, the first and most significant step in the successive stages through which the teaching campaign, inaugurated under the Seven Year Plan, must pass. Whereas the external ornamentation of the Mashriqu'l-Adhkár, under this same Plan, has now entered the final phase in its development, the teaching campaign is still in its initial stages, and is far from having extended effectively its ramifications to either these virgin territories, or to those Republics that are situated in the South American continent. The effort required is prodigious, the conditions under which these preliminary establishments are to be made are often unattractive and unfavourable, the workers who are in a position to undertake such tasks limited, and the resources they can command meagre and inadequate. And yet, how often has the pen of Bahá'u'lláh assured us that *"should a man, all alone, arise in the name of Bahá, and put on the armour of His love, him will the Almighty cause to be victorious, though the forces of earth and heaven be arrayed against him.*"[A] Has He not written: *"By God, besides Whom is none other God! Should anyone arise for the triumph of our Cause, him will God render victorious though tens of thousands of enemies be leagued against him. And if his love for me wax stronger, God will establish his ascendancy over all the powers of earth and heaven.*"[B] *"Consider the work of former generations,"*

'Abdu'l-Bahá has written; *"During the lifetime of Jesus Christ the believing, firm souls were few and numbered, but the heavenly blessings descended so plentifully that in a number of years countless souls entered beneath the shadow of the Gospel. God has said in the Qur'án: 'One grain will bring forth seven sheaves, and every sheaf shall contain one hundred grains.' In other words, one grain will become seven hundred; and if God so wills He will double these also. It has often happened that one blessed soul has become the cause of the guidance of a nation. Now we must not consider our ability and capacity, nay rather we must fix our gaze upon the favours and bounties of God, in these days, Who has made of the drop a sea, and of the atom a sun."*[C] Let those who resolve to be the first to hoist the standard of such a Cause, under such conditions, and in such territories, nourish their souls with the sustaining power of these words, and, *"putting on the armour of His love,"* a love which must *"wax stronger"* as they persevere in their lonesome task, arise to adorn with the tale of their deeds the most brilliant pages ever written in their country's spiritual history.

83   *"Although,"* 'Abdu'l-Bahá, in the Tablets of the Divine Plan, has written, *"in most of the states and cities of the United States, praise be to God, His fragrances are diffused, and souls unnumbered are turning their faces and advancing toward the Kingdom of God, yet in some of the states the Standard of Unity is not yet upraised as it should be, nor are the mysteries of the Holy Books, such as the Bible, the Gospel, and the Qur'án, unravelled. Through the concerted efforts of all the friends the Standard of Unity must needs be unfurled in those states, and the Divine teachings promoted, so that these states may also receive their portion of the heavenly bestowals and a share of the Most Great Guidance."*[A] *"The future of the Dominion of Canada,"* He, in another Tablet of the Divine Plan, has asserted, *"is very great, and the events connected with it infinitely glorious. The eye of God's loving-kindness will be turned towards it, and it shall become the manifestation of the favours of the All-Glorious."*[B] *"Again I repeat,"* He, in that same Tablet reaffirms His previous statement, *"that the future of Canada, whether from a material or a spiritual standpoint, is very great."*[C]

84   No sooner is this initial step taken, involving as it does the formation of at least one nucleus in each of these virgin states and provinces in the North American continent, than the machinery for a tremendous intensification of Bahá'í concerted effort must be set in motion, the purpose of which should be the reinforcement of the noble exertions which only a few isolated believers are now making for the awakening of the nations of Latin America to the Call of Bahá'u'lláh. Not until this second phase of the teaching campaign, under the Seven Year Plan, has been entered can the campaign be regarded as fully launched, or the Plan itself as having attained the most decisive stage in its evolution. So powerful will be the effusions of Divine grace that will be poured forth upon a valiant community that has already in the administrative sphere erected, in all the glory of its exterior ornamentation, its chief Edifice, and in the teaching field raised aloft, in every state and province, in the North American continent the banner of its Faith—

so great will be these effusions that its members will find themselves overpowered by the evidences of their regenerative power.

85 The Inter-America Committee must, at such a stage, nay even before it is entered, rise to the level of its opportunities, and display a vigour, a consecration, and enterprise as will be commensurate with the responsibilities it has shouldered. It should not, for a moment, be forgotten that Central and Southern America embrace no less than twenty independent nations, constituting approximately one-third of the entire number of the world's sovereign states, and are destined to play an increasingly important part in the shaping of the world's future destiny. With the world contracting into a neighbourhood, and the fortunes of its races, nations and peoples becoming inextricably interwoven, the remoteness of these states of the Western Hemisphere is vanishing, and the latent possibilities in each of them are becoming increasingly apparent.

86 When this second stage in the progressive unfoldment of teaching activities and enterprises, under the Seven Year Plan, is reached, and the machinery required for its prosecution begins to operate, the American believers, the stout-hearted pioneers of this mighty movement, must, guided by the unfailing light of Bahá'u'lláh, and in strict accordance with the Plan laid out by 'Abdu'l-Bahá, and acting under the direction of their National Spiritual Assembly, and assured of the aid of the Inter-America Committee, launch an offensive against the powers of darkness, of corruption, and of ignorance, an offensive that must extend to the uttermost end of the Southern continent, and embrace within its scope each of the twenty nations that compose it.

19.3   Enhancing community diversity

In paragraph 81, Shoghi Effendi stresses the importance of increasing the diversity of the American Bahá'í community by attracting African Americans, the American Indians, the Eskimos, the Jews and other ethnic groups into the Faith. He considers the blending of such diverse groups of people into the Bahá'í community and assimilating them in the Bahá'í Administrative Order as a major achievement. The history of the American Bahá'í community shows that increasing the diversity of the community has been an unceasingly pursued goal.

Immigration has been a major factor in enhancing the diversity of the Bahá'í community. During the Vietnam War, ethnic Chinese and Hmong people were attracted to the Faith. They were among those who fled Vietnam. A big effort has been made to teach Cambodians and Laotians in refugee camps, many of whom settled in the United States. Southeast Asian Bahá'ís form the majority or at least a substantial minority of the communities in the cities of Portland, Oregon and Lowell, Massachusetts. After the Islamic Revolution in Írán, tens of thousands of Persian Bahá'ís had to flee Írán and many settled in the US.

The rest of this section briefly studies two important and significant developments in increasing the numbers of African Americans and Native Americans in the North America Bahá'í community.

19.3.1   African American Bahá'ís

The first African American to accept Bahá'u'lláh, as attested by Shoghi Effendi in *God Passes By*,[1] was Robert Turner. He was born as a slave in 1855 and was freed by the Thirteenth Amendment on 18 December 1863. He then worked for an early Bahá'í, Mrs Phoebe Hearst, as a butler. Around 1898, he sent his photograph with a letter to 'Abdu'l-Bahá. In response 'Abdu'l-Bahá revealed the following Tablet that was sent to him through Phoebe Hearst:[2]

> *O thou who art pure in heart, sanctified in spirit, peerless in character, beauteous in face! Thy photograph hath been received revealing thy physical frame in the utmost grace and the best appearance. Thou art dark in countenance and bright in character. Thou art like unto the pupil of the eye which is dark in colour, yet it is the fount of light and the revealer of the contingent world.*

> *I have not forgotten nor will I forget thee. I beseech God that He may graciously make thee the sign of His bounty amidst mankind, illumine thy face with the light of such blessings as are vouchsafed by the merciful Lord, single thee out for His love in this age which is distinguished among all the past ages and centuries.*[3]

Robert Turner was with the first Western pilgrims, including Edward and Lua Getsinger, Mrs Thornburgh-Cropper and Phoebe Hearst, who visited 'Abdu'l-Bahá in the Holy Land in December 1898.[4] 'Abdu'l-Bahá showed a great deal of affection and love to Robert Turner, contrary to the interracial relationship in the West at that time. Shoghi Effendi has named Robert Turner as one of the nineteen disciples of 'Abdu'l-Bahá.[5]

Robert Turner opened the way for African Americans, particularly women to enrol in the Faith. Amongst the most prominent women was Mrs Susie C. Steward who accepted the Faith in 1911. She was one of the first African American Bahá'ís involved in raising funds for building the Bahá'í House of Worship in Wilmette, Illinois.[6]

An African American Bahá'í, who played a major role in race relations, was Louis Gregory who joined the Bahá'í community in 1909. Soon after accepting the Faith, he confronted the racial segregation in the Washington DC Bahá'í community. He wrote to 'Abdu'l-Bahá at the same time and in response 'Abdu'l-Bahá wrote back: *"I hope that thou mayest become ... the means whereby the white and coloured people shall close their eyes to racial differences and behold the reality*

---

[1]   Shoghi Effendi, *God Passes By*, p. 259.

[2]   Cited by Christopher Buck, "The Bahá'í 'Race Amity' Movement and the Black Intelligentsia in Jim Crow America: Alain Locke and Robert S. Abbott", *Bahá'í Studies Review* 17(1), September 2012.

[3]   'Abdu'l-Bahá, *Selections from the Writings of 'Abdu'l-Bahá*, p. 114.

[4]   Shoghi Effendi, *This Decisive Hour*, p. 168.

[5]   Cited in *The Bahá'í World*, Vol. IV, p. 118.

[6]   Richard Thomas, *African American Bahá'ís, Race Relations and the Development of the Bahá'í community in the United States*, retrieved from https://bahai-library.com/thomas_race_relations_us.

of humanity."[1] Louis Gregory dedicated his life to serving the Faith as an administrator, teacher and promoter of race amity for decades.

At the time when Southern American society was systematically pursuing segregation between black and white through the Jim Crow laws, the Bahá'í community started Race Amity conferences and conventions to engender a change in race relations. 'Abdu'l-Bahá began the process by instructing Agnes S. Parsons on her second Pilgrimage to Haifa in 1920 to arrange a convention for unity between the white and coloured people. On her return, Agnes Parsons formed an *ad-hoc* race amity convention committee. The first race amity convention was held on 19–21 May 1921 at the Congregational Church in Washington DC under the title "Convention for Amity Between the Coloured and White Races Based on Heavenly Teachings". This resulted in further Race Amity conferences from 1921 to 1936. This was followed by the "Race Unity" period of 1939–1947 comprising a wide range of race relations initiatives.[2] These conferences attracted African-American leaders and scholars to the Faith, strengthened the faith of the African-American Bahá'ís and enhanced interracial relationships within the Bahá'í community.[3]

Such initiatives resulted in significant increase in the number of African American Bahá'ís. There were only two African-American Bahá'ís in 1899. However, membership grew to five percent of the community by 1936. This number rose to around 30% of the American Bahá'í community in early 1970s when the Faith was taught to rural populations especially in South Carolina.[4]

19.3.2   Native American Bahá'ís

As mentioned by Shoghi Effendi in Paragraph 81, 'Abdu'l-Bahá highlights the significance of the native Americans in spiritualising the inhabitants of the world in the Tablets of the Divine Plan. He states: *"Attach great importance to the indigenous population of America. For these souls may be likened unto the ancient inhabitants of the Arabian Peninsula, who, prior to the Mission of Muḥammad, were like unto savages. When the light of Muḥammad shone forth in their midst, however, they became so radiant as to illumine the world. Likewise, these Indians, should they be educated and guided, there can be no doubt that they will become so illumined as to enlighten the whole world."*[5]

Since the 1940's, an increasing number of Native Americans have been attracted to the Bahá'í Faith. Currently, there is no up to date statistics available on the number of Native American Bahá'ís. Stockman estimates that there were

---

[1]   Cited in *To move the world*, p. 7; *Star of the West*, XII:5, p. 103.

[2]   Christopher Buck, "The Bahá'í 'Race Amity' Movement and the Black Intelligentsia in Jim Crow America: Alain Locke and Robert S. Abbott", *Bahá'í Studies Review* 17(1), September 2012.

[3]   Richard Thomas, African American Bahá'ís, Race Relations and the Development of the Bahá'í community in the United States, retrieved from https://bahai-library.com/thomas_race_relations_us.

[4]   Robert Stockman, "The American Bahá'í Community in the Nineties", published in *America's Alternative Religions*, Timothy Miller Editor, Sunny Press, 1995.

[5]   'Abdu'l-Bahá, *The Tablets of the Divine Plan*, p. 33.

several thousand American Indian and Eskimo Bahá'ís in 1995, especially in rural Alaska and on the Navajo and Sioux reservations.[1] In an earlier statistics published in 1963 by the Hands of the Cause of God resident in the Holy Land, 83 Native tribes were mentioned to be part of the North American Bahá'í community.[2]

There have been various initiatives to further develop Native American Bahá'í community such as the Native American Bahá'í Institute that was established in 1980 as a centre of Bahá'í learning with the mission of cultivating the seeds of knowledge, spiritual, and cultural identity in the participants in order to serve the well-being and prosperity of children, youth and families.[3]

19.4   Three stages of the teaching campaign

In paragraph 82, Shoghi Effendi emphasizes the need to strengthen and support Bahá'í groups formed in North America to evolve into fully functioning Assemblies. He then identifies three stages that every teaching campaign of the first Seven Year Plan should pass through:

a)   Sufficient pioneers arise to make the necessary sacrifices to bring these teaching projects to fruition.

b)   The Bahá'í Administrative Order is implanted in the heart of the virgin territories.

c)   The Bahá'í institutions are secured in the hearts and minds of the inhabitants of those territories.

These endeavours, as highlighted by Shoghi Effendi, are challenging and burdensome, but Bahá'u'lláh has promised His assistance and confirmation when one arises to serve. Shoghi Effendi then cites some statements from Bahá'u'lláh and 'Abdu'l-Bahá in paragraphs 82 and 83 on the assurance of assistance vouchsafed for those who sacrificially support the Cause of God.

Such strategies have been reiterated by Shoghi Effendi in his other messages to the North American Bahá'í community. The goals of the first Seven Year Plan were won by the community closely following the guidance of the beloved Guardian.

In a message dated 13 April 1944 written to the American Bahá'í community at the end of the first Seven Year Plan, Shoghi Effendi illustrated the immensity of the victories achieved:

> The one remaining, and indeed the most challenging, task confronting the American Bahá'í Community has at long last been brilliantly accomplished. The structural basis of the Administrative Order of the Faith of Bahá'u'lláh has,

---

[1]   Robert Stockman, "The American Bahá'í Community in the Nineties", *America's Alternative Religions*, Timothy Miller Editor, Sunny Press, 1995.

[2]   Hands of the Cause Residing in the Holy Land, *The Bahá'í Faith: 1844–1963: Information Statistical and Comparative, Including the Achievements of the Ten Year International Bahá'í Teachings and Consolidation Plan 1953–1963, 1963*, p. 19.

[3]   Retrieved from https://www.facebook.com/Native.American.Bahai.Institute/, 1 October 2018.

through this superb victory, and on the very eve of the worldwide celebrations of the Centenary of His Faith, been firmly laid by the champion-builders of His World Order in every state of the Great Republic of the West and in every Province of the Dominion of Canada. In each of the Republics of Central and South America, moreover, the banner of His undefeatable Faith has been implanted by the members of that same community, while in no less than thirteen Republics of Latin America, as well as in two dependencies in the West Indies, Spiritual Assemblies have been established and are already functioning—a feat that has outstripped the goal originally fixed for the valiant members of that community in their intercontinental sphere of Bahá'í activity.[1]

19.5 Second phase of the Seven Year Plan

In paragraph 84, Shoghi Effendi explains the aim and direction of the second phase of the teaching campaign that was initiated to achieve the expansion goals of the Seven Year Plan. After establishing a nucleus of the Bahá'í Administration in every virgin state and province of the North American continent, energies should be focussed on "awaking of the nations of Latin America to the Call of Bahá'u'lláh".

In paragraphs 85 and 86, Shoghi Effendi provides more guidance on the significance and impact of achieving this second phase of the Plan. The 20 independent nations of Central and South America are destined to play an important role in the world's future destiny. Communication advances in the future will overcome the difficulties caused by the distances separating them at that time from the North American continent. Shoghi Effendi specifically states in paragraph 86 that the teaching activities should be followed by an offensive to conquer the forces of darkness, corruption and ignorance.

In the Tablets of the Divine Plan, 'Abdu'l-Bahá identifies specific goals in Central and Southern America, for the American Bahá'ís to achieve. He states:

> *... the republic of Mexico is very important. The majority of the inhabitants of that country are devoted Catholics. They are totally unaware of the reality of the Bible, the Gospel and the new divine teachings. They do not know that the basis of the religions of God is one and that the holy Manifestations are like unto the Sun of Truth, rising from the different dawning-places. Those souls are submerged in the sea of dogmas. If one breath of life be blown over them, great results will issue therefrom. But it is better for those who intend to go to Mexico to teach, to be familiar with the Spanish language.*

> *Similarly, the six Central American republics, situated south of Mexico— Guatemala, Honduras, Salvador, Nicaragua, Costa Rica, Panama and the seventh country Belize or British Honduras. The teachers going to those parts must also be familiar with the Spanish language. ...*

> *All the above countries have importance, but especially the Republic of Panama, wherein the Atlantic and Pacific Oceans come together through the Panama Canal. It is a centre for travel and passage from America to other continents of*

---

[1] Shoghi Effendi, *This Decisive Hour*, pp. 91–92.

the world, and in the future it will gain most great importance. ...

In a similar way, the republics of the continent of South America—Colombia, Ecuador, Peru, Brazil, British Guiana, Dutch Guiana, French Guiana, Bolivia, Chile, Argentina, Uruguay, Paraguay, Venezuela; also the islands to the north, east and west of South America, such as Falkland Islands, the Galapagos, Juan Fernandez, Tobago and Trinidad. Likewise the city of Bahia, situated on the eastern shore of Brazil. Because it is some time that it has become known by this name, its efficacy will be most potent.[1]

Although there was no systematic campaign to realize the vision of 'Abdu'l-Bahá in Central and South America for 20 years, some individuals arose to travel teach and pioneer to Latin America as soon as they learned about the wishes of 'Abdu'l-Bahá. Among them was Martha Root who visited the important cities of South America in 1919 and established valuable contacts. However, with the launch of the first Seven Year Plan, the Guardian called for permanent pioneers to settle in all the countries of Latin America. The National Spiritual Assembly of the Bahá'ís of United States and Canada appointed an Inter-America Committee to coordinate and drive these goals. The first contingent of pioneers left North America for different parts of Central and South America in 1939.

In the message, dated 13 April 1944, to the American Bahá'ís at the end of the first Seven Year Plan, the Guardian spoke of the victories in Latin America:

In each of the Republics of Central and South America, moreover, the banner of His undefeatable Faith has been implanted by the members of that same community, while in no less than thirteen Republics of Latin America as well as in two dependencies in the West Indies, Spiritual Assemblies have been established and are already functioning—a feat that has outstripped the goal originally fixed for the valiant members of that community in their intercontinental sphere of Bahá'í activity.[2]

---

[1]   'Abdu'l-Bahá, *The Tablets of the Divine Plan*, pp. 32–34.

[2]   Shoghi Effendi, *This Decisive Hour*, p. 92.

19.6 Activities

19.6.1 Short answer questions

1. What are the key points of quote 81:A?

    _____

    _____

    _____

    _____

2. What are the implications for present day society of the guidance provided by 'Abdu'l-Bahá in quotes 81:B and 81:C?

    _____

    _____

    _____

    _____

3. What is your understanding of quote 81:D?

    _____

    _____

    _____

    _____

4. Use quote 81:G to answer the following questions.

    a) Who were the Israelites?

    _____

    _____

    _____

    b) Who are the descendants of the Israelites at the time of Bahá'u'lláh and 'Abdu'l-Bahá, and what was their situation?

    _____

    _____

    _____

    c) Are the descendants of the Israelites delivered from obscurity and degradation?

    _____

_____

_____

_____

5. What is the strategy described by Shoghi Effendi in paragraph 82 to win virgin territories in America?

_____

_____

_____

6. Can you identify a hero or heroine of the Faith who illustrates what Bahá'u'lláh has describes in quotes 82:A and 82:B?

_____

_____

_____

7. What are the key points in quote 82:C?

_____

_____

_____

8. What is the "Standard of Unity" mentioned by 'Abdu'l-Bahá in quote 82:B?

_____

_____

_____

9. What is the promise of 'Abdu'l-Bahá about Canada in quotes 83:B and 83:C?

_____

_____

_____

10. What was the second stage of the teaching campaign initiated in the first Seven Year Plan, as mentioned in paragraph 84?

_____

_____

_____

_____

11. What is the guidance provided by Shoghi Effendi for an Inter-America Committee in paragraph 85?

_____

_____

_____

_____

12. What are the manifestations of the powers of darkness, of corruption and of ignorance mentioned in paragraph 86?

_____

_____

_____

_____

19.6.2 *Mini-project*

Conduct research on the development of the Bahá'í community in Greenland and among the Eskimos. Prepare the result of your research as a paper for presentation to a Bahá'í conference or summer school.

20.
Practical guidance

20.1 Introduction

This chapter covers paragraphs 87-94, in which the Guardian, in a most eloquent style based on the Writings of Bahá'u'lláh, describes the needs and condition of those who leave their native homes to pioneer and teach the Cause in virgin territories. He then provides some practical guidance on the teaching campaign initiated to win the goals of the first Seven Year Plan.

In this chapter, you need to reflect on and understand the following key points:

a) Those who intend to pioneer should:

- Place their whole trust in God.
- Teach themselves first.
- Regard the triumph of the Faith as their supreme objective.
- Not consider the largeness or smallness of the hearer's capacity.
- Remember that their love of Bahá'u'lláh will act as a storehouse of treasure for their souls.
- Be as unrestrained as the wind.
- "... teach with enthusiasm, conviction, wisdom and courtesy, but without pressing their hearer ..."
- Teach the Cause for the sake of God.
- Remember that the "*Faithful Spirit*" will strengthen them.
- Keep in mind the greatness of the blessing that is waiting for them.

b) The number of Local Spiritual Assemblies was increased from 14 to 37 during the two-year gap between the first and the second Seven Year Plans.

c) The Ten Year Crusade achieved the goal of forming a National Spiritual Assembly in each of the 20 Latin American Republics.

20.2   Paragraphs under study

87   Let some, at this very moment, gird up the loins of their endeavour, flee their native towns, cities, and states, forsake their country, and, *"putting their whole trust in God as the best provision for their journey,"* set their faces, and direct their steps towards those distant climes, those virgin fields, those unsurrendered cities, and bend their energies to capture the citadels of men's hearts—hearts, which, as Bahá'u'lláh has written, *"the hosts of Revelation and of utterance can subdue."*[A] Let them not tarry until such time as their fellow-labourers will have passed the first stage in their campaign of teaching, but let them rather, from this very hour, arise to usher in the opening phase of what will come to be regarded as one of the most glorious chapters in the international history of their Faith.[B] Let them, at the very outset, *"teach their own selves, that their speech may attract the hearts of their hearers."*[C] Let them regard the triumph of their Faith as their *"supreme objective."*[D]   Let them not *"consider the largeness or smallness of the receptacle"* that carries the measure of grace that God poureth forth in this age.[E] Let them *"disencumber themselves of all attachment to this world and the vanities thereof,"*[F] and, with that spirit of detachment which 'Abdu'l-Bahá exemplified and wished them to emulate, bring these diversified peoples and countries to the remembrance of God and His supreme Manifestation. Let His love be a *"storehouse of treasure for their souls,"* on the day when *"every pillar shall tremble, when the very skins of men shall creep, when all eyes shall stare up with terror."*[G] Let their *"souls be aglow with the flame of the undying Fire that burneth in the midmost heart of the world, in such wise that the waters of the universe shall be powerless to cool down its ardour."*[H] Let them be *"unrestrained as the wind"* which *"neither the sight of desolation nor the evidences of prosperity can either pain or please."*[I]   Let them *"unloose their tongues and proclaim unceasingly His Cause."*[J] Let them *"proclaim that which the Most Great Spirit will inspire them to utter in the service of the Cause of their Lord."*[K] Let them *"beware lest they contend with anyone, nay strive to make him aware of the truth with kindly manner and most convincing exhortation."*[L] Let them *"wholly for the sake of God proclaim His Message, and with that same spirit accept whatever response their words may evoke in their hearers."*[M] Let them not, for one moment, forget that the *"Faithful Spirit shall strengthen them through its power,"* and that *"a company of His chosen angels shall go forth with them, as bidden by Him Who is the Almighty, the All-Wise."*[N] Let them ever bear in mind *"how great is the blessedness that awaiteth them that have attained the honour of serving the Almighty,"* and remember that *"such a service is indeed the prince of all goodly deeds, and the ornament of every goodly act."*[O]

88   And, finally, let these soul-stirring words of Bahá'u'lláh, as they pursue their course throughout the length and breadth of the southern American continent, be ever ready on their lips, a solace to their hearts, a light on their path, a companion in their loneliness, and a daily sustenance in their journeys: *"O wayfarer in the path of God! Take thou thy portion of the ocean of His grace, and deprive not thyself of the things that lie hidden in its depths*

.... A dewdrop out of this ocean would, if shed upon all that are in the heavens and on earth, suffice to enrich them with the bounty of God, the Almighty, the All-Knowing, the All-Wise. With the hands of renunciation draw forth from its life-giving waters, and sprinkle therewith all created things, that they may be cleansed from all man-made limitations, and may approach the mighty seat of God, this hallowed and resplendent Spot. Be not grieved if thou performest it thyself alone. Let God be all-sufficient for thee .... Proclaim the Cause of thy Lord unto all who are in the heavens and on the earth. Should any man respond to thy call, lay bare before him the pearls of the wisdom of the Lord, thy God, which His Spirit hath sent down upon thee, and be thou of them that truly believe. And should anyone reject thy offer, turn thou away from him, and put thy trust and confidence in the Lord of all worlds. By the righteousness of God! Whoso openeth his lips in this day, and maketh mention of the name of his Lord, the hosts of Divine inspiration shall descend upon him from the heaven of my name, the All-Knowing, the All-Wise. On him shall also descend the Concourse on high, each bearing aloft a chalice of pure light. Thus hath it been foreordained in the realm of God's Revelation, by the behest of Him Who is the All-Glorious, the Most Powerful."[A]

89   Let these words of 'Abdu'l-Bahá, gleaned from the Tablets of the Divine Plan, ring likewise in their ears, as they go forth, assured and unafraid, on His mission: *"O ye apostles of Bahá'u'lláh! May my life be sacrificed for you! ... Behold the portals which Bahá'u'lláh hath opened before you! Consider how exalted and lofty is the station you are destined to attain; how unique the favours with which you have been endowed.*"[A] *"My thoughts are turned towards you, and my heart leaps within me at your mention. Could ye know how my soul gloweth with your love, so great a happiness would flood your hearts as to cause you to become enamoured with each other."*[B] *"The full measure of your success is as yet unrevealed, its significance still unapprehended. Erelong ye will, with your own eyes, witness how brilliantly every one of you, even as a shining star, will radiate in the firmament of your country the light of Divine Guidance, and will bestow upon its people the glory of an everlasting life.*"[C] *"I fervently hope that in the near future the whole earth may be stirred and shaken by the results of your achievements."*[D] *"The Almighty will no doubt grant you the help of His grace, will invest you with the tokens of His might, and will endue your souls with the sustaining power of His holy Spirit.*"[E] *"Be not concerned with the smallness of your numbers, neither be oppressed by the multitude of an unbelieving world .... Exert yourselves; your mission is unspeakably glorious. Should success crown your enterprise, America will assuredly evolve into a Centre from which waves of spiritual power will emanate, and the throne of the Kingdom of God will, in the plenitude of its majesty and glory, be firmly established.*"[F]

90   It should be remembered that the carrying out of the Seven Year Plan involves, insofar as the teaching work is concerned, no more than the formation of at least one Centre in each of the Central and South American Republics. The hundredth anniversary of the birth of the Faith of Bahá'u'lláh should witness, if the Plan already launched is to meet with success, the laying, in each of these countries, of a foundation, however rudimentary, on

which the rising generation of the American believers may, in the opening years of the second century of the Bahá'í era, be able to build. Theirs will be the task, in the course of successive decades, to extend and reinforce those foundations, and to supply the necessary guidance, assistance, and encouragement that will enable the widely scattered groups of believers in those countries to establish independent and properly constituted local Assemblies, and thereby erect the framework of the Administrative Order of their Faith. The erection of such a framework is primarily the responsibility of those whom the community of the North American believers have converted to the Divine Message. It is a task which must involve, apart from the immediate obligation of enabling every group to evolve into a local Assembly, the setting up of the entire machinery of the Administrative Order in conformity with the spiritual and administrative principles governing the life and activities of every established Bahá'í community throughout the world. No departure from these cardinal and clearly enunciated principles, embodied and preserved in Bahá'í national and local constitutions, common to all Bahá'í communities, can under any circumstances be tolerated. This, however, is a task that concerns those who, at a later period, must arise to further a work which, to all intents and purposes, has not yet been effectively started.

91 To pave the way, in a more systematic manner, for the laying of the necessary foundation on which such permanent national and local institutions can be reared and securely established is a task that will very soon demand the concentrated attention of the prosecutors of the Seven Year Plan. No sooner has their immediate obligation in connection with the opening up of the few remaining territories in the United States and Canada been discharged, than a carefully laid-out plan should be conceived, aiming at the establishment of such a foundation. As already stated, the provision for these vast, preliminary undertakings, the scope of which must embrace the entire area occupied by the Central and South American Republics, constitutes the very core, and must ultimately decide the fate, of the teaching campaign conducted under the Seven Year Plan. Upon this campaign must depend not only the effectual discharge of the solemn obligations undertaken in connection with the present Plan, but also the progressive unfoldment of the subsequent stages essential to the realization of 'Abdu'l-Bahá's vision of the part the American believers are to play in the worldwide propagation of their Cause.

92 These undertakings, preliminary as they are to the strenuous and organized labours by which future generations of believers in the Latin countries must distinguish themselves, require, in turn, without a moment's delay, on the part of the National Spiritual Assembly and of both the National Teaching and Inter-America Committees, painstaking investigations preparatory to the sending of settlers and itinerant teachers, whose privilege will be to raise the call of the New Day in a new continent.

93 I can only, in my desire to be of some service to those who are to assume such tremendous responsibilities, and to suffer such self-denial, attempt to offer a few helpful suggestions which, I trust, will facilitate the

accomplishment of the great work to be achieved in the very near future. To this work, that must constitute an historical landmark of first-class importance when completed, the energies of the entire community must be resolutely consecrated. The number of Bahá'í teachers, be they settlers or travellers, must be substantially increased. The material resources to be placed at their disposal must be multiplied, and efficiently administered. The literature with which they should be equipped must be vastly augmented. The publicity that should aid them in the distribution of such literature should be extended, centrally organized, and vigorously conducted. The possibilities latent in these countries should be diligently exploited, and systematically developed. The various obstacles raised by the widely varying political and social conditions obtaining in these countries should be closely surveyed and determinedly surmounted. In a word, no opportunity should be neglected, and no effort spared, to lay as broad and solid a basis as possible for the progress and development of the greatest teaching enterprise ever launched by the American Bahá'í community.

94   The careful translation of such important Bahá'í writings as are related to the history, the teachings, or the Administrative Order of the Faith, and their wide and systematic dissemination, in vast quantities, and throughout as many of these Republics as possible, and in languages that are most suitable and needed, would appear to be the chief and most urgent measure to be taken simultaneously with the arrival of the pioneer workers in those fields. "*Books and pamphlets,*" writes 'Abdu'l-Bahá in one of the Tablets of the Divine Plan, "*must be either translated or composed in the languages of these countries and islands, to be circulated in every part and in all directions.*"[A] In countries where no objections can be raised by the civil authorities or any influential circles, this measure should be reinforced by the publication, in various organs of the Press, of carefully worded articles and letters, designed to impress upon the general public certain features of the stirring history of the Faith, and the range and character of its teachings.

20.3   Girding up the loins of endeavour

In paragraphs 87–89, Shoghi Effendi draws on a number of quotations from Bahá'u'lláh and 'Abdu'l-Bahá that would empower and encourage those who arise to pioneer to virgin territories to teach the Cause. In this section, the key points of each quotation is highlighted.

20.3.1   *Paragraph 87*

When intending to pioneer to virgin territories, you should:

- Quote 87:A: Place your whole trust in God, move to virgin territories and conquer the citadels of men's hearts through "*the hosts of Revelation and of utterance*". The complete quote is: "*Dispute not with any one concerning the things of this world and its affairs, for God hath abandoned them to such as have set their affection upon them. Out of the whole world He hath chosen for*

Himself the hearts of men—hearts which the hosts of revelation and of utterance can subdue.[1]

- Sentence 87:B: Do not linger until others have completed the first stage of the teaching campaign, rather immediately arise to open what will be the most glorious chapter in the American Bahá'í community international history.

- Quote 87:C: Teach your own selves at the outset so that your speech can influence the hearts of those you teach.

- Sentence 87:D: Regard victories won for the Faith as your supreme objective.

- Sentence 87:E: Do not consider the largeness or smallness of the hearer's capacity to receive the grace that God that has poured forth in this age. Here is the complete quotation from Bahá'u'lláh: *"The whole duty of man in this Day is to attain that share of the flood of grace which God poureth forth for him. Let none, therefore, consider the largeness or smallness of the receptacle. The portion of some might lie in the palm of a man's hand, the portion of others might fill a cup, and of others even a gallon-measure."*[2]

- Sentence 87:F: Free yourselves from the burden of attachment to this world, and follow the example of 'Abdu'l-Bahá to teach the Faith with a spirit of detachment.

- Quote 87:G: Consider the love of Bahá'u'lláh as a storehouse of treasure for your soul to assist you in teaching others. Here is the complete quotation from Bahá'u'lláh: *"Beware, O men, lest ye be tempted to part with Him in exchange for the gold and silver ye possess. Let His love be a storehouse of treasure for your souls, on the Day when naught else but Him shall profit you, the Day when every pillar shall tremble, when the very skins of men shall creep, when all eyes shall stare up with terror."*[3]

- Quote 87:H: Set your soul aglow with the flame of an undying Fire in a way that all the waters of the earth cannot cool your soul. There are a number of references to *"undying Fire"* in the writings of Bahá'u'lláh, as the Most Great Spirit–the source of revelation.

- Quote 87:I: Be as unrestrained as the wind and be not affected either by signs of destruction or prosperity.

- Quotes 87:J and 87:K: Unloose your tongues and proclaim what the Great Spirit inspires you.

- Quote 87:L: *"... teach with enthusiasm, conviction, wisdom and courtesy, but without pressing their hearer...."*[4]

- Quote 87:M: Teach the Cause for the sake of God and accept without argument the response you receive from the hearer.

- Quote 87:N: Do not forget for a moment that the *"Faithful Spirit"* will strengthen you and a company of Bahá'u'lláh's Angels will accompany you. There are references to the term *"Faithful Spirit"* in other Tablets of

---

[1]   Bahá'u'lláh, *Gleanings from the Writings of Bahá'u'lláh*, p. 279.

[2]   Bahá'u'lláh, *Gleanings from the Writings of Bahá'u'lláh*, p. 8.

[3]   Bahá'u'lláh, *Gleanings from the Writings of Bahá'u'lláh*, p. 38.

[4]   The Universal House of Justice, *Messages from the Universal House of Justice 1963–1986*, p. 514.

Bahá'u'lláh. There is no authoritative explanation of the actual meaning of this term available in the published works. However, the context in which it has been used indicates that the *"Faithful Spirit"* may refer to the Holy Spirit or the Most Great Spirit. For example, in a Tablet Bahá'u'lláh states:

"O concourse of divines! Be fair, I adjure you by God, and nullify not the Truth with the things ye possess. Peruse that which We have sent down with truth. It will, verily, aid you, and will draw you nigh unto God, the Mighty, the Great. Consider and call to mind how when Muḥammad, the Apostle of God, appeared, the people denied Him. They ascribed unto Him what caused the Spirit (Jesus) to lament in His Most Sublime Station, and the Faithful Spirit to cry out."[1]

- Quote 87:O: Keep in mind the greatness of the blessing that is waiting for you and that the service you render is *"the prince of all goodly deeds, and the ornament of every goodly act."*[2]

20.3.2 Paragraph 88

In paragraph 88, Shoghi Effendi cites excerpts from a Tablet of Bahá'u'lláh in which He counsels those who travel to teach His Cause. Here are some of the key points in this Tablet:

- The revelation of Bahá'u'lláh is an ocean, a dewdrop of which is sufficient to enrich the whole earth with the bounty of God.
- Teachers should draw forth from the water of this ocean and sprinkle it on all created things to purify them from all artificial restrictions.
- Teachers should not be grieved if they feel alone since God is with them.

    o They should proclaim the cause.
    o If anyone responds, they should present the Faith to him.
    o If anyone rejects, they should leave him be.

- Anyone opening his mouth to mention the name of Bahá'u'lláh will receive divine inspiration.

    o The Concourse on high will descend on them with a chalice of pure light.

20.3.3 Paragraph 89

In paragraph 89, Shoghi Effendi cites some statements of 'Abdu'l-Bahá from the Tablets of the Divine Plan. Calling on the servants and teachers of the Cause, 'Abdu'l-Bahá stated:

- Quote 89:A: You are destined for a lofty station.
- Quote 89:B: The thoughts of 'Abdu'l-Bahá are turned towards you, His heart leaps with your mention and His soul glows with your love.
- Quote 89:C: The full extent of your success in teaching the cause will be known in the future.
- Quote 89:D: 'Abdu'l-Bahá hopes that the whole earth may be illumined with your endeavours.

---

[1] Bahá'u'lláh, *The Proclamation of Bahá'u'lláh*, p. 78.
[2] Bahá'u'lláh, *Gleanings from the Writings of Bahá'u'lláh*, p. 334.

- Quote 89:E: There is no doubt that you will receive the grace of God and that your soul will be endued with the sustaining power of the Holy Spirit.
- Quote 89:F: Do not be concerned with the small number of believers, or with the large number of unbelievers. You should exert yourself. If successful, America will become a centre from which spiritual waves will emanate to other parts of the world.

20.4   Erecting Administrative Order framework

In paragraph 90, Shoghi Effendi describes how the centres formed in each of the Central and South American Republics during the Seven Year Plan would develop into independent and properly functioning local Assemblies during the second century of the Bahá'í era. The development would be undertaken by those enrolled in the Faith during the teaching campaign. These Assemblies would form the framework of the Administrative Order in Latin America and function according to the key principles embedded in the constitutions of the Local and National Assemblies. Further development of this concept is provided in paragraphs 91–92.

In paragraph 93, Shoghi Effendi provides some guidance for those who assume the responsibility of building this framework:

- There should be a significant increase in the number of Bahá'í teachers.
- The literature supporting the teaching campaign should be expanded.
- The publicity designed to support the distribution of the literature should be extended, centrally organized and vigorously pursued.
- All possibilities for advancing the Faith in every country should be exploited and developed.
- All potential obstacles should be identified and overcome.
- All the important Bahá'í writings should be translated into local languages, and systematically distributed.
- In addition to publication of literature, the history and teachings of the Faith should be disseminated where possible through articles and letters.

The pioneers and travel teachers followed the model described by the Guardian and this resulted in the emergence of the framework envisaged by Shoghi Effendi in the South and Central America. The number of Local Spiritual Assemblies was increased from 14 to 37 during the two-year gap between the first and the second Seven Year Plans through the efforts of the North American pioneers and the new Latin American believers.[1]

The development of the Bahá'í Administrative Order in Latin American produced its first national institutions in 1951, when two international conventions were held in Panama City and Lima, Peru to elect two National Spiritual Assemblies. The convention in Panama City elected the National Spiritual Assembly for Mexico, Central America and the Antilles. The convention in Peru elected the National Spiritual Assembly for South America.

---

[1] Artemus Lamb, *The Beginnings of the Bahá'í Faith in Latin America: Some Remembrances*, November 1995, retrieved from https://bahai-library.com/lamb_bahai_latin_america.

The development of the Bahá'í Administrative framework in Latin America reached new heights during the Ten Year Crusade with the formation of 20 Latin American Republic National Spiritual Assemblies.

20.5   Activities

20.5.1   Short answer questions

1. What does Shoghi Effendi mean by the following statement from sentence 87:A?

    "... bend their energies to capture the citadels of men's hearts—hearts, which, as Bahá'u'lláh has written, 'the hosts of Revelation and of utterance can subdue.'"

    _____

    _____

    _____

    _____

2. What are the two stages of the teaching campaign referred to in sentence 87:B?

    _____

    _____

    _____

    _____

3. How can one teach oneself as mentioned in quote 87:C?

    _____

    _____

    _____

    _____

4. What other objectives motivated pioneers to go to virgin territories (sentence 87:D)?

    _____

    _____

    _____

    _____

5. What are the implications of sentence 87:E in teaching?

    _____

    _____

    _____

    _____

6. How does detachment make teaching more effective (sentence 87:F)?

_____

_____

_____

_____

7. What is the *"Day"* Bahá'u'lláh referring to in quote 87:G?

_____

_____

_____

8. What is your understanding of quote 87:H?

_____

_____

_____

9. What is meant by the *"Most Great Spirit"* in quote 87:K?

_____

_____

_____

10. In the context of quote 87:M, what other motivations are there to teach?

_____

_____

_____

11. What is your understanding of the term *"Faithful Spirit"* (quote 87:N)?

_____

_____

_____

12. Consider quote 88:A.

   a) What is the analogy used by Bahá'u'lláh linking His Revelation and teaching of His Cause?

_____

_____

_____

_____

b) How should the teacher react to the response received from the hearer of the message?

_____

_____

_____

c) What is the promise of Bahá'u'lláh on the divine inspiration bestowed on the teacher?

_____

_____

_____

13. Identify the key points in quote 88:A from Bahá'u'lláh and describe your understanding of each point.

_____

_____

_____

_____

_____

_____

14. Describe your understanding of all the statements of 'Abdu'l-Bahá cited in paragraph 89.

a) Quote 89:A

_____

_____

_____

b) Quote 89:B

_____

_____

_____

_____

c)   Quote 89:C

_____

_____

_____

c)   Quote 89:D

_____

_____

_____

d)   Quote 89:E

_____

_____

_____

e)   Quote 89:F

_____

_____

_____

_____

15.   What is the model described by Shoghi Effendi in paragraph 90 to establish the Faith and the Bahá'í Administrative Order in Latin America?

_____

_____

_____

20.5.2   *Mini-project*

Conduct research on the development of the Latin American Bahá'í community after the completion of the Ten Year Crusade and identify its major achievements. Arrange your findings as a paper for publication in a Bahá'í journal.

21.
More practical guidance

21.1   Introduction

This chapter covers paragraphs 95–102 in which the Guardian provides more practical guidance on different aspects of the teaching campaign initiated to achieve the goals of the first Seven Year Plan, particularly the opening of the virgin territories in Latin America. He also highlights the roles of women and youth in this campaign and the significance of their active participation.

In this chapter, you need to reflect on and understand the following key points:

a)   Shoghi Effendi advises travel teachers and pioneers to mix in a friendly manner with all people in that society, and acquaint themselves with their cultures while concentrating on those who have shown receptivity.

b)   The value of pioneering and travel teaching could not be properly assessed at that time and the reward that pioneers would receive is limitless.

c)   Shoghi Effendi refers to the victories won at the time in Bulgaria and Australasia by the North American believers as good examples of the nature of rewards received in building the Bahá'í community.

d)   Shoghi Effendi admires the work of the women in the West who have made a significant contribution to the progress of the Faith and its establishment throughout the world since the inception of the Cause in the western countries.

e)   The Bahá'í Youth, although they do not have much experience and resources, possess an adventurous spirit, vigour, alertness and optimism.

f)   In the Tablets of the Divine Plan, 'Abdu'l-Bahá has mentioned that all the countries in Latin America, in particular Panama, will become important in the future.

21.2   Paragraphs under study

95   Every labourer in those fields, whether as traveling teacher or settler, should, I feel, make it his chief and constant concern to mix, in a friendly

manner, with all sections of the population, irrespective of class, creed, nationality, or colour, to familiarize himself with their ideas, tastes, and habits, to study the approach best suited to them, to concentrate, patiently and tactfully, on a few who have shown marked capacity and receptivity, and to endeavour, with extreme kindness, to implant such love, zeal, and devotion in their hearts as to enable them to become in turn self-sufficient and independent promoters of the Faith in their respective localities. *"Consort with all men, O people of Bahá,"* is Bahá'u'lláh's admonition, *"in a spirit of friendliness and fellowship. If ye be aware of a certain truth, if ye possess a jewel, of which others are deprived, share it with them in a language of utmost kindliness and goodwill. If it be accepted, if it fulfil its purpose, your object is attained. If anyone should refuse it, leave him unto himself, and beseech God to guide him. Beware lest ye deal unkindly with him. A kindly tongue is the lodestone of the hearts of men. It is the bread of the spirit, it clotheth the words with meaning, it is the fountain of the light of wisdom and understanding."*[A]

96   An effort, moreover, can and should be made, not only by representative Bahá'í bodies, but also by prospective teachers, as well as by other individual believers, deprived of the privilege of visiting those shores or of settling on that continent, to seize every opportunity that presents itself to make the acquaintance, and awaken the genuine interest, of such people who are either citizens of these countries, or are in any way connected with them, whatever be their interests or profession. Through the kindness shown them, or any literature which may be given them, or any connection which they may establish with them, the American believers can thereby sow such seeds in their hearts as might, in future circumstances, germinate and yield the most unexpected results. Care, however, should, at all times, be exercised, lest in their eagerness to further the international interests of the Faith they frustrate their purpose, and turn away, through any act that might be misconstrued as an attempt to proselytize and bring undue pressure upon them, those whom they wish to win over to their Cause.

97   I would particularly direct my appeal to those American believers, sore-pressed as they are by the manifold, the urgent, and ever-increasing issues that confront them at the present hour, who may find it possible, whatever be their calling or employment, whether as businessmen, school teachers, lawyers, doctors, writers, office workers, and the like, to establish permanently their residence in such countries as may offer them a reasonable prospect of earning the means of livelihood. They will by their action be relieving the continually increasing pressure on their Teaching Fund, which in view of its restricted dimensions must provide, when not otherwise available, the traveling and other expenses to be incurred in connection with the development of this vast undertaking. Should they find it impossible to take advantage of so rare and sacred a privilege, let them, mindful of the words of Bahá'u'lláh, determine, each according to the means at his or her disposal, to appoint a deputy who, on that believer's behalf, will arise and carry out so noble an enterprise. *"Centre your energies,"* are Bahá'u'lláh's words, *"in the propagation of the Faith of God. Whoso is worthy of so high a calling, let him arise and promote it. Whoso is unable, it is his duty*

to appoint him who will, in his stead, proclaim this Revelation, whose power hath caused the foundations of the mightiest structures to quake, every mountain to be crushed into dust, and every soul to be dumbfounded."[A]

98 As to those who have been able to leave their homes and country, and to serve in those regions, whether temporarily or permanently, a special duty, which must continually be borne in mind, devolves upon them. It should be one of their chief aims to keep, on the one hand, in constant touch with the National Committee specifically entrusted with the promotion of their work, and to cooperate, on the other, by every possible means and in the utmost harmony, with their fellow-believers in those countries, whatever the field in which they labour, whatever their standing, ability, or experience. Through the performance of their first duty they will derive the necessary stimulus and obtain the necessary guidance that will enable them to prosecute effectively their mission, and will also, through their regular reports to that committee, be imparting to the general body of their fellow-believers the news of the latest developments in their activities. By fulfilling their other duty, they will insure the smooth efficiency, facilitate the progress, and avert any untoward incidents that might handicap the development of their common enterprise. The maintenance of close contact and harmonious relationships between the Inter-America Committee, entrusted with the immediate responsibility of organizing such a far-reaching enterprise, and the privileged pioneers who are actually executing that enterprise, and extending its ramifications far and wide, as well as among these pioneers themselves, would set, apart from its immediate advantages, a worthy and inspiring example to generations still yet to be born who are to carry on, with all its increasing complexities, the work which is being initiated at present.

99 It would, no doubt, be of exceptional importance and value, particularly in these times when the various restrictions imposed in those countries make it difficult for a considerable number of Bahá'í pioneers to establish their residence and earn their livelihood in those states, if certain ones among the believers, whose income, however slender, provides them with the means of an independent existence, would so arrange their affairs as to be able to reside indefinitely in those countries. The sacrifices involved, the courage, faith, and perseverance it demands, are no doubt very great. Their value, however, can never be properly assessed at the present time, and the limitless reward which they who demonstrate them will receive can never be adequately depicted. *"They that have forsaken their country,"* is Bahá'u'lláh's own testimony, *"for the purpose of teaching Our Cause—these shall the Faithful Spirit strengthen through its power .... By My life! No act, however great, can compare with it, except such deeds as have been ordained by God, the All-Powerful, the Most Mighty. Such a service is indeed the prince of all goodly deeds, and the ornament of every goodly act."*[A] Such a reward, it should be noted, is not to be regarded as purely an abstract blessing confined to the future life, but also as a tangible benefit which such courage, faith and perseverance can alone confer in this material world. The solid achievements, spiritual as well as administrative, which in the far-away

continent of Australasia, and more recently in Bulgaria, representative believers from both Canada and the United States have accomplished, proclaim in terms unmistakable the nature of those prizes which, even in this world, such sterling heroism is bound to win. "*Whoso*," Bahá'u'lláh, in a memorable passage, extolling those of His loved ones who have "*journeyed through the countries in His Name and for His praise*," has written, "*hath attained their presence will glory in their meeting, and all that dwell in every land will be illumined by their memory.*"[B]

100 I am moved, at this juncture, as I am reminded of the share which, ever since the inception of the Faith in the West, the handmaidens of Bahá'u'lláh, as distinguished from the men, have had in opening up, single-handed, so many, such diversified, and widely scattered countries over the whole surface of the globe, not only to pay a tribute to such apostolic fervour as is truly reminiscent of those heroic men who were responsible for the birth of the Faith of Bahá'u'lláh, but also to stress the significance of such a preponderating share which the women of the West have had and are having in the establishment of His Faith throughout the whole world. "*Among the miracles*," 'Abdu'l-Bahá Himself has testified, "*which distinguish this sacred Dispensation is this, that women have evinced a greater boldness than men when enlisted in the ranks of the Faith.*"[A] So great and splendid a testimony applies in particular to the West, and though it has received thus far abundant and convincing confirmation must, as the years roll away, be further reinforced, as the American believers usher in the most glorious phase of their teaching activities under the Seven Year Plan. The "boldness" which, in the words of 'Abdu'l-Bahá, has characterized their accomplishments in the past must suffer no eclipse as they stand on the threshold of still greater and nobler accomplishments. Nay rather, it must, in the course of time and throughout the length and breadth of the vast and virgin territories of Latin America, be more convincingly demonstrated, and win for the beloved Cause victories more stirring than any it has as yet achieved.

101 To the Bahá'í youth of America, moreover, I feel a word should be addressed in particular, as I survey the possibilities which a campaign of such gigantic proportions has to offer to the eager and enterprising spirit that so powerfully animates them in the service of the Cause of Bahá'u'lláh. Though lacking in experience and faced with insufficient resources, yet the adventurous spirit which they possess, and the vigour, the alertness, and optimism they have thus far so consistently shown, qualify them to play an active part in arousing the interest, and in securing the allegiance, of their fellow youth in those countries. No greater demonstration can be given to the peoples of both continents of the youthful vitality and the vibrant power animating the life, and the institutions of the nascent Faith of Bahá'u'lláh than an intelligent, persistent, and effective participation of the Bahá'í youth, of every race, nationality, and class, in both the teaching and administrative spheres of Bahá'í activity. Through such a participation the critics and enemies of the Faith, watching with varying degrees of scepticism and resentment, the evolutionary processes of the Cause of God and its

institutions, can best be convinced of the indubitable truth that such a Cause is intensely alive, is sound to its very core, and its destinies in safe keeping. I hope, and indeed pray, that such a participation may not only redound to the glory, the power, and the prestige of the Faith, but may also react so powerfully on the spiritual lives, and galvanize to such an extent the energies of the youthful members of the Bahá'í community, as to empower them to display, in a fuller measure, their inherent capacities, and to unfold a further stage in their spiritual evolution under the shadow of the Faith of Bahá'u'lláh.

102 Faithful to the provisions of the Charter laid down by the pen of 'Abdu'l-Bahá, I feel it my duty to draw the special attention of those to whom it has been entrusted to the urgent needs of, and the special position enjoyed by, the Republic of Panama, both in view of its relative proximity to the heart and Centre of the Faith in North America, and of its geographical position as the link between two continents. *"All the above countries,"* 'Abdu'l-Bahá, referring to the Latin States in one of the Tablets of the Divine Plan, has written, *"have importance, but especially the Republic of Panama, wherein the Atlantic and Pacific Oceans come together through the Panama Canal. It is a Centre for travel and passage from America to other continents of the world, and in the future it will gain most great importance."* *"Likewise,"* He again has written, *"ye must give great attention to the Republic of Panama, for in that point the Occident and the Orient find each other united through the Panama Canal, and it is also situated between the two great oceans. That place will become very important in the future. The teachings, once established there, will unite the East and the West, the North and the South."* So privileged a position surely demands the special and prompt attention of the American Bahá'í community. With the Republic of Mexico already opened up to the Faith, and with a Spiritual Assembly properly constituted in its capital city, the southward penetration of the Faith of Bahá'u'lláh into a neighbouring country is but a natural and logical step, and should, it is to be hoped, prove to be not a difficult one. No efforts should be spared, and no sacrifice be deemed too great, to establish even though it be a very small group in a Republic occupying, both spiritually and geographically, so strategic a position—a group which, in view of the potency with which the words of 'Abdu'l-Bahá have already endowed it, cannot but draw to itself, as soon as it is formed, the outpouring grace of the Abhá Kingdom, and evolve with such marvellous swiftness as to excite the wonder and the admiration of even those who have already witnessed such stirring evidences of the force and power of the Faith of Bahá'u'lláh. Preference, no doubt, should be given by all would-be pioneers, as well as by the members of the Inter-America Committee, to the spiritual needs of this privileged Republic, though every effort should, at the same time, be exerted to introduce the Faith, however tentatively, to the Republics of Guatemala, Honduras, El Salvador, Nicaragua, and Costa Rica which would link it, in an unbroken chain, with its mother Assemblies in the North American continent. Obstacles, however formidable, should be surmounted, the resources of the Bahá'í treasury should be liberally expended on its behalf, and the ablest and most precious exertions should be consecrated to the cause of its awakening. The erection

of yet another outpost of the Faith, in its heart, will constitute, I firmly believe, a landmark in the history of the Formative Period of the Faith of Bahá'u'lláh in the New World. It will create limitless opportunities, galvanize the efforts, and reinvigorate the life, of those who will have accomplished this feat, and infuse immense courage and boundless joy into the hearts of the isolated groups and individuals in the neighbouring and distant Republics, and exert intangible yet powerful spiritual influences on the life and future development of its people.

21.3   More counsels

In paragraphs 95–99, Shoghi Effendi provides further counsels for the teachers and pioneers who rose during the Seven Year Plan to open the virgin territories to the Faith.

- In paragraph 95, Shoghi Effendi recommends that the travel teachers and pioneers should mix in a friendly manner with all the local people and acquaint themselves with every aspect of their culture while concentrating on those souls who have shown receptivity. Shoghi Effendi then cites a statement (quote 95:A) from Bahá'u'lláh on how the teachings of the Faith should be shared with others.
- In paragraph 96, Shoghi Effendi counsels every individual believer, whether a member of a Bahá'í institution or a prospective teacher of the Faith to seize any opportunity to get to know people who are citizens of pioneering countries or have some connection with them. They should plant the seeds of belief in their hearts through kindness and sharing the literature of the Faith, without placing any pressure on them or attempting to proselytize.
- In paragraph 97, Shoghi Effendi calls on American believers with professions to permanently live and work in pioneering posts, where they can earn their means of livelihood. This will help to reduce the increasing pressures on the Teaching Fund. If it proves impossible to take advantage of such a privilege, they should appoint a deputy to pioneer and teach the Faith on their behalf. Shoghi Effendi then cites a statement (quote 97:A) from Bahá'u'lláh on teaching deputization.
- In paragraph 98, Shoghi Effendi states that pioneers and travel teachers should be in constant communication with the National Committee of North America to receive stimulus and necessary guidance. They should also co-operate with fellow believers in their pioneering countries to facilitate the progress of the Faith. This will set an example for the future generations who will continue the work.
- In paragraph 99, Shoghi Effendi acknowledges the difficulty of the task of establishing a residence and earning a livelihood for a considerable number of Bahá'í pioneers. It would be of great importance if some pioneers can live on an income from their home country, even though sparse, and reside indefinitely in the pioneering countries. Shoghi Effendi then cites an utterance (quote 99:A) in which Bahá'u'lláh exhorts those who forsake their country to teach the Faith.

21.4 Limitless reward

In paragraph 99, Shoghi Effendi states that the value of pioneering and travel teaching cannot be properly assessed at this time and the reward that pioneers receive is limitless. The reward for a pioneer is more than a blessing conferred on those souls in the future life and will include solid spiritual and administrative achievements. The victories won at the time in Bulgaria and Australasia by the North American believers were good examples of the nature of these rewards. This section undertakes a brief review of those achievements.

21.4.1 *Victories in Bulgaria*

Based on other messages of Shoghi Effendi, it can be suggested that the reference to Bulgaria in paragraph 99 is to the sacrifices made and the victories achieved by Marion Jack, a Canadian Bahá'í pioneer to Bulgaria.

Marion Jack was born in Saint John, New Brunswick, Canada, on 1 December 1866. She studied art in England and France, and specialized in landscape painting. She was introduced to the Faith at a social gathering while she was studying in Paris. In 1908, she travelled to the Holy Land and spent some time in 'Akká teaching English to 'Abdu'l-Bahá's grandchildren. During this period, she had the privilege of spending time with 'Abdu'l-Bahá. 'Abdu'l-Bahá admired her sense of humour, cheerfulness and certitude, and gave her the nickname "General Jack". She was back in North American by 1914.

Marion Jack was among the first to respond to 'Abdu'l-Bahá's call in the Tablets of the Divine Plan, pioneering to Alaska and travel teaching in Toronto, Montreal and many other places. She also spent a large amount of time at Green Acre Bahá'í School in Eliot, Maine, where she helped with the teaching work while continuing her painting.

In 1930, Marion Jack returned to Haifa and, following this visit, went to Sofia, Bulgaria. In Sofia, she started to teach the Faith by holding public meetings that were attended by many people of capacity. However, as the Bahá'í Faith was not amongst the religions permitted in Bulgaria, her meetings were deemed illegal and had to be curtailed to include only selected guests. Other difficulties were the scarcity of English speakers and the total lack of Bulgarian translations of Bahá'í literature.

Marion Jack was living on a small pension that did not always reach her. This was during the Great Depression so conditions were hard, but the situation was to become far worse with the start of World War II. The Guardian suggested that she should move to Switzerland to avoid the hardships caused by the war. However, she pleaded to stay in Sofia and Shoghi Effendi accepted her decision. During the war, Marion experienced aerial bombing and the threats of a pro-Nazi government, throughout which she demonstrated her fearlessness and steadfastness. Unfortunately, her financial situation deteriorated further under the post-war Stalinist-style regime. She lived in a damp, rented room with no windows, and suffered serious health problems due to inadequate food, heating and clothing. She passed away on 27 March 1954, aged 87.

The Guardian sent the following message on 29 March 1954 to the Bahá'í world announcing her ascension to the Abhá Kingdom:

> Mourn loss of immortal heroine, Marion Jack, greatly loved and deeply admired by 'Abdu'l-Bahá, a shining example to pioneers of present and future generations of East and West, surpassed in constancy, dedication, self-abnegation and fearlessness by none except the incomparable Martha Root. Her unremitting, highly meritorious activities in the course of almost half a century, both in North America and Southeast Europe, attaining their climax in the darkest, most dangerous phase of the second World War, shed imperishable lustre on contemporary Bahá'í history.
>
> This triumphant soul is now gathered to the distinguished band of her co-workers in the Abhá Kingdom; Martha Root, Lua Getsinger, May Maxwell, Hyde Dunn, Susan Moody, Keith Ransom-Kehler, Ella Bailey and Dorothy Baker, whose remains, lying in such widely scattered areas of the globe as Honolulu, Cairo, Buenos Aires, Sydney, Ṭihrán, Iṣfahán, Tripoli and the depths of the Mediterranean Sea attest the magnificence of the pioneer services rendered by the North American Bahá'í Community in the Apostolic and Formative Ages of the Bahá'í Dispensation. ...[1]

In a message written on his behalf to the European Teaching Committee, dated 24 May 1954, Shoghi Effendi referred to Marion Jack as an example for those who leave their homes to serve in foreign lands:

> For over thirty years, with an enlarged heart, and many other ailments, she remained at her post in Bulgaria. Never well-to-do, she often suffered actual poverty and want; want of heat, want of clothing, want of food, when her money failed to reach her because Bulgaria had come under the Soviet zone of influence. She was bombed, lost her possessions, she was evacuated, she lived in drafty, cold dormitories for many, many months in the country, she returned valiant to the capital of Bulgaria after the war, and continued, on foot, to carry out her teaching work. ... He thinks that every Bahá'í, and most particularly those who have left their homes and gone to serve in foreign fields, should know of, and turn their gaze to, Marion Jack.[2]

21.4.2 *Victories in Australasia*

The achievements in Australasia mentioned by Shoghi Effendi refer to the emergence and development of the Faith there as a result of the work of Clara and Hyde Dunn, who left their home in the United States and took the message of Bahá'u'lláh to Australia.

Hyde Dunn[3] was born in London in 1855 and worked as a travelling salesman in Britain and continental Europe before migrating to the United States. At a tinsmith shop in Seattle in 1905, Dunn saw the shopkeeper in conversation with a man (Ward Fitzgerald) who had just returned from the prison of 'Akká where he

---

1   Shoghi Effendi, *Citadel of Faith*, p. 164.

2   Written on behalf of Shoghi Effendi, cited in *Lights of Guidance*, p. 573.

3   Extracts from *Dunn, Clara and Hyde* by Graham Hassall, retrieved from https://bahai-library.com/hassall_clara_hyde_dunn.

had met 'Abdu'l-Bahá. He overheard the man quoting the words spoken by Bahá'u'lláh to E. G. Browne: "This earth is one country and mankind its citizens, regard ye not one another as strangers" (an early translation). Hyde was attracted to these words and soon accepted the Faith.

Hyde Dunn met Clara David in 1907 in Washington and taught her the Faith, which she accepted after a while. Both Clara and Hyde met 'Abdu'l-Bahá in California in 1912. Being in the presence of 'Abdu'l-Bahá gave them both a spiritual strength that sustained them through the remainder of their lives. Dunn and Clara married in 1917 and settled in Berkley.

In 1919, they learned of the call of 'Abdu'l-Bahá in the Tablets of the Divine Plan to the Bahá'ís of North America to take the message of Bahá'u'lláh to distant lands to which He was not able to travel Himself. They decided to rise to the call and take the Faith to Australia. To reduce the cost, Clara suggested that Hyde might go alone. They sent a cable to 'Abdu'l-Bahá, asking what course of action to take. He replied that they both should go together.

They arrived in Sydney on 3 February 1920. They initially had some financial constraints until Clara found a job. Hyde started work as a travelling salesman within a year, working in country towns during the week and returning home on weekends. Clara stayed in Sydney, inviting people to the meetings organized for the weekends in which Hyde spoke.

Hyde and Clara Dunn managed to foster the development of small and isolated Bahá'í communities across Australia and New Zealand. The first Australian Local Assembly was established in Melbourne in December 1923, followed by others in Perth in July 1924, Adelaide in December 1924, and Sydney in April 1925. A Local Assembly was formed in Auckland in 1923.

Shoghi Effendi stressed the necessity of forming a National Assembly in Australia and New Zealand when Clara met him during her pilgrimage in 1932. The National Spiritual Assembly for Australia and New Zealand was elected in 1934. Hyde passed away in Sydney on 7 February 1941.

After the passing of Hyde, Bahá'ís turned to Clara and expected her to give talks to them. In 1943, she settled in Brisbane for several months. She then resumed her travels, which had been interrupted by Hyde's illness, visiting Bahá'ís in major cities and country towns. Shoghi Effendi appointed Clara Dunn and Hyde Dunn (posthumously) as Hands of the Cause on 29 February 1952. After many years of service, Clara passed away on 18 November 1960.

In *God Passes By*, Shoghi Effendi refers to the opening of Australia and New Zealand by "the great-hearted and heroic Hyde Dunn":

"A new continent was opened to the Cause when, in response to the Tablets of the Divine Plan unveiled at the first Convention after the war, the great-hearted and heroic Hyde Dunn, at the advanced age of sixty-two, promptly forsook his home in California, and, seconded and accompanied by his wife, settled as a pioneer in Australia, where he was able to carry the Message to no less than seven hundred towns throughout that Commonwealth."[1]

21.5   Handmaidens of Bahá'u'lláh in the West

In paragraph 100, Shoghi Effendi admires the work of the women in the West who have made a significant contribution to the progress of the Faith and its establishment throughout the world since the inception of the Cause in western countries. He cites a statement from 'Abdu'l-Bahá declaring that one of the miracles of the dispensation of Bahá'u'lláh is that women have shown greater boldness than men. Shoghi Effendi then emphasizes the necessity for women to demonstrate this "boldness" more evidently throughout the virgin territories of Latin America to achieve great victories for the Faith.

The early history of the Faith in Europe and North America clearly shows that women played a critical role in establishing the Faith in those regions as well as taking the message of Bahá'u'lláh to virgin territories around the world.

We have already briefly reviewed the services rendered by Martha Root (section 7.5), Marion Jack (section 21.4.1) and Clara Dunn (section 21.4.2). In this section, the lives of a number of other handmaidens of Bahá'u'lláh in the West are briefly covered.

21.5.1   Lady Sara Blomfield

Sara Louisa Blomfield was born in Ireland in 1859 but lived primarily in London. She married Arthur Blomfield (1829-1899) on 21 April 1887 and became Lady Blomfield when he was knighted on 4 June 1889. She accepted the Faith in 1907 and became an outstanding Bahá'í. Lady Sara Blomfield hosted 'Abdu'l-Bahá in London and accompanied Him in Paris. She took detailed notes of 'Abdu'l-Bahá's talks in Paris that were later published as *Paris Talks*. 'Abdu'l-Bahá gave Lady Blomfield the Persian name "Sitárih Khánum", where "*sitárih*" means "star" and "*khánum*" means "madam" or "lady".

Shoghi Effendi was in England when he heard the news of the passing of 'Abdu'l-Bahá in 1921. Lady Sara Blomfield accompanied him on his return to Haifa. In Haifa, Lady Sara Blomfield recorded her experience of spending time with the Holy family and her conversations with them. She later published those notes together with her recollections of the days when she had hosted 'Abdu'l-Bahá in London in *The Chosen Highway*.

Lady Blomfield was a strong supporter of the rights of children. She assisted in the establishment of the Save the Children Fund and advocated the Geneva Declaration of the Rights of the child developed by League of Nations.

Lady Sara Blomfield passed away on 31 December 1939.[2]

---

[1]   Shoghi Effendi, *God Passes By*, p. 308.

[2]   Information from "A memorial to Lady Blomfield", *Bahá'í Journal UK*, Volume 20, No.1, May/June 2003/160 BE; and *Lady Blomfield: Her Life and Times*, Robert Weinberg. George Ronald, Oxford. 2012.

21.5.2 Corinne True

Corinne Knight True was born near Louisville, Kentucky, on 1 November 1861. After the Great Chicago Fire in 1871, the family moved to Chicago where her father had invested in Chicago real estate. In the late 1870s she married Moses True despite her father's opposition. Corinne and Moses settled in Chicago and became active members of a Protestant Church. They had eight children within 10 years. The family was very happy until their nine-year-old daughter, Harriet, fell down the basement steps and died. Following this incident, Corinne and Moses left the church and searched for an alternative Christian church.

In 1899, the loss of a son to diphtheria profoundly disturbed the family. Corinne started to search more widely for answers to her deep questions. She learned about Bahá'u'lláh in late 1899 and immediately accepted the Faith. Soon afterwards Corinne lost her seven-year-old son. 'Abdu'l-Bahá sent her a Tablet counselling her on the death of her son. In 1906, her 21-year old son died in a sailing accident.

On 25 February 1907, Corinne arrived in Palestine to see 'Abdu'l-Bahá. During her visit, 'Abdu'l-Bahá charged her with the responsibility of building the House of Worship in Chicago and provided her with detailed instructions on how to achieve it. On her return, Corinne facilitated the creation of a national body consisting of both men and women to coordinate the work of establishing the temple[1]. At the first convention held in Chicago in March 1909, delegates elected nine people to the Executive Board of the Bahá'í Temple Unity, including Corinne True.

Corinne suffered more emotionally when her husband died from a heart attack and her last surviving son caught tuberculosis in 1910. The son died three years later, the night before 'Abdu'l-Bahá laid the temple's cornerstone in Wilmette. 'Abdu'l-Bahá asked Corrine to join Him at the Plaza Hotel after she had buried her son in the morning. 'Abdu'l-Bahá had also lost all five of His sons.

'Abdu'l-Bahá called Corinne True the "Mother of the Temple". She was instrumental in initiating the construction of the Temple by finding suitable land, organizing meetings and raising the funds for it.

Corinne met Shoghi Effendi a number of times in her pilgrimages to the Holy land. The last time she met Shoghi Effendi was in Haifa in 1952 when she was 91 years old. Shoghi Effendi appointed her as a Hand of the Cause of God on 29 February 1952. She was one of several Hands who attended the dedication of the House of Worship in Wilmette on 2 May 1953.

Corinne True passed away in her home in Wilmette on 3 April 1961, when she was one hundred years old.[2]

---

[1] At the time, Chicago had two parallel Bahá'í organizations, one confined to men, the other to women. When, at Corinne True's instigation, a new national body was created to coordinate the work of the temple, 'Abdu'l-Bahá made it clear that it must include women.

[2] Notes from Robert Stockman, *True, Corinne*, 1995, retrieved from http://bahai-library.com/stockman_true.

21.5.3 May Maxwell

May Ellis Maxwell is known as the "mother of the Bahá'í community of Canada". Together with her husband, William Sutherland Maxwell, she established the first Bahá'í community in Montréal in 1902. May was born in Englewood, New Jersey on 14 January 1870.

May first met 'Abdu'l-Bahá on 17 February 1899 during a pilgrimage she made to Palestine with a group of American believers.

She met her future husband, William Maxwell, while living in Paris with her mother and brother in October 1899. On May 1902, they married in London, England, and moved to Montréal, where they started to build a Bahá'í community. Their home was known as a vibrant hub where people were taught about the Faith. Many early believers learned about the Faith in the Maxwells' home.

When 'Abdu'l-Bahá visited Montréal after five months travelling in the United States, He accepted the invitation of the Maxwells and stayed with them for four days. During that period, 'Abdu'l-Bahá gave seven public talks in addition to numerous interviews with various groups and individuals. After the visit, 'Abdu'l-Bahá praised May Maxwell for the arrangements she had made.

Despite poor health, May Maxwell served the Bahá'í community of Canada from 1902 until 1940. She made significant contributions to the establishment of the Bahá'í communities of St. John's, Brockville, Ottawa, Toronto, Calgary and Vancouver. She passed away shortly after pioneering to Argentine in 1940.[1] On 3 March 1940, Shoghi Effendi cabled the following to the Bahá'í world:

"ABDU'L-BAHÁ'S BELOVED HANDMAID DISTINGUISHED DISCIPLE MAY MAXWELL (is) GATHERED (into the) GLORY (of the) ABHÁ KINGDOM. HER EARTHLY LIFE SO RICH EVENTFUL INCOMPARABLY BLESSED (is) WORTHILY ENDED. TO SACRED TIE HER SIGNAL SERVICES HAD FORGED (the) PRICELESS HONOUR (of a) MARTYR'S DEATH. (A) DOUBLE CROWN DESERVEDLY WON. (The) SEVEN YEAR PLAN PARTICULARLY (the) SOUTH AMERICAN CAMPAIGN DERIVE FRESH IMPETUS (from the) EXAMPLE (of) HER GLORIOUS SACRIFICE. SOUTHERN OUTPOST (of) FAITH GREATLY ENRICHED THROUGH ASSOCIATION (with) HER HISTORIC RESTING-PLACE DESTINED REMAIN (a) POIGNANT REMINDER (of the) RESISTLESS MARCH (of the) TRIUMPHANT ARMY (of) BAHÁ'U'LLÁH. ADVISE BELIEVERS (of) BOTH AMERICAS (to) HOLD BEFITTING MEMORIAL GATHERINGS."[2]

21.5.4 Dorothy Baker

Dorothy Baker, née Dodds, was born on 21 December 1898 in Newark, New Jersey[3]. Her grandmother, Ellen Tuller Beecher, was one of the first Bahá'ís in

---

[1] Notes from The Bahá'í Community of Canada webpage on May Maxwell, retrieved from https://www.ca.bahai.org/canadian-bah%C3%A1%C3%AD-history/may-maxwell-1870%E2%80%931940.

[2] Shoghi Effendi, *This Decisive Hour*, p. 52.

[3] Notes from resources on *Heroes and Heroines, Core Curriculum*, retrieved from http://corecurriculum.bahai.us/downloads/2009_0818_Youth_Empowerment_Heroes_and_Heroines_Resource.pdf.

North America, and was known as "Mother Beecher". Ellen Tuller Beecher took her granddaughter to New York to see 'Abdu'l-Bahá when Dorothy was 13 years old. When they entered the room, 'Abdu'l-Bahá greeted Mother Beecher and directed Dorothy to sit on a footstool at His feet, facing the audience. As 'Abdu'l-Bahá spoke, Dorothy gradually turned to Him, gazing with adoration.

Dorothy studied at the Montclair Normal College in New Jersey and graduated in 1918. She met Frank Baker in September 1920 and they were married at Budd Lake, New Jersey on 21 June 1921. The family moved to Lima, Ohio, in 1927.

Dorothy Baker was an enthusiastic Bahá'í teacher and a powerful speaker. She used to spend a great deal of time studying the Bahá'í writings, and prayed daily and fervently. She served on the National Spiritual Assembly of the Bahá'ís of the United States for 14 years, worked on nine national committees, and travelled extensively, visiting many Bahá'í communities in the Americas and Europe. She gave lectures on the Bahá'í Faith to one hundred and forty American colleges and universities. She was appointed a Hand of the Cause in 1951.

Dorothy Baker died on 10 January 1954 in an airplane crash in the Mediterranean Sea near the island of Elba. She was only 56 years old.

On the passing of Dorothy Baker, Shoghi Effendi sent the following message, dated 13 January 1954 to the Bahá'í community:

> Hearts grieved at lamentable, untimely passing of Dorothy Baker, distinguished Hand of the Cause, eloquent exponent of its teachings, indefatigable supporter of its institutions, valiant defender of its precepts. Her long record of outstanding service has enriched the annals of the concluding years of the Heroic and the opening epoch of the Formative Age of the Bahá'í Dispensation. Fervently praying for the progress of her soul in the Abhá Kingdom.

> Assure relatives of profound loving sympathy. Her noble spirit is reaping bountiful reward.

> Advise hold memorial gathering in the Temple befitting her rank and imperishable services ....[1]

21.5.5   Effie Baker

Euphemia Eleanor Baker was the first Australian woman to accept the Faith of Bahá'u'lláh. Nicknamed Effie, she was born on 25 March 1880 at Goldsborough, Victoria, Australia. She studied visual arts and developed a great love for photography. In 1922, she became a Bahá'í after attending a talk given by Hyde Dunn on the Bahá'í Faith. She started her travel teaching by accompanying the Dunns to Tasmania and Western Australia in 1923. She visited New Zealand in 1924 with Martha Root. In New Zealand, she decided to join four Bahá'ís who were planning to make a pilgrimage to the Bahá'í holy places in Haifa. The pilgrims departed from Adelaide on January 1925.

---

[1]   Shoghi Effendi, *Citadel of Faith*, p. 161.

After the pilgrimage, Effie spent some weeks in England. She then returned to Haifa on the invitation of Shoghi Effendi to stay there as the hostess of a new pilgrim-house built for Western believers. Shoghi Effendi soon learnt of Effie's talent in photography and model making. At that time, Shoghi Effendi was preparing the first *Bahá'í Yearbook*, a publication reporting on worldwide Bahá'í activities, later to be renamed *Bahá'í World*. The early volumes of the publication include many photographs taken by Effie Baker of the Bahá'í monument gardens on Mt Carmel and the Bahá'í holy places in Haifa and 'Akká. Effie also constructed some models of the landscapes designed by Shoghi Effendi.

In 1930, Shoghi Effendi asked Effie Baker to travel to Írán to photograph places associated with the early history of the Bábí and Bahá'í religions. This was an urgent task since many places were being razed by the Persian Government's modernization program. At that time, Shoghi Effendi was completing his translation of *Nabil's Narrative* and he required her photographs for the first edition of the book. This was a dangerous assignment for Effie Baker not only because of the hostility of Persian authorities towards Bahá'ís, but also because of their attitude towards women and particularly to westerners.

Arriving in Írán via 'Iráq, Effie Baker travelled around the country, moving from one place to another by car, train, on horseback or riding a donkey. Her photographic equipment had to be kept hidden, and she often had to disguise herself by wearing a black "chador". She had to extend the length of her trip from three months to eight months. She used to process her films secretly at night to check that she had a good print of a site before travelling to the next location. By the time she returned to Haifa, she had over one thousand good prints, around 400 of which have been published.

Effie Baker returned to Goldsborough, Victoria, in February 1936 and remained there until she moved to Sydney in 1963. She died in January 1968.[1]

21.5.6 *Amelia Collins*

Amelia Engelder Collins, nicknamed Millie, was born on 7 June 1873 to a Lutheran family in Pittsburgh, Pennsylvania. She married mining engineer Thomas H. Collins and lived in Calumet, Michigan, and later Bisbee, Arizona, where Thomas developed porphyry copper operations with great success. Millie became a Bahá'í in the 1920s after the family moved to California. She made her first pilgrimage to the Bahá'í Holy places in Haifa in early 1923, accompanied by her husband, Thomas.

Millie was elected to the first National Spiritual Assembly of the Bahá'ís of the United States and Canada (1925) and remained a member until 1933. She was re-elected in 1938 and served until she was asked by Shoghi Effendi to serve at the Bahá'í World Centre. She travelled extensively throughout the United States and Canada as well as Central and South America during the first and the second Seven Year Plans, assisting the communities with the consolidation and teaching work.

---

[1] Graham Hassall, "Baker, Euphemia Eleanor", *Australian Dictionary of Biography*, Volume 14: 1940–1980, ed. John Ritchie, Melbourne University Publishing, 1996.

Although Thomas never formally embraced the Faith, he supported Millie in her Bahá'í work and her financial contributions to the Faith. He died suddenly of a heart attack in 1937. Later that year, Millie made her second pilgrimage to Haifa. On her return, she received a letter from Shoghi Effendi:

> The days you spent under the shadow of the Holy Shrines will long be remembered with joy and gratitude. I have during these days increasingly appreciated and admired the profound sense of devotion, the passionate fervour, the intense love and attachment that animates you in the service of this Holy Cause. For such noble qualities I feel thankful, and I am certain that the fruits they will yield will be equally outstanding and memorable. Rest assured and be happy.[1]

Millie was appointed by Shoghi Effendi as a Hand of the Cause God in 1947. She continued her travels within America as well as to Europe, Turkey and Egypt on various missions at the request of Shoghi Effendi.

In 1944, Millie sent a generous contribution to the Guardian to cover most of the cost of constructing the superstructure of the Shrine of the Báb. In 1953, Shoghi Effendi acknowledged the major financial contributions made by Millie to various Bahá'í projects and named the main gate to the Shrine of Bahá'u'lláh as Collin's Gate in her honour. In 1951, the Guardian appointed Millie Collins as the vice President of the International Bahá'í Council in 1951 and she spent her final years in Haifa.

Millie Collins passed to the Abhá Kingdom on the afternoon of 1 January 1962 while being held in the arms of Rúḥíyyih Khánum.[2]

21.6   Bahá'í youth

In paragraph 101, Shoghi Effendi highlights the importance of Bahá'í youth. Although they do not have much experience and resources, they possess an adventurous spirit, vigour, alertness and optimism. Hence, the Guardian asks them to play an active role in the Seven-Year Plan to teach the youth of their country. It is essential to demonstrate that the youth have an intelligent, persistent and effective participation in both the teaching work and the administrative work of the Faith. This will convince the critics of the Faith that the Cause:

- is intensely alive
- has a sound core
- has a safe-guarded future.

Such participation will contribute to the progress of the Faith, will affect the youths themselves, and spiritually empower them to display their inherent capacities to unfold a further stage of their spiritual evolution.

---

[1] Shoghi Effendi, cited in *The Bahá'í World*, Vol. 13, p. 836.

[2] Notes from *Collins, Amelia: The fulfilled Hope of 'Abdu'l-Bahá* by Richard Francis, retrieved from https://bahai-library.com/francis_collins_biography.

21.7   Importance of Panama

In paragraph 102, the Guardian refers to the importance of Panama and cites some statements from 'Abdu'l-Bahá in this regard. In the Tablets of the Divine Plan, 'Abdu'l-Bahá mentions that all the countries in Latin America, in particular Panama, will become important in the future. This is because of the strategic position of Panama where two oceans are connected through the Panama Canal. The Guardian then asks the Bahá'í community to pay special attention to this Republic.

21.8   Activities

21.8.1   Short answer questions

1.   What are the implications of the quote 95:A in the context of paragraph 95?

_____

_____

_____

_____

2.   Provide some examples of opportunities that may arise for a pioneer to awaken genuine interest in the Faith in local people as described in paragraph 96.

_____

_____

_____

_____

3.   What is the key point of quote 97:A in the context of paragraph 97?

_____

_____

_____

_____

4.   What would have been the advantages of close contact between the Inter-America Committee and pioneers as described in paragraph 98?

_____

_____

_____

_____

5.   What are the key points of quote99:A in the context of paragraph 99?

_____

_____

_____

_____

6.   What are the key points of quote 99:B?

_____

_____

_____

_____

7. In your opinion, what is meant by the "boldness" shown by women in this dispensation?

_____

_____

_____

_____

8. In one paragraph, summarize the most significant achievement of each of the following heroines of the Faith:

a) Lady Sara Blomfield

_____

_____

_____

_____

b) Corinne True

_____

_____

_____

_____

c) May Maxwell

_____

_____

_____

_____

d) Dorothy Baker

_____

_____

_____

_____

e) Effie Baker

_____

_____

_____

---

f)   Amelia Collins

---

9.   Why does the participation of the youth in the work of the Faith demonstrate that the Cause is alive, is sound and has a destiny, as described by Shoghi Effendi in paragraph 101?

---

10.   What is meant by "intelligent, persistent and effective" participation of the youth in the teaching and administrative work of the Cause?

---

11.   What are the key points mentioned by Shoghi Effendi in paragraph 102 regarding the Latin American countries?

21.8.2   Mini-project

Conduct research to identify other heroines of the Faith in the early history of the West who contributed significantly to the establishment of the Bahá'í Faith in America, Europe and the rest of the world.

22.
Going from strength to strength

22.1 Introduction

This chapter covers paragraphs 103–107, in which Shoghi Effendi warns the North American Bahá'í community of events of unimaginable magnitude in the remaining years of the first century of the Bahá'í Era that may threaten and undermine the efforts of the community in winning the goals of the Seven Year Plan. Such events are the result of the decay of the old order driven by the two processes of integration and disintegration towards the establishment of the World Order of Bahá'u'lláh. He also emphasizes the first Seven Year Plan as the initial stage in the implementation of the Tablets of the Divine Plan and a stepping-stone to the accelerated expansion of the Faith in the second century of the Bahá'í Era.

In this chapter, you need to reflect on and understand the following key points:

a) The outbreak of the Second World War foreshadowed a time of inconceivable horror.

- This war embroiled more than 30 countries.
- There are estimates that around 35–60 million people were killed.
- Millions of people were the victims of famine and disease epidemics.
- Around 5,700,000 Jews, half of them from Poland, died in Nazi concentration and death camps.

b) The two processes of integration and disintegration are two aspects of a greater plan of God, whose ultimate objectives are the unity of the human race and the peace of all mankind.

c) The integration process is the result of the steady consolidation and growth of the Faith.

d) The disintegration process is the decline and annihilation of outworn religious and secular institution of the old order.

e)   The first Seven Year Plan was a preliminary stage in the great scheme envisioned for the North American Bahá'í community in undertaking the responsibilities they were charged with by 'Abdu'l-Bahá in the Tablets of the Divine Plan.

f)   Shoghi Effendi stresses that the North American Bahá'í community should not be content with what they achieve in the first Seven Year Plan, but should reach for greater victories in future plans.

22.2   Paragraphs under study

103   Such, dearly beloved friends, is the vista that stretches before the eyes, and challenges the resources, of the American Bahá'í community in these, the concluding years of the First Century of the Bahá'í Era. Such are the qualities and qualifications demanded of them for the proper discharge of their responsibilities and duties. Such are the requirements, the possibilities, and the objectives of the Plan that claims every ounce of their energy. Who knows but that these few remaining, fast-fleeting years, may not be pregnant with events of unimaginable magnitude, with ordeals more severe than any that humanity has as yet experienced, with conflicts more devastating than any which have preceded them. Dangers, however sinister, must, at no time, dim the radiance of their new-born faith. Strife and confusion, however bewildering, must never befog their vision. Tribulations, however afflictive, must never shatter their resolve. Denunciations, however clamorous, must never sap their loyalty. Upheavals, however cataclysmic, must never deflect their course. The present Plan, embodying the budding hopes of a departed Master, must be pursued, relentlessly pursued, whatever may befall them in the future, however distracting the crises that may agitate their country or the world. Far from yielding in their resolve, far from growing oblivious of their task, they should, at no time, however much buffeted by circumstances, forget that the synchronization of such world-shaking crises with the progressive unfoldment and fruition of their divinely appointed task is itself the work of Providence, the design of an inscrutable Wisdom, and the purpose of an all-compelling Will, a Will that directs and controls, in its own mysterious way, both the fortunes of the Faith and the destinies of men. Such simultaneous processes of rise and of fall, of integration and of disintegration, of order and chaos, with their continuous and reciprocal reactions on each other, are but aspects of a greater Plan, one and indivisible, whose Source is God, whose author is Bahá'u'lláh, the theatre of whose operations is the entire planet, and whose ultimate objectives are the unity of the human race and the peace of all mankind.

104   Reflections such as these should steel the resolve of the entire Bahá'í community, should dissipate their forebodings, and arouse them to rededicate themselves to every single provision of that Divine Charter whose outline has been delineated for them by the pen of 'Abdu'l-Baha. The Seven Year Plan, as already stated, is but the initial stage, a stepping-stone to the unfoldment of the implications of this Charter. The impulse, originally generated through the movement of that pen, and which is now driving forward, with increasing momentum, the machinery of the Seven Year Plan, must, in the opening years of the next century, be further accelerated, and

impel the American Bahá'í community to launch further stages in the unfoldment of the Divine Plan, stages that will carry it far beyond the shores of the Northern Hemisphere, into lands and among peoples where that community's noblest acts of heroism are to be performed.

105 Let anyone inclined to doubt the course which this enviable community is destined to follow, turn to and meditate upon these words of 'Abdu'l-Bahá, enshrined, for all time, in the Tablets of the Divine Plan, and addressed to the entire community of the believers of the United States and Canada: *"The full measure of your success,"* He informs them, *"is as yet unrevealed, its significance still unapprehended. Erelong, ye will, with your own eyes, witness how brilliantly every one of you, even as a shining star, will radiate, in the firmament of your country, the light of Divine Guidance, and will bestow upon its people the glory of an everlasting life .... The range of your future achievements still remains undisclosed. I fervently hope that in the near future the whole earth may be stirred and shaken by the results of your achievements. The hope, therefore, which 'Abdu'l-Bahá cherishes for you is that the same success which has attended your efforts in America may crown your endeavours in other parts of the world, that through you the fame of the Cause of God may be diffused throughout the East and the West, and the advent of the Kingdom of the Lord of Hosts be proclaimed in all the five continents of the globe."*[A] *"The moment,"* He most significantly adds, *"this Divine Message is carried forward by the American believers from the shores of America, and is propagated throughout the continents of Europe, of Asia, of Africa, and of Australasia, and as far as the islands of the Pacific, this community will find itself securely established upon the throne of an everlasting dominion. Then will all the peoples of the world witness that this community is spiritually illumined and divinely guided. Then will the whole earth resound with the praises of its majesty and greatness."*[B]

106 No reader of these words, so vibrant with promises that not even the triumphant consummation of the Seven Year Plan can fulfil, can expect a community that has been raised so high, and endowed so richly, to remain content with any laurels it may win in the immediate future. To rest upon such laurels would indeed be tantamount to a betrayal of the trust placed in that community by 'Abdu'l-Bahá. To cut short the chain of victories that must lead it on to that supreme triumph when *"the whole earth may be stirred and shaken"* by the results of its achievements would shatter His hopes. To vacillate, and fail to *"propagate through the continents of Europe, of Asia, of Africa, and of Australasia, and as far as the islands of the Pacific"* a Message so magnificently proclaimed by it in the American continent would deprive it of the privilege of being *"securely established upon the throne of an everlasting dominion."* To forfeit the honour of proclaiming *"the advent of the Kingdom of the Lord of Hosts"* in *"all the five continents of the globe"* would silence those *"praises of its majesty and greatness"* that otherwise would echo throughout *"the whole earth."*

107 Such vacillation, failure, or neglect, the American believers, the ambassadors of the Faith of Bahá'u'lláh, will, I am firmly convinced, never permit. Such a trust will never be betrayed, such hopes can never be shattered, such a

privilege will never be forfeited, nor will such praises remain unuttered. Nay rather the present generation of this blessed, this repeatedly blessed, community will go from strength to strength, and will hand on, as the first century draws to a close, to the generations that must succeed it in the second the torch of Divine Guidance, undimmed by the tempestuous winds that must blow upon it, that they in turn, faithful to the wish and mandate of 'Abdu'l-Bahá, may carry that torch, with that self-same vigour, fidelity, and enthusiasm, to the darkest and remotest corners of the earth.

22.3   Events of unimaginable magnitude

In paragraph 103, Shoghi Effendi highlights that what he described in the previous paragraphs were the qualities and qualifications expected from the North American Bahá'ís, and the "requirements, the possibilities and the objectives" of the first Seven Year Plan set to conclude the First Century of the Bahá'í Era in 1944. The seven-year duration of the Plan, Shoghi Effendi points out, may be pregnant with "events of unimaginable magnitude". The North American Bahá'ís, he emphasizes, must not be deflected from their focus and resolution by the crises and dangers that may affect their country and the world during that period. He specifically points out that:

- Dangers should not diminish their new-born faith.
- Strife and confusion must not darken their vision.
- Tribulations must not shake their will.
- Threats must not undermine their loyalty.
- Upheavals must not turn them away from their direction of action.

This is a theme found in earlier messages of Shoghi Effendi in which he spells out the calamities that lie ahead and the forces causing them. For example, in a message that he wrote to the Bahá'í communities in the West a year earlier, dated 11 March 1937, he states:

The passionate and violent happenings that have, in recent years, strained to almost the point of complete breakdown the political and economic structure of society are too numerous and complex to attempt, within the limitations of this general survey, to arrive at an adequate estimate of their character. Nor have these tribulations, grievous as they have been, seemed to have reached their climax, and exerted the full force of their destructive power. The whole world, wherever and however we survey it, offers us the sad and pitiful spectacle of a vast, an enfeebled, and moribund organism, which is being torn politically and strangulated economically by forces it has ceased to either control or comprehend. The Great Depression, the aftermath of the severest ordeals humanity had ever experienced, the disintegration of the Versailles system, the recrudescence of militarism in its most menacing aspects, the failure of vast experiments and new-born institutions to safeguard the peace and tranquillity of peoples, classes and nations, have bitterly disillusioned humanity and prostrated its spirits. Its hopes are, for the most part, shattered, its vitality is ebbing, its life strangely disordered, its unity severely compromised.[1]

22.3.1   Crises caused by the Second World War

Two years into the Plan, on September 1, 1939, the Second World War broke out and continued until September 2, 1945, one year after the end of the Seven Year Plan. This war enmeshed more than 30 countries of the world representing more than 100 million people grouped into two opposing alliances. The major players were the Axis Powers—Germany, Italy and Japan and the Allies—France, Great Britain, the United States and the Soviet Union as well as China to a lesser extent. Although there are no accurate figures available, there are estimates that around 35–60 million people were killed. It has been challenging to determine the number of people who were injured or permanently disabled, making it the most violent and the largest war in human history. Eastern Europe had the highest human loss with Poland losing 20 percent of its pre-war population, Yugoslavia and the Soviet Union around 10 per cent.[2]

There were millions who became the victims of famine and disease epidemics in China and East Asia in addition to those who died in battles or as the result of bombardment. Around 5,700,000 Jews, half of them from Poland died in Nazi concentration and death camps. It is difficult to estimate the material and the human cost of the war and the degree of misery, deprivation, suffering and dislocation of masses. Many countries in the Far East such as China, Burma, India and Philippines either suffered exploitation and abuse under Japanese occupation or were inflicted by famine and epidemics. In Japan, 40 percent of the built-up areas of 66 Japanese cities were destroyed. The two cities of Hiroshima and Nagasaki were annihilated by the atomic bombs used by the United States.[3]

22.3.2   In the clutches of a cleansing force

In a statement made in 1941, Shoghi Effendi warns humanity of the calamities that were destined to inflict humanity:

> A tempest, unprecedented in its violence, unpredictable in its course, catastrophic in its immediate effects, unimaginably glorious in its ultimate consequences, is at present sweeping the face of the earth. Its driving power is remorselessly gaining in range and momentum. Its cleansing force, however much undetected, is increasing with every passing day. Humanity, gripped in the clutches of its devastating power, is smitten by the evidences of its resistless fury. It can neither perceive its origin, nor probe its significance, nor discern its outcome. Bewildered, agonized and helpless, it watches this great and mighty wind of God invading the remotest and fairest regions of the earth, rocking its foundations, deranging its equilibrium, sundering its nations, disrupting the homes of its peoples, wasting its cities, driving into exile its kings, pulling down its bulwarks, uprooting its institutions, dimming

---

[1]   Shoghi Effendi, *The World Order of Bahá'u'lláh*, p. 188.

[2]   John Graham Royde-Smith, Thomas A. Hughes, *World War II*, retrieved from *Encyclopaedia Britannica*, https://www.britannica.com/event/World-War-II.

[3]   John Graham Royde-Smith, Thomas A. Hughes, *World War II*, retrieved from *Encyclopaedia Britannica*, https://www.britannica.com/event/World-War-II.

its light, and harrowing up the souls of its inhabitants.[1]

In *Century of Light*, the ruin that human race has brought upon itself during the twenties century as a result of the process of disintegration is portrayed:

> The loss of life alone has been beyond counting. The disintegration of basic institutions of social order, the violation—indeed, the abandonment—of standards of decency, the betrayal of the life of the mind through surrender to ideologies as squalid as they have been empty, the invention and deployment of monstrous weapons of mass annihilation, the bankrupting of entire nations and the reduction of masses of human beings to hopeless poverty, the reckless destruction of the environment of the planet—such are only the more obvious in a catalogue of horrors unknown to even the darkest of ages past.[2]

22.4   Processes of integration and disintegration

In paragraph 103, Shoghi Effendi, describes the two parallel and synchronized processes of the unfoldment of the Divine Plan and the "world-shaking crises" as the design and the work of the Divine Will, directing and controlling the fortunes of the Faith and the destiny of humanity.

22.4.1   *Nature of integration and disintegration processes*

The integration process is the progression of steady consolidation and growth of the Faith whereas the disintegration process is the decline and annihilation of outworn religious and secular institutions of the old world order.

In a number of messages, Shoghi Effendi describes the historical process unfolding in the 20th century in the context of the two processes of integration and disintegration. In a letter dated 5 July 1938 to the National Spiritual Assembly of the United States and Canada, Shoghi Effendi reiterates the crises facing humanity in the remaining years of the First Century of the Bahá'í Era by stating:

> Pregnant indeed are the years looming ahead of us all. The twin processes of internal disintegration and external chaos are being accelerated and every day and are inexorably moving towards a climax. The rumblings that must precede the eruption of those forces that must cause 'the limbs of humanity to quake' can already be heard. 'The time of the end,' 'the latter years,' as foretold in the Scriptures, are at long last upon us. The Pen of Bahá'u'lláh, the voice of 'Abdu'l-Bahá, have time and again, insistently and in terms unmistakable, warned an unheeding humanity of impending disaster. The Community of the Most Great Name, the leaven that must leaven the lump, the chosen remnant that must survive the rolling up of the old, discredited, tottering Order, and assist in the unfoldment of a new one in its stead, is standing ready, alert, clear-visioned, and resolute.[3]

In another message, Shoghi Effendi identifies the evidences of disintegration:

> Beset on every side by the cumulative evidences of disintegration, of turmoil

---

[1]   Shoghi Effendi, *The Promised Day is Come*, p. 3.

[2]   Prepared under supervision of the Universal House of Justice, *Century of Light*, p. 2.

[3]   Shoghi Effendi, *This Decisive Hour*, p. 23.

and of bankruptcy, serious-minded men and women, in almost every walk of life, are beginning to doubt whether society, as it is now organized, can, through its unaided efforts, extricate itself from the slough into which it is steadily sinking. Every system, short of the unification of the human race, has been tried, repeatedly tried, and been found wanting. Wars again and again have been fought, and conferences without number have met and deliberated. Treaties, pacts and covenants have been painstakingly negotiated, concluded and revised. Systems of government have been patiently tested, have been continually recast and superseded. Economic plans of reconstruction have been carefully devised, and meticulously executed. And yet crisis has succeeded crisis, and the rapidity with which a perilously unstable world is declining has been correspondingly accelerated.[1]

22.4.2   *Comparison of twin processes*

Comparing the two processes of integration and disintegration, Shoghi Effendi exclaims: "How striking, how edifying the contrast between the process of slow and steady consolidation that characterizes the growth of its [the Faith's] infant strength and the devastating onrush of the forces of disintegration that are assailing the outworn institutions, both religious and secular, of present-day society!"[2]

In another message he states:

"The contrast between the accumulating evidences of steady consolidation that accompany the rise of the Administrative Order of the Faith of God, and the forces of disintegration which batter at the fabric of a travailing society, is as clear as it is arresting. Both within and outside the Bahá'í world the signs and tokens which, in a mysterious manner, are heralding the birth of that World Order, the establishment of which must signalize the Golden Age of the Cause of God, are growing and multiplying day by day. No fair-minded observer can any longer fail to discern them. He cannot be misled by the painful slowness characterizing the unfoldment of the civilization which the followers of Bahá'u'lláh are labouring to establish. Nor can he be deluded by the ephemeral manifestations of returning prosperity which at times appear to be capable of checking the disruptive influence of the chronic ills afflicting the institutions of a decaying age. The signs of the times are too numerous and compelling to allow him to mistake their character or to belittle their significance. He can, if he be fair in his judgment, recognize in the chain of events which proclaim on the one hand the irresistible march of the institutions directly associated with the Revelation of Bahá'u'lláh and foreshadow on the other the downfall of those powers and principalities that have either ignored or opposed it—he can recognize in them all evidences of the operation of God's all-pervasive Will, the shaping of His perfectly ordered and world-embracing Plan."[3]

---

[1]   Shoghi Effendi, *The World Order of Bahá'u'lláh*, p. 160.
[2]   Shoghi Effendi, *The World Order of Bahá'u'lláh*, pp. 154–155.
[3]   Shoghi Effendi, *The World Order of Bahá'u'lláh*, p. 161.

22.4.3   Fortunes of the Faith rising amidst the chaos

Shoghi Effendi identifies "the two parallel processes of integration and disintegration associated respectively with the rising fortunes of God's infant Faith and the sinking fortunes of the institutions of a declining civilization."[1] He also refers to the process of disintegration as one of the two things that will attract people to the Faith. In a letter written on his behalf to an individual dated July 3, 1948, he states:

"There are two things which will contribute greatly to bringing more people into the Cause more swiftly: one is the maturity of the Bahá'ís within their Communities, functioning according to Bahá'í laws and in the proper spirit of unity, and the other is the disintegration of society and the suffering it will bring in its wake. When the old forms are seen to be hopelessly useless, the people will stir from their materialism and spiritual lethargy, and embrace the Faith."[2]

In another message, Shoghi Effendi expands further on how the leaders of religion and politics should turn their attention to the Revelation of Bahá'u'lláh when they experience the bankruptcy of their ideas and the disintegration of the systems in which they once believed:

"Leaders of religion, exponents of political theories, governors of human institutions, who at present are witnessing with perplexity and dismay the bankruptcy of their ideas, and the disintegration of their handiwork, would do well to turn their gaze to the Revelation of Bahá'u'lláh, and to meditate upon the World Order which, lying enshrined in His teachings, is slowly and imperceptibly rising amid the welter and chaos of present-day civilization. They need have no doubt or anxiety regarding the nature, the origin or validity of the institutions which the adherents of the Faith are building up throughout the world. For these lie embedded in the teachings themselves, unadulterated and unobscured by unwarrantable inferences, or unauthorized interpretations of His Word."[3]

The Guardian also warns us that we should be conscious not to be affected by the dark force generated through the disintegration process. In a letter written on his behalf to the Spiritual Assembly of Atlanta, dated February 5, 1957, he states:

"The friends must, at all times, bear in mind that they are, in a way, like soldiers under attack. The world is at present in an exceedingly dark condition spiritually; hatred and prejudice, of every sort, are literally tearing it to pieces. We, on the other hand, are the custodians of the opposite forces, the forces of love, of unity, of peace and integration, and we must constantly be on our guard, whether as individuals or as an Assembly or Community, lest through us these destructive, negative forces enter into our midst. In other words we must beware lest the darkness of society become reflected in our acts and

---

[1]   Shoghi Effendi, *Messages to the Bahá'í World: 1950–1957*, p. 102.

[2]   Shoghi Effendi, *Promoting Entry by Troops*, p. 4.

[3]   Shoghi Effendi, *The World Order of Bahá'u'lláh*, p. 23.

attitudes, perhaps all unconsciously. Love for each other, the deep sense that we are a new organism, the dawn-breakers for a New World Order, must constantly animate our Bahá'í lives, and we must pray to be protected from the contamination of society which is so diseased with prejudice."[1]

The two processes of integration and disintegration have been accelerating day by day since the time of Shoghi Effendi, resulting in the deepening of the crises facing humanity and advancement of the Faith and its institutions. In a letter from the Universal House of Justice, dated 27 April 2017, written to an individual, the features of the disintegration process in the context of the society we live in are described:

"One of the current features of the process of the disintegration of the old world order manifest in the United States is the increasing polarization and fragmentation that has come to characterize so much of political and social life. There has been a hardening of viewpoints, increased incivility, an unwillingness to compromise or even entertain differing perspectives, and a tendency to automatically take sides and fight. Science and religion, two great lights that should guide human progress, are often compromised or swept aside. Matters of moral principle and questions of justice are reduced to intractable liberal or conservative viewpoints, and the country is increasingly divided along divergent lines."[2]

22.5   Beyond Seven Year Plan

In paragraph 104, Shoghi Effendi refers to the first Seven Year Plan as the initial stage in the implementation of the Tablets of the Divine Plan and a stepping-stone to the accelerated expansion of the Faith in the second century of the Bahá'í Era. In paragraph 105, Shoghi Effendi cites 'Abdu'l-Bahá (quote 105:A) explaining that the full measure of the success of the North American Bahá'í community is still unknown. 'Abdu'l-Bahá hopes that the community in its world-wide efforts, will be as successful as it has been at the home-front. He then promises that when the American Bahá'í community takes the message of Bahá'u'lláh to the far corners of the earth, as far as Australasia and the islands of the South Pacific, it will find itself securely established. Then will all the peoples of the earth praise this community for its majesty and greatness.

Shoghi Effendi continues this theme in paragraphs 106 and 107. He stresses that the North American Bahá'í community should not remain content with what they achieve in the first Seven Year Plan as it would be equivalent to a betrayal of the trust placed on them by 'Abdu'l-Bahá. The American Bahá'ís, he is confident, will not permit "such vacillation, failure, or neglect".

Such remarks, clearly show that Shoghi Effendi considered the first Seven Year Plan only as a preliminary stage in the great scheme he had envisioned for the North American Bahá'í community in undertaking the responsibilities with which

---

[1]   Shoghi Effendi, *Lights of Guidance*, pp. 404–405.

[2]   The Universal House of Justice, letter to an individual, retrieved from https://www.bahai.org/library/authoritative-texts/the-universal-house-of-justice/messages/20170427_001/1#551493752.

they were charged by 'Abdu'l-Bahá in the Tablets of the Divine Plan. The consecutive plans introduced by Shoghi Effendi after the first Seven Year Plan for the North American Bahá'í community as well as other Bahá'í communities around the world well demonstrate his systematic approach and genius in developing the Bahá'í Administrative Order and preparing the Bahá'í community worldwide for the election of the Universal House of Justice. In the following sections a brief review of the plans during the ministry of Shoghi Effendi, in which the North American Bahá'í community played a major role, is presented.

22.5.1 Second Seven Year Plan

Following the completion of the first Seven Year Plan, the North American Bahá'í community had two years of respite to consolidate the victories achieved during the Plan. In 1946, the Guardian called upon the North American Bahá'í community to undertake its second Seven Year Plan, the completion of which would coincide with the Centenary of the birth of the Bahá'í Revelation in 1953. In a message sent to the 38th American Annual National Convention, reproduced in section 22.7, Shoghi Effendi articulated the objectives of the new plan:

- "THE FIRST OBJECTIVE (of the) NEW PLAN (is) CONSOLIDATION (of) VICTORIES (already) WON THROUGHOUT (the) AMERICAS, INVOLVING MULTIPLICATION (of) BAHÁ'Í CENTRES, BOLDER PROCLAMATION (of the) FAITH (to the) MASSES.
- (The) SECOND OBJECTIVE (is) COMPLETION (of the) INTERIOR ORNAMENTATION (of the) HOLIEST HOUSE (of) WORSHIP (in the) BAHÁ'Í WORLD DESIGNED (to) COINCIDE (with the) FIFTIETH ANNIVERSARY (of the) INCEPTION (of this) HISTORIC ENTERPRISE.
- (The) THIRD OBJECTIVE (is the) FORMATION (of) THREE NATIONAL ASSEMBLIES, PILLARS (of the) UNIVERSAL HOUSE (of) JUSTICE, (in the) DOMINION (of) CANADA, CENTRAL (and) SOUTH AMERICA.
- (The) FOURTH OBJECTIVE (is the) INITIATION (of) SYSTEMATIC TEACHING ACTIVITY (in) WAR-TORN, SPIRITUALLY FAMISHED EUROPEAN CONTINENT, CRADLE (of) WORLD-FAMED CIVILIZATIONS, TWICE-BLEST (by) 'ABDU'L-BAHÁ'S VISITS, WHOSE RULERS BAHÁ'U'LLÁH SPECIFICALLY (and) COLLECTIVELY ADDRESSED, AIMING (at) ESTABLISHMENT (of) ASSEMBLIES (in the) IBERIAN PENINSULA, (the) LOW COUNTRIES, (the) SCANDINAVIAN STATES, (and) ITALY."[1]

In order to pursue the goals in the new spiritual frontier—Western Europe—a European National Teaching Committee was formed to pursue the processes of expansion and consolidation of the Faith in the ten countries of Portugal, Spain, Italy, Switzerland, Luxemburg, Belgium, Holland and Denmark. Four new National Assemblies were formed during this Plan: Canada, Central America, South America and Italo-Swiss. Hence, there were 12 National Assemblies functioning in the Bahá'í world by Riḍván 1953.

Shoghi Effendi encouraged the newly formed National Assemblies immediately to adopt expansion and consolidation plans, referring to them as

---

1   Shoghi Effendi, *This Decisive Hour*, p. 113. Bullets are added for emphasis.

"accessory plans" in one of his letters.[1] The National Assemblies were guided by the Guardian to deploy the methods and instruments developed by the North American Bahá'í community during their first Seven Year Plan. A summary of the accessory plans is provided in Table 22.1.

National plans	Duration	Date
Australia & New Zealand	Six-Year Plan	1947–1953
British Isles	Six-Year Plan	1944–1950
	Two-Year Plan	1951–1953
Egypt & Sudan	Five-Year Plan	1948–1953
Germany & Austria	Five-Year Plan	1948–1953
India, Pakistan & Burma	Four-&-half Year Plan	Jan. 1946–July 1950
	Nineteen-month Plan	Sep. 1951–April 1953
Iraq	Three-Year Plan	1947–1950
Persia	Forty-five-month Plan concurrent with	Oct. 1946–July 1950
	Women's Four-year Plan	1946–1950

Table 22.1: **National plans outside the North American continent**[2]

22.5.2 *Ten Year Crusade*

The Ten Year Crusade was a plan launched by Shoghi Effendi in 1953 to significantly expand the Faith throughout the world and to build the administrative structure on the basis of which the Universal House of Justice could be elected. The chain of messages of Shoghi Effendi, particularly to the North American Bahá'í community, shows that the Guardian had been preparing the Bahá'í world for such a Plan since the launch of the first Seven Year Plan. His guidance and statements in the paragraphs studied in this part of the book set out his hopes and future goals.

Early in 1953, Shoghi Effendi announced the goals and objectives of the Ten Year Crusade in his message to the International Conference for the Western Hemisphere. At the same time, he released the details of the Plan in a 27 page document that was published as a booklet in Britain and the United States. He also included the major objectives for each continent in his message to each of the four continental conferences. In 12 messages, each one of which was addressed to a particular National Assembly, he described the major objectives of the Plan as well as the supplementary goals designated for that specific country or region.

The four major objectives of the Ten Year Plan were:

First, development of the institutions at the World Centre of the Faith in the Holy Land. Second, consolidation, through carefully devised measures on the home front of the twelve territories destined to serve as administrative bases for the operations of the twelve National Plans. Third, consolidation of all

---

[1] Mentioned by 'Alí Na<u>kh</u>javání, "The Ten Year Crusade", *Journal of Bahá'í Studies*, 14:3–4, Ottawa: Association for Bahá'í Studies North America, 2004. https://bahai-studies.ca/wp-content/uploads/2014/03/14.3-4.Nakhjavani1.pdf.

[2] 'Alí Na<u>kh</u>javání, "The Ten Year Crusade", *Journal of Bahá'í Studies*, 14:3–4, Ottawa: Association for Bahá'í Studies North America, 2004.

territories already opened to the Faith. Fourth, the opening of the remaining chief virgin territories on the planet through specific allotments to each National Assembly functioning in the Bahá'í world.[1]

This is how Shoghi Effendi describes the nature of the Ten Year Crusade in his message dated 4 May 1953:

> The avowed, the primary aim of this Spiritual Crusade is none other than the conquest of the citadels of men's hearts. The theatre of its operations is the entire planet. Its duration a whole decade. Its commencement synchronizes with the centenary of the birth of Bahá'u'lláh's Mission. Its culmination will coincide with the centenary of the declaration of that same Mission. The agencies assisting in its conduct are the nascent administrative institutions of a steadily evolving divinely appointed order. Its driving force is the energizing influence generated by the Revelation heralded by the Báb and proclaimed by Bahá'u'lláh. Its Marshal is none other than the Author of the Divine Plan. Its standard-bearers are the Hands of the Cause of God appointed in every continent of the globe. Its generals are the twelve national spiritual assemblies participating in the execution of its design. Its vanguard is the chief executors of 'Abdu'l-Bahá's master plan, their allies and associates. Its legions are the rank and file of believers standing behind these same twelve national assemblies and sharing in the global task embracing the American, the European, the African, the Asiatic and Australian fronts. The charter directing its course is the immortal Tablets that have flowed from the pen of the Centre of the Covenant Himself. The armour with which its onrushing hosts have been invested is the glad tidings of God's own message in this day, the principles underlying the order proclaimed by His Messenger, and the laws and ordinances governing His Dispensation. The battle cry animating its heroes and heroines is the cry of Yá Bahá'u'l-Abhá, Yá 'Alíyyu'l-A'lá.[2]

22.6   Inauguration of the second Seven Year Plan

On April 25, 1946, Shoghi Effendi announced the objectives of the second Seven Year Plan of the American Bahá'í Community in a message he wrote to the 1946 Bahá'í Convention:

> Hail with joyous heart the delegates of the American Bahá'í Community assembled beneath the dome of the Mother Temple of the West in momentous Convention of the first year of peace. The souls are uplifted in thanksgiving for the protection vouchsafed by Providence to the preeminent community of the Bahá'í world enabling its members to consummate, despite the tribulations of a world-convulsing conflict, the first stage of 'Abdu'l-Bahá's Plan. The Campaign culminating the Centenary of the inauguration of the Bahá'í Era completed sixteen months ere the appointed time the exterior ornamentation of the Mashriqu'l-Adhkár, laid the basis of the administrative order in every virgin state and province of the North American Continent, almost doubled the Assemblies established since the inception of the Faith, established Assemblies in fourteen republics of Latin America, constituted

---

[1]   Shoghi Effendi, *Messages to the Bahá'í World: 1950–1957,* p. 42.
[2]   Shoghi Effendi, *Messages to the Bahá'í World: 1950–1957,* pp. 152–153.

active groups in remaining republics, swelled to sixty the sovereign states within the pale of the Faith.

The two-year respite, well-earned after the expenditure of such a colossal effort, covering such a tremendous range, during so dark a period, is now ended. The prosecutors of the Plan who in the course of six war-ridden years achieved such prodigies of service in the Western Hemisphere from Alaska to Magallanes are now collectively summoned to assume in the course of the peaceful years ahead still weightier responsibilities for the opening decade of the Second Century. The time is ripe, events are pressing. Hosts on high are sounding the signal for inauguration of second Seven Year Plan designed to culminate first Centennial of the year Nine marking the mystic birth of Bahá'u'lláh's prophetic mission in Síyáh-Chál at Ṭihrán.

A two-fold responsibility urgently calls the vanguard of the dawn-breakers of Bahá'u'lláh's Order, torch-bearers of world civilization, executors of 'Abdu'l-Bahá's mandate, to arise and simultaneously bring to fruition the tasks already undertaken and launch fresh enterprises beyond the borders of the Western Hemisphere.

The first objective of the new Plan is consolidation of victories already won throughout the Americas, involving multiplication of Bahá'í centres, bolder proclamation of the Faith to the masses. The second objective is completion of the interior ornamentation of the holiest House of Worship in the Bahá'í world designed to coincide with the fiftieth anniversary of the inception of this historic enterprise. The third objective is the formation of three national Assemblies, pillars of the Universal House of Justice, in the Dominion of Canada, Central and South America. The fourth objective is the initiation of systematic teaching activity in war-torn, spiritually famished European continent, cradle of world-famed civilizations, twice-blest by 'Abdu'l-Bahá's visits, whose rulers Bahá'u'lláh specifically and collectively addressed, aiming at establishment of Assemblies in the Iberian Peninsula, the Low Countries, the Scandinavian states, and Italy. No effort is too great for community belonging to the continent whose rulers Bahá'u'lláh addressed in the Most Holy Book, whose members were invested with spiritual primacy by 'Abdu'l-Bahá and named by Him apostles of His Father, whose country was the first western nation to respond to the Divine Message and deemed worthy to be first to build the Tabernacle of the Most Great Peace, whose administrators evolved the pattern of the embryonic world order, consummated the first stage of the Divine Plan, and whose elevation to the throne of everlasting dominion the Centre of the Covenant confidently anticipated. As the resistless impulse propelling the Plan accelerates, the American Community must rise to new levels of potency in response to the divine mandate, scale loftier heights of heroism, insure fuller participation of the rank and file of members, and closer collaboration with the agencies designed to insure attainment of the fourfold objectives, and evince greater audacity in tearing down the barriers in its path.

Upon the success of the second Seven Year Plan depends the launching, after a respite of three brief years, of a yet more momentous third Seven Year Plan which, when consummated through the establishment of the structure of the administrative order in the remaining sovereign states and chief dependencies of the entire globe, must culminate in and be befittingly commemorated through worldwide celebrations marking the Centennial of the formal assumption by Bahá'u'lláh of the prophetic office associated with Daniel's prophecy and the world triumph of the Bahá'í revelation and signalizing the termination of the initial epoch in the evolution of the Plan whose mysterious, resistless processes must continue to shed ever-increasing lustre on successive generations of both the Formative and Golden Ages of the Faith of Bahá'u'lláh. ... Pledging ten thousand dollars as my initial contribution for the furtherance of the manifold purposes of a glorious crusade surpassing every enterprise undertaken by the followers of the Faith of Bahá'u'lláh in the course of the first Bahá'í century.[1]

---

[1] Shoghi Effendi, *This Decisive Hour*, pp. 112–113.

22.7 Activities

22.7.1 *Short answer questions*

1. Describe the events and conflicts mentioned by Shoghi Effendi in the following statement from paragraph 103?

    "Who knows but that these few remaining, fast-fleeting years, may not be pregnant with events of unimaginable magnitude, with ordeals more severe than any that humanity has as yet experienced, with conflicts more devastating than any which have preceded them."

    _____

    _____

    _____

    _____

2. What is your understanding of the following statement from paragraph 103?

    "Dangers, however sinister, must, at no time, dim the radiance of their new-born faith. Strife and confusion, however bewildering, must never befog their vision. Tribulations, however afflictive, must never shatter their resolve. Denunciations, however clamorous, must never sap their loyalty. Upheavals, however cataclysmic, must never deflect their course. The present Plan, embodying the budding hopes of a departed Master, must be pursued, relentlessly pursued, whatever may befall them in the future, however distracting the crises that may agitate their country or the world."

    _____

    _____

    _____

    _____

3. What are the two processes of integration and disintegration referred to in paragraph 103?

    _____

    _____

    _____

    _____

4. What are the reciprocal reactions of the two processes of integration and disintegration on each other as mentioned in paragraph 103?

    _____

    _____

    _____

    _____

5. What does Shoghi Effendi mean by "stepping-stone" in the following statement form paragraph 104?

    "The Seven Year Plan, as already stated, is but the initial stage, a stepping-stone to the unfoldment of the implications of this Charter."

    _____
    _____
    _____
    _____

6. Consider the last sentence of paragraph 104.

    a) What is meant by "impulse" in terms of the Seven Year Plan?

        _____
        _____
        _____
        _____

    b) What does Shoghi Effendi mean by "that pen"?

        _____
        _____
        _____
        _____

    c) What are the processes driven by the "impulse" as described in the statement?

        _____
        _____
        _____
        _____

    d) What are the key points of quote 105:A?

        _____
        _____
        _____
        _____

    e) What are the key points of quote 105:B?

        _____
        _____

7. Answer the following questions based on the first two sentences of paragraph 106.

    a) What are "laurels"?

    _____

    _____

    _____

    _____

    b) What is the "betrayal of the trust"?

    _____

    _____

    _____

    _____

8. What are the key points in the last three sentences of paragraph 106?

    _____

    _____

    _____

    _____

    _____

    _____

    _____

    _____

22.7.2 Mini-project

Study the second Seven Year Plan of the North American Bahá'í community. Compare its goals and objectives with the goals of the first Seven Year Plan. How do the differences reflect the growth and evolution of the North American Bahá'í community? Write up your findings and analysis as a paper for publication in a Bahá'í journal.

23.
Bahá'u'lláh's sublime utterances

23.1 Introduction

This chapter covers paragraphs 108–115, in which the Guardian cites some of the then unpublished and untranslated Writings of the Bahá'u'lláh regarding teaching and pioneering initiatives. The statements are grouped around a specific theme in several paragraphs.

Here are the major topics covered by the statements:

a) The virtues and favours bestowed on the followers of Bahá'u'lláh and their duty to teach the cause.
b) The station of a true believer.
c) The transforming power of Bahá'u'lláh.
d) The greatness of this Day.
e) The dangers foreshadowed by Bahá'u'lláh.
f) Tolerance and patience under adversities.
g) The paramount importance of teaching the Cause.
h) Those who arise to aid Bahá'u'lláh

To facilitate the study of these paragraphs, the major key points of each quotation are highlighted in the body of this chapter. The key points assist you to obtain a deeper understanding of each quotation. Read each quotation in conjunction with the highlighted key points. When you have grasped the full meaning of each quotation, you will be able to answer the questions at the end of the chapter.

23.2 Paragraphs under study

108 Dearly beloved friends! I can do no better, eager as I am to extend to every one of you any assistance in my power that may enable you to discharge more effectively your divinely appointed, continually multiplying duties, than to direct your special attention, at this decisive hour, to these immortal

passages, gleaned in part from the great mass of Bahá'u'lláh's unpublished and untranslated writings. Whether in His revelation of the station and functions of His loved ones, or His eulogies of the greatness of His Cause, or His emphasis on the paramount importance of teaching, or the dangers which He foreshadows, the counsels He imparts, the warnings He utters, the vistas He discloses, and the assurances and promises He gives, these dynamic and typical examples of Bahá'u'lláh's sublime utterance, each having a direct bearing on the tasks which actually face or lie ahead of the American Bahá'í community, cannot fail to produce on the minds and hearts of any one of its members, who approaches them with befitting humility and detachment, such powerful reactions as to illuminate his entire being and intensify tremendously his daily exertions.

109 *"O friends! Be not careless of the virtues with which ye have been endowed, neither be neglectful of your high destiny .... Ye are the stars of the heaven of understanding, the breeze that stirreth at the break of day, the soft-flowing waters upon which must depend the very life of all men, the letters inscribed upon His sacred scroll."*[A] *"O people of Bahá! Ye are the breezes of spring that are wafted over the world. Through you We have adorned the world of being with the ornament of the knowledge of the Most Merciful. Through you the countenance of the world hath been wreathed in smiles, and the brightness of His light shone forth. Cling ye to the Cord of steadfastness, in such wise that all vain imaginings may utterly vanish. Speed ye forth from the horizon of power, in the name of your Lord, the Unconstrained, and announce unto His servants, with wisdom and eloquence, the tidings of this Cause, whose splendour hath been shed upon the world of being. Beware lest anything withhold you from observing the things prescribed unto you by the Pen of Glory, as it moved over His Tablet with sovereign majesty and might. Great is the blessedness of him that hath hearkened to its shrill voice, as it was raised, through the power of truth, before all who are in heaven and all who are on earth .... O people of Bahá! The river that is Life indeed hath flowed for your sakes. Quaff ye in My name, despite them that have disbelieved in God, the Lord of Revelation. We have made you to be the hands of Our Cause. Render ye victorious this Wronged One, Who hath been sore-tried in the hands of the workers of iniquity. He, verily, will aid everyone that aideth Him, and will remember everyone that remembereth Him. To this beareth witness this Tablet that hath shed the splendour of the loving-kindness of your Lord, the All-Glorious, the All-Compelling."*[B] *"Blessed are the people of Bahá! God beareth Me witness! They are the solace of the eye of creation. Through them the universes have been adorned, and the Preserved Tablet embellished. They are the ones who have sailed on the ark of complete independence, with their faces set towards the Dayspring of Beauty. How great is their blessedness that they have attained unto what their Lord, the Omniscient, the All-Wise, hath willed. Through their light the heavens have been adorned, and the faces of those that have drawn nigh unto Him made to shine."*[C] *"By the sorrows which afflict the beauty of the All-Glorious! Such is the station ordained for the true believer that if to an extent smaller than a needle's eye the glory of that station were to be unveiled to mankind, every beholder would be consumed away in his longing to attain it. For this reason it hath been decreed that in this earthly life the full measure*

of the glory of his own station should remain concealed from the eyes of such a believer."[D] *"If the veil be lifted, and the full glory of the station of those who have turned wholly towards God, and in their love for Him renounced the world, be made manifest, the entire creation would be dumbfounded."*[E]

110 *"Verily I say! No one hath apprehended the root of this Cause. It is incumbent upon everyone, in this day, to perceive with the eye of God, and to hearken with His ear. Whoso beholdeth Me with an eye besides Mine own will never be able to know Me. None among the Manifestations of old, except to a prescribed degree, hath ever completely apprehended the nature of this Revelation."*[A] *"I testify before God to the greatness, the inconceivable greatness of this Revelation. Again and again have We, in most of Our Tablets, borne witness to this truth, that mankind may be roused from its heedlessness."*[B] *"How great is the Cause, how staggering the weight of its Message!"*[C] *"In this most mighty Revelation all the Dispensations of the past have attained their highest, their final consummation."*[D] *"That which hath been made manifest in this preeminent, this most exalted Revelation, stands unparalleled in the annals of the past, nor will future ages witness its like."*[E] *"The purpose underlying all creation is the revelation of this most sublime, this most holy Day, the Day known as the Day of God, in His Books and Scriptures—the Day which all the Prophets, and the Chosen Ones, and the holy ones, have wished to witness."*[F] *"The highest essence and most perfect expression of whatsoever the peoples of old have either said or written hath, through this most potent Revelation, been sent down from the heaven of the Will of the All-Possessing, the Ever-Abiding God."*[G] *"This is the Day in which God's most excellent favours have been poured out upon men, the Day in which His most mighty grace hath been infused into all created things."*[H] *"This is the Day whereon the Ocean of God's mercy hath been manifested unto men, the Day in which the Daystar of His loving-kindness hath shed its radiance upon them, the Day in which the clouds of His bountiful favour have overshadowed the whole of mankind."*[I] *"By the righteousness of Mine own Self! Great, immeasurably great is this Cause! Mighty, inconceivably mighty is this Day!"*[J] *"Every Prophet hath announced the coming of this Day, and every Messenger hath groaned in His yearning for this Revelation—a revelation which, no sooner had it been revealed than all created things cried out saying, 'The earth is God's, the Most Exalted, the Most Great!'"*[K] *"The Day of the Promise is come, and He Who is the Promised One loudly proclaimeth before all who are in heaven and all who are on earth, 'Verily there is none other God but He, the Help in Peril, the Self-Subsisting!' I swear by God! That which had been enshrined from eternity in the knowledge of God, the Knower of the seen and unseen, is revealed. Happy is the eye that seeth, and the face that turneth towards, the Countenance of God, the Lord of all being."*[L] *"Great indeed is this Day! The allusions made to it in all the sacred Scriptures as the Day of God attest its greatness. The soul of every Prophet of God, of every Divine Messenger, hath thirsted for this wondrous Day. All the divers kindreds of the earth have, likewise, yearned to attain it."*[M] *"This Day a door is open wider than both heaven and earth. The eye of the mercy of Him Who is the Desire of the worlds is turned towards all men. An act, however infinitesimal, is, when viewed in the mirror of the knowledge of God, mightier*

than a mountain. Every drop proffered in His path is as the sea in that mirror. For this is the Day which the one true God, glorified be He, hath announced in all His Books, unto His Prophets and His Messengers."[N] *"This is a Revelation, under which, if a man shed for its sake one drop of blood, myriads of oceans will be his recompense."*[O] *"A fleeting moment, in this Day, excelleth centuries of a bygone age …. Neither sun nor moon hath witnessed a day such as this Day."*[P] *"This is the Day whereon the unseen world crieth out, 'Great is thy blessedness, O earth, for thou hast been made the footstool of thy God, and been chosen as the seat of His mighty throne.'"*[Q] *"The world of being shineth, in this Day, with the resplendency of this Divine Revelation. All created things extol its saving grace, and sing its praises. The universe is wrapt in an ecstasy of joy and gladness. The Scriptures of past Dispensations celebrate the great Jubilee that must needs greet this most great Day of God. Well is it with him that hath lived to see this Day, and hath recognized its station."*[R] *"This Day a different Sun hath arisen, and a different Heaven hath been adorned with its stars and its planets. The world is another world, and the Cause another Cause."*[S] *"This is the Day which past ages and centuries can never rival. Know this, and be not of the ignorant."*[T] *"This is the Day whereon human ears have been privileged to hear what He Who conversed with God [Moses] heard upon Sinai, what He Who is the Friend of God [Muḥammad] heard when lifted up towards Him, what He Who is the Spirit of God [Jesus] heard as He ascended unto Him, the Help in Peril, the Self-Subsisting."*[U] *"This Day is God's Day, and this Cause His Cause. Happy is he who hath renounced this world, and clung to Him Who is the Dayspring of God's Revelation."*[V] *"This is the King of Days, the Day that hath seen the coming of the Best Beloved, He Who through all eternity hath been acclaimed the Desire of the World."*[W] *"This is the Chief of all days and the King thereof. Great is the blessedness of him who hath attained, through the sweet savour of these days, unto everlasting life, and who, with the most great steadfastness, hath arisen to aid the Cause of Him Who is the King of Names. Such a man is as the eye to the body of mankind."*[X] *"Peerless is this Day, for it is as the eye to past ages and centuries, and as a light unto the darkness of the times."*[Y] *"This Day is different from other days, and this Cause different from other causes. Entreat ye the one true God that He may deprive not the eyes of men from beholding His signs, nor their ears from hearkening unto the shrill voice of the Pen of Glory."*[Z] *"These days are God's days, a moment of which ages and centuries can never rival. An atom, in these days, is as the sun, a drop as the ocean. One single breath exhaled in the love of God and for His service is written down by the Pen of Glory as a princely deed. Were the virtues of this Day to be recounted, all would be thunderstruck, except those whom thy Lord hath exempted."*[AA] *"By the righteousness of God! These are the days in which God hath proved the hearts of the entire company of His Messengers and Prophets, and beyond them those that stand guard over His sacred and inviolable Sanctuary, the inmates of the celestial Pavilion and dwellers of the Tabernacle of Glory."*[BB] *"Should the greatness of this Day be revealed in its fullness, every man would forsake a myriad lives in his longing to partake, though it be for one moment, of its great glory—how much more this world and its corruptible treasures!"*[CC] *"God the true One is My Witness!*

This is the Day whereon it is incumbent upon everyone that seeth to behold, and every ear that hearkeneth to hear, and every heart that understandeth to perceive, and every tongue that speaketh to proclaim unto all who are in heaven and on earth, this holy, this exalted, and all-highest Name."[DD] *"Say, O men! This is a matchless Day. Matchless must, likewise, be the tongue that celebrateth the praise of the Desire of all nations, and matchless the deed that aspireth to be acceptable in His sight. The whole human race hath longed for this Day, that perchance it may fulfil that which well beseemeth its station and is worthy of its destiny."*[EE]

111 *"Through the movement of Our Pen of Glory We have, at the bidding of the Omnipotent Ordainer, breathed a new life into every human frame, and instilled into every word a fresh potency. All created things proclaim the evidences of this worldwide regeneration."*[A] *"O people! I swear by the one true God! This is the Ocean out of which all Seas have proceeded, and with which every one of them will ultimately be united. From Him all the Suns have been generated, and unto Him they will all return. Through His potency the Trees of Divine Revelation have yielded their fruits, every one of which hath been sent down in the form of a Prophet, bearing a Message to God's creatures in each of the worlds whose number God, alone, in His all-encompassing knowledge, can reckon. This He hath accomplished through the agency of but one Letter of His Word, revealed by His Pen—a Pen moved by His directing Finger—His Finger itself sustained by the power of God's Truth."*[B] *"By the righteousness of the one true God! If one speck of a jewel be lost and buried beneath a mountain of stones, and lie hidden beyond the seven seas, the Hand of Omnipotence would assuredly reveal it in this Day, pure and cleansed from dross."*[C] *"Every single letter proceeding from Our mouth is endowed with such regenerative power as to enable it to bring into existence a new creation—a creation the magnitude of which is inscrutable to all save God. He verily hath knowledge of all things."*[D] *"It is in Our power, should We wish it, to enable a speck of floating dust to generate, in less than the twinkling of an eye, suns of infinite, of unimaginable splendour, to cause a dewdrop to develop into vast and numberless oceans, to infuse into every letter such a force as to empower it to unfold all the knowledge of past and future ages."*[E] *"We are possessed of such power which, if brought to light, will transmute the most deadly of poisons into a panacea of unfailing efficacy."*[F]

112 *"The days are approaching their end, and yet the peoples of the earth are seen sunk in grievous heedlessness, and lost in manifest error."*[A] *"Great, great is the Cause! The hour is approaching when the most great convulsion will have appeared. I swear by Him Who is the Truth! It shall cause separation to afflict everyone, even those who circle around Me."*[B] *"Say: O concourse of the heedless! I swear by God! The promised day is come, the day when tormenting trials will have surged above your heads, and beneath your feet, saying: 'Taste ye what your hands have wrought!'"*[C] *"The time for the destruction of the world and its people hath arrived. He Who is the Pre-Existent is come, that He may bestow everlasting life, and grant eternal preservation, and confer that which is conducive to true living."*[D] *"The day is approaching when its [civilization's] flame will devour the cities, when the Tongue of Grandeur will*

proclaim: 'The Kingdom is God's, the Almighty, the All-Praised!'"[E] "O ye that are bereft of understanding! A severe trial pursueth you, and will suddenly overtake you. Bestir yourselves, that haply it may pass and inflict no harm upon you."[F] "O ye peoples of the world! Know, verily, that an unforeseen calamity is following you, and that grievous retribution awaiteth you. Think not the deeds ye have committed have been blotted from My sight."[G] "O heedless ones! Though the wonders of My mercy have encompassed all created things, both visible and invisible, and though the revelations of My grace and bounty have permeated every atom of the universe, yet the rod with which I can chastise the wicked is grievous, and the fierceness of Mine anger against them terrible."[H] "Grieve thou not over those that have busied themselves with the things of this world, and have forgotten the remembrance of God, the Most Great. By Him Who is the Eternal Truth! The day is approaching when the wrathful anger of the Almighty will have taken hold of them. He, verily, is the Omnipotent, the All-Subduing, the Most Powerful. He shall cleanse the earth from the defilement of their corruption, and shall give it for an heritage unto such of His servants as are nigh unto Him."[I] "Soon will the cry, 'Yea, yea, here am I, here am I' be heard from every land. For there hath never been, nor can there ever be, any other refuge to fly to for anyone."[J] "And when the appointed hour is come, there shall suddenly appear that which shall cause the limbs of mankind to quake. Then, and only then, will the Divine Standard be unfurled, and the Nightingale of Paradise warble its melody."[K]

113 "In the beginning of every Revelation adversities have prevailed, which later on have been turned into great prosperity."[A] "Say: O people of God! Beware lest the powers of the earth alarm you, or the might of the nations weaken you, or the tumult of the people of discord deter you, or the exponents of earthly glory sadden you. Be ye as a mountain in the Cause of your Lord, the Almighty, the All-Glorious, the Unconstrained."[B] "Say: Beware, O people of Bahá, lest the strong ones of the earth rob you of your strength, or they who rule the world fill you with fear. Put your trust in God, and commit your affairs to His keeping. He, verily, will, through the power of truth, render you victorious, and He, verily, is powerful to do what He willeth, and in His grasp are the reins of omnipotent might."[C] "I swear by My life! Nothing save that which profiteth them can befall My loved ones. To this testifieth the Pen of God, the Most Powerful, the All-Glorious, the Best Beloved."[D] "Let not the happenings of the world sadden you. I swear by God! The sea of joy yearneth to attain your presence, for every good thing hath been created for you, and will, according to the needs of the times, be revealed unto you."[E] "O my servants! Sorrow not if, in these days and on this earthly plane, things contrary to your wishes have been ordained and manifested by God, for days of blissful joy, of heavenly delight, are assuredly in store for you. Worlds, holy and spiritually glorious, will be unveiled to your eyes. You are destined by Him, in this world and hereafter, to partake of their benefits, to share in their joys, and to obtain a portion of their sustaining grace. To each and every one of them you will, no doubt, attain."[F]

114 "This is the day in which to speak. It is incumbent upon the people of Bahá to strive, with the utmost patience and forbearance, to guide the peoples of the

world to the Most Great Horizon. Everybody calleth aloud for a soul. Heavenly souls must needs quicken, with the breath of the Word of God, the dead bodies with a fresh spirit. Within every word a new spirit is hidden. Happy is the man that attaineth thereunto, and hath arisen to teach the Cause of Him Who is the King of Eternity."[A] "Say: O servants! The triumph of this Cause hath depended, and will continue to depend, upon the appearance of holy souls, upon the showing forth of goodly deeds, and the revelation of words of consummate wisdom."[B] "Centre your energies in the propagation of the Faith of God. Whoso is worthy of so high a calling, let him arise and promote it. Whoso is unable, it is his duty to appoint him who will, in his stead, proclaim this Revelation, whose power hath caused the foundations of the mightiest structures to quake, every mountain to be crushed into dust, and every soul to be dumbfounded."[C] "Let your principal concern be to rescue the fallen from the slough of impending extinction, and to help him embrace the ancient Faith of God. Your behaviour towards your neighbour should be such as to manifest clearly the signs of the one true God, for ye are the first among men to be re-created by His Spirit, the first to adore and bow the knee before Him, the first to circle round His throne of glory."[D] "O ye beloved of God! Repose not yourselves on your couches, nay, bestir yourselves as soon as ye recognize your Lord, the Creator, and hear of the things which have befallen Him, and hasten to His assistance. Unloose your tongues, and proclaim unceasingly His Cause. This shall be better for you than all the treasures of the past and of the future, if ye be of them that comprehend this truth."[E] "I swear by Him Who is the Truth! Erelong will God adorn the beginning of the Book of Existence with the mention of His loved ones who have suffered tribulation in His path, and journeyed through the countries in His name and for His praise. Whoso hath attained their presence will glory in their meeting, and all that dwell in every land will be illumined by their memory."[F] "Vie ye with each other in the service of God and of His Cause. This is indeed what profiteth you in this world, and in that which is to come. Your Lord, the God of Mercy, is the All-Informed, the All-Knowing. Grieve not at the things ye witness in this day. The day shall come whereon the tongues of the nations will proclaim: 'The earth is God's, the Almighty, the Single, the Incomparable, the All-Knowing!'"[G] "Blessed is the spot, and the house, and the place, and the city, and the heart, and the mountain, and the refuge, and the cave, and the valley, and the land, and the sea, and the island, and the meadow where mention of God hath been made, and His praise glorified."[H] "The movement itself from place to place, when undertaken for the sake of God, hath always exerted, and can now exert, its influence in the world. In the Books of old the station of them that have voyaged far and near in order to guide the servants of God hath been set forth and written down."[I] "I swear by God! So great are the things ordained for the steadfast that were they, so much as the eye of a needle, to be disclosed, all who are in heaven and on earth would be dumbfounded, except such as God, the Lord of all worlds, hath willed to exempt."[J] "I swear by God! That which hath been destined for him who aideth My Cause excelleth the treasures of the earth."[K] "Whoso openeth his lips in this day, and maketh mention of the name of his Lord, the hosts of Divine inspiration shall descend upon him from the heaven of My name, the All-Knowing, the All-Wise. On him shall also descend the Concourse on high, each bearing aloft a chalice of pure light. Thus hath it been foreordained in the realm of God's Revelation, by the behest of Him Who is the All-Glorious, the Most Powerful."[L] "By the righteousness of Him Who, in this day, crieth within the inmost heart of all created things, 'God, there is none other God besides Me!' If any man were to arise to defend, in his writings, the Cause of God against its assailants, such a man, however inconsiderable his share, shall be so honoured in the world to come that the Concourse on high would envy his glory. No pen can depict the loftiness of his station, neither can any tongue describe its splendour."[M] "Please God ye may all be strengthened to carry out that which is the Will of God, and may be graciously assisted to appreciate the rank conferred upon such of His loved ones as have arisen to serve Him and magnify His name. Upon them be the glory of God, the glory of all that is in the heavens and all that is on earth, and the glory of the inmates of the most exalted Paradise, the heaven of heavens."[N] "O people of Bahá! That there is none to rival you is a sign of mercy. Quaff ye of the Cup of Bounty the wine of immortality, despite them that have repudiated God, the Lord of names and Maker of the heavens."[O]

115 "I swear by the one true God! This is the day of those who have detached themselves from all but Him, the day of those who have recognized His unity, the day whereon God createth, with the hands of His power, divine beings and imperishable essences, every one of whom will cast the world and all that is therein behind him, and will wax so steadfast in the Cause of God that every wise and understanding heart will marvel."[A] "There lay concealed within the Holy Veil, and prepared for the service of God, a company of His chosen ones who shall be manifested unto men, who shall aid His Cause, who shall be afraid of no one, though the entire human race rise up and war against them. These are the ones who, before the gaze of the dwellers on earth and the denizens of heaven, shall arise and, shouting aloud, acclaim the name of the Almighty, and summon the children of men to the path of God, the All-Glorious, the All-Praised."[B] "The day is approaching when God will have, by an act of His Will, raised up a race of men the nature of which is inscrutable to all save God, the All-Powerful, the Self-Subsisting."[C] "He will, erelong, out of the Bosom of Power, draw forth the Hands of Ascendancy and Might—Hands who will arise to win victory for this Youth, and who will purge mankind from the defilement of the outcast and the ungodly. These Hands will gird up their loins to champion the Faith of God, and will, in My name, the Self-Subsistent, the Mighty, subdue the peoples and kindreds of the earth. They will enter the cities, and will inspire with fear the hearts of all their inhabitants. Such are the evidences of the might of God; how fearful, how vehement is His might!"[D]

23.3   Station of true believer

Below are the key points of the quotations in paragraph 109:

- Quote 109:A: Bahá'u'lláh counsels His followers not to be careless of the virtues with which they are endowed.
- Quote 109:B: Bahá'u'lláh highlights the station and duties of his followers and counsels them to stay steadfast, obey His commandments and aid His Cause.

- Quote 109:C: Bahá'u'lláh describes the blessings bestowed on His followers.
- Quote 109:D: If Bahá'u'lláh were to reveal the glory of the station of the true believer to an extent smaller than a needle's eye, every observer would die to attain it.
- Quote 109:E: If Bahá'u'lláh were to reveal the glory of the station of those who have turned towards God, the entire creation would be dumbfounded.

23.4   Greatness of this Day

Below are the key points of the quotations in paragraph 110:

- Quote 110:A

    o   No one has understood the root of the Cause of Bahá'u'lláh.
    o   Everyone must perceive the Cause with the eye of God and listen to the Word with His ear.
    o   The past Manifestations of God understood only to a prescribed degree the nature of the Revelation of Bahá'u'lláh.

- Quote 110:B: Bahá'u'lláh testifies before God to the greatness of His Revelation.

- Quote 110:C: The Cause of Bahá'u'lláh is great and the weight of its Message is astonishing.

- Quote 110:D: With the Revelation of Bahá'u'lláh, all previous revelations have attained their ultimate perfection.

- Quote 110:E: Compared to what has been recorded in the past, all that has been manifested in the Revelation of Bahá'u'lláh is unique and will not be witnessed again in the future.

- Quote 110:F

    o   The purpose underlying all creation is the revelation of this Day, known as the Day of God.
    o   Past Prophets, the Chosen Ones and the holy ones longed to witness this Day.

- Quote 110:G: In the Revelation of Bahá'u'lláh, the essence and the perfect expression of anything said or written in the past are revealed.
- Quote 110:H: This is the Day that the favours of God have been poured down on mankind and His mercy has permeated all created things.
- Quote 110:I: In this Day, the mercy, the loving kindness and the bountiful favours of God have been manifested unto men.
- Quote 110:J: Great is the Cause of Bahá'u'lláh and mighty is this Day.
- Quote 110:K: All the Prophets of the past have announced the coming of this Day.

- Quote 110:L

    o   The Promised Day has come.
    o   The Promised One has appeared.

- o That which had been embodied in the knowledge of God is revealed in this Day.

- Quote 110:M

  - o The Greatness of this Day is evident from the references made to it in the previous revelations as the Day of God.
  - o The soul of every Divine Messenger has thirsted for this Day.
  - o All people of the past have yearned to attain this Day.

- Quote 110:N

  - o An act, however negligible, when viewed in the mirror of the knowledge of God is greater than a mountain.
  - o Every drop offered in His path is like an ocean in the mirror of the knowledge of God.

- Quote 110:O: In this Revelation, if a drop of blood is sacrificed in His path, a multitude of oceans will be the reward.
- Quote 110:P

  - o A brief moment in this Day excels centuries in the past.
  - o Neither sun nor moon have witnessed such a Day.

- Quote 110:Q: This is the Day in which the earth has become the footstool of God and the seat of His mighty throne.
- Quote 110:R: In this Day, the world of being is illumined with the Revelation of Bahá'u'lláh, the universe is in joy, and the Scriptures of the past celebrate the "great Jubilee" that must greet this Day.
- Quote 110:S

  - o In this day, a different Sun has arisen and a different Heaven with its stars and planet has appeared.
  - o This is another world and another Cause.

- Quote 110:T: The past ages and centuries cannot match this Day.
- Quote 110:U: In this Day, the human ear can hear what Moses heard on Sinai and Muḥammad heard in His Ascent (Miʻráj),[1] and Jesus heard when He ascended to heaven.
- Quote 110:V: This is God's Day. Happy is the one who has renounced this world and adhered to Bahá'u'lláh.
- Quote 110:W: This is the King of Days, the Day in which the Best Beloved and the Desire of the World has come.
- Quote 110:X: This is the Chief and King of all days. Blessed is the one who has arisen with steadfastness to aid the Cause of Bahá'u'lláh. Such a person is the eye to the body of humankind.
- Quote 110:Y: This is a peerless Day as it is as the eye of past ages and centuries and as a light to the darkness of our time.
- Quote 110:Z

---

[1] Reference to Muḥammad's vision of His night journey to the outermost mosque and His ascent to the heavens.

- o This is a different Day and Cause.
  - o Beseech God that He does not deprive the eyes of men to see His signs and their ears to hear the shrill voice of His pen.
- Quote 110:AA: These are God's days, a moment of which the ages and centuries cannot match; in which an atom is as the sun and a drop as the ocean; and in which a single breath exhaled in the love of God and His service is counted as a princely deed.
- Quote 110:BB: These are the days in which God has demonstrated the truth of the hearts of the Messengers, Prophets and the dwellers of the Abhá Kingdom.
- Quote 110:CC: If the greatness of this Day is fully revealed, everyone would sacrifice countless lives, how much more the corruptible treasures of this world, to partake of its great Glory even for one moment.
- Quote 110:DD: In this Day, everyone who see must observe, every ear that listens must hear, every heart that understands must perceive, and every tongue that speaks must proclaim the name of Bahá'u'lláh to all who are in heaven and on earth.
- Quote 110:EE

  - o This is a matchless Day; matchless should be the tongue that praises Bahá'u'lláh and matchless the deed that aims for acceptance in His sight.
  - o The whole human race has yearned for this Day.

23.5 His transforming power

Below are the key points of the quotes in paragraph 111:

- Quote 111:A

  - o Bahá'u'lláh has breathed a new life into every human frame through the movement of His pen.
  - o The evidences of this worldwide regeneration are proclaimed by all created things.

- Quote 111:B

  - o The Revelation of Bahá'u'lláh is an Ocean out of which all Seas have originated, and within it all unite.
  - o From Bahá'u'lláh all Suns have been generated and unto Him all return.
  - o Through His potency, the fruits of the Tree of Divine Revelation have been sent down in the form of a Prophet with a Message to God's creatures in each of the worlds of God whose number only God knows.
  - o He has achieved this by one Letter of His Word, revealed by His Pen, a Pen moved by His Finger, the Finger powered by God's Truth.

- Quote 111:C: In this Day, the Hand of Omnipotence can reveal in all its purity a muddied particle of jewel buried under a mountain of stones that lie beyond the seven seas.
- Quote 111:D: Every letter originated from the mouth of Bahá'u'lláh has such regenerating power that can bring into being a new creation.

- Quote 111:E

  - Bahá'u'lláh has the power to enable a speck of dust to generate suns of infinite and unimaginable splendour.
  - He has the power to cause a dewdrop to develop into vast and numberless oceans.
  - He has the power to infuse such a force into every letter to unfold all the knowledge of the past and future.

- Quote 111:F: Bahá'u'lláh is possessed of such power that can transform the most deadly of poisons into a panacea.

23.6 Dangers foreshadowed by Bahá'u'lláh

Below are the key points of the quotes in paragraph 112:

- Quote 112:A: The peoples of the earth are sunk in heedlessness and error, ignorant of the Day of Bahá'u'lláh.
- Quote 112:B: The most great convulsion is imminent, in which everyone will feel the pangs of severance—even those closest to Bahá'u'lláh.
- Quote 112:C: The promised day is come when all will be encompassed by agonising trials.

- Quote 112:D

  - This is the time for the destruction of the world and its people.
  - Bahá'u'lláh, the Pre-Existent is come to confer true life.

- Quote 112:E: The day is approaching when the flame of civilization will engulf the cities.
- Quote 112:F: A severe trial pursues and will suddenly overtake the people who lack understanding. Make an effort that it may not harm you.
- Quote 112:G: An unforeseen calamity is following the people of the world and grievous retributions await them. Bahá'u'lláh has not forgotten what they committed.
- Quote 112:H: Although the mercy of Bahá'u'lláh has encompassed all created things and His grace has permeated every atom in the universe, the rod with which He chastises the wicked is severe and His anger against them fierce.
- Quote 112:I

  - Do not grieve over those who have busied themselves with the world as the day is approaching when Bahá'u'lláh's anger will have taken hold of them.
  - He will clean the earth from their corruption and give it as a heritage to those who are close to Him.

- Quote 112:J: Soon the cry *"Yea, yea, here am I, here am I"* will be heard from every land.[1] There has never been or will ever be any other refuge for anyone.

- Quote 112:K

---

[1]   This is a reference to the spread of the Faith to every corner of the earth.

- At the appointed time, calamities that shall cause the limbs of mankind to quake will suddenly appear.
- Then the Divine Standard will be unrolled and the Nightingale of Paradise will sing its melody.

23.7 Tolerance and patience under adversities

Below are the key points of quotes in paragraph 113:

- Quote 113:A: In every Revelation, early adversities are turned later into great prosperity.

- Quote 113:B
  - Let not the powers of the earth alarm you, the might of nations weaken you or the clamour of enemies discourage you.
  - Stay as steadfast as a mountain in the Cause.

- Quote 113:C
  - Let not the strong rulers of the world rob you of your strength and fill you with fear.
  - Trust in God and He will render you victorious.

- Quote 113:D: The loved ones of Bahá'u'lláh shall be protected.

- Quote 113:E
  - Do not be saddened by the happenings of the world.
  - Every good thing is created for you and will be revealed to you at the appropriate time.

- Quote 113:F: Do not be saddened if things contrary to your wishes occur as days of joy and heavenly delight are destined for you in this world and the next. You will attain them and partake of their benefits.

23.8 Paramount importance of teaching the Cause

Below are the key points of quotes in paragraph 114:

- Quote 114:A
  - In this Day, the people of Bahá should guide the people of the world to the Revelation of Bahá'u'lláh.
  - The Word of God has the power to refresh the spiritually dead with a new spirit.
  - Happy is the man who arises to teach the Cause of Bahá'u'lláh.

- Quote 114:B: The victory of the Faith is dependent on the appearance of holy souls with good deeds and perfect wisdom.

- Quote 114:C
  - Focus your energies on propagation of the Faith.
  - Those who can should arise to teach the Faith, otherwise they should appoint someone to teach on their behalf.

- Quote 114:D

    o   Your main concern should be rescuing the fallen from extinction and assisting them to embrace the Faith.

    o   You should manifest the signs of the one true God in dealing with your neighbour.

- Quote 114:E: Upon recognition of Bahá'u'lláh, arise to proclaim His Cause. This will be better for you than the treasures of the past and the future.

- Quote 114:F: The beginning of the Book of Existence will be adorned with those who have suffered tribulations in the path of Bahá'u'lláh and have travelled through countries to proclaim His Cause.

- Quote 114:G

    o   Vie with each other in the service of God and His Cause.

    o   Do not grieve at the things you see in this Day as the day will come when all nations proclaim that the earth is God's.

- Quote 114:H: Blessed is any spot where mention of God is made.
- Quote 114:I: Movement for the sake of God exerts its influence.
- Quote 114:J: If but an iota of that which is ordained for the steadfast were to be disclosed, all in heaven and on earth would be dumbfounded except those who have been exempted by God.
- Quote 114:K: That which is ordained for those who aid the Cause of Bahá'u'lláh surpasses all the treasures of the earth.
- Quote 114:L: Anyone who makes mention of Bahá'u'lláh will receive divine inspiration.
- Quote 114:M: If any man defends the Cause in his writings, he will be so honoured in the next world that the Concourse on high will envy him.
- Quote 114:N: Bahá'u'lláh hopes that all are strengthened to carry out the Will of God and are assisted to appreciate the rank conferred on those who arise to serve Him.
- Quote 114:O: This is a sign of His mercy that no one can rival the people of Bahá.

23.9   Those who arise to aid Bahá'u'lláh

Below are the key points of quotes in paragraph 115:

- Quote 115:A: This is the day of those who have detached themselves from all but God and have recognized the unity of God, the Day on which God creates those who will cast away the world and stay so steadfast that every understanding heart will be amazed.
- Quote 115:B: There is a company of chosen ones hidden in the Holy Veil who will be manifested to aid the Cause of Bahá'u'lláh. They will be afraid of no one, proclaim the name of Bahá'u'lláh, and call humanity to the path of God.
- Quote 115:C: The day is approaching when God will raise up a race of man whose nature is unknown to all but God.

- Quote 115:D: Before long, God will reveal the Hands of Ascendency and Might who will arise to win victory for Bahá'u'lláh by overcoming the peoples of the earth, and entering into cities to inspire the inhabitants.

23.10 Activities

23.10.1 Short answer questions

1. Consider quote 109:A. What are the implications and meanings of the following metaphors Bahá'u'lláh has used to describe the virtues and high destiny of the people of Bahá?

    a) *"stars of the heaven of understanding"*

    _____

    _____

    _____

    _____

    b) *"the breeze that stirreth at the break of day"*

    _____

    _____

    _____

    _____

    c) *"the soft-flowing waters upon which must depend the very life of all men"*

    _____

    _____

    _____

    _____

    d) *"the letters inscribed upon His sacred scroll"*

    _____

    _____

    _____

    _____

2. In quote 109:B, Bahá'u'lláh counsel us: *"Cling ye to the Cord of steadfastness, in such wise that all vain imaginings may utterly vanish."* How does steadfastness cause vain imaginings to utterly vanish?

    _____

    _____

    _____

    _____

3. In quote 109:B, Bahá'u'lláh states: *"He, verily, will aid everyone that aideth Him, and will remember everyone that remembereth Him."*

a)   How does God aid those who aid Him?

_____

_____

_____

_____

b)   How does God remember those who remember Him?

_____

_____

_____

_____

4.   What are the qualities of the people of Bahá described in quote 109:C?

_____

_____

_____

_____

5.   Why is the station of the true believer concealed in this life (quotes 109:D and 109:E)?

_____

_____

_____

_____

6.   What is the meaning of *"perceiving with eye of God"* and *"hearing with the Ear of God"* as mentioned in quote 110:A?

_____

_____

_____

_____

7.   What is meant by the statement *"all the Dispensations of the past have attained their highest, their final consummation"* in quote 110:D?

_____

_____

_____

_____

8. Will future ages witness a revelation similar to the Revelation of Bahá'u'lláh (quote 110:E)?

    _____

    _____

    _____

    _____

9. What is the purpose underlying all creation as mentioned in quote 110:F?

    _____

    _____

    _____

    _____

10. What is meaning of *"This Day a door is open wider than both heaven and earth"* in quote 110:N?

    _____

    _____

    _____

    _____

11. What is the recompense of shedding one drop of blood for Bahá'u'lláh (quote 110:P)?

    _____

    _____

    _____

    _____

12. What is meant by quote 110:T?

    _____

    _____

    _____

13. What happens if the full measure of this Day is revealed (quote 110:CC)?

    _____

    _____

    _____

    _____

14. How has Bahá'u'lláh breathed a new life into every human frame (quote 111:A)?

_____

_____

_____

_____

15. What is the meaning of *"This is the Ocean out of which all Seas have proceeded, and with which every one of them will ultimately be united. From Him all the Suns have been generated, and unto Him they will all return."* (quote 111:B)?

_____

_____

_____

_____

16. What is the power of a single letter proceeding from the Mouth of Bahá'u'lláh (quote 111:D)?

_____

_____

_____

_____

17. What are the consequences of the most great convulsion as described by Bahá'u'lláh in quote 112:B?

_____

_____

_____

_____

18. How evident are the signs of destruction in our present society as mentioned by Bahá'u'lláh in quote 112:E?

_____

_____

_____

_____

19. What happens to those who have busied themselves with the things of this world (quote 112:I)?

_____

_____

_____

_____

20. When will the *"Divine Standard be unfurled"* and the *"Nightingale of Paradise warble its melody"* (quote 112:K)?

_____

_____

_____

_____

21. Why does Bahá'u'lláh ask us not to be sad in this earthly plane (quotes 113:E and 113:F)?

_____

_____

_____

_____

22. What does the triumph of the Cause depend on (quote 114:B)?

_____

_____

_____

_____

23. According to quote 114:D, what should be your principal concern?

_____

_____

_____

_____

24. For what can we vie with each other (quote 114:H)?

_____

_____

_____

_____

25. What is the effect of movement from one place to another for the sake of God (quote 114:I)?

_____

_____

---

26. What are the promises of Bahá'u'lláh for those who make mention of Him (quote 114:L)?

---

27. What is the reward of the person who defends the Faith in writing (quote 114:M)?

---

28. How will God win victory in the future (quotes 115:B and 115:C)?

23.10.2 Mini-project

Consider the statements cited in paragraph 112. To what extent do these statements describe the challenges faced by humanity worldwide at the present time? Arrange your thoughts and papers in a presentation for the members of your community.

24.
American nation

24.1   Introduction

This chapter covers the concluding paragraphs (116–124) of *The Advent of Divine Justice*. The focus of these paragraphs is on the future and destiny of the American nation to become the first nation *"to build the Tabernacle of the Great Peace, and proclaim the oneness of mankind"*, and to lead all nations spiritually as foretold by 'Abdu'l-Bahá. Shoghi Effendi explains that their role will unfold through various stages. Two factors will force the American nation to abandon its current isolationism: on the one hand, the continuing deterioration in the world political situation and, on the other hand, the advances in travel and communications that will bridge the distances between the American continent and other parts of the world. The immediate future for America will be dark and oppressive. Through the crises prophesied by Bahá'u'lláh, this nation will emerge determined to seize its opportunity and, in conjunction with its sister nations in both the East and West, will solve the colossal problems of the world.

In this chapter, you need to reflect on and understand the following key points:

a)   The capacities and powers of America have been generated as the result the creative energies of the World Order of Bahá'u'lláh released within this nation.

b)   The God-given capacities conferred on the American nation are manifested through two distinctive processes.

    i)   The followers of Bahá'u'lláh in America manifest these capacities by building the Bahá'í Administrative Order and teaching the Faith.

    ii)   These same capacities affect the American government and its people, and shape the destiny of the nation under the influence of world political and economic forces.

c)   'Abdu'l-Bahá advised a very high government official that the best way for him to serve his country was to contribute towards applying the principle of federalism, underlying the American government, to the nations of the world.

d)   President Woodrow Wilson was considerably influenced by the Bahá'í teachings.

e)   Shoghi Effendi identifies the dangers threatening the world in connection with the looming Second World War.

f)   After the dark period, the American nation will raise its voice in the councils of the nations and lay the cornerstone of universal peace, proclaiming the unity of mankind and becoming the example of the prophecies of 'Abdu'l-Bahá.

24.2   Paragraphs under study

116 One more word in conclusion. Among some of the most momentous and thought-provoking pronouncements ever made by 'Abdu'l-Bahá, in the course of His epoch-making travels in the North American continent, are the following: *"May this American Democracy be the first nation to establish the foundation of international agreement. May it be the first nation to proclaim the unity of mankind. May it be the first to unfurl the Standard of the Most Great Peace."*[A] And again: *"The American people are indeed worthy of being the first to build the Tabernacle of the Great Peace, and proclaim the oneness of mankind .... For America hath developed powers and capacities greater and more wonderful than other nations .... The American nation is equipped and empowered to accomplish that which will adorn the pages of history, to become the envy of the world, and be blest in both the East and the West for the triumph of its people. .... The American continent gives signs and evidences of very great advancement. Its future is even more promising, for its influence and illumination are far-reaching. It will lead all nations spiritually."*[B]

117 The creative energies, mysteriously generated by the first stirrings of the embryonic World Order of Bahá'u'lláh, have, as soon as released within a nation destined to become its cradle and champion, endowed that nation with the worthiness, and invested it with the powers and capacities, and equipped it spiritually, to play the part foreshadowed in these prophetic words. The potencies which this God-given mission has infused into its people are, on the one hand, beginning to be manifested through the conscious efforts and the nationwide accomplishments, in both the teaching and administrative spheres of Bahá'í activity, of the organized community of the followers of Bahá'u'lláh in the North American continent. These same potencies, apart from, yet collateral with these efforts and accomplishments, are, on the other hand, insensibly shaping, under the impact of the world political and economic forces, the destiny of that nation, and are influencing the lives and actions of both its government and its people.

118 To the efforts and accomplishments of those who, aware of the Revelation of Bahá'u'lláh, are now labouring in that continent, to their present and future course of activity, I have, in the foregoing pages sufficiently referred. A word, if the destiny of the American people, in its entirety, is to be correctly apprehended, should now be said regarding the orientation of that nation as a whole, and the trend of the affairs of its people. For no matter how ignorant

of the Source from which those directing energies proceed, and however slow and laborious the process, it is becoming increasingly evident that the nation as a whole, whether through the agency of its government or otherwise, is gravitating, under the influence of forces that it can neither comprehend nor control, towards such associations and policies, wherein, as indicated by 'Abdu'l-Bahá, her true destiny must lie. Both the community of the American believers, who are aware of that Source, and the great mass of their countrymen, who have not as yet recognized the Hand that directs their destiny, are contributing, each in its own way, to the realization of the hopes, and the fulfilment of the promises, voiced in the above-quoted words of 'Abdu'l-Bahá.

119   The world is moving on. Its events are unfolding ominously and with bewildering rapidity. The whirlwind of its passions is swift and alarmingly violent. The New World is being insensibly drawn into its vortex. The potential storm centres of the earth are already casting their shadows upon its shores. Dangers, undreamt of and unpredictable, threaten it both from within and from without. Its governments and peoples are being gradually enmeshed in the coils of the world's recurrent crises and fierce controversies. The Atlantic and Pacific Oceans are, with every acceleration in the march of science, steadily shrinking into mere channels. The Great Republic of the West finds itself particularly and increasingly involved. Distant rumblings echo menacingly in the ebullitions of its people. On its flanks are ranged the potential storm centres of the European continent and of the Far East. On its southern horizon there looms what might conceivably develop into another Centre of agitation and danger. The world is contracting into a neighbourhood. America, willingly or unwillingly, must face and grapple with this new situation. For purposes of national security, let alone any humanitarian motive, she must assume the obligations imposed by this newly created neighbourhood. Paradoxical as it may seem, her only hope of extricating herself from the perils gathering around her is to become entangled in that very web of international association which the Hand of an inscrutable Providence is weaving. 'Abdu'l-Bahá's counsel to a highly placed official in its government comes to mind, with peculiar appropriateness and force: You can best serve your country if you strive, in your capacity as a citizen of the world, to assist in the eventual application of the principle of federalism, underlying the government of your own country, to the relationships now existing between the peoples and nations of the world. The ideals that fired the imagination of America's tragically unappreciated President, whose high endeavours, however much nullified by a visionless generation, 'Abdu'l-Bahá, through His own pen, acclaimed as signalizing the dawn of the Most Great Peace, though now lying in the dust, bitterly reproach a heedless generation for having so cruelly abandoned them.

120   That the world is beset with perils, that dangers are now accumulating and are actually threatening the American nation, no clear-eyed observer can possibly deny. The earth is now transformed into an armed camp. As much as fifty million men are either under arms or in reserve. No less than the sum of three billion pounds is being spent, in one year, on its armaments. The

light of religion is dimmed and moral authority disintegrating. The nations of the world have, for the most part, fallen a prey to battling ideologies that threaten to disrupt the very foundations of their dearly won political unity. Agitated multitudes in these countries seethe with discontent, are armed to the teeth, are stampeded with fear, and groan beneath the yoke of tribulations engendered by political strife, racial fanaticism, national hatreds, and religious animosities. *"The winds of despair,"* Bahá'u'lláh has unmistakably affirmed, *"are, alas, blowing from every direction, and the strife that divides and afflicts the human race is daily increasing. The signs of impending convulsions and chaos can now be discerned ...."*[A] *"The ills,"* 'Abdu'l-Bahá, writing as far back as two decades ago, has prophesied, *"from which the world now suffers will multiply; the gloom which envelops it will deepen. The Balkans will remain discontented. Its restlessness will increase. The vanquished Powers will continue to agitate. They will resort to every measure that may rekindle the flame of war. Movements, newly born and worldwide in their range, will exert their utmost for the advancement of their designs. The Movement of the Left will acquire great importance. Its influence will spread."*[B] As to the American nation itself, the voice of its own President, emphatic and clear, warns his people that a possible attack upon their country has been brought infinitely closer by the development of aircraft and by other factors. Its Secretary of State, addressing at a recent Conference the assembled representatives of all the American Republics, utters no less ominous a warning. "These resurgent forces loom threateningly throughout the world—their ominous shadow falls athwart our own Hemisphere." As to its Press, the same note of warning and of alarm at an approaching danger is struck. "We must be prepared to defend ourselves both from within and without .... Our defensive frontier is long. It reaches from Alaska's Point Barrow to Cape Horn, and ranges the Atlantic and the Pacific. When or where Europe's and Asia's aggressors may strike at us no one can say. It could be anywhere, any time .... We have no option save to go armed ourselves .... We must mount vigilant guard over the Western Hemisphere."

121   The distance that the American nation has travelled since its formal and categoric repudiation of the Wilsonian ideal, the changes that have unexpectedly overtaken it in recent years, the direction in which world events are moving, with their inevitable impact on the policies and the economy of that nation, are to every Bahá'í observer, viewing the developments in the international situation, in the light of the prophecies of both Bahá'u'lláh and 'Abdu'l-Bahá, most significant, and highly instructive and encouraging. To trace the exact course which, in these troubled times and pregnant years, this nation will follow would be impossible. We can only, judging from the direction its affairs are now taking, anticipate the course she will most likely choose to pursue in her relationships with both the Republics of America and the countries of the remaining continents.

122   A closer association with these Republics, on the one hand, and an increased participation, in varying degrees, on the other, in the affairs of the whole world, as a result of recurrent international crises, appear as the most likely

developments which the future has in store for that country. Delays must inevitably arise, setbacks must be suffered, in the course of that country's evolution towards its ultimate destiny. Nothing, however, can alter eventually that course, ordained for it by the unerring pen of 'Abdu'l-Bahá. Its federal unity having already been achieved and its internal institutions consolidated—a stage that marked its coming of age as a political entity—its further evolution, as a member of the family of nations, must, under circumstances that cannot at present be visualized, steadily continue. Such an evolution must persist until such time when that nation will, through the active and decisive part it will have played in the organization and the peaceful settlement of the affairs of mankind, have attained the plenitude of its powers and functions as an outstanding member, and component part, of a federated world.

123 The immediate future must, as a result of this steady, this gradual, and inevitable absorption in the manifold perplexities and problems afflicting humanity, be dark and oppressive for that nation. The world-shaking ordeal which Bahá'u'lláh, as quoted in the foregoing pages, has so graphically prophesied, may find it swept, to an unprecedented degree, into its vortex. Out of it will probably emerge, unlike its reactions to the last world conflict, consciously determined to seize its opportunity, to bring the full weight of its influence to bear upon the gigantic problems that such an ordeal must leave in its wake, and to exorcise forever, in conjunction with its sister nations of both the East and the West, the greatest curse which, from time immemorial, has afflicted and degraded the human race.

124 Then, and only then, will the American nation, moulded and purified in the crucible of a common war, inured to its rigors, and disciplined by its lessons, be in a position to raise its voice in the councils of the nations, itself lay the cornerstone of a universal and enduring peace, proclaim the solidarity, the unity, and maturity of mankind, and assist in the establishment of the promised reign of righteousness on earth. Then, and only then, will the American nation, while the community of the American believers within its heart is consummating its divinely appointed mission, be able to fulfil the unspeakably glorious destiny ordained for it by the Almighty, and immortally enshrined in the writings of 'Abdu'l-Bahá. Then, and only then, will the American nation accomplish *"that which will adorn the pages of history,"* *"become the envy of the world and be blest in both the East and the West."*[A]

24.3 Two processes driving America

In paragraphs 116–118, the Guardian highlights the destiny of the American people viewed in the context of the utterances made by 'Abdu'l-Bahá (particularly quotes 116:A and 116:B). 'Abdu'l-Bahá hoped (quote 116:A) that the American Democracy would be the first nation to:

• Establish international agreements.
• Announce the unity of mankind.
• Unfurl the banner of the Most Great Peace.

'Abdu'l-Bahá explained (quote 116:B) the reasons why the American nation was worthy of being the first to establish the Great Peace and of proclaiming the oneness of mankind:

- *"For America hath developed powers and capacities greater and more wonderful than other nations.*
- *... The American nation is equipped and empowered to accomplish that which will adorn the pages of history, to become the envy of the world, and be blest in both the East and the West for the triumph of its people.*
- *... The American continent gives signs and evidences of very great advancement.*
- *Its future is even more promising, for its influence and illumination are far-reaching.*
- *It will lead all nations spiritually."*[1]

In paragraph 117, Shoghi Effendi explains that the capacities and powers referred to by 'Abdu'l-Bahá for America were generated as the result the creative energies of the World Order of Bahá'u'lláh being released within this nation. The God-given potentialities conferred on the American nation are manifested through two distinctive processes. In the first process, the followers of Bahá'u'lláh in America are manifesting these capacities by building the Bahá'í Administrative Order and teaching the Faith. In the second process, these same capacities are affecting the American government and its people, and shaping the destiny of the nation under the influence of world political and economic forces.

In paragraph 118, Shoghi Effendi confirms that both the American Bahá'í community, through conscious efforts, and their countrymen, unconsciously, are contributing towards the realization of the hopes of 'Abdu'l-Bahá and His promises for America.

In a letter dated June 5, 1947, Shoghi Effendi, further highlights the nature of these two processes:

> Indeed if we would read aright the signs of the times, and appraise correctly the significances of contemporaneous events that are impelling forward both the American Bahá'í Community and the nation of which it forms a part on the road leading them to their ultimate destiny, we cannot fail to perceive the workings of two simultaneous processes, generated as far back as the concluding years of the Heroic Age of our Faith, each clearly defined, each distinctly separate, yet closely related and destined to culminate, in the fullness of time, in a single glorious consummation.

> One of these processes is associated with the mission of the American Bahá'í Community, the other with the destiny of the American nation. The one serves directly the interests of the Administrative Order of the Faith of Bahá'u'lláh, the other promotes indirectly the institutions that are to be associated with the establishment of His World Order.[2]

---

[1] Bullets are added for emphasis.
[2] Shoghi Effendi, *Citadel of Faith*, pp. 31–32.

These two processes are similar to the concept of the Major and Minor Plans of God. According to the Universal House of Justice, the Major Plan of God

... tumultuous in its progress, working through mankind as a whole, tearing down barriers to world unity and forging humankind into a unified body in the fires of suffering and experience. This process will produce, in God's due time, the Lesser Peace, the political unification of the world. Mankind at that time can be likened to a body that is unified but without life.[1]

The Minor Plan of God, on the other hand, is

... the task of breathing life into this unified body—of creating true unity and spirituality culminating in the Most Great Peace—is that of the Bahá'ís, who are labouring consciously, with detailed instructions and continuing Divine guidance, to erect the fabric of the Kingdom of God on earth, into which they call their fellowmen, thus conferring upon them eternal life.

... God's Major Plan proceeds mysteriously in ways directed by Him alone, but the Minor Plan that He has given us to execute, as our part in His grand design for the redemption of mankind, is clearly delineated.[2]

24.4 Moving out of isolationism

During the 1930s, the memory of the tragic losses during the First World War and the Great Depression pushed public opinion and government policies towards isolationism. Such an orientation meant non-involvement in European and Asian conflicts as well as international politics. This, however, did not stop America maintaining its interest in Latin America. The Atlantic and Pacific Oceans securing America from the East and the West assisted the country to maintain its isolation from European conflicts.

In paragraph 119, Shoghi Effendi explains that in light of the deterioration of the world political situation on all fronts and the steady shrinking of the travel and communication times between the American continent and other parts of the world, the American nation would not be able to continue its isolationism and it has no option but to play a more active role in world affairs. This could be driven either by national security or humanitarian motives.

Shoghi Effendi then cites the counsel of 'Abdu'l-Bahá to a very high government official that the best way for him to serve his country was to contribute towards applying the principle of federalism underlying the American government to the nations of the world. This was the ideal that President Woodrow Wilson tried unsuccessfully to achieve.

24.5 Unappreciated president

In paragraph 119, Shoghi Effendi refers to President Woodrow Wilson as an "unappreciated President" whose ideals were repealed by a "visionless

---

[1] The Universal House of Justice, *Messages from the Universal House of Justice 1963–1986*, p. 126.

[2] The Universal House of Justice, *Messages from the Universal House of Justice 1963–1986*, p. 127.

generation". Woodrow Wilson (1856–1924) was the 28th president of the United States who served two terms from 1913 to 1921. He was an advocate of world peace and is ranked as one of the greatest presidents of the US.

President Wilson tried to keep the United States neutral during World War I, but ultimately called on Congress to declare war against Germany in 1917 when German submarines attacked US merchant ships. After the war, he helped to develop a peace treaty that included the establishment of the League of Nations as part of the Treaty of Versailles, as covered in section 4.4. The Senate did not agree to the United States being a member of the League of Nations. Despite this, President Wilson was awarded the Noble Peace prize in 1919. According to 'Abdu'l-Bahá, this initiative of President Wilson signalized the dawn of the Most Great Peace, as attested by Shoghi Effendi in paragraph 119.

In one of His Tablets 'Abdu'l-Bahá makes mention of President Wilson to be

... indeed serving the Kingdom of God for he is restless and strives day and night that the rights of all men may be preserved safe and secure, that even small nations, like greater ones, may dwell in peace and comfort, under the protection of Righteousness and Justice. This purpose is indeed a lofty one. I trust that the incomparable Providence will assist and confirm such souls under all conditions.[1]

In one of his letters highlighting the blessings conferred on the American nation, Shoghi Effendi states:

"To her President, the immortal Woodrow Wilson, must be ascribed the unique honour, among the statesmen of any nation, whether of the East or of the West, of having voiced sentiments so akin to the principles animating the Cause of Bahá'u'lláh, and of having more than any other world leader, contributed to the creation of the League of Nations—achievements which the pen of the Centre of God's Covenant acclaimed as signalizing the dawn of the Most Great Peace, whose sun, according to that same pen, must needs arise as the direct consequence of the enforcement of the laws of the Dispensation of Bahá'u'lláh"[2]

In a letter dated March 17, 1925, written on behalf of Shoghi Effendi, he states:

"With regard to Ex-President Wilson and Dr Jordan, it seems fairly clear that both of these men were considerably influenced by the Bahá'í Teachings; but at the same time it is well to avoid making dogmatic statements that they got all their principles from Bahá'u'lláh, or the like as we are not in a position to prove such statements, and to make claims which we cannot prove weakens instead of strengthening our position."[3]

The Dr Jordan mentioned in this letter is David Starr Jordan (19 January 1851–19 September 1931) who was a leading eugenicist, ichthyologist, educator and peace activist. He was president of Indiana University and Stanford University.

[1] 'Abdu'l-Bahá, *Selections from the Writings of 'Abdu'l-Bahá*, p. 108.
[2] Shoghi Effendi, *Citadel of Faith*, p. 35.
[3] Written on behalf of Shoghi Effendi, cited in *Lights of Guidance*, p. 452.

He also served as a Director of the Sierra Club from 1892 to 1903. During His journeys in the United States, 'Abdu'l-Bahá spoke at Leland Stanford Junior University in Palo Alto and afterwards He had lunch with Dr Jordan at his home.[1]

24.6   Impending convulsions

In paragraph 120, Shoghi Effendi identifies the dangers threatening the world at that time, in particular:

- About 50 million men were either in military service or in the reserves.
- The world spent three billion pounds annually on armaments.
- The light of religion was dimmed and moral authority was breaking up.
- The world nations had become victims to battling ideologies, threatening their political unity.
- The citizens of countries were discontented with politics, were "armed to the teeth", were "stampeded with fear", and groaned "beneath the yoke of tribulations engendered by political strife, racial fanaticism, national hatreds, and religious animosities."

Such warnings were connected with the looming Second World War. Shoghi Effendi then cites an utterance of Bahá'u'lláh (quote 120:A) to indicate that the convulsions experienced at the time were prophesied by Bahá'u'lláh. He also cites a statement (quote 120:B) from 'Abdu'l-Bahá revealed in January 1920,[2] in which He makes a number of prophecies about the chaos that would surround humanity:

- *"The ills from which the world now suffers will multiply;*
- *the gloom which envelops it will deepen.*
- *The Balkans will remain discontented. Its restlessness will increase.*
- *The vanquished Powers will continue to agitate. They will resort to every measure that may rekindle the flame of war.*
- *Movements, newly born and worldwide in their range, will exert their utmost for the advancement of their designs.*
- *The Movement of the Left will acquire great importance. Its influence will spread."*[3]

The Balkans, also known as the Balkan Peninsula, consists of the three southern peninsulas in the easternmost area of Europe. The area is now divided up into Albania, Bosnia and Herzegovina, Bulgaria, Croatia, Kosovo, Macedonia, Republic of Montenegro, Romania, Serbia, Slovenia and portions of Greece and Turkey. Over its history, the Balkans has been characterized by disunity between different ethnic groups.

Shoghi Effendi provides some explanation on these prophecies made by 'Abdu'l-Bahá in a message dated 4 June 1947:

"The agitation in the Balkan Peninsula; the feverish activity in which Germany

---

[1] 'Abdu'l-Bahá in America, 1912– 2012, retrieved from https://centenary. bahai.us/photo/dr-david-starr-jordan-1851-1931-president-stanford-university.

[2] Shoghi Effendi, *The World Order of Bahá'u'lláh*, p. 30.

[3] Bullet is added for emphasis.

and Italy played a disastrous role, culminating in the outbreak of the second World War; the rise of the Fascist and Nazi movements, which spread their ramifications to distant parts of the globe; the spread of communism which, as a result of the victory of Soviet Russia in that same war, has been greatly accelerated—all these happenings, some unequivocally, others in veiled language, have been forecast in this Tablet, the full force of whose implications are as yet undisclosed, and which, we may well anticipate, the American nation, as yet insufficiently schooled by adversity, must sooner or later experience."[1]

This statement of Shoghi Effendi indicates that "vanquished Powers" is a reference to Germany and Italy, the "newly born movements" are Fascism and Nazism, and the "Movement of the Left" refers to communism.

In the remainder of the paragraph, "the voice of its President" is a reference to President Franklin D. Roosevelt who was elected in 1933 and served four terms as the President of the United States until his death in 1945. The Secretary of State at the time was Codell Hull (2 October 1871—23 July 1955) who served in that position for 11 years from 1933–1944).

24.7   Destiny of America

In paragraphs 121–124, Shoghi Effendi describes the future and destiny of America. He states that it is rather difficult to identify the exact course that the American nation will follow in the coming years. It is however possible to anticipate the direction it will follow in its relationship with its neighbours and other parts of the world. A closer relationship with its neighbours and greater involvement in world affairs will be unavoidable.

Setbacks and delays will occur but the evolution of this nation towards its destiny foretold in the prophecies of 'Abdu'l-Bahá will continue until the time when America assumes a leading role in the peaceful settlement of the affairs of mankind and attains its station as an outstanding member of a federal world.

However, the immediate future is dark and oppressive for the American nation. Through the crises prophesied by Bahá'u'lláh, this nation will emerge determined to seize its opportunities and in conjunction with its sister nations in both the East and West, will solve the gigantic problems of the world.

Then the American nation will raise its voice in the councils of the nations and lay the cornerstone of universal peace. It will proclaim the unity of mankind, and achieve the destiny foretold in the prophecies of 'Abdu'l-Bahá, in which it will adorn the pages of history and become the envy of the world.

In a letter written on behalf of the Guardian to the National Spiritual Assembly of the United States, dated 20 June 1954, he explains that the Bahá'ís should not dwell on the dark future facing the world:

> He has been told that some of the friends are disturbed over reports brought back by the pilgrims concerning the dangers facing America in the future whenever another world conflagration breaks out.

---

[1]   Shoghi Effendi, *Citadel of the Faith*, p. 37.

He does not feel that the Bahá'ís should waste time dwelling on the dark side of things. Any intelligent person can understand from the experiences of the last world war, and keeping abreast of what modern science has developed in the way of weapons for any future war, that big cities all over the world are going to be in tremendous danger. This is what the Guardian has said to the pilgrims.[1]

---

[1] Written on behalf of Shoghi Effendi, *Lights of Guidance*, p. 134.

24.8 Activities

24.8.1 Short answer questions

1. In quote 116:B, 'Abdu'l-Bahá describes some of the reasons why the American people are worthy of *"being the first to build the Tabernacle of the Great Peace, and proclaim the oneness of mankind ...."* Summarize these reasons in bullet form.

    _____

    _____

    _____

    _____

2. In paragraph 117, Shoghi Effendi explains how the American nation has become the cradle and champion of the Faith. Share your understanding of his explanation.

    _____

    _____

    _____

    _____

3. What are the two processes through which the American Bahá'í community and the American nation are contributing towards the realization of the hopes of 'Abdu'l-Bahá and His promises for America?

    _____

    _____

    _____

    _____

4. In paragraph 119, Shoghi Effendi explains the forces that would drive America to abandon its isolationism during the 1930's. Identify the key points in this analysis and list them as bullet form.

    _____

    _____

    _____

    _____

5. Who was the "unappreciated President" as referred to by Shoghi Effendi in paragraph 119?

    _____

    _____

    _____

6. In paragraph 120, Shoghi Effendi warns Bahá'ís of the immediate dangers that were threatening the world at that time. What specific events is he referring to?

    _____

    _____

    _____

    _____

7. Consider quote 120:B. What does 'Abdu'l-Bahá mean by each of the following terms?

    a) The vanquished Powers:

    _____

    _____

    _____

    _____

    b) Newly born movements:

    _____

    _____

    _____

    _____

    c) The Movement of the Left:

    _____

    _____

    _____

    _____

8. How were the prophecies made by 'Abdu'l-Bahá in quote 120:B to be realized?

    _____

    _____

    _____

    _____

9. What are the different stages that the American nation will pass through before it can accomplish "that which will adorn the pages of history", "become the envy of the world and be blest in both the East and the West."?

_____

_____

_____

_____

10. In the context of the analysis provided by Shoghi Effendi in paragraphs 121–124 for the evolution of the United States towards its destiny, what stage of its evolution has it currently reached?

_____

_____

_____

_____

24.8.2   Mini-project

Conduct research to identify how the United States abandoned its isolationism as explained by Shoghi Effendi in paragraph 119, assumed a major role in the world affairs, and developed new relationships with other nations. Organize your findings as a paper for publication in a Bahá'í journal.

Appendix
Tablets of the Divine Plan

This Appendix reproduces 'Abdu'l-Bahá's 14 Tablets of the Divine Plan addressed to the Bahá'ís of various regions.

1. The Northeastern States

Revealed on 26 March 1916, in 'Abdu'l-Bahá's room at the house in Bahjí, addressed to the Bahá'ís of nine Northeastern States of the United States: Maine, Massachusetts, New Hampshire, Rhode Island, Connecticut, Vermont, Pennsylvania, New Jersey and New York.

O ye heavenly heralds:

These are the days of Naw-Rúz. I am always thinking of those kind friends! I beg for each and all of you confirmations and assistance from the threshold of oneness, so that those gatherings may become ignited like unto candles, in the republics of America, enkindling the light of the love of God in the hearts; thus the rays of the heavenly teachings may begem and brighten the states of America like the infinitude of immensity with the stars of the Most Great Guidance.

The Northeastern States on the shores of the Atlantic—Maine, New Hampshire, Massachusetts, Rhode Island, Connecticut, Vermont, Pennsylvania, New Jersey and New York—in some of these states believers are found, but in some of the cities of these states up to this date people are not yet illumined with the lights of the Kingdom and are not aware of the heavenly teachings; therefore, whenever it is possible for each one of you, hasten ye to those cities and shine forth like unto the stars with the light of the Most Great Guidance. God says in the glorious Qur'án: "The soil was black and dried. Then we caused the rain to descend upon it and immediately it became green, verdant, and every kind of plant sprouted up luxuriantly."[1] In other words, He says the earth is black, but when the spring showers descend upon it that black soil is quickened, and variegated flowers are

---

[1]   Qur'án 22:5.

pushed forth. This means the souls of humanity belonging to the world of nature are black like unto the soil. But when the heavenly outpourings descend and the radiant effulgences appear, the hearts are resuscitated, are liberated from the darkness of nature and the flowers of divine mysteries grow and become luxuriant. Consequently man must become the cause of the illumination of the world of humanity and propagate the holy teachings revealed in the sacred books through the divine inspiration. It is stated in the blessed Gospel: Travel ye toward the East and toward the West and enlighten the people with the light of the Most Great Guidance, so that they may take a portion and share of eternal life.[1] Praise be to God, that the Northeastern States are in the utmost capacity. Because the ground is rich, the rain of the divine outpouring is descending. Now you must become heavenly farmers and scatter pure seeds in the prepared soil. The harvest of every other seed is limited, but the bounty and the blessing of the seed of the divine teachings is unlimited. Throughout the coming centuries and cycles many harvests will be gathered. Consider the work of former generations. During the lifetime of Jesus Christ the believing, firm souls were few and numbered, but the heavenly blessings descended so plentifully that in a number of years countless souls entered beneath the shadow of the Gospel. God has said in the Qur'án: "One grain will bring forth seven sheaves, and every sheaf shall contain one hundred grains."[2] In other words, one grain will become seven hundred; and if God so wills He will double these also. It has often happened that one blessed soul has become the cause of the guidance of a nation. Now we must not consider our ability and capacity, nay, rather, we must fix our gaze upon the favours and bounties of God, in these days, Who has made of the drop a sea, and of the atom a sun.

Upon you be greeting and praise!

---

[1]   cf. Mark 16:15.

[2]   cf. Qur'án 2:261.

2. The Southern States

Revealed on 27 March 1916, in the garden adjacent to the Shrine of Bahá'u'lláh, addressed to the Bahá'ís of sixteen Southern States of the United States: Delaware, Maryland, Virginia, West Virginia, North Carolina, South Carolina, Georgia, Florida, Alabama, Mississippi, Tennessee, Kentucky, Louisiana, Arkansas, Oklahoma and Texas.

O ye heralds of the Kingdom of God:

A few days ago an epistle was written to those divine believers, but because these days are the days of Naw-Rúz, you have come to my mind and I am sending you this greeting for this glorious feast. All the days are blessed, but this feast is the national fête of Persia. The Persians have been holding it for several thousand years past. In reality every day which man passes in the mention of God, the diffusion of the fragrances of God and calling the people to the Kingdom of God, that day is his feast. Praise be to God that you are occupied in the service of the Kingdom of God and are engaged in the promulgation of the religion of God by day and by night. Therefore all your days are feast days. There is no doubt that the assistance and the bestowal of God shall descend upon you.

In the Southern States of the United States, the friends are few, that is, in Delaware, Maryland, Virginia, West Virginia, North Carolina, South Carolina, Georgia, Florida, Alabama, Mississippi, Tennessee, Kentucky, Louisiana, Arkansas, Oklahoma and Texas. Consequently you must either go yourselves or send a number of blessed souls to those states, so that they may guide the people to the Kingdom of Heaven. One of the holy Manifestations, addressing a believing soul, has said that, if a person become the cause of the illumination of one soul, it is better than a boundless treasury. "O 'Alí! If God guide, through thee, one soul, it is better for thee than all the riches!" Again He says, "Direct us to the straight path!"[1] that is, Show us the right road. It is also mentioned in the Gospel: Travel ye to all parts of the world and give ye the glad tidings of the appearance of the Kingdom of God.[2]

In brief, I hope you will display in this respect the greatest effort and magnanimity. It is assured that you will become assisted and confirmed. A person declaring the glad tidings of the appearance of the realities and significances of the Kingdom is like unto a farmer who scatters pure seeds in the rich soil. The spring cloud will pour upon them the rain of bounty, and unquestionably the station of the farmer will be raised in the estimation of the lord of the village, and many harvests will be gathered.

Therefore, ye friends of God! Appreciate ye the value of this time and be ye engaged in the sowing of the seeds, so that you may find the heavenly blessing and the lordly bestowal. Upon you be Bahá'u'l-Abhá!

---

[1] Qur'án 1:6.

[2] cf. Mark 16:15.

3.   The Central States

Revealed on 29 March 1916, outside the house in Bahjí, and addressed to the Bahá'ís of twelve Central States of the United States: Michigan, Wisconsin, Illinois, Indiana, Ohio, Minnesota, Iowa, Missouri, North Dakota, South Dakota, Nebraska and Kansas.

O ye heavenly souls, O ye spiritual assemblies, O ye lordly meetings:

For some time past correspondence has been delayed, and this has been on account of the difficulty of mailing and receiving letters. But because at present a number of facilities are obtainable, therefore, I am engaged in writing you this brief epistle so that my heart and soul may obtain joy and fragrance through the remembrance of the friends. Continually this wanderer supplicates and entreats at the threshold of His Holiness the One and begs assistance, bounty and heavenly confirmations in behalf of the believers. You are always in my thoughts. You are not nor shall you ever be forgotten. I hope by the favour of His Holiness the Almighty that day by day you may add to your faith, assurance, firmness and steadfastness, and become instruments for the promotion of the holy fragrances.

Although in the states of Illinois, Wisconsin, Ohio, Michigan and Minnesota—praise be to God—believers are found who are associating with each other in the utmost firmness and steadfastness—day and night they have no other intention save the diffusion of the fragrances of God, they have no other hope except the promotion of the heavenly teachings, like the candles they are burning with the light of the love of God, and like thankful birds are singing songs, spirit-imparting, joy-creating, in the rose garden of the knowledge of God—yet in the states of Indiana, Iowa, Missouri, North Dakota, South Dakota, Nebraska and Kansas few of the believers exist. So far the summons of the Kingdom of God and the proclamation of the oneness of the world of humanity has not been made in these states systematically and enthusiastically. Blessed souls and detached teachers have not travelled through these parts repeatedly; therefore these states are still in a state of heedlessness. Through the efforts of the friends of God souls must be likewise enkindled in these states, with the fire of the love of God and attracted to the Kingdom of God, so that section may also become illumined and the soul imparting breeze of the rose garden of the Kingdom may perfume the nostrils of the inhabitants. Therefore, if it is possible, send to those parts teachers who are severed from all else save God, sanctified and pure. If these teachers be in the utmost state of attraction, in a short time great results will be forthcoming. The sons and daughters of the kingdom are like unto the real farmers. Through whichever state or country they pass they display self-sacrifice and sow divine seeds. From that seed harvests are produced. On this subject it is revealed in the glorious Gospel: When the pure seeds are scattered in the good ground heavenly blessing and benediction is obtained.[1] I hope that you may become assisted and confirmed, and never lose courage in the promotion of the divine teachings. Day by day may you add to your effort, exertion, and magnanimity.

Upon you be greeting and praise!

---

[1]   cf. Matthew 13:23.

4.   The Western States

Revealed on 1 April 1916, in 'Abdu'l-Bahá's room at the house in Bahjí, addressed to the Bahá'ís of eleven Western States of the United States: New Mexico, Colorado, Arizona, Nevada, California, Wyoming, Utah, Montana, Idaho, Oregon and Washington.

He is God!
O ye sons and daughters of the Kingdom:

Day and night I have no other occupation than the remembrance of the friends, praying from the depth of my heart in their behalf, begging for them confirmation from the Kingdom of God and supplicating the direct effect of the breaths of the Holy Spirit. I am hopeful from the favours of His Highness the Lord of Bestowals, that the friends of God during such a time may become the secret cause of the illumination of the hearts of humanity, breathing the breath of life upon the spirits—whose praiseworthy results may become conducive to the glory and exaltation of humankind throughout all eternity. Although in some of the Western States, like California, Oregon, Washington and Colorado, the fragrances of holiness are diffused, numerous souls have taken a share and a portion from the fountain of everlasting life, they have obtained heavenly benediction, have drunk an overflowing cup from the wine of the love of God and have hearkened to the melody of the Supreme Concourse—yet in the states of New Mexico, Wyoming, Montana, Idaho, Utah, Arizona and Nevada, the lamp of the love of God is not ignited in a befitting and behoving manner, and the call of the Kingdom of God has not been raised. Now, if it is possible, show ye an effort in this direction. Either travel yourselves, personally, throughout those states or choose others and send them, so that they may teach the souls. For the present those states are like unto dead bodies: they must breathe into them the breath of life and bestow upon them a heavenly spirit. Like unto the stars they must shine in that horizon and thus the rays of the Sun of Reality may also illumine those states.

God says in the great Qur'án: "Verily God is the helper of those who have believed. He will lead them from darkness into light."[1] This means: God loves the believers, consequently He will deliver them from darkness and bring them into the world of light.

It is also recorded in the blessed Gospel: Travel ye throughout the world and call ye the people to the Kingdom of God.[2] Now this is the time that you may arise and perform this most great service and become the cause of the guidance of innumerable souls. Thus through this superhuman service the rays of peace and conciliation may illumine and enlighten all the regions and the world of humanity may find peace and composure.

During my stay in America I cried out in every meeting and summoned the people to the propagation of the ideals of universal peace. I said plainly that the continent of Europe had become like unto an arsenal and its conflagration was dependent upon one spark, and that in the coming years, or within two years, all

---

[1]   Qur'án 2:257.
[2]   cf. Mark 16:15.

that which is recorded in the Revelation of John and the Book of Daniel would become fulfilled and come to pass. This matter, in all probability, was published in the San Francisco Bulletin, October 12, 1912. You may refer to it, so that the truth may become clear and manifest; thus ye may fully realize that this is the time for the diffusion of the fragrances.

The magnanimity of man must be heavenly or, in other words, it must be assisted by the divine confirmation, so that he may become the cause of the illumination of the world of humanity.

Upon you be greeting and praise!

5. Canada and Greenland

Revealed on 5 April 1916, in the garden adjacent to the Shrine of Bahá'u'lláh, and addressed to the Bahá'ís of Canada—Newfoundland, Prince Edward Island, Nova Scotia, New Brunswick, Quebec, Saskatchewan, Manitoba, Ontario, Alberta, British Columbia, Yukon, Mackenzie, Keewatin, Ungava, Franklin Islands—and Greenland.

He is God!
O ye daughters and sons of the Kingdom:

Although in most of the states and cities of the United States, praise be to God, His fragrances are diffused, and souls unnumbered are turning their faces and advancing toward the Kingdom of God, yet in some of the states the Standard of Unity is not yet upraised as it should be, nor are the mysteries of the Holy Books, such as the Bible, the Gospel, and the Qur'án, unravelled. Through the concerted efforts of all the friends the Standard of Unity must needs be unfurled in those states, and the divine teachings promoted, so that these states may also receive their portion of the heavenly bestowals and a share of the Most Great Guidance. Likewise in the provinces of Canada, such as Newfoundland, Prince Edward Island, Nova Scotia, New Brunswick, Quebec, Ontario, Manitoba, Saskatchewan, Alberta, British Columbia, Ungava, Keewatin, Mackenzie, Yukon, and the Franklin Islands in the Arctic Circle—the believers of God must become self-sacrificing and like unto the candles of guidance become ignited in the provinces of Canada. Should they show forth such a magnanimity, it is assured that they will obtain universal divine confirmations, the heavenly cohorts will reinforce them uninterruptedly, and a most great victory will be obtained. God willing, the call of the Kingdom may reach the ears of the Eskimos, the inhabitants of the Islands of Franklin in the north of Canada, as well as Greenland. Should the fire of the love of God be kindled in Greenland, all the ice of that country will be melted, and its cold weather become temperate—that is, if the hearts be touched with the heat of the love of God, that territory will become a divine rose garden and a heavenly paradise, and the souls, even as fruitful trees, will acquire the utmost freshness and beauty. Effort, the utmost effort, is required. Should you display an effort, so that the fragrances of God may be diffused among the Eskimos, its effect will be very great and far-reaching. God says in the great Qur'án: A day will come wherein the lights of unity will enlighten all the world. "The earth will be irradiated with the light of its Lord."[1] In other words, the earth will become illumined with the light of God. That light is the light of unity. "There is no God but God." The continent and the islands of Eskimos are also parts of this earth. They must similarly receive a portion of the bestowals of the Most Great Guidance.

Upon you be greeting and praise!

---

[1] Qur'án 39:69.

6. The United States and Canada

Revealed on 8 April 1916, in the garden outside the Shrine of Bahá'u'lláh, and addressed to the Bahá'ís of the United States and Canada.

He is God!
O ye blessed souls:

I desire for you eternal success and prosperity and beg perfect confirmation for each one in the divine world. My hope for you is that each one may shine forth like unto the morning star from the horizon of the world and in this Garden of God become a blessed tree, producing everlasting fruits and results.

Therefore I direct you to that which is conducive to your heavenly confirmation and illumination in the Kingdom of God!

It is this: Alaska is a vast country; although one of the maidservants of the Merciful has hastened to those parts, serving as a librarian in the public library, and according to her ability is not failing in teaching the Cause, yet the call of the Kingdom of God is not yet raised through that spacious territory.

His Holiness Christ says: Travel ye to the East and to the West of the world and summon the people to the Kingdom of God.[1] Hence the mercy of God must encompass all humanity. Therefore do ye not think it permissible to leave that region deprived of the breezes of the Morn of Guidance. Consequently, strive as far as ye are able to send to those parts fluent speakers, who are detached from aught else save God, attracted with the fragrances of God, and sanctified and purified from all desires and temptations. Their sustenance and food must consist of the teachings of God. First they must themselves live in accordance with those principles, then guide the people. Perchance, God willing, the lights of the Most Great Guidance will illuminate that country, and the breezes of the rose garden of the love of God will perfume the nostrils of the inhabitants of Alaska. Should you be aided to render such a service, rest ye assured that your heads shall be crowned with the diadem of everlasting sovereignty, and at the threshold of oneness you will become the favoured and accepted servants.

Likewise the republic of Mexico is very important. The majority of the inhabitants of that country are devoted Catholics. They are totally unaware of the reality of the Bible, the Gospel and the new divine teachings. They do not know that the basis of the religions of God is one and that the holy Manifestations are like unto the Sun of Truth, rising from the different dawning-places. Those souls are submerged in the sea of dogmas. If one breath of life be blown over them, great results will issue therefrom. But it is better for those who intend to go to Mexico to teach, to be familiar with the Spanish language.

Similarly, the six Central American republics, situated south of Mexico— Guatemala, Honduras, Salvador, Nicaragua, Costa Rica, Panama and the seventh country Belize or British Honduras. The teachers going to those parts must also be familiar with the Spanish language.

---

[1] cf. Mark 16:15.

Attach great importance to the indigenous population of America. For these souls may be likened unto the ancient inhabitants of the Arabian Peninsula, who, prior to the Mission of Muḥammad, were like unto savages. When the light of Muḥammad shone forth in their midst, however, they became so radiant as to illumine the world. Likewise, these Indians, should they be educated and guided, there can be no doubt that they will become so illumined as to enlighten the whole world.

All the above countries have importance, but especially the Republic of Panama, wherein the Atlantic and Pacific Oceans come together through the Panama Canal. It is a centre for travel and passage from America to other continents of the world, and in the future it will gain most great importance.

Likewise the islands of the West Indies, such as Cuba, Haiti, Puerto Rico, Jamaica, the islands of the Lesser Antilles, Bahama Islands, even the small Watling Island, have great importance; especially the two black republics, Haiti and Santo Domingo, situated in the cluster of the Greater Antilles. Likewise the cluster of the islands of Bermuda in the Atlantic Ocean have importance.

In a similar way, the republics of the continent of South America—Colombia, Ecuador, Peru, Brazil, British Guiana, Dutch Guiana, French Guiana, Bolivia, Chile, Argentina, Uruguay, Paraguay, Venezuela; also the islands to the north, east and west of South America, such as Falkland Islands, the Galápagos, Juan Fernandez, Tobago and Trinidad. Likewise the city of Bahia, situated on the eastern shore of Brazil. Because it is some time that it has become known by this name, its efficacy will be most potent.

In short, O ye believers of God! Exalt your effort and magnify your aims. His Holiness Christ says: *Blessed are the poor, for theirs shall be the Kingdom of Heaven.*[1] In other words: Blessed are the nameless and traceless poor, for they are the leaders of mankind. Likewise it is said in the Qur'án: "And We desire to show favour to those who were brought low in the land, and to make them spiritual leaders among men, and to make of them Our heirs."[2] *Or, we wish to grant a favour to the impotent souls and suffer them to become the inheritors of the Messengers and Prophets.*

Now is the time for you to divest yourselves of the garment of attachment to this world that perisheth, to be wholly severed from the physical world, become heavenly angels, and travel to these countries. I swear by Him, besides Whom there is none other God, that each one of you will become an Isráfíl of Life, and will blow the Breath of Life into the souls of others.

Upon you be greeting and praise!

Supplication

O Thou Incomparable God! O Thou Lord of the Kingdom! These souls are Thy heavenly army. Assist them and, with the cohorts of the Supreme Concourse, make them victorious, so that each one of them may become like unto a regiment and

---

[1] cf. Matthew 5:3.

[2] Qur'án 28:5.

conquer these countries through the love of God and the illumination of divine teachings.

O God! Be Thou their supporter and their helper, and in the wilderness, the mountain, the valley, the forests, the prairies and the seas, be Thou their confidant— so that they may cry out through the power of the Kingdom and the breath of the Holy Spirit.

Verily, Thou art the Powerful, the Mighty and the Omnipotent, and Thou art the Wise, the Hearing and the Seeing.

7. The United States and Canada

Revealed on 11 April 1916, in 'Abdu'l-Bahá's room at the house in Bahjí, and addressed to the Bahá'ís of the United States and Canada.

He is God!
O ye real Bahá'ís of America:

Praise be to His Highness the Desired One that ye have become confirmed in the promotion of divine teachings in that vast Continent, raised the call of the Kingdom of God in that region and announced the glad tidings of the manifestation of the Lord of Hosts and His Highness the Promised One. Thanks be unto the Lord that ye have become assisted and confirmed in this aim. This is purely through the confirmations of the Lord of Hosts and the breaths of the Holy Spirit. The full measure of your success is as yet unrevealed, its significance still unapprehended. Erelong ye will, with your own eyes, witness how brilliantly every one of you, even as a shining star, will radiate in the firmament of your country the light of divine Guidance, and will bestow upon its people the glory of an everlasting life.

Consider! The station and the confirmation of the apostles in the time of Christ was not known, and no one looked on them with the feeling of importance—nay, rather, they persecuted and ridiculed them. Later on it became evident what crowns studded with the brilliant jewels of guidance were placed on the heads of the apostles, Mary Magdalene and Mary the mother of John.

The range of your future achievements still remains undisclosed. I fervently hope that in the near future the whole earth may be stirred and shaken by the results of your achievements. The hope, therefore, which 'Abdu'l-Bahá cherishes for you is that the same success which has attended your efforts in America may crown your endeavours in other parts of the world, that through you the fame of the Cause of God may be diffused throughout the East and the West and the advent of the Kingdom of the Lord of Hosts be proclaimed in all the five continents of the globe.

The moment this divine Message is carried forward by the American believers from the shores of America and is propagated through the continents of Europe, of Asia, of Africa and of Australasia, and as far as the islands of the Pacific, this community will find itself securely established upon the throne of an everlasting dominion. Then will all the peoples of the world witness that this community is spiritually illumined and divinely guided. Then will the whole earth resound with the praises of its majesty and greatness. A party speaking their languages, severed, holy, sanctified and filled with the love of God, must turn their faces to and travel through the three great island groups of the Pacific Ocean—Polynesia, Micronesia and Melanesia, and the islands attached to these groups, such as New Guinea, Borneo, Java, Sumatra, Philippine Islands, Solomon Islands, Fiji Islands, New Hebrides, Loyalty Islands, New Caledonia, Bismarck Archipelago, Ceram, Celebes, Friendly Islands, Samoa Islands, Society Islands, Caroline Islands, Low Archipelago, Marquesas, Hawaiian Islands, Gilbert Islands, Moluccas, Marshall Islands, Timor and the other islands. With hearts overflowing with the love of God, with tongues commemorating the mention of God, with eyes turned to the Kingdom of God, they must deliver the glad tidings of the manifestation of the Lord of Hosts to all the people. Know ye of a certainty that whatever gathering ye enter, the waves of the

Holy Spirit are surging over it, and the heavenly grace of the Blessed Beauty encompasseth that gathering.

Consider ye, that Miss Agnes Alexander, the daughter of the Kingdom, the beloved maidservant of the Blessed Perfection, travelled alone to the Hawaiian Islands, to the Island of Honolulu, and now she is gaining spiritual victories in Japan! Reflect ye how this daughter was confirmed in the Hawaiian Islands. She became the cause of the guidance of a gathering of people.

Likewise Miss Knobloch travelled alone to Germany. To what a great extent she became confirmed! Therefore, know ye of a certainty that whosoever arises in this day to diffuse the divine fragrances, the cohorts of the Kingdom of God shall confirm him and the bestowals and the favours of the Blessed Perfection shall encircle him.

O that I could travel, even though on foot and in the utmost poverty, to these regions, and, raising the call of "Yá Bahá'u'l-Abhá" in cities, villages, mountains, deserts and oceans, promote the divine teachings! This, alas, I cannot do. How intensely I deplore it! Please God, ye may achieve it.

At this time, in the Hawaiian Islands, through the efforts of Miss Alexander, a number of souls have reached the shore of the sea of faith! Consider ye, what happiness, what joy is this! I declare by the Lord of Hosts that had this respected daughter founded an empire, that empire would not have been so great! For this sovereignty is eternal sovereignty and this glory is everlasting glory.

Likewise, if some teachers go to other islands and other parts, such as the continent of Australia, New Zealand, Tasmania, also to Japan, Asiatic Russia, Korea, French Indochina, Siam, Straits Settlements, India, Ceylon and Afghanistan, most great results will be forthcoming. How good would it be were there any possibility of a commission composed of men and women, to travel together through China and Japan—so that this bond of love may become strengthened, and through this going and coming they may establish the oneness of the world of humanity, summon the people to the Kingdom of God and spread the teachings.

Similarly, if possible, they should travel to the continent of Africa, Canary Islands, Cape Verde Islands, Madeira Islands, Réunion Islands, St. Helena, Zanzibar, Mauritius, etc., and in those countries summon the people to the Kingdom of God and raise the cry of "Yá Bahá'u'l-Abhá!" They must also upraise the flag of the oneness of the world of humanity in the island of Madagascar.

Books and pamphlets must be either translated or composed in the languages of these countries and islands, to be circulated in every part and in all directions.

It is said that in South Africa, a diamond mine is discovered. Although this mine is most valuable, yet after all it is stone. Perchance, God willing, the mine of humanity may be discovered and the brilliant pearls of the Kingdom be found.

In brief, this world-consuming war has set such a conflagration to the hearts that no word can describe it. In all the countries of the world the longing for universal peace is taking possession of the consciousness of men. There is not a soul who does not yearn for concord and peace. A most wonderful state of receptivity is being realized. This is through the consummate wisdom of God, so that capacity may be created, the standard of the oneness of the world of humanity be upraised, *and the fundamental of universal peace and the divine principles be promoted in the East and the West.*

Therefore, O ye believers of God! Show ye an effort and after this war spread ye the synopsis of the divine teachings in the British Isles, France, Germany, Austria-Hungary, Russia, Italy, Spain, Belgium, Switzerland, Norway, Sweden, Denmark, Holland, Portugal, Rumania, Serbia, Montenegro, Bulgaria, Greece, Andorra, Liechtenstein, Luxemburg, Monaco, San Marino, Balearic Isles, Corsica, Sardinia, Sicily, Crete, Malta, Iceland, Faroe Islands, Shetland Islands, Hebrides and Orkney Islands.

In all these countries, like unto the morning stars shine ye forth from the horizon of guidance. Thus far ye have been untiring in your labours. Let your exertions henceforth increase a thousandfold. Summon the people in these countries, capitals, islands, assemblies and churches to enter the Abhá Kingdom. The scope of your exertions must needs be extended. The wider its range, the more striking will be the evidence of divine assistance.

You have observed that while ‘Abdu’l-Bahá was in the utmost bodily weakness and feebleness, while he was indisposed, and had not the power to move—notwithstanding this physical state he travelled through many countries, in Europe and America, and in churches, meetings and conventions was occupied with the promotion of the divine principles and summoned the people to the manifestation of the Kingdom of Abhá. You have also observed how the confirmations of the Blessed Perfection encompassed all. What result is forthcoming from material rest, tranquillity, luxury and attachment to this corporeal world? It is evident that the man who pursues these things will in the end become afflicted with regret and loss.

Consequently, one must close his eyes wholly to these thoughts, long for eternal life, the sublimity of the world of humanity, the celestial developments, the Holy Spirit, the promotion of the Word of God, the guidance of the inhabitants of the globe, the promulgation of universal peace and the proclamation of the oneness of the world of humanity! This is the work! Otherwise like unto other animals and birds one must occupy himself with the requirements of this physical life, the satisfaction of which is the highest aspiration of the animal kingdom, and one must stalk across the earth like unto the quadrupeds.

Consider ye! No matter how much man gains wealth, riches and opulence in this world, he will not become as independent as a cow. For these fattened cows roam freely over the vast tableland. All the prairies and meadows are theirs for grazing, and all the springs and rivers are theirs for drinking! No matter how much they graze, the fields will not be exhausted! It is evident that they have earned these material bounties with the utmost facility.

Still more ideal than this life is the life of the bird. A bird, on the summit of a mountain, on the high, waving branches, has built for itself a nest more beautiful than the palaces of the kings! The air is in the utmost purity, the water cool and clear as crystal, the panorama charming and enchanting. In such glorious surroundings, he expends his numbered days. All the harvests of the plain are his possessions, having earned all this wealth without the least labour. Hence, no matter how much man may advance in this world, he shall not attain to the station of this bird! Thus it becomes evident that in the matters of this world, however much man may strive and work to the point of death, he will be unable to earn the abundance, the freedom and the independent life of a small bird. This proves and establishes the fact that man is not created for the life of this ephemeral world— nay, rather, is he created for the acquirement of infinite perfections, for the attainment to the sublimity of the world of humanity, to be drawn nigh unto the divine threshold, and to sit on the throne of everlasting sovereignty!

Upon you be Bahá'u'l-Abhá!

Whoever sets out on a teaching journey to any place, let him recite this prayer day and night during his travels in foreign lands:

O God, my God! Thou seest me enraptured and attracted toward Thy glorious kingdom, enkindled with the fire of Thy love amongst mankind, a herald of Thy kingdom in these vast and spacious lands, severed from aught else save Thee, relying on Thee, abandoning rest and comfort, remote from my native home, a wanderer in these regions, a stranger fallen upon the ground, humble before Thine exalted threshold, submissive toward the heaven of Thine omnipotent glory, supplicating Thee in the dead of night and at the break of dawn, entreating and invoking Thee at morn and at eventide to graciously aid me to serve Thy Cause, to spread abroad Thy teachings and to exalt Thy Word throughout the East and the West.

O Lord! Strengthen my back, enable me to serve Thee with the utmost endeavour, and leave me not to myself, lonely and helpless in these regions.

O Lord! Grant me communion with Thee in my loneliness, and be my companion in these foreign lands.

Verily, Thou art the Confirmer of whomsoever Thou willest in that which Thou desirest, and, verily, Thou art the All-Powerful, the Omnipotent.

8. The United States and Canada

Revealed on 19 April 1916, in 'Abdu'l-Bahá's room at the house in Bahjí; on April 20, in the pilgrims' quarters of the house in Bahjí; on April 22, in the garden adjacent to the Shrine of Bahá'u'lláh, and addressed to the Bahá'ís of the United States and Canada.

He is God!
O ye Apostles of Bahá'u'lláh!
May my life be sacrificed for you!

The Blessed Person of the Promised One is interpreted in the Holy Book as the Lord of Hosts—the heavenly armies. By heavenly armies those souls are intended who are entirely freed from the human world, transformed into celestial spirits and have become divine angels. Such souls are the rays of the Sun of Reality who will illumine all the continents. Each one is holding in his hand a trumpet, blowing the breath of life over all the regions. They are delivered from human qualities and the defects of the world of nature, are characterized with the characteristics of God, and are attracted with the fragrances of the Merciful. Like unto the apostles of Christ, who were filled with Him, these souls also have become filled with His Holiness Bahá'u'lláh; that is, the love of Bahá'u'lláh has so mastered every organ, part and limb of their bodies, as to leave no effect from the promptings of the human world.

These souls are the armies of God and the conquerors of the East and the West. Should one of them turn his face toward some direction and summon the people to the Kingdom of God, all the ideal forces and lordly confirmations will rush to his support and reinforcement. He will behold all the doors open and all the strong fortifications and impregnable castles razed to the ground. Singly and alone he will attack the armies of the world, defeat the right and left wings of the hosts of all the countries, break through the lines of the legions of all the nations and carry his attack to the very centre of the powers of the earth. This is the meaning of the Hosts of God.

Any soul from among the believers of Bahá'u'lláh who attains to this station will become known as the Apostle of Bahá'u'lláh. Therefore strive ye with heart and soul so that ye may reach this lofty and exalted position, be established on the throne of everlasting glory, and crown your heads with the shining diadem of the Kingdom, whose brilliant jewels may irradiate upon centuries and cycles.

O ye kind friends! Uplift your magnanimity and soar high toward the apex of heaven so that your blessed hearts may become illumined more and more, day by day, through the rays of the Sun of Reality, that is, His Holiness Bahá'u'lláh; at every moment the spirits may obtain a new life, and the darkness of the world of nature may be entirely dispelled; thus you may become incarnate light and personified spirit, become entirely unaware of the sordid matters of this world and in touch with the affairs of the divine world.

Behold the portals which Bahá'u'lláh hath opened before you! Consider how exalted and lofty is the station you are destined to attain; how unique the favours with which you have been endowed. Should we become intoxicated with this cup, the sovereignty of this globe of earth will become lower in our estimation than children's play. Should they place in the arena the crown of the government of the whole world, and invite each one of us to accept it, undoubtedly we shall not condescend, and shall refuse to accept it.

To attain to this supreme station is, however, dependent on the realization of certain conditions:

The first condition is firmness in the Covenant of God. For the power of the Covenant will protect the Cause of Bahá'u'lláh from the doubts of the people of error. It is the fortified fortress of the Cause of God and the firm pillar of the religion of God. Today no power can conserve the oneness of the Bahá'í world save the Covenant of God; otherwise differences like unto a most great tempest will encompass the Bahá'í world. It is evident that the axis of the oneness of the world of humanity is the power of the Covenant and nothing else. Had the Covenant not come to pass, had it not been revealed from the Supreme Pen and had not the Book of the Covenant, like unto the ray of the Sun of Reality, illuminated the world, the forces of the Cause of God would have been utterly scattered and certain souls who were the prisoners of their own passions and lusts would have taken into their hands an axe, cutting the root of this Blessed Tree. Every person would have pushed forward his own desire and every individual aired his own opinion! Notwithstanding this great Covenant, a few negligent souls galloped with their chargers into the battlefield, thinking perchance they might be able to weaken the foundation of the Cause of God: but praise be to God all of them were afflicted with regret and loss, and erelong they shall see themselves in poignant despair. Therefore, in the beginning the believers must make their steps firm in the Covenant so that the confirmations of Bahá'u'lláh may encircle them from all sides, the cohorts of the Supreme Concourse may become their supporters and helpers, and the exhortations and advices of 'Abdu'l-Bahá, like unto the pictures engraved on stone, may remain permanent and ineffaceable in the tablets of all hearts.

The second condition: Fellowship and love amongst the believers. The divine friends must be attracted to and enamoured of each other and ever be ready and willing to sacrifice their own lives for each other. Should one soul from amongst the believers meet another, it must be as though a thirsty one with parched lips has reached to the fountain of the water of life, or a lover has met his true beloved. For one of the greatest divine wisdoms regarding the appearance of the holy Manifestations is this: The souls may come to know each other and become intimate with each other; the power of the love of God may make all of them the waves of one sea, the flowers of one rose garden, and the stars of one heaven. This is the wisdom for the appearance of the holy Manifestations! When the most great bestowal reveals itself in the hearts of the believers, the world of nature will be transformed, the darkness of the contingent being will vanish, and heavenly illumination will be obtained. Then the whole world will become the Paradise of Abhá, every one of the believers of God will become a blessed tree, producing wonderful fruits.

O ye friends! Fellowship, fellowship! Love, love! Unity, unity!—so that the power of the Bahá'í Cause may appear and become manifest in the world of existence. My thoughts are turned towards you, and my heart leaps within me at your mention. Could ye know how my soul glows with your love, so great a happiness would flood your hearts as to cause you to become enamoured with each other.

The third condition: Teachers must continually travel to all parts of the continent, nay, rather, to all parts of the world, but they must travel like 'Abdu'l-Bahá, who journeyed throughout the cities of America. He was sanctified and free from every attachment and in the utmost severance. Just as His Holiness Christ says: Shake off the very dust from your feet.[1]

You have observed that while in America many souls in the utmost of supplication and entreaty desired to offer some gifts, but this servant, in accord with the exhortations and behests of the Blessed Perfection, never accepted a thing, although on certain occasions we were in most straitened circumstances. But on the other hand, if a soul for the sake of God, voluntarily and out of his pure desire, wishes to offer a contribution (toward the expenses of a teacher) in order to make the contributor happy, the teacher may accept a small sum, but must live with the utmost contentment.

The aim is this: The intention of the teacher must be pure, his heart independent, his spirit attracted, his thought at peace, his resolution firm, his magnanimity exalted and in the love of God a shining torch. Should he become as such, his sanctified breath will even affect the rock; otherwise there will be no result whatsoever. As long as a soul is not perfected, how can he efface the defects of others? Unless he is detached from aught else save God, how can he teach severance to others?

In short, O ye believers of God! Endeavour ye, so that you may take hold of every means in the promulgation of the religion of God and the diffusion of the fragrances of God.

Amongst other things is the holding of the meetings for teaching so that blessed souls and the old ones from amongst the believers may gather together the youths of the love of God in schools of instruction and teach them all the divine proofs and irrefragable arguments, explain and elucidate the history of the Cause, and interpret also the prophecies and proofs which are recorded and are extant in the divine books and epistles regarding the manifestation of the Promised One, so that the young ones may go in perfect knowledge in all these degrees.

Likewise, whenever it is possible a committee must be organized for the translation of the Tablets. Wise souls who have mastered and studied perfectly the Persian, Arabic, and other foreign languages, or know one of the foreign languages, must commence translating Tablets and books containing the proofs of this Revelation, and publishing those books, circulate them throughout the five continents of the globe.

Similarly, the magazine, the Star of the West, must be edited with the utmost regularity, but its contents must be the promulgation of the Cause of God that both East and West may become informed of the most important events.

In short, in all the meetings, whether public or private, nothing should be discussed save that which is under consideration, and all the articles be centred around the Cause of God. Promiscuous talk must not be dragged in and contention is absolutely forbidden.

---

[1]   cf. Matthew 10:14.

The teachers traveling in different directions must know the language of the country in which they will enter. For example, a person being proficient in the Japanese language may travel to Japan, or a person knowing the Chinese language may hasten to China, and so forth.

In short, after this universal war, the people have obtained extraordinary capacity to hearken to the divine teachings, for the wisdom of this war is this: That it may become proven to all that the fire of war is world-consuming, whereas the rays of peace are world-enlightening. One is death, the other is life; this is extinction, that is immortality; one is the most great calamity, the other is the most great bounty; this is darkness, that is light; this is eternal humiliation and that is everlasting glory; one is the destroyer of the foundation of man, the other is the founder of the prosperity of the human race.

Consequently, a number of souls may arise and act in accordance with the aforesaid conditions, and hasten to all parts of the world, especially from America to Europe, Africa, Asia and Australia, and travel through Japan and China. Likewise, from Germany teachers and believers may travel to the continents of America, Africa, Japan and China; in brief, they may travel through all the continents and islands of the globe. Thus in a short space of time, most wonderful results will be produced, the banner of universal peace will be waving on the apex of the world and the lights of the oneness of the world of humanity may illumine the universe.

In brief, O ye believers of God! The text of the divine Book is this: If two souls quarrel and contend about a question of the divine questions, differing and disputing, both are wrong. The wisdom of this incontrovertible law of God is this: That between two souls from amongst the believers of God, no contention and dispute may arise; that they may speak with each other with infinite amity and love. Should there appear the least trace of controversy, they must remain silent, and both parties must continue their discussions no longer, but ask the reality of the question from the Interpreter. This is the irrefutable command!

Upon you be Bahá'u'l-Abhá!

Supplication

O God, my God! Thou seest how black darkness is enshrouding all regions, how all countries are burning with the flame of dissension, and the fire of war and carnage is blazing throughout the East and the West. Blood is flowing, corpses bestrew the ground, and severed heads are fallen on the dust of the battlefield.

O Lord! Have pity on these ignorant ones and look upon them with the eye of forgiveness and pardon. Extinguish this fire, so that these dense clouds which obscure the horizon may be scattered, the Sun of Reality shine forth with the rays of conciliation, this intense gloom be dispelled and the resplendent light of peace shed its radiance upon all countries.

O Lord! Draw up the people from the abyss of the ocean of hatred and enmity, and deliver them from this impenetrable darkness. Unite their hearts, and brighten their eyes with the light of peace and reconciliation. Deliver them from the depths of war and bloodshed, and free them from the darkness of error. Remove the veil from their eyes, and enlighten their hearts with the light of guidance. Treat them with Thy tender mercy and compassion, and deal not with them according to Thy justice and wrath which cause the limbs of the mighty to quake.

O Lord! Wars have persisted. Distress and anxiety have waxed great and every flourishing region is laid waste.

O Lord! Hearts are heavy, and souls are in anguish. Have mercy on these poor souls and do not leave them to the excesses of their own desires.

O Lord! Make manifest in Thy lands humble and submissive souls, their faces illumined with the rays of guidance, severed from the world, extolling Thy Name, uttering Thy praise, and diffusing the fragrance of Thy holiness amongst mankind.

O Lord! Strengthen their backs, gird up their loins, and enrapture their hearts with the most mighty signs of Thy love.

O Lord! Verily, they are weak, and Thou art the Powerful and the Mighty; they are impotent, and Thou art the Helper and the Merciful.

O Lord! The ocean of rebellion is surging, and these tempests will not be stilled save through Thy boundless grace which hath embraced all regions.

O Lord! Verily, the people are in the abyss of passion, and naught can save them but Thine infinite bounties.

O Lord! Dispel the darkness of these corrupt desires, and illumine the hearts with the lamp of Thy love through which all countries will erelong be enlightened. Confirm, moreover, Thy loved ones, those who, leaving their homelands, their families and their children, have, for the love of Thy Beauty, travelled to foreign countries to diffuse Thy fragrances and promulgate Thy teachings. Be Thou their companion in their loneliness, their helper in a strange land, the remover of their sorrows, their comforter in calamity. Be Thou a refreshing draught for their thirst, a healing medicine for their ills and a balm for the burning ardour of their hearts.

Verily, Thou art the Most Generous, the Lord of grace abounding, and, verily, Thou art the Compassionate and the Merciful.

9. The Northeastern States

Revealed on 2 February 1917, in Ismá'íl Áqá's room at the house of 'Abdu'l-Bahá in Haifa, and addressed to the Bahá'ís of the nine Northeastern States of the United States: Maine, Massachusetts, New Hampshire, Rhode Island, Connecticut, Vermont, Pennsylvania, New Jersey and New York.

He is God!
O ye real friends:

All countries, in the estimation of the one true God, are but one country, and all cities and villages are on an equal footing. Neither holds distinction over another. All of them are the fields of God and the habitation of the souls of men. Through faith and certitude, and the precedence achieved by one over another, however, the dweller conferreth honour upon the dwelling, some of the countries achieve distinction, and attain a preeminent position. For instance, notwithstanding that some of the countries of Europe and of America are distinguished by, and surpass other countries in, the salubrity of their climate, the wholesomeness of their water, and the charm of their mountains, plains and prairies, yet Palestine became the glory of all nations inasmuch as all the holy and divine Manifestations, from the time of Abraham until the appearance of the Seal of the Prophets (Muḥammad), have lived in, or migrated to, or travelled through, that country. Likewise, Mecca and Medina have achieved illimitable glory, as the light of Prophethood shone forth therein. For this reason Palestine and Ḥijáz have been distinguished from all other countries.

Likewise, the continent of America is, in the eyes of the one true God, the land wherein the splendours of His light shall be revealed, where the mysteries of His Faith shall be unveiled, where the righteous will abide and the free assemble. Therefore, every section thereof is blessed: but because these nine states have been favoured in faith and assurance, hence through this precedence they have obtained spiritual privilege. They must realize the value of this bounty; because they have obtained such a favour and in order to render thanksgiving for this most great bestowal, they must arise in the diffusion of divine fragrances so that the blessed verse of the Qur'án, "God is the light of heaven and earth: the similitude of His light is a niche in a wall, wherein a lamp is placed, and the lamp enclosed in a case of glass; the glass appears as if it were a shining star. It is lighted with the oil of a Blessed Tree, an olive neither of the East, nor of the West; it wanteth little but that the oil thereof would give light, although no fire touched it. This is the light added unto light. God will direct unto His light whom He pleaseth"[1]—may be realized.

He says: The world of nature is the world of darkness, because it is the origin of a thousand depravities; nay, rather, it is darkness upon darkness. The illumination of the world of nature is dependent upon the splendour of the Sun of Reality. The grace of guidance is like unto the candle which is enkindled in the glass of knowledge and wisdom and that glass of knowledge and wisdom is the mirror of the heart of humanity. The oil of that luminous lamp is from the fruits of the Blessed Tree and that oil is so refined that it will burn without light. When the intensity of the light

---

[1]   Qur'án 24:35.

and the translucency of the glass and the purity of the mirror are brought together, it will become light upon light.

In brief, in these nine blessed states 'Abdu'l-Bahá journeyed and travelled from place to place, explained the wisdom of the heavenly books and diffused the fragrances. In most of these states he founded the divine Edifice and opened the door of teaching. In those states he sowed pure seeds and planted blessed trees.

Now the believers of God and the maidservants of the Merciful must irrigate these fields and with the utmost power engage themselves in the cultivation of these heavenly plantations so that the seeds may grow and develop, prosperity and blessing be realized and many rich and great harvests be gathered in.

The Kingdom of God is like unto a farmer who comes into possession of a piece of pure and virgin soil. Heavenly seeds are scattered therein, the clouds of divine providence pour down and the rays of the Sun of Reality shine forth.

Now all these bounties exist and appear in full in these nine states. The divine Gardener passed by that holy ground and scattered pure seeds from the lordly teachings in that field; the rain of the bounties of God poured down and the heat of the Sun of Reality—that is, the merciful confirmations—shone with the utmost splendour. It is my hope that each one of those blessed souls may become a peerless and unique irrigator and the East and the West of America may become like unto a delectable paradise so that all of you may hear from the Supreme Concourse the cry of "Blessed are you, and again blessed are you!"

Upon you be greeting and praise!

The following supplication is to be read by the teachers and friends daily:

O Thou kind Lord! Praise be unto Thee that Thou hast shown us the highway of guidance, opened the doors of the kingdom and manifested Thyself through the Sun of Reality. To the blind Thou hast given sight; to the deaf Thou hast granted hearing; Thou hast resuscitated the dead; Thou hast enriched the poor; Thou hast shown the way to those who have gone astray; Thou hast led those with parched lips to the fountain of guidance; Thou hast suffered the thirsty fish to reach the ocean of reality; and Thou hast invited the wandering birds to the rose garden of grace.

O Thou Almighty! We are Thy servants and Thy poor ones; we are remote and yearn for Thy presence, are athirst for the water of Thy fountain, are ill, longing for Thy healing. We are walking in Thy path and have no aim or hope save the diffusion of Thy fragrance, so that all souls may raise the cry: O God, "Guide us to the straight path."[1] May their eyes be opened to behold the light, and may they be freed from the darkness of ignorance. May they gather around the lamp of Thy guidance. May every portionless one receive a share. May the deprived become the confidants of Thy mysteries.

O Almighty! Look upon us with the glance of mercifulness. Grant us heavenly confirmation. Bestow upon us the breath of the Holy Spirit, so that we may be assisted in Thy service and, like unto brilliant stars, shine in these regions with the light of Thy guidance.

---

[1]   Qur'án 1:6.

Fazel Naghy

Verily, Thou art the Powerful, the Mighty, the Wise and the Seeing.

10. The Southern States

Revealed on 3 February 1917, in Haifa in Ismá'íl Áqá's room, and addressed to the Bahá'ís of the sixteen Southern States of the United States: Delaware, Maryland, Virginia, West Virginia, North Carolina, South Carolina, Georgia, Florida, Alabama, Mississippi, Tennessee, Kentucky, Louisiana, Arkansas, Oklahoma and Texas.

O ye blessed, respected souls:

The philosophers of the ancients, the thinkers of the Middle Ages and the scientists of this and the former centuries have all agreed upon the fact that the best and the most ideal region for the habitation of man is the temperate zone, for in this belt the intellects and thoughts rise to the highest stage of maturity, and the capability and ability of civilization manifest themselves in full efflorescence. When you read history critically and with a penetrating eye, it becomes evident that the majority of the famous men have been born, reared and have done their work in the temperate zone, while very, very few have appeared from the torrid and frigid zones.

Now these sixteen Southern States of the United States are situated in the temperate zone, and in these regions the perfections of the world of nature have been fully revealed. For the moderation of the weather, the beauty of the scenery and the geographical configuration of the country display a great effect in the world of minds and thoughts. This fact is well demonstrated through observation and experience.

Even the holy, divine Manifestations have had a nature in the utmost equilibrium, the health and wholesomeness of their bodies most perfect, their constitutions endowed with physical vigour, their powers functioning in perfect order, and the outward sensations linked with the inward perceptions, working together with extraordinary momentum and coordination.

Therefore in these sixteen states, because they are contiguous to other states and their climate being in the utmost of moderation, unquestionably the divine teachings must reveal themselves with a brighter effulgence, the breaths of the Holy Spirit must display a penetrating intensity, the ocean of the love of God must be stirred with higher waves, the breezes of the rose garden of the divine love be wafted with higher velocity, and the fragrances of holiness be diffused with swiftness and rapidity.

Praise be to God that the divine outpourings are infinite, the melody of the lordly principles is in the utmost efficacy, the most great Orb shining with perfect splendour, the cohorts of the Supreme Concourse are attacking with invincible power, the tongues are sharper than the swords, the hearts are more brilliant than the light of electricity, the magnanimity of the friends precedes all the magnanimities of the former and subsequent generations, the souls are divinely attracted, and the fire of the love of God is enkindled.

At this time and at this period we must avail ourselves of this most great opportunity. We must not sit inactive for one moment; we must sever ourselves from composure, rest, tranquillity, goods, property, life and attachment to material things. We must sacrifice everything to His Highness, the Possessor of existence, so that the powers of the Kingdom may show greater penetration and the brilliant effulgence in this New Cycle may illumine the worlds of minds and ideals.

It is about twenty-three years that the fragrances of God have been diffused in America, but no adequate and befitting motion has been realized, and no great acclamation and acceleration has been witnessed. Now it is my hope that through the heavenly power, the fragrances of the Merciful, the attraction of consciousness, the celestial outpourings, the heavenly cohorts and the gushing forth of the fountain of divine love, the believers of God may arise and in a short time the greatest good may unveil her countenance, the Sun of Reality may shine forth with such intensity that the darkness of the world of nature may become entirely dispelled and driven away; from every corner a most wonderful melody may be raised, the morning birds may break into such a song that the world of humanity may be quickened and moved, the solid bodies may become liquefied, and the souls who are like unto adamantine rocks may open their wings and through the heat of the love of God fly heavenward.

Nearly two thousand years ago, Armenia was enveloped with impenetrable darkness. One blessed soul from among the disciples of Christ hastened to that part, and through his effort, erelong that province became illumined. Thus it has become evident how the power of the Kingdom works!

Therefore, rest ye assured in the confirmations of the Merciful and the assistance of the Most High; become ye sanctified above and purified from this world and the inhabitants thereof; suffer your intentions to work for the good of all; cut your attachment to the earth and like unto the essence of the spirit become ye light and delicate. Then with a firm resolution, a pure heart, a rejoiced spirit, and an eloquent tongue, engage your time in the promulgation of the divine principles so that the oneness of the world of humanity may pitch her canopy in the apex of America and all the nations of the world may follow the divine policy. This is certain, that the divine policy is justice and kindness toward all mankind. For all the nations of the world are the sheep of God, and God is the kind shepherd. He has created these sheep. He has protected them, sustained and trained them. What greater kindness than this? And every moment we must render a hundred thousand thanksgivings that, praise be to God, we are freed from all the ignorant prejudices, are kind to all the sheep of God, and our utmost hope is to serve each and all, and like unto a benevolent father educate every one.

Upon you be greeting and praise!

Every soul who travels through the cities, villages and hamlets of these states and is engaged in the diffusion of the fragrances of God, should peruse this commune every morning:

O My God! O my God! Thou seest me in my lowliness and weakness, occupied with the greatest undertaking, determined to raise Thy word among the masses and to spread Thy teachings among Thy peoples. How can I succeed unless Thou assist me with the breath of the Holy Spirit, help me to triumph by the hosts of Thy glorious kingdom, and shower upon me Thy confirmations, which alone can change a gnat into an eagle, a drop of water into rivers and seas, and an atom into lights and suns? O my Lord! Assist me with Thy triumphant and effective might, so that my tongue may utter Thy praises and attributes among all people and my soul overflow with the wine of Thy love and knowledge.

Thou art the Omnipotent and the Doer of whatsoever Thou willest.

11. The Central States

Revealed on 8 February 1917, in Bahá'u'lláh's room at the house of Abbúd in 'Akká, and addressed to the Bahá'ís of the twelve Central States of the United States: Michigan, Wisconsin, Illinois, Indiana, Ohio, Minnesota, Iowa, Missouri, North Dakota, South Dakota, Nebraska and Kansas.

He is God!
O ye old believers and intimate friends:

God says in the great Qur'án: "He specializes for His Mercy whomsoever He willeth."[1]

These twelve Central States of the United States are like unto the heart of America, and the heart is connected with all the organs and parts of man. If the heart is strengthened, all the organs of the body are reinforced, and if the heart is weak all the physical elements are subjected to feebleness.

Now praise be to God that Chicago and its environs from the beginning of the diffusion of the fragrances of God have been a strong heart. Therefore, through divine bounty and providence it has become confirmed in certain great matters.

First: The call of the Kingdom was in the very beginning raised from Chicago. This is indeed a great privilege, for in future centuries and cycles, it will be as an axis around which the honour of Chicago will revolve.

Second: A number of souls with the utmost firmness and steadfastness arose in that blessed spot in the promotion of the Word of God and even to the present moment, having purified and sanctified the heart from every thought, they are occupied with the promulgation of the teachings of God. Hence the call of praise is raised uninterruptedly from the Supreme Concourse.

Third: During the American journey 'Abdu'l-Bahá several times passed through Chicago and associated with the friends of God. For some time he sojourned in that city. Day and night he was occupied with the mention of the True One and summoned the people to the Kingdom of God.

Fourth: Up to the present time, every movement initiated in Chicago, its effect was spread to all parts and to all directions, just as everything that appears in and manifests from the heart influences all the organs and limbs of the body.

Fifth: The first Mashriqu'l-Adhkár in America was instituted in Chicago, and this honour and distinction is infinite in value. Out of this Mashriqu'l-Adhkár, without doubt, thousands of Mashriqu'l-Adhkárs will be born.

Likewise (were instituted in Chicago) the general Annual Conventions, the foundation of the Star of the West, the Publishing Society for the publication of books and Tablets and their circulation in all parts of America, and the preparations now under way for the celebration of the Golden Centenary Anniversary of the Kingdom of God. I hope that this Jubilee and this Exhibition may be celebrated in the utmost perfection so that the call to the world of unity, "There is no God but One God, and all the Messengers, from the beginning to the Seal of the Prophets

---

[1] Qur'án 2:105, 3:74.

(Muḥammad) were sent on the part of the True One!" may be raised; the flag of the oneness of the world of humanity be unfurled, the melody of universal peace may reach the ears of the East and the West, all the paths may be cleared and straightened, all the hearts may be attracted to the Kingdom of God, the tabernacle of unity be pitched on the apex of America, the song of the love of God may exhilarate and rejoice all the nations and peoples, the surface of the earth may become the eternal paradise, the dark clouds may be dispelled and the Sun of Truth may shine forth with the utmost intensity.

O ye friends of God! Exert ye with heart and soul, so that association, love, unity and agreement be obtained between the hearts, all the aims may be merged into one aim, all the songs become one song and the power of the Holy Spirit may become so overwhelmingly victorious as to overcome all the forces of the world of nature. Exert yourselves; your mission is unspeakably glorious. Should success crown your enterprise, America will assuredly evolve into a centre from which waves of spiritual power will emanate, and the throne of the Kingdom of God will, in the plentitude of its majesty and glory, be firmly established.

This phenomenal world will not remain in an unchanging condition even for a short while. Second after second it undergoes change and transformation. Every foundation will finally become collapsed; every glory and splendour will at last vanish and disappear, but the Kingdom of God is eternal and the heavenly sovereignty and majesty will stand firm, everlasting. Hence in the estimation of a wise man the mat in the Kingdom of God is preferable to the throne of the government of the world.

Continually my ear and eye are turned toward the Central States; perchance a melody from some blessed souls may reach my ears—souls who are the dawning-places of the love of God, the stars of the horizon of sanctification and holiness—souls who will illumine this dark universe and quicken to life this dead world. The joy of 'Abdu'l-Bahá depends upon this! I hope that you may become confirmed therein.

Consequently, those souls who are in a condition of the utmost severance, purified from the defects of the world of nature, sanctified from attachment to this earth, vivified with the breaths of eternal life—with luminous hearts, with heavenly spirit, with attraction of consciousness, with celestial magnanimity, with eloquent tongues and with clear explanations—such souls must hasten and travel through all parts of the Central States. In every city and village they must occupy themselves with the diffusion of the divine exhortations and advices, guide the souls and promote the oneness of the world of humanity. They must play the melody of international conciliation with such power that every deaf one may attain hearing, every extinct person may be set aglow, every dead one may obtain new life and every indifferent soul may find ecstasy. It is certain that such will be the consummation.

Let the spreaders of the fragrances of God recite this prayer every morning:

O Lord, my God! Praise and thanksgiving be unto Thee for Thou hast guided me to the highway of the kingdom, suffered me to walk in this straight and far-stretching path, illumined my eye by beholding the splendours of Thy light, inclined my ear to the melodies of the birds of holiness from the kingdom of mysteries and attracted my heart with Thy love among the righteous.

O Lord! Confirm me with the Holy Spirit, so that I may call in Thy Name amongst the nations, and give the glad tidings of the manifestation of Thy kingdom amongst mankind.

O Lord! I am weak, strengthen me with Thy power and potency. My tongue falters, suffer me to utter Thy commemoration and praise. I am lowly, honour me through admitting me into Thy kingdom. I am remote, cause me to approach the threshold of Thy mercifulness. O Lord! Make me a brilliant lamp, a shining star and a blessed tree, adorned with fruit, its branches overshadowing all these regions. Verily, Thou art the Mighty, the Powerful and Unconstrained.

12. The Western States

Revealed on 15 February 1917, in Bahá'u'lláh's room at the house of Abbúd in 'Akká, and addressed to the Bahá'ís of the eleven Western States of the United States: New Mexico, Colorado, Arizona, Nevada, California, Wyoming, Utah, Montana, Idaho, Oregon and Washington.

He is God!
O ye friends and the maidservants of the Merciful, the chosen ones of the Kingdom:

The blessed state of California bears the utmost similarity to the Holy Land, that is, the country of Palestine. The air is of the utmost temperance, the plain very spacious, and the fruits of Palestine are seen in that state in the utmost of freshness and delicacy. When 'Abdu'l-Bahá was traveling and journeying through those states, he found himself in Palestine, for from every standpoint there was a perfect likeness between this region and that state. Even the shores of the Pacific Ocean, in some instances, show perfect resemblance to the shores of the Holy Land—even the flora of the Holy Land have grown on those shores—the study of which had led to much speculation and wonder.

Likewise, in the state of California and other Western states, wonderful scenes of the world of nature, which bewilder the minds of men, are manifest. Lofty mountains, deep canyons, great and majestic waterfalls, and giant trees are witnessed on all sides, while its soil is in the utmost fertility and richness. That blessed state is similar to the Holy Land and that region and that country like unto a delectable paradise, is in many ways identical with Palestine. Now just as there are natural resemblances, heavenly resemblances must also be acquired.

The lights of the divine traces are manifest in Palestine. The majority of the Israelitish Prophets raised the call of the Kingdom of God in this holy ground. Having spread the spiritual teachings, the nostrils of the spiritually-minded ones became fragrant, the eyes of the illumined souls became brightened, the ears were thrilled through this song, the hearts obtained eternal life from the soul-refreshing breeze of the Kingdom of God and gained supreme illumination from the splendour of the Sun of Reality. Then from this region the light was spread to Europe, America, Asia, Africa and Australia.

Now California and the other Western States must earn an ideal similarity with the Holy Land, and from that state and that region the breaths of the Holy Spirit be diffused to all parts of America and Europe, that the call of the Kingdom of God may exhilarate and rejoice all the ears, the divine principles bestow a new life, the different parties may become one party, the divergent ideas may disappear and revolve around one unique centre, the East and the West of America may embrace each other, the anthem of the oneness of the world of humanity may confer a new life upon all the children of men, and the tabernacle of universal peace be pitched on the apex of America; thus Europe and Africa may become vivified with the breaths of the Holy Spirit, this world may become another world, the body politic may attain to a new exhilaration, and just as in the state of California and other Western States the marvellous scenes of the world of nature are evident and manifest, the great signs of the Kingdom of God may also be unveiled so that the body may correspond with the spirit, the outward world may become a symbol of the inward world, and the mirror of the earth may become the mirror of the Kingdom, reflecting the ideal virtues of heaven.

During My journey and traveling in those parts, I beheld wonderful scenes and beautiful panoramas of nature, orchards and rivers; national parks and general conclaves; deserts, plains, meadows and prairies; and the grains and fruits of that region greatly attracted My attention; even to the present moment they are in My mind.

Particularly was I greatly pleased with the meetings in San Francisco and Oakland, the gatherings in Los Angeles, and the believers who came from the cities of other states. Whenever their faces cross My memory, immediately infinite happiness is realized.

Therefore I hope that the divine teachings like unto the rays of the sun may be diffused in all the Western States, and the blessed verse of the Qur'án, "It is a good City and the Lord is the Forgiver!"[1] may become realized. Likewise, the significance of another Qur'anic verse, "Do ye not travel through the land?"[2] and of the verse, "Behold the traces of the Mercy of God!"[3] become revealed in the utmost effulgence.

Praise be to God that through the divine bounty and providence, in that region the field of service is vast, the minds are in the utmost degree of intelligence and progress, sciences and arts are being promoted, the hearts like unto mirrors are in the utmost state of purity and translucency, and the friends of God are in perfect attraction. Therefore it is hoped that meetings for teaching will be organized and instituted, and for the diffusion of the fragrances of God wise teachers may be sent to cities, even to villages.

The teachers of the Cause must be heavenly, lordly and radiant. They must be embodied spirit, personified intellect, and arise in service with the utmost firmness, steadfastness and self-sacrifice. In their journeys they must not be attached to food and clothing. They must concentrate their thoughts on the outpourings of the Kingdom of God and beg for the confirmations of the Holy Spirit. With a divine power, with an attraction of consciousness, with heavenly glad tidings and celestial holiness they must perfume the nostrils with the fragrances of the Paradise of Abhá.

The following commune is to be read by them every day:

O God! O God! This is a broken-winged bird and his flight is very slow—assist him so that he may fly toward the apex of prosperity and salvation, wing his way with the utmost joy and happiness throughout the illimitable space, raise his melody in Thy Supreme Name in all the regions, exhilarate the ears with this call, and brighten the eyes by beholding the signs of guidance.

O Lord! I am single, alone and lowly. For me there is no support save Thee, no helper except Thee and no sustainer beside Thee. Confirm me in Thy service, assist

---

1   Qur'án 34:15.
2   Qur'án 30:9, 40:82, 47:10.
3   Qur'án 30:50.

me with the cohorts of Thine angels, make me victorious in the promotion of Thy Word and suffer me to speak out Thy wisdom amongst Thy creatures. Verily, Thou art the helper of the weak and the defender of the little ones, and verily Thou art the Powerful, the Mighty and the Unconstrained.

13. Canada and Greenland

Revealed on 21 February 1917, in Bahá'u'lláh's room at the house of Abbúd in 'Akká, and addressed to the Bahá'ís of Canada—Newfoundland, Prince Edward Island, Nova Scotia, New Brunswick, Quebec, Saskatchewan, Manitoba, Ontario, Alberta, British Columbia, Yukon, Mackenzie, Keewatin, Ungava, Franklin Islands—and Greenland.

He is God!
O ye kind friends and the maidservants of the Merciful:

In the great Qur'án, God says: "Thou shalt see no difference in the creatures of God."[1] In other words, He says: From the ideal standpoint, there is no variation between the creatures of God, because they are all created by Him. From the above premise, a conclusion is drawn, that there is no difference between countries. The future of the Dominion of Canada, however, is very great, and the events connected with it infinitely glorious. It shall become the object of the glance of providence, and shall show forth the bounties of the All-Glorious.

'Abdu'l-Bahá during his journey and sojourn through that Dominion obtained the utmost joy. Before My departure, many souls warned Me not to travel to Montreal, saying, the majority of the inhabitants are Catholics, and are in the utmost fanaticism, that they are submerged in the sea of imitations, that they have not the capability to hearken to the call of the Kingdom of God, that the veil of bigotry has so covered the eyes that they have deprived themselves from beholding the signs of the Most Great Guidance, and that the dogmas have taken possession of the hearts entirely, leaving no trace of reality. They asserted that should the Sun of Reality shine with perfect splendour throughout that Dominion, the dark, impenetrable clouds of superstitions have so enveloped the horizon that it would be utterly impossible for anyone to behold its rays.

But these stories did not have any effect on the resolution of 'Abdu'l-Bahá. He, trusting in God, turned his face toward Montreal. When he entered that city he observed all the doors open, he found the hearts in the utmost receptivity and the ideal power of the Kingdom of God removing every obstacle and obstruction. In the churches and meetings of that Dominion he called men to the Kingdom of God with the utmost joy, and scattered such seeds which will be irrigated with the hand of divine power. Undoubtedly those seeds will grow, becoming green and verdant, and many rich harvests will be gathered. In the promotion of the divine principles he found no antagonist and no adversary. The believers he met in that city were in the utmost spirituality, and attracted with the fragrances of God. He found that through the effort of the maidservant of God Mrs Maxwell a number of the sons and daughters of the Kingdom in that Dominion were gathered together and associated with each other, increasing this joyous exhilaration day by day. The time of sojourn was limited to a number of days, but the results in the future are inexhaustible. When a farmer comes into the possession of a virgin soil, in a short time he will bring under cultivation a large field. Therefore I hope that in the future Montreal may become so stirred, that the melody of the Kingdom may travel to all parts of the

---

[1]   Qur'án 67:3.

world from that Dominion and the breaths of the Holy Spirit may spread from that centre to the East and the West of America.

O ye believers of God! Be not concerned with the smallness of your numbers, neither be oppressed by the multitude of an unbelieving world. Five grains of wheat will be endued with heavenly blessing, whereas a thousand tons of tares will yield no results or effect. One fruitful tree will be conducive to the life of society, whereas a thousand forests of wild trees offer no fruits. The plain is covered with pebbles, but precious stones are rare. One pearl is better than a thousand wildernesses of sand, especially this pearl of great price, which is endowed with divine blessing. Erelong thousands of other pearls will be born from it. When that pearl associates and becomes the intimate of the pebbles, they also all change into pearls.

Again I repeat that the future of Canada, whether from a material or a spiritual standpoint, is very great. Day by day civilization and freedom shall increase. The clouds of the Kingdom will water the seeds of guidance which have been sown there. Consequently, rest ye not, seek ye no composure, attach not yourselves to the luxuries of this ephemeral world, free yourselves from every attachment, and strive with heart and soul to become fully established in the Kingdom of God. Gain ye the heavenly treasures. Day by day become ye more illumined. Draw ye nearer and nearer unto the threshold of oneness. Become ye the manifestors of spiritual favours and the dawning-places of infinite lights! If it is possible, send ye teachers to other portions of Canada; likewise, dispatch ye teachers to Greenland and the home of the Eskimos.

As regards the teachers, they must completely divest themselves from the old garments and be invested with a new garment. According to the statement of Christ, they must attain to the station of rebirth—that is, whereas in the first instance they were born from the womb of the mother, this time they must be born from the womb of the world of nature. Just as they are now totally unaware of the experiences of the foetal world, they must also forget entirely the defects of the world of nature. They must be baptized with the water of life, the fire of the love of God and the breaths of the Holy Spirit; be satisfied with little food, but take a large portion from the heavenly table. They must disengage themselves from temptation and covetousness, and be filled with the spirit. Through the effect of their pure breath, they must change the stone into the brilliant ruby and the shell into pearl. Like unto the cloud of vernal shower, they must transform the black soil into the rose garden and orchard. They must make the blind seeing, the deaf hearing, the extinguished one enkindled and set aglow, and the dead quickened.

Upon you be greeting and praise!

Praise be to Thee, O my God! These are Thy servants who are attracted by the fragrances of Thy mercifulness, are enkindled by the fire burning in the tree of Thy singleness, and whose eyes are brightened by beholding the splendours of the light shining in the Sinai of Thy oneness.

O Lord! Loose their tongues to make mention of Thee amongst Thy people, suffer them to speak forth Thy praise through Thy grace and loving-kindness, assist them with the cohorts of Thine angels, strengthen their loins in Thy service, and make them the signs of Thy guidance amongst Thy creatures.

Verily, Thou art the All-Powerful, the Most Exalted, the Ever-Forgiving, the All-Merciful.

The spreaders of the fragrances of God should recite this prayer every morning:

O God, my God! Thou beholdest this weak one begging for celestial strength, this poor one craving Thy heavenly treasures, this thirsty one longing for the fountain of eternal life, this afflicted one yearning for Thy promised healing through Thy boundless mercy which Thou hast destined for Thy chosen servants in Thy kingdom on high.

O Lord! I have no helper save Thee, no shelter besides Thee, and no sustainer except Thee. Assist me with Thine angels to diffuse Thy holy fragrances and to spread abroad Thy teachings amongst the choicest of Thy people.

O my Lord! Suffer me to be detached from aught else save Thee, to hold fast to the hem of Thy bounty, to be wholly devoted to Thy Faith, to remain fast and firm in Thy love and to observe what Thou hast prescribed in Thy Book.

Verily, Thou art the Powerful, the Mighty, the Omnipotent.

14. **The United States and Canada**

Revealed on 8 March 1917, in the summerhouse (Ismá'íl Áqá's room) at 'Abdu'l-Bahá's house in Haifa, and addressed to the Bahá'ís of the United States and Canada.

He is God!
O ye heavenly souls, sons and daughters of the Kingdom:

God says in the Qur'án: "Take ye hold of the Cord of God, all of you, and become ye not disunited."[1]

In the contingent world there are many collective centres which are conducive to association and unity between the children of men. For example, patriotism is a collective centre; nationalism is a collective centre; identity of interests is a collective centre; political alliance is a collective centre; the union of ideals is a collective centre, and the prosperity of the world of humanity is dependent upon the organization and promotion of the collective centres. Nevertheless, all the above institutions are, in reality, the matter and not the substance, accidental and not eternal—temporary and not everlasting. With the appearance of great revolutions and upheavals, all these collective centres are swept away. But the Collective Centre of the Kingdom, embodying the institutions and divine teachings, is the eternal Collective Centre. It establishes relationship between the East and the West, organizes the oneness of the world of humanity, and destroys the foundation of differences. It overcomes and includes all the other collective centres. Like unto the ray of the sun, it dispels entirely the darkness encompassing all the regions, bestows ideal life, and causes the effulgence of divine illumination. Through the breaths of the Holy Spirit it performs miracles; the Orient and the Occident embrace each other, the North and South become intimates and associates, conflicting and contending opinions disappear, antagonistic aims are brushed aside, the law of the struggle for existence is abrogated, and the canopy of the oneness of the world of humanity is raised on the apex of the globe, casting its shade over all the races of men. Consequently, the real Collective Centre is the body of the divine teachings, which include all the degrees and embrace all the universal relations and necessary laws of humanity.

Consider! The people of the East and the West were in the utmost strangeness. Now to what a high degree they are acquainted with each other and united together! How far are the inhabitants of Persia from the remotest countries of America! And now observe how great has been the influence of the heavenly power, for the distance of thousands of miles has become identical with one step! How various nations that have had no relations or similarity with each other are now united and agreed through this divine potency! Indeed to God belongs power in the past and in the future! And verily God is powerful over all things!

Consider the flowers of a garden. Though differing in kind, colour, form, and shape, yet, inasmuch as they are refreshed by the waters of one spring, revived by the breath of one wind, invigorated by the rays of one sun, this diversity increaseth their charm, and addeth unto their beauty. How unpleasing to the eye if all the

---

[1] Qur'án 3:103.

flowers and plants, the leaves and blossoms, the fruits, the branches and the trees of that garden were all of the same shape and colour! Diversity of hues, form and shape, enricheth and adorneth the garden, and heighteneth the effect thereof. In like manner, when divers shades of thought, temperament and character, are brought together under the power and influence of one central agency, the beauty and glory of human perfection will be revealed and made manifest. Naught but the celestial potency of the Word of God, which ruleth and transcendeth the realities of all things, is capable of harmonizing the divergent thoughts, sentiments, ideas, and convictions of the children of men.

Therefore, the believers of God throughout all the republics of America, through the divine power, must become the cause of the promotion of heavenly teachings and the establishment of the oneness of humanity. Every one of the important souls must arise, blowing over all parts of America the breath of life, conferring upon the people a new spirit, baptizing them with the fire of the love of God, the water of life, and the breaths of the Holy Spirit so that the second birth may become realized. For it is written in the Gospel: "That which is born of the flesh is flesh; and that which is born of the Spirit is spirit."[1]

Therefore, O ye believers of God in the United States and Canada! Select ye important personages, or else they by themselves, becoming severed from rest and composure of the world, may arise and travel throughout Alaska, the republic of Mexico, and south of Mexico in the Central American republics, such as Guatemala, Honduras, Salvador, Nicaragua, Costa Rica, Panama and Belize; and through the great South American republics, such as Argentina, Uruguay, Paraguay, Brazil, French Guiana, Dutch Guiana, British Guiana, Venezuela, Ecuador, Peru, Bolivia and Chile; also in the group of the West Indies islands, such as Cuba, Haiti, Puerto Rico, Jamaica and Santo Domingo, and the group of islands of the Lesser Antilles, the Islands of Bahama and the Islands of Bermuda; likewise to the islands to the east, west and north of South America, such as Trinidad, Falkland Islands, Galápago Islands, Juan Fernandez and Tobago. Visit ye especially the city of Bahia, on the eastern shore of Brazil. Because in the past years this city was christened with the name, BAHIA, there is no doubt that it has been through the inspiration of the Holy Spirit.

Consequently, the believers of God must display the utmost effort, upraise the divine melody throughout those regions, promulgate the heavenly teachings and waft over all the spirit of eternal life, so that those republics may become so illumined with the splendours and the effulgences of the Sun of Reality that they may become the objects of the praise and commendation of all other countries. Likewise, ye must give great attention to the Republic of Panama, for in that point the Occident and the Orient find each other united through the Panama Canal, and it is also situated between the two great oceans. That place will become very important in the future. The teachings, once established there, will unite the East and the West, the North and the South.

Hence the intention must be purified, the effort ennobled and exalted, so that you may establish affinity between the hearts of the world of humanity. This glorious

---

[1]   John 3:6.

aim will not become realized save through the promotion of divine teachings which are the foundations of the holy religions.

Consider how the religions of God served the world of humanity! How the religion of Torah became conducive to the glory and honour and progress of the Israelitish nation! How the breaths of the Holy Spirit of His Holiness Christ created affinity and unity between divergent communities and quarrelling families! How the sacred power of His Holiness Muḥammad became the means of uniting and harmonizing the contentious tribes and the different clans of Peninsular Arabia—to such an extent that one thousand tribes were welded into one tribe; strife and discord were done away with; all of them unitedly and with one accord strove in advancing the cause of culture and civilization, and thus were freed from the lowest degree of degradation, soaring toward the height of everlasting glory! Is it possible to find a greater Collective Centre in the phenomenal world than this? In comparison to this divine Collective Centre, the national collective centre, the patriotic collective centre, the political collective centre and the cultural and intellectual collective centre are like child's play!

Now strive ye that the Collective Centre of the sacred religions—for the inculcation of which all the Prophets were manifested and which is no other than the spirit of the divine teachings—be spread in all parts of America, so that each one of you may shine forth from the horizon of reality like unto the morning star, divine illumination may overcome the darkness of nature, and the world of humanity may become enlightened. This is the most great work! Should you become confirmed therein, this world will become another world, the surface of the earth will become the delectable paradise, and eternal Institutions be founded.

Let whosoever travels to different parts to teach, peruse over mountain, desert, land and sea this supplication:

O God! O God! Thou seest my weakness, lowliness and humility before Thy creatures; nevertheless, I have trusted in Thee and have arisen in the promotion of Thy teachings among Thy strong servants, relying on Thy power and might.

O Lord! I am a broken-winged bird and desire to soar in Thy limitless space. How is it possible for me to do this save through Thy providence and grace, Thy confirmation and assistance.

O Lord! Have pity on my weakness, and strengthen me with Thy power. O Lord! Have pity on my impotence, and assist me with Thy might and majesty.

O Lord! Should the breath of the Holy Spirit confirm the weakest of creatures, he would attain all to which he aspireth and would possess anything he desireth. Indeed, Thou hast assisted Thy servants in the past and, though they were the weakest of Thy creatures, the lowliest of Thy servants and the most insignificant of those who lived upon the earth, through Thy sanction and potency they took precedence over the most glorious of Thy people and the most noble of mankind. Whereas formerly they were as moths, they became as royal falcons, and whereas before they were as brooks, they became as seas, through Thy bestowal and Thy mercy. They became, through Thy most great favour, stars shining on the horizon of guidance, birds singing in the rose gardens of immortality, lions roaring in the forests of knowledge and wisdom, and whales swimming in the oceans of life.

Verily, Thou art the Clement, the Powerful, the Mighty, and the Most Merciful of the merciful.

Bibliography

'Abdu'l-Bahá. *A Traveller's Narrative Written to Illustrate the Episode of the Báb.* Tr. E. G. Browne. Bahá'í Publishing Trust, Wilmette, Ill. 1980.

_____. *'Abdu'l-Bahá in London: Addresses and Notes of Conversations.* Bahá'í Publishing Trust, London. 1982.

_____. *Divine Philosophy.* Compilation compiled by Soraya (Isabel Fraser) Chamberlain. The Tudor Press, Boston. 1918.

_____. *Foundations of World Unity: Compiled from Addresses and Tablets of 'Abdu'l-Bahá.* Bahá'í Publishing Trust, Wilmette, Ill. 1972.

_____. *Paris Talks: Addresses Given by 'Abdu'l-Bahá in Paris in 1911–1912.* Bahá'í Publishing Trust, London. 1969.

_____. *Selections from the Writings of 'Abdu'l-Bahá.* Translated by a Committee at the Bahá'í World Centre and Marzieh Gail. Haifa: Bahá'í World Centre. 1978.

_____. *Some Answered Questions.* Collected and translated by Laura Clifford Barney. 2nd edn. Bahá'í World Centre, Haifa, 2014.

_____. Tablet to August Forel. *The Bahá'í World*, vol. XV, pp. 37–43.

_____. Tablet to the Hague. Part of the Tablet is in *Selections from the Writings of 'Abdu'l-Bahá*, pp. 296–307, and in *The Bahá'í Revelation*, pp. 208–19. Refer to https://www.bahai.org/library/authoritative-texts/abdul-baha/tablets-hague-abdul-baha/ for recent full translation of both Tablets.

_____. *Tablets of Abdul-Baha Abbas.* 3 vols. Bahá'í Publishing Society, New York. 1909–16.

_____. *Tablets of the Divine Plan: Revealed by 'Abdu'l-Bahá to the North American Bahá'ís.* Bahá'í Publishing Trust, Wilmette, Ill. 1993.

_____. *The Promulgation of Universal Peace: Talks Delivered by 'Abdu'l-Bahá during His Visit to the United States and Canada in 1912.* 2nd ed. Compiled by Howard MacNutt. Bahá'í Publishing Trust, Wilmette, Ill. 1982.

_____. *The Secret of Divine Civilization.* Tr. Marzieh Gail and Ali-Kuli Khan. Bahá'í Publishing Trust, Wilmette, Ill. 1990.

Báb, The. *Selections from the Writings of the Báb.* Compiled by the Research Department of the Universal House of Justice. Tr. Habib Taherzadeh *et al.* Haifa: Bahá'í World Centre, 1976.

Bahá'í International Community. *Conservation and Sustainable Development in the Bahá'í Faith.* Statement to Summit on the Alliance Between Religions and Conservation. UK. 1995.

_____. *The Prosperity of Humankind.* Presented to the plenary session of the United Nations World Summit on Social Development, Vienna, Austria, 6 March 1995.

Bahá'í Prayers, A Selection of Prayers Revealed by Bahá'u'lláh, The Báb, and 'Abdu'l-Bahá. Bahá'í Publishing Trust, Wilmette, Ill. 1991.

Bahá'í Scriptures. Compiled by Horace Holley. Bahá'í Publishing Committee, New York. 1928.

The Bahá'í World: A Biennial International Record, vol. XV, 1968–1973. Compiled by the Universal House of Justice. Haifa: Bahá'í World Centre, 1975.

Bahá'í World Faith: Selected Writings of Bahá'u'lláh and 'Abdu'l-Bahá. Bahá'í Publishing Trust, Wilmette, Ill. 1976.

Bahá'u'lláh. *Epistle to the Son of the Wolf.* Tr. Shoghi Effendi. Bahá'í Publishing Trust, Wilmette, Ill. 1988.

_____. *Gems of Divine Mysteries (Javáhiru'l-Asrár).* Bahá'í World Centre. 2002.

_____. *Gleanings from the Writings of Bahá'u'lláh.* Tr. Shoghi Effendi. Bahá'í Publishing Trust, Wilmette, Ill. 1983.

_____. *Prayers and Meditations by Bahá'u'lláh.* Tr. Shoghi Effendi. Bahá'í Publishing Trust, Wilmette, Ill. 1987.

_____. *Tablets of Bahá'u'lláh revealed after the Kitáb-i-Aqdas.* Tr. Habib Taherzadeh *et al.* Bahá'í Publishing Trust, Wilmette, Ill. 1988.

_____. *The Hidden Words.* Trans. Shoghi Effendi. Bahá'í Publishing Trust, Wilmette, Ill. 1939.

_____. *The Kitáb-i-Aqdas: The Most Holy Book.* Bahá'í Publishing Trust, Wilmette, Ill. 1993.

_____. *The Kitáb-i-Íqán: The Book of Certitude.* Tr. Shoghi Effendi. Bahá'í Publishing Trust, Wilmette, Ill. 1983.

_____. *The Proclamation of Bahá'u'lláh: To the Kings and Leaders of the World.* Bahá'í World Centre. 1991.

_____. *The Seven Valleys and The Four Valleys.* Trans. Marzieh Gail. Bahá'í Publishing Trust, Wilmette, Ill. 1986.

_____. The Seven Valleys and The Four Valleys *in Call of the Divine Beloved.* Revised tr. Bahá'í World Centre, Haifa. 2019

_____. *The Summons of the Lord of Hosts: Tablets of Bahá'u'lláh.* Bahá'í World Centre, Haifa. 2002.

Balyuzi, H. M. *Khadíjih Bagum: the Wife of the Báb.* George Ronald. 1981.

The Compilation of Compilations, Vols I & II, compiled by Research Department of the Universal House of Justice. Bahá'í Publications Australia, Mona Vale. 1991.

Esslemont, J. E. *Bahá'u'lláh and the New Era: An Introduction to the Bahá'í Faith.* Bahá'í Publishing Trust, Wilmette, Ill. 1980.

Giachery, Ugo. *Shoghi Effendi: Recollections.* George Ronald, Oxford. 1973.

Gail, Marzieh. *Arches of the Years.* George Ronald, Oxford. *1991.*

_____. *Six Lessons on Islám.* Bahá'í Publishing Trust. 1953.

The Importance of Obligatory Prayer and Fasting. A compilation compiled by the Research Department of the Universal House of Justice. Bahá'í Publications Australia, Mona Vale. 2000. Also published in *The American Bahá'í,* 31:7, pp. 3–6. 27 Sep 2000.

Ives, Howard Colby. *Portals to Freedom.* George Ronald, Oxford. 1983.

Japan Will Turn Ablaze! Tablets of 'Abdu'l-Bahá, Letters of Shoghi Effendi and the Universal House of Justice, and Historical Notes About Japan. Compiled by Barbara R. Sims. Bahá'í Publishing Trust of Japan. 1992.

Khan, Janet A. *Prophet's Daughter: The Life and Legacy of Bahíyyih* Khánum, *Outstanding Heroine of the Bahá'í Faith.* Bahá'í Publishing Wilmette, IL. 2005.

The Light of Divine Guidance. Vol. 2. Bahá'í-Verlag, Hofheim. 1985.

Lights of Guidance: A Bahá'í Reference File. Compiled by Helen Hornby. New Delhi: Bahá'í Publishing Trust, 1994.

Messages from the Universal House of Justice 1963–1986: The Third Epoch of the Formative Age. Comp. Geoffrey W. Marks. Bahá'í Publishing trust, Wilmette, Ill. 1996.

Messages from the Universal House of Justice 1986–2001: The Fourth Epoch of the Formative Age. Comp. Geoffrey W. Marks. Bahá'í Publishing trust, Wilmette, Ill. 2009.

Momen, Moojan. *Hinduism and Bahá'í Faith.* George Ronald, Oxford. 1990.

Nabíl-i-A'ẓam (Muḥammad-i-Zarandí). *The Dawn-Breakers: Nabíl's Narrative of the Early Days of the Bahá'í Revelation.* Tr. & ed. Shoghi Effendi. Bahá'í Publishing Trust, Wilmette, Ill. 1932.

Naghdy, Fazel. *Knowing my inner self: Applied Spirituality for Teenagers.* Kindle Direct Publishing, an Amazon.com company. 2014.

_____. *A Tutorial on the Dispensation of Bahá'u'lláh.* Kindle Direct Publishing, an Amazon.com company. 2012.

_____. *A Tutorial on the Kitáb-i-Íqán.* Kindle Direct Publishing, an Amazon.com company. 2012.

Plato. *Five Dialogues: Euthyphro, Apology, Crito, Meno, Phaedo.* Tr. G. M. A. Grube. Hackett Publishing, Indianapolis. 2002.

Prayer, Meditation, and the Devotional Attitude. A compilation of the Universal House of Justice. Bahá'í Publications Australia, Mona Vale. 1980.

Principles of Bahá'í Administration: A Compilation. Comp. by the National Spiritual Assembly of the Bahá'ís of the United Kingdom. Bahá'í Publishing Trust, London. 1976.

Rabbani, Rúḥíyyih Khánum. *The Priceless Pearl.* Bahá'í Publishing Trust, London. 1969.

Shoghi Effendi. *The Advent of Divine Justice.* Bahá'í Publishing Trust, Wilmette, Ill. 1990.

_____. *Citadel of Faith: Messages to America, 1947–1957.* Bahá'í Publishing Trust, Wilmette, Ill. 1965.

_____. *The Dawn Breakers. Nabil's Narrative of the Early Days of the Bahá'í Revelation,* Bahá'í Publishing Trust. 1974.

_____. *Dawn of a New Day: Messages to India 1923–1957.* Bahá'í Publishing Trust. 1970.

_____. *Directives from the Guardian.* New Delhi: Bahá'í Publishing Trust, [n.d.].

_____. *God Passes By.* Bahá'í Publishing Trust, Wilmette, Ill. 1974.

_____. *High Endeavours, Messages to Alaska.* National Spiritual Assembly of Alaska. 1976.

_____. *Messages to the Bahá'í World: 1950–1957.* Bahá'í Publishing Trust, Wilmette, Ill. 1971.

_____. *The Unfolding Destiny of the British Bahá'í Community: The Messages from the Guardian of the Bahá'í Faith to the Bahá'ís of the British Isles.* Bahá'í Publishing Trust, London. 1981.

_____. *The World Order of Bahá'u'lláh: Selected Letters.* Bahá'í Publishing Trust, Wilmette, Ill. 1991.

Star of the West: The Bahá'í Magazine. Periodical, 25 vols, 1910–1935. Chicago.

Taherzadeh, Adib. *The Revelation of Bahá'u'lláh: Baghdád 1853–63.* vol. 1. George Ronald, Oxford. 1976.

_____. *The Revelation of Bahá'u'lláh: Adrianople 1863–68.* vol. 2. George Ronald, Oxford. 1977.

_____. *The Revelation of Bahá'u'lláh: 'Akká. The Early Years. 1868–77.* vol. 3. George Ronald, Oxford. 1983.

Index of Articles

General Index